# READING GOETHE
# AT MIDLIFE

Life consists of rare individual moments of the highest significance and countless intervals in which at best the phantoms of those moments hover about us. Love, spring, a beautiful melody, the mountains, the moon, the sea—they all speak truly to our heart only once: if they ever do, in fact, truly find speech. For many people never experience these moments at all but are themselves intervals and pauses in the symphony of real life.

—Nietzsche, *Human, All-Too-Human*, vol. 1, §586

Titian, *The Three Ages of Man*

*Zurich Lecture Series in Analytical Psychology*
Murray Stein and Nancy Cater, Co-editors

**ISAP**ZURICH
INTERNATIONAL SCHOOL OF
ANALYTICAL PSYCHOLOGY ZURICH

Previously published in the Series:

John Hill, *At Home in the World: Sounds and
Symmetries of Belonging*

# READING GOETHE
## AT MIDLIFE

*Ancient Wisdom, German
Classicism, and Jung*

PAUL BISHOP

CHIRON PUBLICATIONS • ASHEVILLE, NORTH CAROLINA

www.ChironPublications.com
Previously published by Spring Journal Books
Frontispiece: Caspar David Friedrich, The Stages of Life, Museum der Bildenden Künste, Leipzig, Germany. Bildarchiv Preussischer Kulturbesitz / Art Resource, New York.
Frontispiece: Titian (Tiziano Vecellio), The Three Ages of Man, Edinburgh, National Gallery of Scotland (Bridgewater Loan, 1945)


Printed primarily in the United States of America.


ISBN 978-1-63051-828-8 paperback
ISBN 978-1-63051-829-5 hardcover
ISBN 978-1-63051-829-5 electronic
ISBN 978-1-63051-831-8 limited edition paperback

# Contents

# List of Abbreviations

JUNG

*CW* = C. G. Jung, *Collected Works*, ed. Sir Herbert Read, Michael Fordham, Gerhard Adler, and William McGuire, 20 vols. (London: Routledge and Kegan Paul, 1953-1983)

*JGW* = C. G. Jung, *Gesammelte Werke*, ed. Lilly Jung-Merker, Elisabeth Ruf, and Leonie Zander, 20 vols. (Olten und Freiburg im Breisgau: Walter, 1960-1983)

*L* = C. G. Jung, *Letters*, ed. Gerhard Adler and Aniela Jaffé, trans. R. F. C. Hull, 2 vols. (London: Routledge and Kegan Paul, 1973-1975)

*PU* = C. G. Jung, *Psychology of the Unconscious: A Study of the Transformations and Symbolisms of the Libido: A Contribution to the History of the Evolution of Thought*, trans. Beatrice M. Hinkle, introd. William McGuire (London: Routledge, 1991)

*MDR* = *Memories, Dreams, Reflections: Recorded and edited by Aniela Jaffé*, trans. Richard and Clara Winston (London: Fontana, 1983)

*ETG* = *Erinnerungen, Träume, Gedanken von C. G. Jung: Aufgezeichnet und herausgegeben von Aniela Jaffé* (Olten und Freiburg im Breisgau: Walter-Verlag, 1971)


FREUD

*SE* = Sigmund Freud, *The Standard Edition of the Complete Works of Sigmund Freud*, general eds. J. Strachey and A. Freud, 24 vols. (London: Hogarth Press, 1953-1974)

*FGW* = Sigmund Freud, *Gesammelte Werke: chronologisch geordnet*, ed. Anna Freud et al., 19 vols. (Frankfurt am Main: Fischer, 1952-1987)


GOETHE

*GE* = *Goethe Edition = Goethe's Collected Works*, ed. Victor Lange, Eric A. Blackall, and Cyrus Hamlin, 12 vols. (Boston, MA; New

York: Suhrkamp/Insel Publishers, 1983-1989). The following volumes have been cited:

—*Selected Poems*, ed. Christopher Middleton (Boston: Suhrkamp/Insel Publishers, 1983) [*Goethe Edition*, vol. 1];

—*Essays on Art and Literature*, ed. J. Gearey, trans. Ellen von Nardroff and Ernest H. von Nardroff (New York: Suhrkamp Publishers, 1986) [*Goethe Edition*, vol. 3];

—*From My Life: Poetry and Truth: Parts One to Three*, ed. Thomas P. Saine and Jeffrey L. Sammons, trans. Robert R. Heitner (New York: Suhrkamp Publishers, 1987) [*Goethe Edition*, vol. 4];

—*From My Life: Poetry and Truth: Part Four/Campaign in France 1792. Siege of Mainz*, ed. Thomas P. Saine and Jeffrey L. Sammons, trans. Robert R. Heitner, Thomas P. Saine (New York: Suhrkamp Publishers, 1987) [*Goethe Edition*, vol. 5];

—*Italian Journey*, ed. Thomas P. Saine and Jeffrey L. Sammons, trans. Robert R. Heitner (New York: Suhrkamp Publishers, 1989) [*Goethe Edition*, vol. 6];

—*Wilhelm Meister's Apprenticeship*, ed. and trans. Eric A. Blackall (New York: Suhrkamp Publishers, 1989) [*Goethe Edition*, vol. 9];

—*Conversations of German Refugees/ Wilhelm Meister's Journeyman Years or The Renunciants*, ed. Jane K. Brown, trans. Jan van Heurck, Krishna Winston (New York: Suhrkamp Publishers, 1989) [*Goethe Edition*, vol. 10];

—*Scientific Studies*, ed. and trans. Douglas Miller (New York: Suhrkamp Publishers, 1988) [*Goethe Edition*, vol. 12].

Cited in the text with volume number plus page reference.

*HA =*   *Hamburger Ausgabe = Werke*, ed. Erich Trunz, 14 vols. (Hamburg: Wegner, 1948-1960; Munich: Beck, 1981). Cited as *Werke* [HA]. *Briefe*, ed. Kurt Robert Mandelkow, 4 vols. (Hamburg: Wegner, 1962-1967). Cited as *Briefe* [HA].

*WA =*   *Weimarer Ausgabe = Werke*, ed. on behalf of Großherzogin Sophie von Sachsen, 4 parts, 133 vols. in 143 (Weimar: Böhlau, 1887-1919). Cited as *Werke* [WA].

Where appropriate, German spelling and punctuation have been modernized.

Where not indicated otherwise, translations from foreign languages are by the author.

# Acknowledgments

I am immensely grateful to Nancy Cater for her patience with regard to this project, and for the interest she has taken in it. Without the impetus provided by the kind invitation from her and Murray Stein to give the Zurich Lecture Series in Analytical Psychology for 2010, this project would never have been completed. Equally, I am grateful to the staff of the following libraries for their help and advice during the completion of this study: Glasgow University Library (and, in particular, Graham Whitaker); the British Library, London; the Philologische Bibliothek of the Freie Universität, Berlin; the Leipziger Universitätsbibliothek; and the Deutsche Bücherei, now part of the Deutsche Nationalbibliothek, in Leipzig. I should also like to thank the Erbengemeinschaft C. G. Jung for permission to use materials in the C. G. Jung-Archiv in the ETH-Bibliothek in Zurich, and I am grateful to Michael Gasser and his colleagues in the ETH Spezialsammlungen for their kind assistance during my work in the archive. I have also benefited from discussions about the Orphic mysteries with my colleague Alan Cardew at the University of Essex. I learned much from individual members of the audience at the Zurich Lectures in October 2010, and I am grateful to them all for their reactions and responses. Finally, my thanks to Sylvia Ruud for her skillful copyediting and indexing, which have brought this volume to completion.

In this study I have drawn on the writings of what is, nowadays, a frequently ignored group of Goethe critics, including Werner Danckert, Friedrich Hiebel, Hans Leisegang, Karl Justus Obenauer, Joseph Pieper, and Eduard Spranger. Strangely enough, although both C. G. Jung and Rudolf Steiner drew extensively on Goethe, the latter inspired a number of literary critics to read Goethe afresh, whereas the former never (or rarely) did. To the extent that I have used some of these critics in this study, I hope to draw attention to this (neglected) school of Goethe criticism. At the same time, I have learned much from my colleague at Glasgow, Roger Stephenson, especially his *Studies in Weimar Classicism: Writing as Symbolic Form* (2010), as well as from other recent scholarship on Goethe, including Gernot Böhme's *Goethes "Faust" als philosophischer Text* (2005), John Armstrong's *Love, Life, Goethe: How to Be Happy in an Imperfect World* (2006), and Pierre Hadot's *N'oublie pas de vivre: Goethe et la tradition des exercices spirituels* (2008)—works that, to a greater or lesser extent, belong in the tradition of the aesthetico-existential approach to Goethe, from Robert d'Harcourt's *Gœthe et l'art de vivre* (1935) to Katherina Mommsen's *Goethe's Art of Living* (2003).

My own research would not have been possible—and my own happiness in this imperfect world greatly diminished—without the love and support of Helen Bridge.

# Preface to the second edition

In his correspondence, Goethe says: "The point of life is life itself."[1] But what, in this context, is meant by life? As I have suggested elsewhere, there is a complex relation between the *Red Book* of C.G. Jung and the tradition of German classicism, including its Goethean thematics of *life, the self, death*, and *beauty*.[2] (Indeed, such is the remarkable scope of the *Red Book* that it encompasses not just beauty, but also *the sublime*.)[3] For instance: from the very outset of the *Red Book*, in the first chapter of *Liber primus* which bears the programmatic title "Refinding the Soul," Jung tells his soul: "The one thing I have learned is that one must live this life" (*dass man nämlich dieses Leben leben muss*).[4] In the following chapter, "Soul and God," Jung enquires further: "But how can I attain knowledge of the heart? You can attain this knowledge only by living your life to the full [*Du kannst dieses Wissen nur dadurch erlangen, dass du dein Leben völlig lebst*] [...] It appears as though you want to flee from yourself so as not to have to live what remains unlived until now."[5]

---

[1] Goethe, letter to Johann Heinrich Meyer of 8 February 1796; in Goethe, *Briefe*, ed. Karl Robert Mandelkow, 4 vols (Hamburg: Wegner, 1962-1967), vol. 3, p. 215: *Der Zweck des Lebens ist das Leben selbst.*

[2] For further discussion, see Paul Bishop, "Jung and the Quest for Beauty: *The Red Book* in relation to German classicism," in Thomas Kirsch and George Hogenson (eds), *The Red Book: Reflections on C.G. Jung's "Liber Novus"* (London and New York: Routledge, 2014), pp. 11-35.

[3] For further discussion, see Paul Bishop, "*Wie hast du es mit der Religion?* Lacan, Jung, and the Religious Sublime," in Robin S. Brown (ed.), *Re-Encountering Jung: Analytical Psychology and Contemporary Psychoanalysis* (London and New York: Routledge, 2018), pp. 195-217; reprinted as "Simply Sublime? Lacan, Jung, and the *Red Book*," in Ann Casement and Phil Goss (eds), *The Blazing Sublime: Thresholds and Pathways between Jung and Lacan* (forthcoming).

[4] C.G. Jung, *The Red Book: Liber Novus* [Reader's Edition], ed. Sonu Shamdasani, trans. Mark Kyburz, John Peck, and Sonu Shamdasani (New York and London: Norton, 2009), p. 128.

[5] Jung, *The Red Book: Liber Novus* [Reader's Edition], p. 133.

"But," Jung continues, "you cannot flee from yourself" (*du kannst dir aber nicht entfliehen*),[6] and in so doing he cites directly from the opening stanza of Goethe's poem, "Primal Words. Orphic" (*Urworte. Orphisch*) of 1820: *So mußt du sein, dir kannst du nicht entfliehen* ("So must you be, you cannot flee yourself"). Thus the theme of *life* intersects with the theme of the *self* — and a quotation from Goethe is inscribed at the very heart of the Jungian project of analytical psychology.[7] In fact, it would be no exaggeration to say that the relation between *life* and *the self* underpins the respective Goethean and Jungian conceptions of *the mystery of life.*

Now in his conversation with his confidant Johann Peter Eckermann (1792-1854) of 7 October 1827, Goethe makes the following remark: "We all walk in mysteries. We do not know what is stirring in the atmosphere that surrounds us."[8] This observation prompts us to consider the dimension of mystery of life, not least with reference to the remarkable poem, "Primal Words. Orphic," in which Goethe explored mysteries which, while being neither Eleusinian, nor Bacchic, nor even (despite the title of the poem!) Orphic, are no less mysterious for that.

For these "Orphica" (as Goethe referred to this poem)[9] represent — as Jochen Schmidt has argued — the sum of experience of an older man, whose mature age determines the perspective from which it was written.[10] Precisely this emphasis on experience — on experience gained through life — is central to Goethe's intentions in this work. Rather than with the Orphic mysteries of ancient Greece, his concern is with the "mysteries and wonders" among which, as he told Eckermann, we are all groping. Thus, rather than offering an initiation into the Orphic ancient mysteries, his poem uncovers the mysteriousness of life itself.

---

[6] Jung, *The Red Book: Liber Novus* [Reader's Edition], pp. 133-134.

[7] Bishop, "Jung and the Quest for Beauty," pp. 22-27.

[8] *Conversations of Goethe with Eckermann and Soret*, trans. John Oxenford, vol. 2 (London: Smith, Elder, 1850), p. 19. This preface to the second edition draws on an extended version of a paper given to the Guild of Pastoral Psychology in London on 22 October 2016 and published in an abbreviated form as *"We All Walk in Mysteries: We Do Not Know What is Stirring in the Atmosphere Around Us"* [The Guild of Pastoral Psychology, Guild Paper No. 325]. I am grateful to the Guild for granting permission to re-use this material.

[9] See Goethe's letter to Sulpiz Boisserée of 16 July 1818; Goethe, *Briefe* [Hamburger Ausgabe], ed. Kurt Robert Mandelkow, 4 vols (Hamburg: Wegner, 1962-1967), vol. 3, p. 435.

[10] Jochen Schmidt, *Goethes Altersgedicht "Urworte. Orphisch": Grenzerfahrung und Entgrenzung* (Heidelberg: Winter, 2006), p. 28.

What were the Ancient Mysteries? We cannot tell exactly because they remain, as their name suggests, just that: *mysteries*, something secret and revealed only to the few, if even to them.[11] In this respect, we should pay attention to the etymology of the word "mystery," which tells us all we need (or can) know about this concept. For the modern English word "mystery" can be traced back, through the Middle English word "mysterie," the Ango-Norman word "misterie," and the Old French "mistere," to the Latin word "mysterium" and ultimately to ancient Greek.

In ancient Greek, μυστήριον ("mustérion") means *mystery*, a *secret*, or a *secret rite*, derived from the the word μύστης ("mústēs," i.e., *initiated one*), derived from μύστης (*mústēs*, i.e., *initiated one*), from μυέω ("muéō," i.e., *I initiate*) and in turn μύω ("múō," i.e., *I shut*).

The late eighteenth and early nineteenth centuries — i.e., the age of Goethe, and the intellectual-cultural background to Jung — saw an intensification of interest in the theology and rituals of the ancient Mysteries, which continued well into the twentieth century — i.e., the age of Jung.[12] According to the English Neoplatonist Thomas Taylor (1758-1835), those Mysteries had, according to the translator and commentator Thomas Taylor (1758-1835), been "designed by the ancient theologists, their founders, to signify occultly the condition of the unpurified soul invested with an earthly body, and enveloped in a material and physical nature."[13] Taylor drew attention to the distinction between the Lesser Mysteries of Eleusis which, as Proclus had noted, Heracles had had to undergo in order to enter the underworld — "Hence Hercules being purified by *sacred initiations*, and enjoying undefiled fruits, obtained at length a perfect establishment among the gods" —[14] and the Greater

---

[11] For a general discussion of the religious background formed by ancient Greek mystery cults, see Michael B. Cosmopoulos (ed.), *Greek Mysteries: The Archaeology and Ritual of Ancient Greek Secret Cults* (London and New York: Routledge, 2003); Jennifer Larson, *Ancient Greek Cults: A Guide* (New York and London: Routledge, 2007); Hugh Bowden, *Mystery Cults in the Ancient World* (London: Thames & Hudson, 2010); and Charles Stein, "Ancient Mysteries," in Glenn Alexander Magee (ed.), *The Cambridge Handbook of Western Mysticism and Esotericism* (Cambridge: Cambridge University Press, 2016), pp. 3-12.

[12] For a discussion that places Goethe's poem in the context of the nineteenth-century debate on mythology, see Paul Bishop, "From the Archaic into the Aesthetic: Myth and Literature in the 'Orphic' Goethe," in Leon Burnett, Sanja Bahun, and Roderick Main (eds), *Myth, Literature, and the Unconscious* (London: Karnac, 2013), pp. 189-210.

[13] Taylor, "On the Eleusinian Mysteries," in *Oracles and Mysteries*, in *Oracles and Mysteries* [TTS, vol. 7] (Frome: Prometheus Trust, 2001), p. 60.

[14] Proclus, *Commentary on the Republic of Plato*, cited by Thomas Taylor in *A Dissertation on the Eleusinian and Bacchic Mysteries* [1790], "On the Eleusinian Mysteries," in *Oracles and Mysteries*,

Mysteries of Eleusis (corresponding to the ascent of Heracles to Mount Olympus), whose ceremonies are said to have "obscurely intimated, by mystic and splendid visions, the felicity of the soul both here and hereafter, when purified from the defilements of a material nature, and constantly elevated to the realities of intellectual [spiritual] vision."[15] According to another commentator, the Canadian-born historian of mysticism, Manly P. Hall (1901-1990), the Mysteries' "gloom and depression" had represented "the agony of the spiritual soul unable to express itself because it has accepted the limitations and illusions of the human environment."[16] Yet he also noted that there has been another stage of the Mysteries where the neophyte, in his initiation, entered a series of chambers whose "ever-increasing brilliancy" portrayed "the ascent of the spirit from the lower worlds into the realms of bliss,"[17] perhaps like the journey leading "up to the light, just as some men are said to have gone from Hades up to the gods," of which Socrates had spoken.[18] And one of Jung's closest collaborators, the Hungarian philologist and mythologist Carl Kerényi (1897-1973), also explored the Eleusinian Mysteries on the basis of various ancient depictions in some detail.[19]

Rather than the Eleusinian or the Bacchic, the Mysteries to which Goethe, however obliquely, refers in his poem of 1820 are the Orphic Mysteries, a cult focused on the god ripped to shreds by the Thracian Maenads yet whose head and lyre continued to be the source of music, i.e., aesthetic pleasure, and prophecy long after his death. Even more important than any set of mythological references, however, is the first word of the title of Goethe's poem, i.e., *Urwort*. This word (or *Wort*) is an *Ur-* word, i.e., a primal word, evoking the notion of the primordial or the archaic.[20] In this context, the notion of the primordial or the archaic

---

p. 74; cf. "A History of the Restoration of the Platonic Theology" [1788], in *Oracles and Mysteries*, p. 199.

[15] Taylor, "On the Eleusinian Mysteries," in *Oracles and Mysteries*, p. 77.

[16] Manly P. Hall, *The Secret Teachings of All Ages* (New York: Tarcher/Penguin, 2003), p. 69.

[17] Hall, *Secret Teachings of All Ages*, p. 72.

[18] *Republic*, 521c; in *The Republic of Plato*, ed. and trans. Allan Bloom (New York: Basic Books, 1968), p. 200. This journey signifies "the turning of a soul around from a day that is like night to the true day," in other words "that ascent to what *is*" which constitutes, Socrates affirms, "philosophy."

[19] See Carl Kerényi, *Eleusis: Archetypal Image of Mother and Daughter*, trans. Ralph Manheim (Princeton, NJ: Princeton University Press, 1967, pp. 52-59).

[20] For further discussion of the archaic, see Paul Bishop (ed.), *The Archaic: The Past in the Present* (London and New York: Routledge, 2012); Paul Bishop and Leslie Gardner (eds), *The Ecstatic*

is not meant (just) in a chronological or metaphysical sense, but rather (or as well as) in an existential sense — in the sense that the archaic is the eternal which is always in time.[21]

This relation between the archaic and everyday sense emerges clearly from the wider context of Goethe's remark in his discussion with Eckermann, which deserves further analysis in order to uncover its full signficance. For this conversation and the anecdotes it contains are rich in psychoanalytic resonances, as the American commentator Avital Ronnell has realized.[22] Here is Eckermann's account of a dream he had, and the response it evoked in Goethe, and the subsequent exchange of anecdotes:[23]

I related to Goethe a wonderful dream of my boyish years, which was literally fulfilled the next morning.

"I had," said I, "brought up three young linnets, to which I devoted my whole heart, and which I loved above all things. They flew freely about my chamber, and came towards me and settled on my hand as soon as I entered at the door. One day at noon, I had the misfortune, that, on my entrance into the chamber, one of the birds flew over me, out of the house — I knew not whither. I sought it the whole afternoon, on all the roofs, and was inconsolable when evening came and I had discovered no traces of it. I went to sleep with sad thoughts in my heart, and towards morning I had the following dream: — Methought I roamed about the neighbouring houses in search of my lost bird. All at once I heard the sound of its voice, and saw it behind the garden of our cottage, seated upon the roof of a neighbour's house. I called to it, and it approached me, moved its wings towards me as if asking for food, but still it could not venture to fly down to my hand. I ran quickly

---

*and the Archaic: An Analytical Psychological Inquiry* (London and New York: Routledge, 2018); and Paul Bishop, Leslie Gardner, and Terence Dawson (eds), *Katabasis and the Archaic: Depth Psychology and the Descent of the Soul*, forthcoming.

[21] For further discussion, see Paul Bishop, "Just a Moment? Or, the Archaic as an Expression of the Eternal in Time," in Angeliki Yiassemides (ed.), *Time and the Psyche: Jungian Perspectives* (London and New York: Routledge, 2017), pp. 87-105.

[22] See Avital Ronnell, *Dictations: On Haunted Writing* [1986] (Lincoln, NE: Bison, 1993), pp. 172-175.

[23] *Conversations of Goethe with Eckermann and Soret*, vol. 2, pp. 18-22.

through our garden into my chamber, and returned with the cup of soaked rape seed; I held the favourite food towards it, and it perched upon my hand, when, full of joy, I carried it back into my chamber to the other two.

"With this dream I awoke; and as it was then broad daylight, I quickly put on my clothes, and with the utmost haste ran down through our little garden to the house where I had seen the bird. But how great was my astonishment when the bird was really there ! Everything happened literally as I had seen it in the dream. I called the bird, it approached, but it hesitated to fly to my hand. I ran back and brought the food, when it flew upon my hand, and I took it back to the others."

"This boyish adventure of yours," said Goethe, "is certainly very remarkable. But there are many such things in nature, though we have not the right key to them. We all walk in mysteries. We are surrounded by an atmosphere of which we do not know what is stirring in it, or how it is connected with our own spirit. So much is certain, — that in particular cases we can put out the feelers of our soul beyond its bodily limits, and that a presentiment, nay, an actual insight into the immediate future, is accorded to it."

"I have lately experienced something similar," returned I. "As I was returning from a walk along the Erfurt road, about ten minutes before I reached Weimar, I had the mental impression that a person whom I had not seen, and of whom I had not even thought for a length of time, would meet me at the corner of the theatre. It troubled me to think that this person might meet me, and great was my surprise when, as I was about to turn the corner, this very person actually met me, in the same place which I had seen in my imagination ten minutes before."

"That is also very wonderful, and more than chance," returned Goethe. "As I said, we are all groping among mysteries and wonders. Besides, one soul may have a decided influence upon another, merely by means of its silent presence, of which I could relate many instances. It has often happened to me that, when I have been walking with an acquaintance, and have had a living image of something in my mind, he has at once begun to speak of that very thing. I have also known a man who, without saying a word, could suddenly silence a party engaged in cheerful conversation, by the mere power of his mind. Nay, he could also introduce a tone which would make everybody feel uncomfortable. We have all something of electrical and magnetic forces within us, and we put forth, like the magnet itself, an attractive or repulsive power, accordingly as we come in contact with something similar or dissimilar. It is possible, nay, even probable, that if a young girl were, without knowing it, to find herself in a dark chamber with a man who designed to murder her, she would have an uneasy sense of his unknown presence, and that an anguish would come over her, which would drive her from the room to the rest of the household."

"I know a scene in an opera," returned I, " in which two lovers, who have long been separated by a great distance, find themselves together in a dark room without knowing it; but they do not remain long together before the magnetic power begins to work; one feels the proximity of the other — they are involuntarily attracted towards each other — and it is not long before the young girl is clasped in the arms of the youth."

"With lovers," answered Goethe, "this magnetic power is particularly strong, and acts even at a distance. In my younger days I have experienced cases enough, when, during solitary walks, I have felt a great desire for the company of a beloved girl, and have thought of her till she has really come to meet me. 'I was so restless in my room,' she has said, 'that I could not help coming here.'

"I recollect an instance during the first years of my residence here, where I soon fell in love again. I had taken a long journey, and had returned some days ; but, being detained late at night by court affairs, I had not been able to visit my mistress; besides, our mutual affection had already attracted attention, and I was afraid to pay my visits by day, lest I should increase the common talk. On the fourth or fifth evening, however, I could resist no longer, and I was on the road to her, and stood before her house, before I had thought of it. I went softly upstairs, and was upon the point of entering her room, when I heard, by the different voices, that she was not alone. I went down again unnoticed, and was quickly in the dark streets, which at that time were not lighted. In an impassioned and angry mood I roamed about the town in all directions, for about an hour, and passed the house once more, full of passionate thoughts of my beloved. At last I was on the point of returning to my solitary room, when I once more went past her house, and remarked that she had no light. 'She must have gone out,' said I, to myself, 'but whither, in this dark night? and where shall I meet her?' I afterwards went through many streets — I met many people, and was often deceived, inasmuch as I often fancied I saw her form and size ; but, on nearer approach invariably found that it was not she. I then firmly believed in a strong mutual influence, and that I could attract her to me by a strong desire. I also believed myself surrounded by invisible beings of a higher order, whom I entreated to direct her steps to me, or mine to her. 'But what a fool thou art!' I then said to myself; 'thou wilt not seek her and go to her again, and yet thou desirest signs and wonders!"

"In the meantime I had gone down the esplanade, and had reached the small house in which Schiller afterwards lived, when it occurred to me to turn back towards the palace, and then go down a little street to the right. I had scarcely taken a hundred steps in this direction, when I saw a female form coming towards me which perfectly resembled her I expected. The street was faintly lighted by the weak rays which now and then shone from a window, and since I had been already often deceived in the course of the evening with an apparent resemblance, I did not feel courage to speak to her in doubt. We passed quite close to each other, so that our arms touched. I stood still and looked about me; she did the same. 'Is it you?' said she, and I recognised her beloved voice. 'At last!' said I, and was enraptured even to tears. Our hands clasped each other. 'Now,' said I, 'my hopes have not deceived me; I have sought you with the greatest eagerness; my feelings told me that I should certainly find you; now I am happy, and I thank God that my forebodings have proved true.' 'But, you wicked one!' said she, 'why did you not come? I heard today, by chance, that you had been back three days, and I have wept the whole afternoon, because I thought you had forgotten me. Then, an hour ago, I was seized with a longing and uneasiness on your account, such as I cannot describe. There were two female friends with me, whose visit appeared interminable. At last, when they were gone, I involuntarily seized my hat and cloak, and was impelled to go out into the air and darkness, I knew not whither; you were constantly in my mind, and I could not help thinking that I should meet you.' Whilst she thus spoke truly from her heart, we still held each other's hands, and pressed them, and gave each other to understand that absence had not cooled our love. I accompanied her to her door, and into the house. She went up the dark stairs before me, holding my hand and drawing me after her. My happiness was indescribable; both because I at last saw her again, and also because my belief had not deceived me, and I had not been deluded in my sense of an invisible influence."

Goethe was in a most amiable mood; I could have listened to him for hours; but he seemed to be gradually growing tired, and so we very soon went to bed in our alcove.

When today we read a passage like this it comes as no surprise to learn how keen the early psychoanalytic community was to apply its insights to Goethe and to the circle around Goethe. In 1930, for instance, the Austrian-American psychoanalyst Eduard Hitschmann (1871-1957) gave a talk about Goethe's personality from a psychoanalytic perspective to the Goethe-Verein in Vienna, later published in *Imago*; and a year later the journal *Psychoanalytische Bewegung* published a psychoanalytic-bio-graphical study of Eckermann.[24] And there are many other examples one could give which, for reasons of space, we must discuss another time.

The dream recounted by Eckermann at the beginning of this passage is described by him as "wonderful," or, in German, *merkwürdig*, i.e., it is worthy of note. Goethe reinforces the choice of this term, describing it as "very remarkable" (i.e., *höchst merkwürdig*). It demonstrates how, in his view, we are all "walking" — moving, travelling, wandering, *wir wandeln* — in mysteries or secrets (*in Geheimissen*). Eckermann's dream prompts Goethe to reflect on the way that our soul

---

[24] Eduard Hitschmann, *Psychoanalytisches zur Persönlichkeit Goethes* (Vienna: International Psychoanalytischer Verlag, 1932); *Johann Peter Eckermann: Eine psychoanalytisch-biographische Studie* (Vienna: Internationaler Psychoanalytischer Verlag, 1933).

or our psyche (*unsere Seele*) can "put out feelers" beyond the body and in this way gain access to "a presentiment," i.e., *ein Vorgefühl* (literally, a preliminary feeling), and hence gain "an actual insight into the immediate future" (*ein wirklicher Blick in die nächste Zukunft*). This presentiment is "actual" or "real" (*wirklich*), because it has or makes an effect; as Jung said, *was wirkt, ist wirklich*.[25]

This thought sparks off in Eckermann a recollection of a recent experience. (Throughout this conversation, the experiential nature of these mysteries or secrets is repeatedly emphasized.) Walking back to Weimar along the Erfurt road, Eckermann suddenly remembered someone he had neither seen or thought of for some time — Auguste Kladzig (1810-1875), a famous singer, actress and author. In 1833, she married and became Auguste von La Roche but, when she was sixteen, the thirty-four-year old Eckermann had fallen in love with her and written her love poems. On the road from Erfurt, Eckermann suddenly remembered her — just before, as he was about to turn a corner, he bumped into her again.

Goethe responds with much enthusiasm to this narrative. What had happened to Eckermann on this occasion was "also very wonderful" (*gleichfalls sehr merkwürdig*) and — in a significant phrase — "more than chance" (*mehr als Zufall*). It is, surely, an example of what Jung would call an example of synchronicity, in accordance with his definition of it as "a case of *meaningful coincidence*, i.e., an acausal connection."[26] Strengthening Goethe in his conviction that "we are all groping [*tappen*] among mysteries and wonders [*in Geheimnissen und Wundern*]," it prompts him to recollect different ways in which, simply through the power of its sheer presence, one soul or psyche can influence another. For instance, the example of two people suddenly thinking about the same thing at the same time, or the example of a man whose mere presence was enough to make everyone fall silent. Goethe describes this power in vitalist or energic terms, akin to electricity or magnetism — those forces that so fascinated writers and thinkers of the classical and Romantic period alike.[27] The notion of animal magnetism was formulated by the

---

[25] For one of the many occasions when Jung uses this phrase, see "The Aims of Psychotherapy," in *The Practice of Psychotherapy* [*Collected Works*, vol. 16], trans. R.F.C. Hull (London: Routledge and Kegan Paul, 1966), §111.

[26] Jung, "Synchronicity: An Acausal Connecting Principle," in *The Structure and Dynamics of the Psyche* [*Collected Works*, vol. 8], trans. R.F.C. Hull (London: Routledge and Kegan Paul, 1969), §827.

[27] For further discussion of the fascination of eighteenth-century writers with electricity and

controversial German physician Franz Friedrich Anton Mesmer (1734-1815) in the 1770s, and it was developed further by some German Romantic "scientists" as Karl Christian Wolfart (1778–1832), Christoph Wilhelm Hufeland (1762-1836), and Johann Karl Passavant (1790-1857). Goethe's third example, that of a girl in a dark room who senses the presence of man who plans to kill her, induces perhaps almost as great an anxiety (*eine Angst*) in us as readers as it does in the girl in the darkness...

In turn, this third example prompts Eckermann to recall a similar moment in an opera, just as a later conversation on 28 May 1830 will spur him on to give an account of a ballet he saw in Mailand. The opera in question in the conversation under discussion is, of course, Beethoven's *Fidelio*. In his prison cell in the dungeons, into which his rival nobleman has thrown him, Florestan does not recognize his wife, Leonore, disguised as a man and calling herself Fidelio. When his rival, Pizarro, turns up in the dungeon and threatens Florestan, Leonore/Fidelio interposes herself between the two men and reveals her identity. With the arrival of Don Fernando and the end of tyranny, all the prisoners are liberated — including Florestan, who is unchained by Leonore, and she is hailed by the crowd as a "fair wife" (*holdes Weib*) (incidentally, an expression that one also finds in Schiller's "Ode to Joy," famously set to music by Beethoven in his Ninth Symphony).

Goethe brings the conversation away from the world of art and back to the world of reality; indeed, back to reality in its erotic dimension. Curiously, the example that Goethe gives in Eckermann's account of the conversation appears to be a projection onto Goethe of an incident that had happened during Eckermann's own infatuation with Augustine Kladzig from 1828 to 1830;[28] or perhaps the example of the lovers thinking of each other and eventually encountering each other in the street is one that happened all the time in Weimar; or, for that matter, in any time or place? Closer to our psychoanalytic home, however, is the striking parallel between Goethe imagining the face of his lover in the faces of everyone else he sees in the street and what happened to Freud at the height of his friendship with Jung. For as Freud wrote to Jung on 4 October 1909: "The day after we separated an incredible number of

---

magnetism, see Robert J. Richards, *The Romantic Conception of Life: Science and Philosophy in the Age of Goethe* (Chicago and London: University of Chicago Press, 2002).

[28] Eduard Castle, *Anmerkungen und Register zu Eckermanns Gesprächen mit Goethe* (Berlin, Leipzig, Vienna and Stuttgart: Bong, 1916), pp. 276-277.

people looked amazingly like you; wherever I went in Hamburg, your light hat with the dark band kept turning up. And the same in Berlin."[29]

The language of Goethe's account of his experience places a strong emphasis the dimensions of emotion and of desire. He paces the streets "in an impassioned and angry mood" (*unmutig und leidenschaftlich*), he is "full of passionate thoughts" (*voll sehnsüchtiger Gedanken*) about his beloved, he talks about his and his lover's "strong mutual influence" (*eine gegenseitige Einwirkung*), about his sensation of being "surrounded by invisible beings of a higher order" (*unsichtbar von höheren Wesen umgeben*), and about "signs and wonders" (*Zeichen und Wunder*). And when he and his lover eventually find each, Goethe says he has been seeking her "with the greatest eagerness" (*mit dem größten Verlangen*), but he has trusted his "feelings" (*Gefühl*); he tells her he had been "seized with a longing and uneasiness on [her] account" (*ergriff mich ein Verlangen und eine Unruhe nach Ihnen*); and he declares, almost as if anticipating the American hit pop song, "you were always on my mind" (*dabei lagen Sie mir immer im Sinn*). Goethe's account of this experience, whether it was his or Eckermann's or of them both, ends on three powerful concepts — "happiness" (*Glück*), "belief" (*Glaube*), and "feeling" or "sense" (*Gefühl*), and not just any ordinary feeling or sense but "a sense of an invisible influence" (*mein Gefühl von einer unsichtbaren Einwirkung*). Indeed, even recounting this experience seems to have had an influence: Goethe was now, Eckermann remembers, in a "most amiable mood," and he (Eckermann) could have listened to him (Goethe) for hours. But even Goethe grew tired, and so they soon retired; exhausted, as it were, from the mere memory of the power of desire.

Nevertheless, we do not have to read this passage from Goethe's conversations with Eckermann along the Freudian lines proposed by Avital Ronell. She refers this conversation of 7 October 1827 back to an earlier conversation of 26 September 1827 and forward to the conversation the next day on 8 October 1827. In so doing, she focuses on an expression used by Goethe, *Vorgefühl* or "presentiment," which she analyses in a Freudian way in two respects.[30] First, by splitting the word up into "a kind of cryptic code" for Eckermann's "deeply felt attachment" to birds or, in German *Vo[r]ge[füh]l= Vogel*. (This attachment to birds manifests itself in various ways, from his father's trade as a seller of raw

[29] *The Freud/Jung Letters: The Correspondence between Sigmund Freud and C.G. Jung*, ed. William McGuire, trans. R.F.C. Hull (Cambridge, MA: Harvard University Press, 1988), p. 258.

[30] Ronell, *Dictations*, p. 161.

quills, via the nest of young warblers someone brings him, to the flock of birds he watches with Goethe, the pair of roasted hens they eat together, and their discussion of the character of the cuckoo.) Second, through the "uncanny link" that Goethe's family name was Vogelhuber (before it was changed to the French Gothé) and, above and beyond this "hidden and discarded patronymic," Goethe's focus in his conversation of 7 October 1828 on accidents (*Zufall*), mystery and secrets (*Geheimnisse*), the other side of which is the "uncanny" or "un-secret" (*unheimlich — un-heimlich*) itself. These terms are constellated around the governing notion of *Vorgefühl* or presentiment or even telepathy.

And here lies the basis for a Jungian approach to these passages. Not simply through the motif of the occult, in which Jung was indeed interested for a while,[31] and yet which should nevertheless not define the scope of his work, as Freud suggested (in "On the History of the Psychoanalytic Movement" [1914]) by asserting that both Jung and Alfred Adler "court a favourable opinion by putting forward certain lofty ideas, which view things, as it were, *sub specie aeternitatis*" and criticizing in particular those members of the Jungian school who had, in Freud's words, "picked out a few cultural overtones from the symphony of life" and "once more failed to hear the mighty and primordial melody of the instincts."[32] Rather, a Jungian approach to the conversations between Goethe and Eckermann will focus on the notion of the secret or *Geheimnis* — the Jungian counterpart to the Freudian emphasis on the uncanny or *unheimlich*.

Once again, etymology can help discern these subterranean (and, in this sense, unconscious) links. For the English word "secret" derives from the modern and old French word *secret*, and in turn from the Latin word *secretus* meaning "separate" or "set apart" (cf. the noun *secretum*, i.e., a secret). At the root of this word lies the past participle of *scernere* = *se* + *cernere*, i.e., "to separate" — and conceptually this word would seem to stand at odds with the notion of the holy. Yet the word "holy," deriving from the Old English *hālig*, and in turn from the Old High German *heilag* and the Old Norse *heilagr* from a Germanic base meaning the WHOLE, also means to "set apart for religious use" or "to consecrate."

[31] See C.G. Jung, *Psychology and the Occult* (London: Ark, 1982); and *Jung on Synchronicity and the Paranormal*, ed. Roderick Main (London: Routledge, 1997).

[32] Sigmund Freud, "On the History of the Psychoanalytic Movement," in *Historical and Expository Works on Psychoanalysis* [Penguin Freud Library, vol. 15], ed. Albert Dickinson, trans. James Strachey (Harmondsworth: Penguin, 1993), pp. 57-128 (pp. 119 and 124).

Here lies the etymological and conceptual link with two other related terms — with sacrifice and mystery. For "sacrifice" derives from the Latin *sacrificare*, and correspondingly *sacrificium* means "a sacrifice," cf. *sacrificus* which derives from *sacer*, i.e., "sacred," "holy" and *ficus*; a sacrifice is thus something that makes something holy.[33] And the word *mystery*, as we saw above, has Greek roots mediated to other modern European languages: via the Anglo-Norman equivalent of the Old French *mistere* (cf. in modern French *mystère*), in turn from the Latin *mysterium* and ultimately the Greek *mustērion*, a "sacred thing or ceremony," from the base of *mustikos*, i.e., "secret" — and hence the source of the word "mystic" as well.

The linguistic nexus surrounding the German word for "secret" (i.e., *Geheimnis*) and the German word for "the uncanny" (i.e., *das Unheimliche*) is equally insightful. After all, both the word *heimlich*, i.e., "secret," and *heimisch*, i.e., "homely" or "familiar," are related to the word for "home," i.e., *das Heim*. Within the word for "secret," i.e. *Geheimnis*, the word for "home" is literally "at home," for it lies at the very heart of the word — *Ge-heim-nis*. The "secret" is also the "mystery," something which is "secretive" or "mysterious," i.e., *geheimnisvoll*. And etymologically what is secret is related to "the uncanny," i.e., *das Unheimliche*, something which is "un-homely" and yet nevertheless is related to one's home. On this etymological account, embraced by Freud in his essay on "The Uncanny" (*Das Unheimliche*) of 1919, home is where the uncanny is at home.[34]

A cursory glance at these etymological links and relations thus pushes us in the direction of a "dialectic of the secret," of the kind that has been proposed by the French philosopher and theologian Bertrand Vergely. In a talk given at I.D.E.E. PSY in Paris on 5 September 2012, Vergely outlined the contours of the dialectic of the secret as follows:

> When a soul suffers, sometimes it cries out, sometimes it whispers. Between what is too much and what is too little, however, there exists a happy medium which is defined by the secret. The secret is something one hides. But it also

---

[33] For a fascinating overview of the notion of sacrifice, particularly in relation to contemporary approaches, see Dennis King Keenan, *The Question of Sacrifice* (Bloomington and Indianapolis: Indiana University Press, 2005).

[34] See "The Uncanny" (1919), in Sigmund Freud, *Art and Literature* [Penguin Freud Library, vol. 14], ed. Albert Dickson, trans. James Strachey (Harmondsworth: Penguin, 1990), pp. 335-376.

something one reveals to someone else in a privileged one-to-one. This is not a contradiction. One never says anything better than what one has been able to conceal. A word speaks when it emerges from a weight of silence. For then it secretes [*secrète*] something, just as one says that a perfume secretes a nectar. This is what illuminates our sufferings. Do we not suffer from a lack of a secret? It is not because of a lack of a secret that one cries out or whispers? This is the question we have to ask.[35]

Someone who did not have any lack of secrets was Carl Jung, who places the notion of the secret in the foreground of his autobiographical work (constructed by Aniela Jaffé), *Memories, Dreams, Reflections* (1962).

For reasons of space it is not possible to quote extensively from *Memories, Dreams, Reflections*, and the reader is advised to go (back) to this work and read it with an eye alert to all those passages where Jung refers, implicitly or explicitly, to the idea of the secret. For instance, there is the childhood dream of the subterranean phallus that initiates him into "the secrets of the earth"; when reading out of *Orbis Pictus*, Jung describes his feeling of affinity with the illustrations of Brahma, Vishnu, and Shiva as "a secret I must never betray"; when as a child he played the game of sitting on a stone, and wondering whether he was the one sitting on the stone or the stone on which he is sitting, he sensed that "this stone stood in some secret relationship to me"; he recounts how this sense of secret was embodied in the little mannikin he carved out of the end of a ruler, "an inviolable secret which must never be betrayed"; he describes "the possession of a secret" as having "a very powerful formative influence on my character" and as "the essential factor of my boyhood"; as he moved away from Christianity, Jung was constantly "on the lookout for something mysterious [*nach etwas Geheimnisvollem*]," while realizing that the subterranean phallus was "something very secret and other [*etwas sehr geheimes Anderes*] that people don't know about"; finally, with the vision of God and Basel Cathedral, Jung had "something tangible that was part of the great secret."[36] Small wonder, then, that Jung comes to the

---

[35] Bertrand Vergely, "La dialectique du secret." Available online HTTP: <http://psycho-ressources.com/blog/la-dialectique-du-secret/>.

[36] Jung, *Memories, Dreams, Reflections*, ed. Aniela Jaffé, trans. Richard and Clara Winston (London: Fontana, 1967), pp. 30, 33, 36, 37, 38, and 58.

following conclusion about the role of the secret in the development of his life (and, by the same token, in the constitution of his thought):

> My entire youth can be understood in terms of this secret.
> It induced in me an almost unendurable loneliness. My one
> great achievement during those years was that I resisted the
> temptation to talk about it with anyone. Thus the pattern
> of my relationship to the world was already prefigured:
> today as then I am a solitary, because I know things and
> must hint at things which other people do not know, and
> usually do not even want to know.[37]

In this passage it is almost as if Jung wants to say alongside Kafka in his famous diary entry of 1913: "What I have achieved is only a result of being solitary" (*Was ich geleistet habe, ist nur ein Erfolg des Alleinseins*).[38] This, then, is Jung's secret — that he has a secret, and it is in this existential sense that we should approach the great secrets or the great mysteries of Goethe's poem, "Primal Words. Orphic" (*Urworte. Orphisch*).

As I undertook to argue in the Zurich Lecture Series entitled *Reading Goethe At Midlife*, Goethe's poem can be read in the light of Jung's notion of the stages of life and, in particular, his notion of the mid-life crisis.[39] For it takes us through the entire existential dialectic of the human life-cycle: from birth (stanza 1), socialization (stanza 2), and sexual awakening (stanza 3) to conformity to social convention (stanza 4) and rebirth at midlife (stanza 5). The focus shifts, as it does in the life of the human being, from the particular to the general and back again, switching between the individual (stanzas 1 and 3) and society (stanzas 2 and 4). Of all the stanzas in this poem, however, the most relevant to our discussion is the opening one, entitled "DAIMON" (in Greek), "Dämon" (in German), or "Daimon" (in English). The reason why Goethe chooses to start his poem with this stanza (the actual titles of the stanzas were added later) can be understood with reference to remarks by one of Goethe's contemporaries, Arthur Schopenhauer (1788-1860).

---

[37] Jung, *Memories, Dreams, Reflections*, p. 58.

[38] See Kafka's diary entry for 21 July 1913 (Kafka, *Tagebücher 1910-1923*, ed. Max Brod (Frankfurt am Main: Fischer, 1986), p. 228.

[39] See Paul Bishop, *Reading Goethe At Midlife: Ancient Wisdom, German Classicism & Jung* (New Orleans, LA: Spring Journal Books, 2011).

In his short essays collected under the magnificent title *Parerga and Paralipomena*, Schopenhauer includes one with the programmatic title, "Transcendent Speculation on the Apparent Deliberateness in the Fate of the Individual." In this essay Schopenhauer examines the notion that "*a secret and inexplicable power* guides all the twists and turns in the course of our lives" — and that it does so "often contrary to our temporary motive, but in such a way as to be appropriate to its objective integrity and subjective purposiveness, hence to be conducive to our actual true benefit, so that we often afterwards recognize the foolishness of our desires leading in the opposite direction."[40] This is the sense given by Schopenhauer to a fragment by Cleanthes (§527) cited in Seneca's *Epistles* (letter 107): "Aye, the willing soul / Fate leads, but the unwilling drags along."[41] Expressed in more philosophical terms, this is the notion that there exists, within each individual, "an unfathomable power, sprung from the unity of the deep-lying root of necessity and chance," and this notion arises, Schopenhauer suggests, from the consideration that "the determinate, highly unique *individuality* of each human being in physical, moral, and intellectual respects […] is everything about him [or her] and, consequently, must have sprung from the highest metaphysical necessity."[42] Expressed in mythological terms, this is the idea of destiny, *heimarmenē, peprōmene, fatum*, or "the guiding genius of each individual"; in Christian terms, it is providence or *pronoia*.[43] Whether called destiny, genius, or providence, this concept is trying to name "the root of that inexplicable unity of the contingent and the necessary, which constitutes the secret controller of all being."[44]

As is evident from his poem, Goethe opts for the ancient notion of the genius or *daimon*, that is, a spirit that is (in Schopenhauer's words) "attached to all individuals and presiding over their courses of life," a notion that is of Etruscan origin but widespread among the ancients.[45]

---

[40] Schopenhauer, "Transcendent Speculation on the Apparent Deliberateness in the Fate of the Individual," in *Parerga and Paralipomena: Short Philosophical Essays*, vol. 1, ed. and trans. Sabine Roehr and Christopher Janaway (Cambridge: Cambridge University Press, 2014), pp. 177-197 (p. 185).

[41] Seneca, *Ad Lucilium Epistulæ Morales*, trans. Richard M. Gummere, vol. 3 (Cambridge, MA; London: Harvard University Press; Heinemann, 1921), p. 229.

[42] Schopenhauer, "Transcendent Speculation," p. 185.

[43] Schopenhauer, "Transcendent Speculation," p. 185.

[44] Schopenhauer, "Transcendent Speculation," p. 185.

[45] Schopenhauer, "Transcendent Speculation," p. 186. For further discussion of the notion of the *daimon* (and many other related themes in Goethe's poem), see Peter Kingsley, *Catafalque:*

Schopenhauer cites a wide variety of ancient sources, and it is worth pausing for a moment on these, because these are likely also to have been sources known to Goethe and to Jung alike. The essential idea of the genius or *daimon* is contained, Schopenhauer says, in a verse of Menander cited by Plutarch (in his essay "On Tranquillity of Mind" in his *Moralia*, chapter 15, 474b), by Stobaeus (in his *Eclogues*, 1.6.4), and by Clement of Alexandria (in his *Stromata*, book 5, 15):

> By every man at birth a Spirit stands,
> A guide of virtue for life's mysteries;[46]

In the myth of Er in book 10 of the *Republic*, Socrates explains how, prior to its rebirth, each soul chooses its life together with the appropriate personality, and is assigned the corresponding *daimon*: "When all the souls had chosen lives, in the same order as the lots they had drawn, they went forward to Lachesis" — i.e., the second of the Three Fates or Moirai; the others are Clotho and Atropos — "and she sent with each the demon he had chosen as the guardian of the life and a fulfiller of what was chosen":

> The demon first led the soul to Clotho — under her hand as it turned the whirling spindle — thus ratifying the fate it had drawn and chosen. After touching her, he next led it to the spinning of Atropos, thus making the threads irreversible. And from there, without turning round, they went under Necessity's throne.[47]

Schopenhauer notes that Porphyry has provided "a commentary on this passage that is very much worth reading,"[48] and he notes that Socrates

---

*Carl Jung and the End of Humanity*, 2 vols (London: Catafalque Press, 2018), vol. 1, pp. 86-89, and vol. 2, pp. 521-522.

[46] Plutarch, *Moralia*, trans. W.C. Helmbold, vol. 6 (Cambridge, MA: Harvard University Press, 1939), p. 221. In fact, Plutarch takes issue with this line from Menander, and to it he opposes the view found in Empedocles (Diels-Kranz, fragment 122) that "two Fates, as it were, or Spirits, receive in their care each one of us at birth and consecrate us": "Chthonia was there and far-seeing Heliopê, / And bloody Deris, grave-eyed Harmonia, / Callisto, Aeschra, Thoösa, and Denaea, / Lovely Nemertes, dark-eyed Asapheia" (i.e., Earth-maiden, Sun-maiden; Discord, Harmony; Beauty, Ugliness; Swiftness, Slowness; Truth, Uncertainty) (p. 221).

[47] *Republic*, 620d-621a; *The Republic of Plato*, trans. Bloom, p. 303.

[48] Schopenhauer, "Transcendent Speculation on the Apparent Deliberateness in the Fate of the Individual," p. 186. For further discussion, see Dorian Gieseler Greenbaum, *The Daimonic in Hellenistic Astrology: Origins and Influence* (Leiden: Brill, 2016), chapter 7, "Porphyry, the *Oikodespotēs* and the Personal Daimon," pp. 236-277.

had earlier recounted to Glaucon how each soul in the afterlife hears "the speech of Necessity's maiden daughter, Lachesis": "A demon will not select you, but you will choose a demon. Let him who gets the first lot make the first choice of a life to which he will be bound by necessity."[49] And the idea is picked up by Horace and expressed in the following "beautiful" manner, defing the genius as

> the god who accompanies our birth-star
> And rules it, who is what mortal men are, and whose face
> Varies for each of us from fair to foul [*vultu mutabilis, albus et ater*].[50]

(Jung had a particular interest in this passage; see his early article "The Significance of the Father in the Destiny of the Individual" (1909; 1927; 1949), where in the original version he expresses the hope that "experience in the years to come will sink deeper shafts into this obscure territory, on which I have been able to shed but a fleeting light, and will discover more about the secret workshop of the demon who shapes our fate.")[51] And Schopenhauer mentions further Apuleius's "On the God of Socrates," which discusses daimons in general as well as "the peculiar dæmon" who, according to Plato (see above), is "allotted to every man, who is a witness and a guardian of his conduct in life, who, without being visible to any one, is always present, and who is an arbitrator not only of his deeds, but also of his thought."[52] Schopenhauer refers to the "short but important" chapter on the "peculiar dæmon" in section 9, §6, of Iamblichus's *On the Mysteries of the Egyptians, Chaldeans and Assyrians*.[53] And he cites the

---

[49] *Republic*, 617d-e; *The Republic of Plato*, trans. Bloom, p. 300.

[50] Horace, *Epistles, Book II and Epistle to the Pisones*, ed. and trans. Niall Rudd (Cambridge: Cambridge University Press, 1989), p. 57.

[51] Jung, *Freud and Psychoanalysis* [*Collected Works*, vol. 4], trans. R.F.C. Hull (London and New York: Routledge and Kegan Paul, 1961), §693-§744 (§744, note 226); cf. Foreword to the Second Edition (p. 302); and cf. Jung's letter to Carl Kerényi of 12 July 1951 where he wrote: "I can imagine that for a mythologist the collision with living archetypes is something quite special. [..] It means an intensification and enhancement of life — with a pensive side-glance at the genius *vultu mutabilis, albus et ater*" (C.G. Jung, *Letters*, ed. Gerhard Adler and Aniela Jaffé, trans. R.F.C. Hull, vol. 2, *1951-1961* (Princeton, NJ: Princeton University Press, 1975), p. 19).

[52] Apuleius, *Golden Ass, or The Metamorphosis and other Philosophical Writings*, trans. Thomas Taylor [TTS, vol. 14] (Frome: Prometheus Trust, 1997), pp. 233-255 (p. 245).

[53] Iamblichus, *On the Mysteries of the Egyptians, Chaldeans, and Assyrians and Life of Pythagoras*, trans. Thomas Taylor [TTS, vol. 17] (Sturminster Newton: Prometheus Trust, 1999), pp. 1-195 (p. 146).

passage in the commentary on Plato's *First Alcibiades* where Proclus writes: "For he who guides aright our whole life, fulfilling both the choices we have made before our birth, the gifts of fate and of the gods who guide it, and further bestowing in due measure the illuminations of providence, such is our guardian spirit."[54] Finally, Schopenhauer considers the notion of *fate* in Paracelsus and in Plutarch's "On the Sign of Socrates" (*Moralia*, book 7), as well as the Christian notion of providence, as "figurative, allegorical conceptions of the matter being discussed, since it is not granted to us to grasp the most profound and hidden truths other than through image and simile."[55]

And if we examine the first stanza of Goethe's "Primal Words. Orphic" (and, indeed, his poem as a whole) it emerges that the central secret or mystery than it is addressing is the individual as the meeting point of chance and necessity. True, he presents this secret or mystery in astrological terms, playing with astrological symbolism (ll. 1-2) much as he does in the opening lines of his autobiographical work, *Poetry and Truth* (*Dichtung und Wahrheit*), book 1.[56] But this is not in itself an astrological argument; rather, his case rests on the amazing expression that he uses at the end of the first stanza where he defines the living self as "the minted form that lives and living grows" (Middleton), as "imprinted form informing living matter" (Whaley), as *Geprägte Form, die lebend sich entwickelt*.

This is the central mystery, and it is one that we find addressed in various ways in Goethe's works (not least in his *Faust*, which deserves further consideration on its own). We find it, for example, in his evocation of the *magical world* we find in one of his early essays, "On Falconet and about Falconet" (1776):

---

[54] Proclus, *Commentary on the First Alcibiades*, ed. L.G. Westerink, trans. William O'Neill [Platonic Texts and Translations, vol. 6] (Westbury: Prometheus Trust, 2011), p. 102.

[55] Schopenhauer, "Transcendent Speculation on the Apparent Deliberateness in the Fate of the Individual," p. 188.

[56] For further discussion of the role of astrology in Goethe's thought, see Albert Kniepf, "Goethe und die Astrologie," *Psychische Studien*, vol. 45, no. 6 (June, 1918), 256-264; Julius Schiff, "Goethe und die Astrologie," *Preußische Jahrbücher*, 210 (1927), 86-96; and Johannes Hoffmeister, "Goethe und die Astrologie," *Geisteskultur*, vol. 39, nos 11-12 (1930), 278-286. And for further discussion of the role of astrology in Jung's thought, see Liz Greene, *Jung's Studies in Astrology: Prophecy, Magic, and the Qualities of Time* (London and New York: Routledge, 2018); and Liz Greene, *The Astrological World of Jung's "Liber Novus": Daimons, Gods, and the Planetary Journey* (London and New York: Routledge, 2018).

[The artist] may enter the workshop of the cobbler or a
stable; he may look at the face of his beloved, his boots or
the world of antiquity, everywhere he sees sacred vibrations
[…], with which nature joins together all things […] With
every step he takes is revealed a *magic world*, which
intimately and steadfastly surrounded all great masters,
whose works will forever inspire reverence in the striving
artist […] Every human being has felt several times in his
or her life the force of this magic […] Who has never been
overcome by a shudder when entering a sacred forest?
Whom has all-embracing night never shaken with an
uncanny horror? To whom has, in the presence of his lover,
the entire world not appeared golden? […] This is what […]
weaves its way through the soul of the artist, what presses
forward in him […] to the most understandable expression,
without going through the power of cognition.[57]

(For an analysis of this passage from a vitalist perspective, see the
comments made by the vitalist philosopher Ludwig Klages (1872-1956),
who used it to argue that Romanticism had only gone further along a
path opened up by Goethe.)[58] And we find it, again with reference to the
Platonic notion of weaving in a passage from *Faust* —

True, the tissue of thought hath warp and weft,
Like a masterpiece of the weaver's craft.
One tread, and a thousand threads do flit,
Hitherward, thitherward, shoots the shuttle;
The threads flow out, unseen and subtle;
One stroke, and a thousand knots are knit.[59]

[57] See "Nach Falconet und über Falconet" in *Aus Goethes Brieftasche* (1776), discussing the
work of the French sculptor Étienne Maurice Falconet (1716-1791); translated in *Goethe on Art*, ed.
John Gage (Berkeley and Los Angeles: University of California Press, 1980), pp. 17-20. For further
discussion of this unusual text by Goethe, see W.D. Robson-Scott, *The Younger Goethe and the Visual
Arts* (Cambridge: Cambridge University Press, 1981), pp. 53-56.

[58] Ludwig Klages, *Der Geist als Widersacher der Seele* [1929-1932], 6th edn (Bonn: Bouvier
Verlag Herbert Grundmann, 1962), pp. 1117-1118). For further discussion, see Raymond Furness,
*Zarathustra's Children: A Study of a Lost Generation of German Writers* (Rochester, NY; Camden House,
2000), pp. 99-122; and Paul Bishop, *Ludwig Klages and the Philosophy of Life: A Vitalist Toolkit* (London and New York: Routledge, 2018), esp. pp. 143-144.

[59] *Faust I*, ll. 1924-1927; in Goethe, *Faust: Parts I and II*, trans. Albert G. Latham (London;
New York: Dent; Dutton, 1908), pp. 86-87.

— which Goethe later reworked as a poem "Antepirrhema" (c. 1819) that concludes his scientific essay "Indecision and Surrender" (1820):

> Thus view with unassuming eyes
> The Weaver Woman's masterpiece:
> One pedal shifts a thousand strands,
> The shuttles back and forward flying,
> Each fluent strand with each complying,
> One stroke a thousand links commands;
> No patchwork, this, of rang and tatter.
> Since time began She plots the matter,
> So may the Master, very deft,
> Insert with confidence the weft.[60]

(As Goethe noted in his letter to Humboldt of 17 March 1832, where he uses the analogy in an explicitly psychological context, "consciousness and the unconscious are related as the weft is to the warp, an analogy that I like to use.")[61]

And finally the Fates are replaced by the Muses in the concluding stanza of Goethe's poem, "Permanence in Change" (*Dauer im Wechsel*) of 1803, which contains in its very title another aspect of the paradoxical tension that constitutes the individual:

> Let the start and end so fusing
> Join in One and unify!
> Swifter than the things you're losing
> You must let yourself go by!
> Thanks the Muses for bestowing
> Favour of a lasting kind:
> Import from your heart outflowing
> And the form within your mind.[62]

The Muses as goddesses of memory, as well as goddesses of science and art, enable us to transform the past — and, in so doing, to open the way

---

[60] Goethe, "Antepirrhema," translated Christopher Middleton, in *Selected Poems*, p. 163; cf. "Indecision and Surrender," in Jeremy Naydler (ed. and trans.), *Goethe on Science: An Anthology of Goethe's Scientific Writings* (Edinburgh: Floris Books, 1996), pp. 98-100.

[61] Goethe, *Briefe* [Hamburger Ausgabe], vol. 4, p. 480.

[62] Goethe, *Selected Poems*, trans. Whaley, p. 87.

to the future — and they enable us to do this through art. Through a combination of hope (cf. the final stanza of "Primal Words. Orphic"), imagination, and memory, fused together in the (aesthetic) symbol, we are able to change, to develop and thus (in Nietzsche's words) to become more truly who we are. This is indeed a miracle — and it is the miracle of transformation about which Jung spoke at length in *Symbols of Transformation* (1952), his reworking of the book he had originally published as *Transformations and Symbols of Libido* (1911-1912).[63] Against the cosmic backdrop of the rising and setting sun — "the sun, rising triumphant, tears himself from the enveloping womb of the sea, and leaving behind him the noonday zenith and all its glorious works, sinks down again into the maternal depths, into all-enfolding and all-regenerating night"; the reference to the Mothers of Goethe's *Faust*, Part Two — "always he imagines his worst enemy within himself — a deadly longing for the abyss, a longing to drown in his own source, to be sucked down to the realm of the Mothers"; and the allusion to the legend of Theseus and Peirithous — "if, like Peirithous, he tarries too long in this abode of rest and peace, he is overcome by apathy, and the poison of the serpent paralyses him for all time," Jung drives home the existential implications of his message which is ultimately a Goethean one (§553).

For "the mind shies away," Jung writes, "but life wants to flow down to the depths," and so "the daimon throws us down" and "makes us traitors to our ideals and cherished convictions — traitors to the selves we thought we were" (§553). Jung contrasts this situation, which he describes as "an *unwilling* sacrifice," with what happens when the sacrifice is *voluntary*: then "things go very differently." An *involuntary* sacrifice involves "an overthrow, a 'transvaluation of all values,' the destruction of all we held sacred"; it is, despite that Nietzschean echo, something essentially negative. By contrast, a *voluntary* sacrifice brings "transformation and conservation" (§553). Striking an elegaic note, Jung writes that "everything grows old, all beauty fades, all heat cools, all brightness dims, and every truth becomes stale and trite"; thanks to "the working of time," all things "age, sicken, crumble to dust" — *unless, that is, 'they change"* (§553). This experience of transformative change involves an act of descent — "And let those that go down the sunset way do so with open eyes," Jung warns, "for it is a sacrifice which daunts even the gods" (§553) —, but also an act of ascent, or a moment in which, as Jung promises us,

---

[63] C.G. Jung, *Symbols of Transformation* [*Collected Works*, vol. 5], trans. R.F.C. Hull (Princeton, NJ: Princeton University Press, 1967).

"the vanishing shapes are shaped anew," in which truth "suffers change and bears new witness in new images, in new tongues" (§553). When this happens, we understand why, for Plato,[64] as it is for Aristotle,[65] a sense of wonder is the beginning of philosophy. And we are also tempted to exclaim, along with Goethe in his poem "Parabase" (c. 1820), *Zum Erstaunen bin ich da*, "Wonder of wonders, I am here."[66]

Paul Bishop, Glasgow, November 2019

---

[64] See *"Theaetetus"*, 155c-d; in *The Being of the Beautiful: Plato's "Theaetetus", "Sophist", and "Statesman"*, trans. Seth Benardete (Chicago and London: University of Chicago Press, 1984), p. I.19. For further discussion, see David W. Bollert, "The Wonder of Humanity in Plato's Dialogues," in *Kritike: An Online Journal of Philosophy*, vol. 4, no. 1 (June, 2010), 174-198; and Laura-Lee Kearns, "Subjects of Wonder: Toward an Aesthetics, Ethics, and Pedagogy of Wonder," *The Journal of Aesthetic Education*, vol. 49, no. 1 (Spring, 2015), 98-119.

[65] See *Metaphysics*, 982b; in *Complete Works of Aristotle*, ed. Jonathan Barnes, vol. 2 (Princeton, NJ: Princeton University Press, 1984, p. 1554). For further discussion, see Bertrand Vergely, *Retour à l'émerveillement* (Paris: Albin Michel, 2010).

[66] Goethe, "Parabase" (c. 1820), trans. Middleton, in *Selected Poems*, ed. Middleton, p. 155.

## A note on Goethe's text

Various translations of *Urworte. Orphisch* exist, including versions by Christopher Middleton,[67] John Whaley,[68] and David Luke.[69] For completeness, a fourth version by James F. Clarke is offered here in full,[70] followed by the complete text of Goethe's own notes on the poem as translated by John S. Dwight.[71]

ORPHIC SAYINGS

I. Destiny
According as the sun and planets saw,
    From their bright thrones, the moment of thy birth,
Such is thy Destiny; and by that Law
    Thou must go on — and on — upon the earth.
Such *must* thou be; Thyself thou canst not fly;
    So still do Sibyls speak, have Prophets spoken.
The living stamp, received from Nature's die,
    No time can ever change, no art has ever broken.

II. Chance
Yet through these limits, sternly fixed to bound us,
    A pleasing, wandering form goes with and round us.
Thou art not lonely — thou hast many brothers —
    Learning and acting, still art moved by others.
Chances takes or gives the thing while we pursue it:
    Our life's a trifle, and we trifle through it.
The circling years go round. All keeps the same;
    The lamp stands waiting for the kindling flame.

---

[67] Goethe, *Selected Poems*, ed. Christopher Middleton [Goethe Edition, vol. 1] (Boston: Suhrkamp/Insel Publishers, 1983), pp. 231-233.

[68] Goethe, *Selected Poems*, trans. John Whaley (London: Dent, 1998), pp. 123-125.

[69] Goethe, *Selected Poems*, ed. and trans. David Luke (Harmondsworth: Penguin, 1964), pp. 302-304.

[70] *Select Minor Poems of Goethe and Schiller*, ed. and trans. John S. Dwight (Boston: Hilliard, Gray, 1839), pp. 160-161.

[71] *Select Minor Poems of Goethe and Schiller*, trans. Dwight, pp. 417-421.

III. Love

It comes at last. From heaven it falls, down-darting,
    Whither from ancient chaos up it flew;
    Around it floats, now near, and then departing.
It fans the brow and breast the Spring-day through:
    Mournful though sweet, a saddened bliss imparting,
Rousing vague longings for the Fair and True,
    While most hearts fade away, unfixed, alone,
The noblest is devoted to the **One**.

IV. Necessity

And so, once more, 'tis as the planets would;
    Conditions, limits, laws, our fate decide;
We *will* the right, because we see we *should*;
    And thus by our own hands our limbs are tied.
The heart drives out its hope, a much-loved brood;
    At the stern *must* wishes and whims subside;
So, after many years, in seeming free,
    More closely fettered than at first are we.

V. Hope

Yet shall these gates unfold, these walls give way.
    These barriers, rooted in the ancient hill,
Are firm as primal rock; but rocks decay;
    One essence moves in life and freedom still;
Through cloud, and mist, and storm, to upper day
    Lifts the sad heart, weak thoughts, and fainting will;
Through every zone she ranges unconfined;
    She waves her wing — we leave time, space, behind!

*The following, in explanation of this poem, is from the ninth volume of Goethe's Posthumous Works.*

The following five stanzas have been already printed in the second volume of the "Morphology," but they deserve to be made known to a wider public. Friends, too, have wished that something might be added for a clearer understanding of the same, that their meaning may no longer be matter of conjecture merely, but obvious and determined.

The aim here has been, to present poetically, in a compendious, laconic style, whatever has been handed down of older and later Orphic doctrines. These few strophes contain much that is significant, in an order, which, once known, introduces the mind easily into the midst of the weightiest reflections.

## 1. Δαίμων, Destiny.

The relation of the title to the strophe requires explanation. The "Daemon" here signifies the necessary, limited individuality of a person, determined at birth, — the characteristic by which each distinguishes himself from every other, however great their resemblance. This determination they used to ascribe to some overruling planet; and the infinitely various motions and relations of the heavenly bodies to each other and to the earth were construed into an apt correspondence with the manifold vicissitudes of births. Out of this was the whole future fate of the man to proceed; and one may well grant, that inborn powers and peculiarities, more than all else, determine the fate of men.

Accordingly this strophe asserts, with repeated emphasis, the unchangeableness of the Individual. The ever so marked peculiarity may be disturbed, indeed, like every thing finite; but, so long as its kernel holds together, it cannot be split in pieces, or dissolved, even through long generations.

This firm, tough nature, developing itself out of itself, comes, indeed, into all sorts of external relations, whereby its first and original character is hemmed in in its workings, and hindered in its tendencies; and this new power, which now comes in, our philosophy names

## 2. Τύχη, Chance.

However, it is not accident that one is descended from this or that nation, race, or family; for the nations spread over the earth, as well as their various ramifications, are to be regarded as individuals; and Tyche (Chance) can only enter by amalgamation and crossing of bloods.[72] We

---

[72] Goethe's biologistic thinking raises problems for contemporary readers, as it does in the case of Nietzsche; see Greg Moore, *Nietzsche, Biology and Metaphor* (Cambridge: Cambridge University Press, 2002).

see a striking example of the stiff-necked personality of such races in the Jews: European nations, removed to other parts of the world, do not lay aside their character; and in North America, after several centuries, the Englishman, the Frenchman, the German, is distinctly recognized; but where amalgamations have taken place, the operations of Tyche instantly appear; thus, for instance, the Mestizo is known by the clear skin. In education, if it be not public and national, Tyche maintains her versatile rights. Nurse and maid, father or guardian, teacher or overseer, as well as all the early circumstances, as of playmates, country or city life, &c, all modify the peculiarity, by earlier development, by check or by furtherance; the "Daemon," indeed, holds his own through all; and this is the personal nature, the " old Adam," as it may be called, which, as often as it may get driven out, comes back ever more indomitable.

In this sense, of a necessary constitutional individuality, they have ascribed to every man his "Daemon," who occasionally whispers in his ear what is the very thing to be done. So Socrates chose the hemlock, because it behoved him to die.[73]

Yet Tyche desists not. She works constantly upon Youth, which, with its inclinations, its plays, its associations, and its volatile essence, throws itself this way and that way, and finds no hold or satisfaction. Then arises and grows with every day a more earnest un-rest, a deeper fundamental longing; it awaits the coming of a new divinity.

3. Ἔρως, Love.

Under this is contained all, from the gentlest inclination to the most passionate madness, which can be thought of; here the individual Demon and misleading Tyche form an alliance; the man seems only to obey himself, to let his own will have its way, to give the reins to his impulses; and yet there are contingences which will intrude, foreign forces which will turn him out of his path; he thinks to get, and he is caught; he thinks to have won, and he is already lost. Here, too, Tyche drives her trade again; she entices the wanderer into new labyrinths; here are no limits to his wandering, for the way is error. And now we fall into the danger of losing ourselves in the thought, that what seemed most characteristic and individual will float away and dissolve into the Universal. Hence the

---

[73] See Nietzsche, "The Problem of Socrates," §12: "Socrates *wanted* to die: not Athens, but he himself chose the hemlock; he forced Athens to sentence him" (*The Portable Nietzsche*, ed. and trans. Walter Kaufmann (New York: Viking Penguin, 1968), p. 479).

abrupt entrance of the two last lines will give us a distinct hint, how alone one may escape this error and gain instead a life-long security.

For now is it first seen of what the Demon is capable; he, the self-subsisting self-seeker, who, with unconditioned will, reached forth into the world, and only felt chagrin when Tyche, hero and there, stepped in his way, — he now feels that he is not determined and stamped by nature alone; now is he in his inmost soul sure that he can determine himself, — that the object which Fate brings in his way, he can not only take strong hold of, but also appropriate it, and, what is more, embrace a second being, like himself, with eternal, indestructible fondness.

No sooner is this step taken, than freedom by a free resolution is given up. Two souls must fit themselves to one body, two bodies to one soul; and whilst such an alliance is brought about, soon steps in, by mutual fond necessity, a third; parents and children again must form themselves into one whole; great is the common satisfaction, but greater the want. The body, consisting of so many members, by its earthly fate grows sick in some one of its parts; instead of enjoying itself in the whole, it suffers in details, and yet, in spite of that, is such a relation found to be as desirable as it is necessary. The advantage attracts every one, and to the disadvantages he lets himself become reconciled. Family links itself to family, clan to clan; a whole people finds itself together, and finds, too, that that is for the good of the whole, which the one shall decide ; it erects that decision irrevocably into a law; what was once free, spontaneous affection now becomes duty, out of which a thousand duties disclose themselves; and, that all may be settled for time and for eternity, there is no lack of ceremonies for state, church, or family. All parties provide by the strictest contracts, by all possible public testimonials, that the whole shall in no smallest part be endangered through private will or caprice.

4. Ἀνάγκη, Necessity.

This verse needs no remark. There is no one whose own experience does not furnish notes enough to such a text, — no one who has not felt himself painfully constrained at the recollection of such circumstances; nay, many a one might well despair, if the Present held him bound in the same way. How gladly we hasten hence to the last lines, to which every fine spirit will cheerfully undertake to supply the commentary, both moral and religious!

*An die Hoffnung!*

# Part One

At that time, in the fortieth year of my life, I had achieved everything that I wished for myself. I had achieved honor, power, wealth, knowledge, and every human happiness. Then my desire for the increase of these trappings ceased, the desire ebbed from me and horror overcame me.

—Jung, *The Red Book*

In the second half of life you may begin to understand that life is a comedy all round, in every respect, and that nothing is quite true and even that is not quite true; and by such insight you slowly begin to step out of life without risking a neurosis.

—Jung, Seminar on Nietzsche's *Zarathustra*,
7 December 1938

# CHAPTER 1

# The Stages of Life and the Midlife Crisis: A Brief History of an Idea

The notion of the midlife crisis is one of the key ideas associated with Jung's analytical psychology, although the actual phrase was probably not coined by Jung himself.[1] In his standard account of Jung's ideas, Anthony Storr presents the idea of the stages of life in the context of another of Jung's central categories, the process of individuation.[2] While Jung's outline of the stages of life has, as we shall see, been developed by several Jungian analysts, including Murray Stein (1983) and Verena Kast (1986), it has also been regarded by other Jungians as problematic. For example, in their entry on the "stages of life" in *A Critical Dictionary of Jungian Analysis*, its editors raise three questions about his schema, concluding with this final, and highly negative, point: "Jung's adherence to the theory of opposites makes the division [between the first and the second half of life] somewhat pat and rigid."[3] And in his outline presentation of Jung's thought, David Tacey remarks that Jung's theory of the midlife crisis is "slightly dated" and "reflects a time in which society

---

[1] See Elliott Jaques, "Death and the Mid-Life Crisis," *International Journal of Psycho-Analysis* 46 (1965): 502-514 (which the *Oxford English Dictionary* cites as the source of the expression). According to Jaques, the midlife crisis occurs at the age of 35. Although Jaques makes no mention of Jung, his paper is entirely compatible with Jung's earlier essay of 1930/1931 (see chapter 2, below).

[2] Anthony Storr, *Jung* (London: Fontana, 1973), pp. 80-93.

[3] Andrew Samuels, Bani Shorter, and Fred Plaut, *A Critical Dictionary of Jungian Analysis* (London and New York: Routledge, 1986), p. 143.

was more stable than it is today," arguing that "the theory of the stages of life needs some postmodern modifications."[4]

Yet Jung's principle of individual psychobiography is, in fact, a traditional topos of classical thought. Concomitant with the notion of life conceived as a sequence of stages is the notion of a major dividing point or caesura, usually called the "midlife crisis." Likewise, this is in many ways an ancient idea, albeit one that has, over the last half century or so, come to the fore in psychoanalytic (and indeed, popular psychological) discourse. According to a widespread misconception, the Chinese ideogram for "crisis"—the word *weiji* (危機)—consists of the two characters for "danger" and "opportunity." It is a topos to which the literature on "midlife crisis" frequently refers,[5] even though it is, in fact, untrue.[6] At least, it is untrue in terms of philology, although the fanciful derivation may conceal a deeper, psychological truth.

In this study, on which a series of talks given in 2010 as the Zurich Lecture Series in Analytical Psychology was based, I shall explore Jung's theory of the midlife crisis, not least by means of a close reading of his paper *"Die Lebenswende"*—a title translated by R. F. C. Hull, not entirely accurately, as "The Stages of Life." The turning point between, on the one hand, the first and second stages of life (childhood and youth), and, on the other, the third and final (old age and death), is what Jung called the "midlife crisis," and represents what I shall call "the Orphic moment": a moment of crisis, yes, but also a moment of decision, of opportunity—of hope. A chance to heed ancient wisdom, and to listen for "the call of the Self."

In this opening chapter, I provide a brief historical survey of the stages of life and its related concept, the midlife crisis. Necessarily there will be gaps in such a historical overview—yet consideration of some of the major instances of the use of the term provides a useful historical context in which to set Jung's paper "The Stages of Life" (1930), and a major poem from Goethe's late period, "Primal Words. Orphic" (*Urworte. Orphisch*) (1817), both of which make use of these ancient topoi. Then,

---

[4]David Tacey, *How To Read Jung* (London: Granta, 2006), p. 49.

[5]See, for example, Jim Conway, *Men in Mid-Life Crisis* [1978] (Exeter: Paternoster, 1983), pp. 14-15. The suggestiveness of this combination of lines constituted the starting point for a recent radio discussion of the midlife crisis: *Sound Advice*, BBC Radio 4, 29 July 2006.

[6]For further discussion, see the online article by Victor H. Mair, "How A Misunderstanding about Chinese Characters Has Led Many Astray," at http://pinyin.info/chinese/crisis.html, accessed 28 September 2007.

in chapter 2, I offer a detailed analysis of Jung's paper on "The Stages of Life," relating it to major concepts in his other works and essays. In chapter 3, I examine the intellectual and cultural background to "Primal Words. Orphic," while in chapter 4 I offer a close reading of this text, drawing on Goethe's own commentary and on relevant background material to help elucidate its message, and using Jungian ideas to explore the psychological implications of Goethe's work. Without diverging too far from Goethe's original text, this chapter tries to highlight the remarkable symmetry between Goethean and Jungian ideas. Throughout this study, I balance Jung's sense of crisis, resolved by the "call of the Self," with Goethe's emphasis on the importance of hope, seeking to widen the discussion and to delineate the cosmic dimension, as sought by Goethe, to the outcome of the Orphic moment: the happy human being.

## Two Visual Starting Points

As a visual *entrée en matière* into our discussion, let us consider briefly two paintings that, between them, provide a kind of visual contextualization to frame our discussion: a work by a classical painter—a member of the sixteenth-century Venetian school and a major exponent of the Italian Renaissance—Titian (c. 1485-1576), and one by an iconic representative of the German Romantic school, Caspar David Friedrich (1774-1840).[7]

Belonging to the Duke of Sutherland Collection and displayed in the National Gallery of Scotland, *The Three Ages of Man* is one of Titian's early paintings (Figure 1, frontispiece).[8] Described by one commentator as "a poetic meditation on the transience of human life and love set in an

[7]Titian's classical temperament and the clarity of his colors doubtless explain his appeal to Goethe, whereas the latter's condemnatory remarks, made in 1826 to Friedrich Förster (*Goethes Gespräche*, ed. Flodoard von Biedermann, 5 vols. [Leipzig: Biedermann, 1909-1911], vol. 3, pp. 309-310), about the painting *Cloister Graveyard in Snow* by the Berlin-based artist Karl Friedrich Lessing (1808-1880), could equally well apply to some of Friedrich's paintings; see *Goethe und die Kunst*, ed. Sabine Schulze (Ostfildern: Hatje, 1994), p. 461.

[8]For discussion of the painting, see Aidon Weston-Lewis, "Titian: Three Ages of Man," in *A Companion Guide to the National Gallery of Scotland* (Edinburgh: National Galleries of Scotland, 2000), pp. 32-33 (p. 32); and *Titian*, ed. David Jaffé (London: National Gallery, 2003), pp. 88-89. Jaffé provides a full bibliography documenting discussion of this painting, including Erwin Panofsky, *Problems in Titian, Mostly Iconographic* (London: Phaidon, 1969), pp. 94-99; Charles Hope, *Titian* (London: Jupiter Books, 1980), pp. 18-23; Hugh Brigstocke, *Italian and Spanish Paintings in the National Gallery of Scotland* (Edinburgh: Trustees of the National Gallery of Scotland, 1993), pp. 172-177; and Paul Joannides, *Titian to 1518: The Assumption of Genius* (New Haven and London: Yale University Press, 2001), pp. 193-201.

idyllic pastoral landscape,"[9] this painting depicts the "three ages" in three groups: on the right, two sleeping and rather tubby infants, over whom an equally portly Cupid clambers, represent the blissful innocence of childhood; to the left, (sexual) maturity is symbolized by two lovers—a nearly naked shepherd, and an amorous and somewhat *deshabillé* country girl—who gaze into each other's eyes, his legs and her arms intertwined, as she clasps in her hands two musical pipes; and, positioned to the right of the center, an old man—in the manner of penitent St. Jerome—contemplates one skull held in his right hand, holding a second skull in his left hand. These symbols of Eros and Thanatos are set against a landscape (as Vasari noted) of "exceptional beauty,"[10] and the painting's implicit equation of sleep and death—the infants are sleeping, the old man is exhausted, and the pose of the lovers suggests postcoital fatigue—underscores its classic message of *memento mori*.

In *Der Mensch als Symbol* (The Human Being as a Symbol) (1933), the psychoanalyst Georg Groddeck (1866-1934) discusses, apparently without knowledge of Titian's original, the copy of the painting in the Galleria Borghese in Rome, attributed to (Giovanni Battista Salvi da) Sassoferrato (1605-1685).[11] Not surprisingly, since the painting is nothing less than a gift for psychoanalysts, Groddeck highlights the persistent phallic symbolism in the work: the two (testicular) children sleep in front of the upright tree stump, symbolizing both erection and castration anxiety; the suggestive positioning of the pipes requires no commentary, but Groddeck emphasizes the active role of the shepherdess in initiating the "pipe-play of love" (*das Flötenspiel der Liebe*);[12] while the old man, sadly incapable of an erection, instead can only stretch out his foot. In Groddeck's view, the painting depicts something "fundamentally human" (*Urmenschliches*), by representing life (*Leben*) in the form of the drive (*Trieb*). Yet something about it, he contends, is unusual: "In it, what

---

[9] Weston-Lewis, "Titian: Three Ages of Man," p. 32.

[10] Giorgio Vasari, *Lives of the Artists*, ed. and trans. George Bull (Harmondsworth: Penguin, 1971), p. 448.

[11] Georg Groddeck, *Der Mensch als Symbol: Unmaßgebliche Meinungen über Kunst und Sprache* [1933] (Frankfurt am Main: Fischer, 1989), pp. 33-36.

[12] Groddeck comments specifically: "In the Fall of Man, which was in fact not a Fall at all, but was invented for the benefit of human life, because without a feeling of guilt all pride and all human sensation would remain dead, the woman carries the culpability of innocence [*ist unschuldig schuldig*]; she is attracted by the phallus, the man's snake. That the gift of transforming the penis into a phallus [*des Gliedes in den Phallus*] does not belong to the woman, however, is made plain by the image of childhood with its tree-clambering Eros: erection can take place without a woman" (*Der Mensch als Symbol*, p. 34).

is masculine comes into being, persists, and decays, whereas the feminine, shown in just a single figure, neither comes into being nor disappears, but remains unchanging" (*daß in ihm Männliches wird, ist und vergeht, während das Weibliche, in einer einzigen Figur gezeigt, weder entsteht noch vergeht, sondern unverändert immer ist*).[13]

Nevertheless, in Titian's painting, the "three ages" to which its title refers are youth, sexual maturity, and old age—understood as a set of dis-crete, if interrelated, stages, the third and final one of which is, so it inti-mates, distinctly gloomy. Another visual *point d'entrée* that relates even more closely in our thematic discussion is a painting entitled *The Stages of Life* (*Die Lebensstufen*) by the German Romantic painter Caspar David Friedrich (Figure 2, Frontispiece). Dated to around 1834 or 1835, and thus completed over three centuries after Titian's painting, this work—displayed in Leipzig's Museum der bildenden Künste—is equally, or even more, enigmatic.[14]

Now, Friedrich completed this work (long believed to have been painted before 1815) in 1835, shortly before a massive stroke brought his career as a painter to an end, and five years before his eventual death. Not simply for this reason are an awareness of mortality and a powerful sense of life's transience major themes of the work. On the shore of the sea, an old man—Friedrich himself?—walks towards a group of four figures: a man in a top hat who turns in greeting, a young woman who gestures with her finger, and two children at play (each of whom has been identified as a relation of Friedrich). The presence in the children's hands of the Swedish flag—Greifswald, Friedrich's hometown, had passed along with the rest of Pomerania from Swedish to Prussian control in 1815—and the old man's nationalist garb suggest a political message in the painting, but a religious dimension opens up with the correspondence (and/or contrast) between each of the figures and the presence of five ships in the background. If the children, young woman, middle-aged man, and old man represent the stages of life, the ships making their way back to the shore surely symbolize the final return, while the upturned boat in the fore-

[13]*Ibid.*, p. 36.

[14]See Dietulf Sander, "Caspar David Friedrich: Lebensstufen," in *Museum der bildenden Künste Leipzig: Museumsführer*, ed. Hans-Werner Schmidt (Munich and Berlin: Deutscher Kunstverlag, 2004), pp. 134-135. See also Jens Christian Jensen, *Caspar David Friedrich: Leben und Werk* (Cologne: DuMont, 1983), pp. 216-218; William Vaughan, *Friedrich* (London: Phaidon, 2004), pp. 297-300; and Norbert Wolf, *Caspar David Friedrich 1774-1840: Der Maler der Stille* (Cologne: Taschen, 2007), pp. 12, 89, and 90-91.

ground on the right is more than reminiscent of a coffin. The end of life as
shipwreck?—or as a safe return to harbor? The sticks to the left, it has
been suggested, mark the location of the nets—ready to be hauled in. And
the warm, glowing light of the setting sun engulfs the entire setting, as the
moon gently rises...

The crucial figure here is surely the middle-aged man in the top hat,
who turns to look at the old man—who, with his back to us, stands in the
same relation to him as does the viewer—and addresses him with an
ambiguous, not entirely benevolent, gesture. In a way, this figure sums up
the questions posed by the midlife crisis: Does it beckon us on to contemplate the children at play, a symbol of fresh life and renewal, or to medi-
tate that the journey on which we are embarked has only one final, and
inevitable, destination?

## From the Ages of Humankind...

In Friedrich Schiller's philosophical poem or cultural-historical ballad,
"The Four Ages of the World" (*Die vier Weltalter*) (1802), a minstrel steps
forth before the guests of a feasting assembly and narrates a history of the
world in four epochs: first, a Saturnian period, or the infancy of the world;
second, the Heroic age of work and toil; third, the era of Greek art and
civilization; and finally, the era of medieval Christendom. For the festive
listeners—and for us, as readers—it is the task of the fifth age to remain
true to the vocation of art to retain the youthfulness of the world:

> Then may Bards and fair Dames in eternal band
>   Be conjoin'd, of soft pleasing duty,
> Aye working and weaving, hand in hand,
>   The girdle of Truth and Beauty.
> So Love and the Muse, in blest harmony strung,
> Shall make life ever look bright and young.
>
> [*Drum soll auch ein ewiges zartes Band*
>   *Die Frauen, die Sänger umflechten,*
> *Sie wirken und weben Hand in Hand*
>   *Den Gürtel des Schönen und Rechten.*
> *Gesang und Liebe in schönem Verein,*
> *Sie erhalten dem Leben den Jugendschein.*][15]

[15]Friedrich Schiller, *The Minor Poems*, trans. John Herman Merivale (London: Pickering, 1844),
pp. 288-292 (p. 292); Schiller, *Sämtliche Gedichte und Balladen*, ed. Georg Kurscheidt (Frankfurt am
Main: Insel, 2004), pp. 156-158 (p. 158).

In this poem we find Schiller harking back to the idea, found in the oldest texts of the Western tradition, that humankind goes through a sequence of historical periods or "ages." Thus, way back in the late eighth century BCE, Hesiod relates in his *Works and Days* how gods and mortal humans have a common origin. The gods create five different races of mortals: a first race, made of gold, who "lived like gods without sorrow of heart, remote and free from toil and grief"; a second race, made of silver, and "less noble by far"; next, a third race, "a brazen race [...] terrible and strong," of bronze; then, "a god-like race of hero-men who are called demi-gods"; and finally, "a race of iron"—our race—who will "never rest from labour and sorrow by day, and from perishing by night," and who are destined for destruction by Zeus.[16]

This idea persists, centuries later, in the work of Ovid (43 BCE to 18 CE), whose *Metamorphoses* opens with an account of the four ages of humankind—golden, silver, bronze, and iron[17]—and concludes with the discourses of Pythagoras, including an exposition of his discourse on the four seasons/ages of life. Just as there are four seasons, Pythagoras teaches,

> [Y]ou notice how the year in four
> Seasons revolves, completing one by one
> Fit illustration of our human life.
> The young springtime, the tender suckling spring,
> Is like a child; [...].
> Spring passes, and the year, grown sturdier,
> Rolls on to summer like a strong young man;
> No age so sturdy, none so rich, so warm.
> Then autumn follows, youth's fine fervour spent,
> Mellow and ripe, a temperate time between
> Youth and old age, his temples flecked with grey.
> And last, with faltering footsteps, rough and wild,
> His hair, if any, white, old winter comes.[18]

Ovid—doubtless a source for Shakespeare's later treatment of this theme—emphasizes that, as the seasons change throughout the year, so, too, do we throughout our course of life:

---

[16]Hesiod, *Works and Days*, in *Hesiod, The Homeric Hymns and Homerica*, trans. Hugh G. Evelyn-White (Cambridge, MA: Harvard University Press; London: Heinemann, 1914), ll. 109-181, pp. 11-17.

[17]See Ovid, *Metamorphoses*, book 1, ll. 88-261, in *Metamorphoses*, trans. A. D. Melville (Oxford and New York: Oxford University Press, 1987), pp. 3-8.

[18]Ovid, *Metamorphoses*, book 15, ll. 200-216; p. 358.

> Our bodies too are always, endlessly
> Changing; what we have been, or are today,
> We shall not be tomorrow. Years ago
> We hid, mere seeds and promise, in the womb;
> [...] Born to the shining day, the infant lies
> Strengthless, but soon on all fours like the beasts
> Begins to crawl, and then by slow degrees,
> Weak-kneed and wobbling, clutching for support
> Some helping upright, learns at last to stand.
> Then swift and strong he traverses the span
> Of youth, and when the years of middle life
> Have given their service, too, he glides away
> Down the last sunset slope of sad old age—
> Old age that saps and mines and overthrows
> The strength of earlier years.[19]

Drawing on classical mythology, Ovid sings a paean to the forces of all-devouring Time and jealous Old Age:

> [...] Milo, grown old,
> Sheds tears to see how shrunk and flabby hang
> Those arms on which the muscles used to swell,
> Massive like Hercules; and, when her glass
> Shows every time-worn wrinkle, Helen weeps
> And wonders why she twice was stolen for love.
> Time, the devourer, and the jealous years
> With long corruption ruin all the world
> And waste all things in slow mortality.[20]

At this point, we should note the central importance in this cosmology of the figure of Pythagoras (580-572 BCE – 500-490 BCE), a pre- Socratic philosopher who was associated with the Orphic mysteries.[21] According to Diogenes Laertius (c. 200-250 CE), Pythagoras was born on the island of Samos, but went to Egypt, where he was initiated into their most secret mysteries.[22] While Aristippus claimed that Pythagoras's name derived

---

[19]Ovid, *Metamorphoses*, book 15, ll. 217-229; pp. 358-359.

[20]Ovid, *Metamorphoses*, book 15, ll. 229-237; p. 359.

[21]For the significance of the discourse of Pythagoras in the *Metamorphoses*, see E. J. Kenney, "Introduction," in *Metamorphoses*, pp. xv-xvii. For further discussion of Pythagoras and Pythagoreanism, see B. L. van der Waerden, *Die Pythagoreer: Religiöse Bruderschaft und Schule der Wissenschaft* (Zurich and Munich: Artemis, 1979); and Carl A. Huffman, "The Pythagorean Tradition," in *The Cambridge Companion to Early Greek Philosophy*, ed. A. A. Long (Cambridge: Cambridge University Press, 1999), pp. 66-87.

[22]See Book 8, chapter 1, in Diogenes Laertius, *The Lives and Opinions of Eminent Philosophers*,

"from the fact of his speaking [*agor-*] truth no less than the God at Delphi [*pyth-*],"[23] Pythagoras was, according to Iamblichus, the first person to call himself a philosopher.[24] The Orphic connection was examined in the nineteenth century by Johann Jakob Bachofen (1815-1887),[25] and again in the early twentieth century by the classical philologist Karl Kerényi (1897-1973), in his study on the relation between Pythagoras and Orpheus.[26] Among the features common to both are the perceived need for ritual purification, and the ritual practice of an incubatory descent into a subterranean realm of the dead: according to Hieronymus of Rhodes, Pythagoras had undertaken a *katabasis* or descent to Hades, where he saw the punishments meted out to Hesiod and Homer because of what they had said about the gods, and to those who refrained from sexual intercourse with their wives.[27]

Ovid's account of Pythagorean teaching is supported by Diogenes Laertius in Book 8 of his *Lives and Opinions of Eminent Philosophers*. Here he relates how Pythagoras divided the life of the (male) individual into four stages—"A boy for twenty years; a young man (*neaniskos*) for twenty years; a middle-aged man (*neanias*); an old man for twenty years"—corresponding to the different seasons of the year: "Boyhood answers to spring;

---

trans. C. D. Yonge (London: Bell, 1895), pp. 338-339; a point supported in the biographies by Porphyry (see his *Life of Pythagoras*, §6 and §12) and Iamblichus (see his *Life of Pythagoras*, chapter 4). In the ancient accounts of Pythagoras's life and teaching given by Diogenes Laertius, Porphyry, and Iamblichus, one notes the proximity of the ascetic, even divine figure of Pythagoras to Christ, while key Pythagorean doctrines—dualism, immortality of the soul, and metempsychosis (transmigration of the soul)—reappear in Platonism.

[23]Diogenes, *Lives and Opinions*, book 8, chapter 1, p. 347.

[24]See Iamblichus, *Life of Pythagoras*, chapter 12; for further discussion, see Walter Burkert, "Platon oder Pythagoras? Zum Ursprung des Wortes 'Philosophie,'" *Hermes* 88 (1960): 159-177.

[25]See J. J. Bachofen, *Der Mythus von Orient und Occident: Eine Metaphysik der alten Welt*, ed. Manfred Schröter, introd. Alfred Baeumler (Munich: Beck, 1926), pp. 520-536, "Der Pythagorismus und die späteren Systeme."

[26]Karl Kerényi, "Pythagoras und Orpheus" [1934-1937], in *Humanistische Seelenforschung* (Wiesbaden: VMA-Verlag, 1978), pp. 15-51; and *Pythagoras und Orpheus: Präludien zu einer zukünftigen Geschichte der Orphik und des Pythagoreismus* [Albae Vigilae, NF, No. 9], 3rd ed. (Zurich: Rhein-Verlag, 1950). For further discussion of the Orphic and Pythagorean traditions, see Walter Burkert, *Lore and Science in Ancient Pythagoreanism [Weisheit und Wissenschaft: Studien zu Pythagoras, Philolaos und Platon]* [1962], trans. Edwin L. Minar, Jr. (Cambridge: Harvard University Press, 1972), pp. 125-133; Peter Kingsley, *Ancient Philosophy, Mystery, and Magic: Empedocles and Pythagorean Tradition* (Oxford: Oxford University Press, 1995), pp. 115-116; and Sara Rappe, *Reading Neoplatonism: Non-discursive Thinking in the Texts of Plotinus, Proclus, and Damascius* (Cambridge: Cambridge University Press, 2000), "Pythagoreanism, Oral Teachings, and Neoplatonic Textuality," pp. 117-124.

[27]Diogenes, *Lives and Opinions*, book 8, chap. 1, p. 347.

youth to summer; middle age to autumn; and old age to winter."[28] Thus in Pythagoras we find the fundamental schema of the "seasons of a man's life," which we shall encounter in our historical survey time and again, and we should also note that here, as elsewhere in antiquity, the process of ageing and old age itself are presented in terms of lack or loss, and nearly always as a matter for lament. In Homer's *Iliad*, Diomedes calls out to Hector, "hard old age is upon you," which means that "all your strength is gone [...], your henchman is a man of no worth, and your horses are heavy."[29] When Virgil's Aeneas, accompanied by the Sibyl, makes his descent to the underworld, he first sees in the entrance to Orcus the allegorical figures of Grief, Ever-Haunting Anxiety, Diseases, and—along with Fear, Ill-Prompting Hunger, and Squalid Indigence—Morose Old Age (and, as if to underscore the point, in Book 9 the mother of Euryalus, when she addresses her son, emphasizes her "sere [dry and withered] old age" and tells of how she had been working on a robe for him "to distract my old mind from its troubles").[30] And in Seneca's version of *Oedipus*, Age— bowed down with her heavy burden—features among a similarly allegorical group of figures, including Sorrow, Sickness, and Fear.[31]

### ...TO THE STAGES OF LIFE

Just as, so it was once believed, ontogeny recapitulates phylogeny, so the idea that human history could be divided into various "ages" turned into the concept of different developmental phases in the life of the individual human being: the "stages of life." The idea of dividing the life of the individual into different stages can be found as far back as the surviving fragments of the Athenian statesman and poet Solon (c. 638-559 BCE).[32] In fragment 27 of his poems, Solon divides life into ten stages of seven years—

> A boy, before he has reached adolescence, while still a child,
> grows and casts out his "fence of teeth" within the first seven

[28]Diogenes, *Lives and Opinions*, book 8, chap. 1, p. 342.

[29]Homer, *The Iliad*, trans. Richard Lattimore (Chicago and London: University of Chicago Press, 1951), p. 185 (Book 8, ll. 102-104).

[30]Virgil, *The Aeneid*, trans. C. Day Lewis (Oxford: Oxford University Press, 1986), pp. 164 and 268 (Book 6, ll. 274-276 and Book 9, ll. 483-487).

[31]Seneca, *Thyestes; Phaedra; The Trojan Women; Oedipus; with Octavia*, trans. E. F. Watling (Harmondsworth: Penguin, 1966), p. 232 (Act 3, l. 594).

[32]For further discussion, see *The World of Athens: An Introduction to Classical Athenian Culture*, ed. by the Joint Association of Classical Teachers (Cambridge: Cambridge University Press, 1984), pp. 6-7.

> years. When the god brings to an end the next seven years, he puts forth the signs of adolescence. In the third period, while his limbs are still growing, the down of the beard appears, and his complexion loses its bloom. In the fourth hebdomad, every man is in the prime of his strength; this men have as a sign of their worth. In the fifth, it is seasonable for a man to take thought on marriage, and to seek after a breed of sons to succeed him. In the sixth, the mind of man is in all things fully trained, and he no longer feels the same impulse towards wild behaviour. In the seventh seven he is at his prime in mind and tongue, and in the eighth, the sum of the two being fourteen years. In the ninth, though he still has some strength, his tongue and his wisdom are too feeble for works of mighty worth

—which concludes, as it inevitably must, with the following, final stage:

> If he complete the tenth and reach its full measure, not untimely is it if he meet the fate of death.[33]

Solon takes as his basic unit the number 7—the magic number, and one that will provide the basis for many other schemes. And the stages are presented as simply flowing from the one into the other. There is no crisis; perhaps, in Athenian democracy, its citizens had other (or more interesting) things to concern them.

The idea of the stages of life, although not an elaborate scheme, lies behind an even more ancient tradition—the riddle of the Sphinx, that figure so intimately connected with the history of psychoanalysis.[34] This riddle alludes to the traditional question posed by the Theban oracle, and eventually, so legend has it, solved by Oedipus: "What goes on four feet, on two feet, and three, / But the more feet it goes on the weaker it be?"[35]

---

[33]See Kathleen Freeman, *The Work and Life of Solon: With a Translation of His Poems* (Cardiff: The University of Wales Press Board; London: Humphrey Milford, 1926), pp. 213-214.

[34]According to Freud's biographer, Ernest Jones, his admirers in Vienna presented Freud on his fiftieth birthday with a medallion, depicting on one side a portrait of Freud and on the other an image of Oedipus conversing with the Sphinx, with the inscription from Sophocles' *Oedipus Rex*, "He divined the famous riddle and was a most mighty man." "When Freud read the inscription," Jones reports, "he became pale and agitated and in a strangled voice demanded to know who had thought of it. He behaved as if he had encountered a *revenant*, and so he had. [...] Freud disclosed that as a young student at the University of Vienna he used to stroll around the great arcaded court inspecting the busts of former famous professors of the institution. He then had the phantasy, not merely of seeing his own bust there in the future [...] but of it actually being inscribed with the *identical* words he now saw on the medallion" (Ernest Jones, *The Life and Work of Sigmund Freud*, 3 vols. [New York: Basic Books, 1953-1957], vol. 2, pp. 13-14).

[35]See Ebenezer Cobham Brewer, *Dictionary of Phrase and Fable* (London: Cassell, 1970), p. 1025.

And the idea that we should respond to the stages of life by acknowledging, though not necessarily accepting, the inevitability of death, occurs in the fragmentary remains of another text by Solon, written in response to a Greek elegiac poet, Mimnermus of Colophon in Ionia (second half of seventh century BCE). Of his works, later collected under the title *Nanno* (the name of the flute player whom he loved, and who accompanied him), the following fragment has survived:

> What's life, what's joy, without love's heavenly gold?
>> I hope I die when I no longer care
> For secret closeness, tender favours, bed,
>> Which are the rapturous flowers that grace youth's prime
> For men and women. But when painful age
>> Comes on, that makes a man loathsome and vile,
> Malignant troubles ever vex his heart;
>> Seeing the sunlight gives him joy no more.
> He is abhorred by boys, by women scorned:
>> So hard a thing God made old age to be.[36]

Further on in the fragment, Mimnermus outlines in extensive detail the sufferings of old age, and asks to be relieved from the burden of existence at the age of sixty:

> Most handsome once, perhaps, but when his season's past,
>> He's loathed and slighted even by his sons.
>
> He gave Tithonus an unending bane,
>> Old age, that is more frightful than harsh death.
>
> The sweat runs down me, and my heart's a-flutter,
>> Seeing my generation in its bloom
> Of joy and beauty. Oh, it ought to last
>> For longer! But it's fleeting as a dream,
> Our precious youth; in no time ugly, harsh,
>> Hateful old age is looming over us,
> Unvalued, that enveloping deforms
>> Past recognition, dims both sight and mind.
> I pray my fated death may catch me
>> Hale and hearty at threescore years.[37]

---

[36]M. L. West, trans., *Greek Lyric Poetry* (Oxford: Clarendon Press, 1993), p. 28.

[37]*Ibid.*, pp. 28-29. According to the Homeric Hymn to Aphrodite, Eos asked Zeus to make Tithonus, her lover, immortal, but neglected to ask he be granted eternal youth as well (*The Homeric Hymns*, no. 5, "To Aphrodite," ll. 218-238, in Hesiod, *The Homeric Hymns and Homerica*, trans.

In response to Mimnermus's plea to die at the age of sixty, Solon adds—in line with his own scheme for the stages of life—another twenty years, asking to die at eighty:

> But if even now you will listen to me, delete this word, and do not resent it that my thought was better than yours; alter your poem, sweet singer, and let your song be thus: "In my eightieth year may the lot of death befall me." May my death come not unlamented; when I die, may I leave to my friends a legacy of grief and mourning.[38]

Nevertheless, another fragment contains the (more positive, more hopeful) thought: "Ever as I grow old I learn many things."[39]

Yet whether one dies at sixty or eighty, the longer one lives, the more the problems of old age intensify. Mimnermus was well aware of this:

> But we are like the leaves that flowery spring
>     Puts forth, quick spreading in the sun's warm light:
> For a brief span of time we take our joy
>     In our youth's bloom, the future, good or ill,
> Kept from us, while the twin dark Dooms stand by,
>     One bringing to fulfilment harsh old age,
> The other, death. The ripeness of youth's fruit
>     Is short, short as the sunlight on the earth,
> And once the season of perfection's past,
>     It's better to be dead than stay alive.
> All kinds of worry come. One man's estate
>     Is failing, and there's painful poverty;
> Another has no sons—the keenest need
>     One feels as one goes down below the earth;
> Sickness wears down another's heart. There's none
>     Zeus does not give a multitude of ills.[40]

Mimnermus's account of old age dates from sometime in the seventh century BCE; and in the intervening centuries nothing changed, for a "younger" allegorical poem on old age can be found in the biblical book Ecclesiastes (or "The Preacher"), conventionally attributed to King Solo-

---

Hugh G. Evelyn-White [Cambridge, MA: Harvard University Press; London: Heinemann, 1982], pp. 421-423).

[38]Fragment 19, in Freeman, *The Life and Work of Solon*, p. 212.

[39]Fragment 17, in *ibid.*

[40]West, *Greek Lyric Poetry*, p. 28. The two twin dooms referred to here are the daimons of misfortune and of death.

mon, but most likely to have been composed in the third century BCE. Recent scholarship has ruled out the possibility of links with Cynic, Epicurean, or Stoic philosophy,[41] yet the similarities with Greek philosophy are highly suggestive, and the text remains a fine, moving account of old age:

> Remember now thy Creator in the days of thy youth, while the evil days come not, nor the years draw nigh, when thou shalt say, I have no pleasure in them;
>
> While the sun, or the light, or the moon, or the stars, be not darkened, nor the clouds return after the rain:
>
> In the day when the keepers of the house shall tremble, and the strong men shall bow themselves, and the grinders cease because they are few, and those that look out of the windows be darkened,
>
> And the doors shall be shut in the streets, when the sound of the grinding is low, and he shall rise up at the voice of the bird, and all the daughters of musick shall be brought low;
>
> Also when they shall be afraid of that which is high, and fears shall be in the way, and the almond tree shall flourish, and the grasshopper shall be a burden, and desire shall fail: because man goeth to his long home, and the mourners go about the streets:
>
> Or ever the silver cord be loosed, or the golden bowl be broken, or the pitcher be broken at the fountain, or the wheel broken at the cistern.
>
> Then shall the dust return to the earth as it was; and the spirit shall return unto God who gave it.[42]

Although the implication of some of the metaphors remains somewhat enigmatic, the picture overall is devastatingly clear: the body ages, the legs become bent, the teeth cannot chew, the eyes lose their sight, the hair turns white, the gait becomes hobbled, and sexual desire vanishes ("desire shall fail");[43] all

---

[41] *The New Jerusalem Bible*, ed. Henry Wansborough (London: Darton, Longmann and Todd, 1985), OT, p. 1013.

[42] Ecclesiastes 12:1-7 (Authorized Version).

[43] Literally, "the caper-bush loses its tang" *(New Jerusalem Bible*, p. 1025); cf. note d: "uncertain translation, based on substituting the passive *(wetuppar)* for an unattested form *(wetiphereh).*" Yet the idea of loss of sexual potency seems to be implied somewhere here: the *Oxford Bible Commentary* comments that "if they continue the symbolism of old age, then the almond tree may be the whitening of the hair, and the grasshopper the impotent penis (as suggested in early rabbinic exegesis); the symbolism of the caper is obscure, although it, too, has white flowers" *(The Oxford Bible Commentary*, ed. John Barton and John Muddiman [Oxford: Oxford University Press, 2001], p. 428).

that remains is the loosed silver cord, the broken golden bowl, the broken pitcher, the broken wheel—death. "Vanity of vanities, all is vanity."

In his study of *Rhetoric*, Aristotle (third century BCE) observed that "all the valuable qualities that youth and age divide between them are united in the prime of life," noting that while the body is "in its prime" from the age of 30 to 35, the mind is not in its prime until about 49.[44] So where does this leave the individual who passes these staging posts? What do we do with the body after the age of 35, and the mind after the age of 49?[45] In the case of the Roman satirist Juvenal (born c. 60-70 CE), the answer is: not much. In his tenth Satire, written in the reign of Trajan or Hadrian, Juvenal offered a grim account of old age, mocking those who prayed, "Grant us a long life, Jupiter, O grant us many years," and emphasized "how grisly, how unrelenting / Are longevity's ills." What old age brings, Juvenal insists, is negative for one's appearance—

> Look first at your face, you'll see an ugly
> And shapeless caricature of its former self: your skin
> Has become a scaly hide, you're all chapfallen, the wrinkles
> Scored down your cheeks now make you resemble nothing so
>     much
> As some elderly female baboon in darkest Africa.
> [...]
> But old men all look alike, all share the same bald pate,
> Their noses all drip like an infant's, their voices tremble
> As much as their limbs, they mumble their bread with
>     toothless
> Gums. It's a wretched life for them, they become a burden
> To their wives, their children, themselves [...]

—negative for one's sources of pleasure—

> [...] Their taste-buds are ruined, they get scant pleasure
> From food or wine, sex lies long in oblivion—
> Or if they try, it's hopeless: though they labour all night long
> At that limp and shrivelled object, limp it remains. [...]
>
> [...] Sex is a pretty dead loss—
> The old tag's true—when desire outruns performance.

---

[44] Aristotle, *Rhetoric*, book 2, chapter 13, 1290b, in *The Collected Works*, ed. Richard McKeon (New York: Random House, 1941), p. 1406.

[45] For an account, from the ancient Greek and Roman worlds to today, of the depiction of old age, see *A History of Old Age*, ed. Pat Thane (Los Angeles: The Paul J. Getty Museum, 2005).

—and negative for one's powers of mind:

> [...] But worse than all bodily ills
> Is the senescent mind. Men forget what their own servants
> Are called, they can't recognize yesterday's host at dinner,
> Or, finally, the children they begot and brought up. [...]
> [...]
> If he keeps his wits intact, though, a further ordeal awaits
> The old man: he'll have to bury his sons, he'll witness
> His dear's wife's end, and his brother's, he'll see the urns
> Filled with his sisters' ashes.

In short, Juvenal sees the fruits of old age as decidedly bitter:

> Such are the penalties
> If you live to a ripe old age—perpetual grief,
> Black mourning, a world of sorrow, ever-recurrent
> Family bereavements to haunt your declining years.[46]

The extreme negativity of this account, however, can be read as a calculated riposte to the far more positive outlook of an earlier writer and thinker, the great Roman orator and statesman Cicero (106-43 BCE). Now, Cicero wrote his essay on old age at the beginning of 44 BCE, when he was 62 years old and his addressee, his friend Atticus, 65; thus the "burden" of old age, as Cicero put it, was one that they shared.[47] *De Senectute* takes the form of a conversation between Cato, on the one hand, and Scipio and Laelius, on the other, who "express wonder" at the "ease" with which their host "endures being old."[48]

The leading idea in this essay is the principle, typical of Stoic thought, that Nature offers us "the best guide"; indeed, Scipio says that he follows and obeys her "as a divine being,"[49] and later Cato stipulates that "all things in keeping with nature must be classified as

---

[46]Juvenal, *Satires*, no. 10, ll. 188, 190-194, 198-206, 233-236, 240-242, and 243-245; in Juvenal, *The Sixteen Satires*, trans. Peter Green (Harmondsworth: Penguin, 1974), pp. 211-213.

[47]Cicero, *Selected Works*, trans. Michael Grant (Harmondsworth: Penguin, 1971), pp. 211-247 (p. 213). For an edition with a useful commentary, see Cicero, *On Old Age (De Senectute): Latin Text, Notes, Vocabulary* [1922], ed. Charles E. Bennett (Bristol: Bristol Classical Press; Oak Park, IL: Bolchazy-Carducci Publishers, 1985). In his *Red Book*, Jung quotes a passage from *De Senectute* (C. G. Jung, *The Red Book: Liber Novus*, ed. Sonu Shamdasani, trans. Mark Kyburz, John Peck, and Sonu Shamdasani [New York and London: Norton, 2009], "Liber secundus," chap. 15, "Nox secunda," pp. 294-295, cf. p. 295, n. 176), and his library contains a copy of a translation of Cicero's *De Divinatione* and a two-volume edition of Cicero's letters.

[48]Cicero, *Selected Works*, p. 214.

[49]Cicero, *Selected Works*, p. 215.

good."[50] Its guiding image is that of harvesting, the image of "a time of withering, of readiness to fall, like a ripeness which comes to the fruits of the trees and of the earth."[51] Tied up with this image is the notion that "life's course is invariable," for "nature has one path only, and you cannot travel along it more than once."[52] Here, too, we find the idea that "every stage of life has its own characteristics," so that "boys are feeble, youths in their prime are aggressive, middle-aged men are dignified, old people are mature," and (here is the image again) "each one of these qualities is ordained by nature for harvesting in due season." From all this, Cato derives the following maxim: "Enjoy the blessing of strength while you have it, and have no regrets when it has gone—any more than young men should regret the end of boyhood, or those approaching middle age lament the passing of youth."[53]

For Cato, old age is the philosophical age *par excellence*, for it permits "the study, and the practice, of decent, enlightened living,"[54] and he evokes, using the examples of Plato, Isocrates, and Gorgias, the image of "the tranquil and serene evening of a life spent in peaceful, blameless, enlightened pursuits."[55] True, Cato admits, there are four reasons to regard old age as an "unhappy time," but each of these objections he has an answer. First, it "takes us away from active work," but in fact, he replies, old age is "really very lively, and perpetually active, and still busy with the pursuits of earlier years." For those who regard old age as weakening memory, Cato has the following answer:

> I never heard of an old man forgetting where he had buried his money! Old people remember what interests them: the dates fixed for their lawsuits, and the names of their debtors and creditors. And what about elderly lawyers, priests, augurs, and philosophers? They remember a great many things. Provided the old retain their concentration and application, they stay sound of mind. And that not only applies to well-known public figures, but is equally true of people living quietly in retirement.[56]

[50] Cicero, *Selected Works*, p. 241.
[51] Cicero, *Selected Works*, p. 215.
[52] Cicero, *Selected Works*, p. 226.
[53] Cicero, *Selected Works*, p. 226.
[54] Cicero, *Selected Works*, p. 216.
[55] Cicero, *Selected Works*, p. 218.
[56] Cicero, *Selected Works*, pp. 221-222.

Second, it is said that old age "weakens the body," but Cato responds that "when failures of bodily vigour do occur they are to be blamed upon youthful dissipations more often than upon old age."[57] Moreover, someone who spends his life in study grows old "by stages, imperceptibly; there is no sudden break-up, only a gradual process of extinction."[58] Third, in reply to those who criticize old age because it "deprives us of practically all physical pleasures," particularly "sensual pleasures," Cato responds that "if age really frees us from youth's most dangerous failing, then we are receiving a most blessed gift."[59] Citing the Pythagorean philosopher Archytas of Tarentum, Cato continues that "the most fatal curse given by nature to mankind [...] is sensual greed: this incites men to gratify their lusts heedlessly and uncontrollably, thus bringing about national betrayals, revolutions, and secret negotiations with the enemy," and so "the weakening of temptations to indulge in [pleasures of this kind], far from supplying a pretext to reproach of old age, is a reason for offering it the most cordial compliments."[60]

Finally, following a long, detailed, and eloquent encomium of farming (again the harvest theme), Cato deals with the fourth objection to old age, namely that "it is not far from death." In these passages, the motif of the harvest melds seamlessly with an interrelated set of images related to departure—taking leave and coming home (or, in the imagery of Caspar David Friedrich, entering harbor):

> In the same way as apples, while green, can only be picked by force, but after maturity fall off by themselves, so death comes to the young with violence but to old people when the time is ripe. And the thought of this ripeness so greatly attracts me that as I approach death I feel like a man nearing harbour after a long voyage: I seem to be catching sight of land. [...] What nature gives us is a place to dwell in temporarily, not one to make our own. When I leave life, therefore, I shall feel as if I am leaving a hostel rather than a home.[61]

[57] Cicero, *Selected Works*, p. 224.

[58] Cicero, *Selected Works*, p. 228.

[59] Cicero, *Selected Works*, p. 228.

[60] Cicero, *Selected Works*, pp. 228 and 230. In this context Cicero cites the story, told by Plato in *The Republic*, about how Sophocles was glad that old age had helped him escape "that barbarous, savage master"—making love (Cicero, *Selected Works*, p. 232; cf. Plato, *The Republic*, 329b – 329c). This anecdote is, as we shall see, later cited by Montaigne.

[61] Cicero, *Selected Works*, pp. 241 and 246.

Thus this masterpiece of late Stoicism concludes with the following words, placed into the mouth of Cato by Cicero: "When life's last act, old age, has become wearisome, when we have had enough, the time has come to go."[62]

Cicero's account of old age was taken up by another Stoic philosopher, Seneca (c. 4 BCE to 65 CE). Having spent his life (under Tiberius and Caligula) as a statesman, (under Claudius) as an exile, and (under Nero) as tutor to the emperor and then unofficial minister-in-chief, Seneca—who had also distinguished himself as an orator and a tragedian—retired for the last three years of life from public activity and lived in southern Italy, devoting himself to philosophy and writing. Written c. 62-65 CE, the *Epistulae Morales ad Lucilius* are among the products of these final three years, a sequence of letters expounding Stoic doctrine to the procurator in Sicily. Here Seneca tells Lucilius:

> We should cherish old age and enjoy it. It is full of pleasure if you know how to use it. Fruit tastes most delicious just when its season is ending. The charms of youth are at their greatest at the time of its passing. It is the final glass which pleases the inveterate drinker, the one that sets the crowning touch on his intoxication and sends him off into oblivion. Every pleasure defers till its last its greatest delights. The time of life which offers the greatest delight is the age that sees the downward movement—not the steep decline—already begun; and in my opinion even the age that stands on the brink has pleasures of its own—or else the very fact of not experiencing the want of any pleasures takes their place. How nice it is to have outworn one's desires and left them behind![63]

Although Seneca was in his late fifties or early sixties when he was writing to Lucilius, he had suffered poor health (especially asthma) since his youth and, aware of his physical decline, asked his correspondent to place him "on the list of the decrepit, the ones on the very brink!"[64] Nevertheless, in his old age, Seneca celebrated the eternal vigor of his mind:

> Only my vices and their accessories have decayed: the spirit is full of life, and delighted to be having only limited dealings

---

[62]Cicero, *Selected Works*, p. 247.

[63]Seneca, *Letters to Lucilius*, no. 12; in Seneca, *Letters from a Stoic*, trans. Robin Campbell (Harmondsworth: Penguin, 1969), p. 58.

[64]*Letters to Lucilius*, no. 26; *ibid.*, p. 70.

with the body. It has thrown off a great part of its burden. It's full of vigour, and carrying on an argument with me on the subject of old age, maintaining that these are its finest years.[65]

"Moving to one's end through nature's own gentle process of dissolution—is there a better way," Seneca asked, "of leaving life than that?" Such "serenity and sobriety" were a product, he emphasized, of "philosophy."[66] In fact, in another letter Seneca makes the point to Lucilius that (our) death is inextricably bound up with (our) life:

> We are dying daily, in fact, for daily some part of life is taken from us, and even when we are growing, life is dwindling. We have lost our infancy first, then our childhood, then our youth. All the time that has passed away up to yesterday is gone for ever: the very day we are now spending we share with death. It is not the fall of the last grain that empties the hour-glass, but the trickling away of all that went before: so it is not the last hour—the hour in which we cease to be—that alone makes up death, though it alone makes death complete: only then do we reach death, but we have been on the way a long time.[67]

Both traditions, the classical and the biblical, will have been familiar to St. Augustine (354-430), who wrote his famous autobiographical text, the *Confessions*, at the age of forty-two. In this text, as James J. O'Donnell has pointed out, Augustine operates with, and modifies, the conventional Roman distinctions between the different stages of life. Thus infancy ends and boyhood begins at the age of seven; boyhood ends and adolescence begins at fifteen; adolescence ends and youth begins at thirty—in fact, Augustine extends the period of youth (*iuventus*) to the age of forty-five, which should give us pause for thought… ; maturity (*gravitas*) begins at forty-five and ends at sixty, when old age (*senectus*) begins.[68] As a result, what O'Donnell calls the two "defining moments" in his life—his conversion and the composition of the *Confessions* in 397 or 398-401, and his victory over Donatism at the conference in Carthage, the initiation of

---

[65] *Letters to Lucilius*, no. 26; *ibid.*, pp. 70-71.

[66] *Letters to Lucilius*, no. 26; *ibid.*, p. 70.

[67] Seneca, Letter 24; in *Seneca's Letters to Lucilius*, trans. E. Phillips Barker, 2 vols. (Oxford: Clarendon Press, 1932), vol. 1, p. 84 [translation modified].

[68] James J. O'Donnell, *Augustine: A New Biography* (New York, London, Toronto: Harper Perennial, 2006), pp. 26-27.

work on the *City of God*, and the beginning of his anti-Pelagian campaign in 411-412—coincide with the "threshold ages" of forty-five and sixty.[69]

In his later thought, Augustine finds in the six ages of man an interpretative framework for the seven days of creation, setting up a series of correspondences between the stages of human life and the Christian account of history. Thus to the first stage, infancy, corresponds the time from Adam to Noah; to the second, boyhood, corresponds the time from Noah to Abraham; to adolescence (*adolescentia*), i.e., from fifteen to thirty, corresponds the time from David to the Babylonian exile; to maturity (*gravitas*), the time from the captivity in Babylon to the coming of Christ; to old age corresponds the time between the first coming of Christ and his second, at the end of time; and to the seventh age corresponds the eternal afterlife: the salvation of the individual and the establishment of the city of God.[70]

Indeed, in the Christian liturgical tradition, the various canonical Hours of the Divine Office correspond to the seven stages of life, as the nineteenth-century French novelist Joris-Karl Huysmans (1848-1907) recalled, through the voice of his character Durtal, in his novel *En Route* (1895):

> [Durtal] brought to mind the symbolism of those canonical hours which recalled every day to the Christian the shortness of life in summing up for him its image from infancy to death. Recited soon after dawn, Prime was the figure of childhood; Tierce of youth; Sext the full vigour of age; None the approaches of old age, while Vespers were an allegory of decrepitude. They belonged, moreover, to the Nocturns, and were sung about six o'clock in the evening, at that hour when, at the time of the Equinoxes, the sun sets in the red cinder of the clouds. As for Compline, it resounds when night, the symbol of death, has come. This canonical Office was a marvellous rosary of psalms; every bead of each of these hours bore reference to the different phases of human existence, followed, little by little, the periods of the day, the decline of destiny, to end in

---

[69] *Ibid.*, p. 27.

[70] *Ibid.*, pp. 303-304. As O'Donnell remarks, "the most curious and influential part of this pattern was the gloomy resignation implicit in imagining that the present age, ostensibly the time of redemption and reception of the good news that Jesus represented, is to be understood as old age, and this in an era when old age was likely to be premature, brief, and marked by illness, weakness, and decline"—"hardly an inspirational theme for preaching or leadership" (p. 304), yet the extraordinarily large number of Augustine's sermons that survive testify to his productivity and to the fruitfulness of his insights.

the most perfect of offices, in Compline, that provisional ab-
solution of death, itself represented by sleep.[71]

As becomes clear from E. J. Quigley's study of the breviary, Durtal is
harking back to an ancient motif in the liturgical tradition.[72]

After Augustine, St. Gregory the Great (540-603), in a homily on the
gospel for Septuagesima Sunday, read the references to times of the day in
the parable of the vineyard laborers in relation to the ages of the
world—the morning of the world is from Adam to Noah, the third hour
is from Noah to Abraham, the sixth from Abraham to Moses, the ninth
from Moses until the advent of Christ, and the eleventh until the end of
the world—and to "the changing of the years in the life of every man," a
schema in which, significantly enough, he emphasized the solar cycle:

> The morning is the childhood of our reason. The third hour
> can be interpreted as adolescence, because while the heat of
> youth increases, it is as though the sun mounts higher in the
> sky. The sixth hour is young manhood, because as the sun is
> now as it were at its zenith, so now is the full strength of man-
> hood attained. Mature age is signified by the ninth hour, in
> which the sun descends from its highest point, because in that
> age man already declines from the heat of youth. The eleventh
> hour is that time of life which is called senility or old age.[73]

Just as the early Christian scholar and theologian Origen (c. 185-254) had
offered the "deeper and more mystical exposition" that "the whole life of
man is but one day,"[74] so Gregory discerned in the biblical text the mes-

---

[71]J.-K. Huysmans, *En Route*, trans. W. Fleming [1896] (Sawtry, Cambridgeshire: Dedalus, 2002), p. 268.

[72]Edward J. Quigley, *The Divine Office: A Study of the Roman Breviary* (Dublin: Gill, 1920), p. 5: "The seven canonical hours [...] bear a striking resemblance to the seven ages of man. *Matins*, the night office, typifies the pre-natal stage of life. *Lauds*, the office of dawn, seems to resemble the beginnings of childhood. *Prime* recalls [...] youth. *Terce*, recited when the sun is high in the heavens shedding brilliant light, symbolises early manhood with its strength and glory. *Sext* typifies mature age. *None*, recited when the sun is declining, suggests man in his middle age. *Vespers* reminds all of decrepit age gliding gently down to the grave. *Compline*, night prayer said before sleep, should remind us of the great night, death."

[73]Gregory, "Homily 19 on the Gospels," in J.-P. Migne, *Patrologiae Cursus Completus, Series Latina*, 221 vols (Paris: Migne, 1844-1866), vol. 76, 1153-1159; translated in *The Sunday Sermons of the Great Fathers*, ed. and trans. M. F. Toal, 4 vols. (San Francisco: Ignatius Press, 1996), vol. 1, pp. 379-385 (p. 380). See also Dom Guéranger, *The Liturgical Year [Année Liturgique]* [1949/1841-1847], trans. Dom Laurence Shepherd, 15 vols. (Great Falls, MT: St. Bonaventura Publications, 2000), vol. 4, p. 126.

[74]Origen, "Exposition of the parable," in J.-P. Migne, *Patrologiae Cursus Completus, Series*

sage that "to bear the burden of the day and the heats means to be wearied by the heats of [one's] own flesh throughout the days of a long life."[75]

Other writers have been equally keen to apply the motif of the stages of life to human history, too: to the stages of human (cultural) development (in the phylogenetic, rather than ontogenetic, sense). For example, in his preface to the second edition of the great account of Renaissance art history, *Lives of the Artists* (1550; 1568), the Italian painter, architect, and writer Giorgio Vasari (1511-1574) subsumed the history of the development of art to a pattern of growth and decay—and rebirth:

> From the smallest beginnings art attained the greatest heights, only to decline from its noble position to the most degraded status. Seeing this, artists can also realize the nature of the arts we have been discussing [i.e., sculpture and painting]: these, like the other arts and like human beings themselves, are born, grow up, become old, and die. And they will be able to understand more readily the process by which art has been reborn and reached perfection in our own times.[76]

By referring to his own "times," Vasari means the Renaissance: the "rebirth" of art and culture that began in Italy at the end of the fifteen century and spread across Europe in the first few decades of the sixteenth century—in other words, the start of the period we could describe as "modernity."

## THE STAGES OF LIFE: AN IDEA COMES OF AGE

According to the French philosopher Bertrand Vergely, modernity began "a long time before modernity."[77] He recalls Pascal's suggestion, made in his fragment for a treatise on emptiness, that "the succession of human individuals, in the course of so many centuries, should be considered as a single individual who always exists and continually learns," as a consequence of which "those we call the ancients were indeed new in all things, and formed the infancy of humankind; and as we have added to their knowledge the experience of the centuries that followed them, it is in us

---

*Graeca*, 161 vols. (Paris: Migne, 1857-1887), vol. 13, pp. 1337-1362; translated in Toal, *Sunday Sermons*, vol. 1, pp. 366-374 (p. 373).

[75]Gregory, "Homily 19"; Toal, *Sunday Sermons*, pp. 381-382.

[76]Giorgio Vasari, *Lives of the Artists*, ed. and trans. George Turnbull (Harmondsworth: Penguin, 1971), pp. 46-47.

[77]Bertrand Vergely, *Boulevard des philosophes: De la Renaissance à aujourd'hui* (Toulouse: Milan, 2005), p. 120: *"La modernité a commencé bien avant la modernité."*

that one may find this antiquity we revere in others."[78] Pascal's idea
prompts Vergely to reflect on the dialectical relationship between the
ancient and the modern, the old and the new, as follows:

> The past does not come to an end with the appearance of the
> new—of the modern world. It still lives among us, in myriad
> ways. As Bergson and Proust understood, everything of qual-
> ity knows how to last by remembering itself and imagining it-
> self as a life of its own that never ceases to reappear in the
> present. Thus Pascal was right to say that modernity is the ma-
> turity of the past, indeed its old age. The Ancients are among
> us, today, and not outside us, in the past.[79]

From this reflection, Vergely draws two conclusions—both, in their own
way, highly Jungian. First, that "the present is not the negation of the
past, nor the past the negation of the present," for "it required much
youthfulness on the part of the Ancients to have been what they were able
to be, just as it requires much age and maturity for the Moderns to be
modern." And second, that "everything is always beginning and everything is always beginning again, because everything always continues," so
that "if the genius of the Ancients resides in the way they knew how to begin,
the genius of the Moderns is to have known how to begin again, in order to
bring alive the only message that matters: that of continuing to live."[80]

For Michel de Montaigne (1533-1592), a figure who stands at the
beginning of the period called (by common consent) modernity, old age
is something to be regarded with a considerable degree of skepticism. An

---

[78]Pascal, *Opuscules: Premiére partie*, §5, "Fragment d'un Traité du Vide," in Pascal, *Pensées et Opuscules*, ed. Léon Brunschvicg (Paris: Hachette, [1959]), pp. 80-81; *"La suite des hommes, pendant le cours de tant de siécles, doit être considérée comme un même homme qui subsiste toujours et qui apprend continuellement; Ceux que nous appelons ancient étaient véritablement nouveaux en toutes choses, et formaient l'enfance des hommes proprement; et comme nous avons joint à leurs connaissances l'expérience des siècles qui les ont suivis, c'est en nous que l'on peut trouver cette antiquité que nous révérons dans les autres."*

[79]Vergely, *Boulevard des philosophes*, pp. 120-121: *"Le passé ne s'est achevé avec l'apparition du nouveau du monde moderne. Il vit encore parmi nous, de mille façons. Ainsi que l'ont compris Bergson et Proust, tout ce qui a de la qualité sait durer en se mémorisant et en s'imaginant selon une vie propre quie ne cesse de resurgir dans le présent. Aussi Pascal a-t-il eu raison de dire que la modérnité est la maturité du passé, voire sa vieillesse. Les Anciens sont parmi nous, aujourd'hui, et non hors de nous, dans la passé."*

[80]Vergely, *Boulevard des philosophes*, p. 121; *"Le présent n'est pas la négation du passé, ni le passé la négation du présent; Il a fallu beaucoup de jeunesse aux Anciens pour être ce qu'ils ont su être, comme il a fallu beaucoup de vieillesse et de maturité aux Modernes pour être ce modernes; Tout commence toujours et tout recommence toujours parce que tout continue toujours; Si le génie des Anciens est d'avoir su commencer, le génie des Modernes est d'avoir su recommencer, afin de faire vivre le seul message qui importe: celui de continuer de vivre."*

impetus to Montaigne's turn to a life of philosophical introspection came in the form of his own midlife crisis—an encounter with death that falls into the category of experience Michel Onfray terms an *hapax existentiel* [81] —when he was knocked from his horse and nearly died from the fall.[82] Reflecting in 1588, at the age of fifty-five, on the first edition of his *Essays*, published in 1580, when he was still approaching fifty, he wrote of the intervening years:

> I have long since grown old but not one inch wiser. "I" now and "I" then are certainly twain, but which "I" was better? I know nothing about that. If we were always progressing towards improvement, to be old would be a beautiful thing. But it is a drunkard's progress, formless, staggering, like the reeds which the wind shakes as it fancies, haphazardly.[83]

Montaigne highlights the decline of the body, and he fears the decline of his mind:

> The Ancient[84] who said that he was obliged to the passing years for freeing him from sensual pleasures held a quite different opinion from mine: I could never be grateful to infirmity for any good it might do me. [...] Every day the years read me lectures on lack of ardour and on temperance. My body flees from excess: it is afraid of it. It is its turn now to guide my mind towards amendment of life. It is its turn now to act the professor, and it does so more harshly and imperiously. For one single hour, sleeping or waking, it never allows me to take time off from learning about death, suffering, and penitence.[85]

---

[81] Michel Onfray, *L'Art de jouir* (Paris: Grasset, 1991), p. 27; *Le Désir d'être un volcan: Journal hédoniste I* (Paris: Grasset, 1996), pp. 320-347 (especially p. 324); and *La Puissance d'exister: Manifeste hédoniste* (Paris: Grasset, 2006), pp. 81-85.

[82] Michel Onfray, *Contre-histoire de la philosophie*, vol. 2, *Le christianisme hédoniste* (Paris: Grasset, 2006), pp. 248-250; and Sarah Bakewell, *How to Live: Or, a Life of Montaigne in One Question and Twenty Attempts at an Answer* (London: Chatto and Windus, 2010), pp. 14-22.

[83] Montaigne, *Essais*, book 3, chapter 9, "On vanity"; in Michel de Montaigne, *The Complete Essays*, trans. M. A. Screech (Harmondsworth: Penguin, 2003), p. 1091. For further discussion of old age as a theme, see Dorothy Gabe Coleman, *Montaigne's "Essais"* (London: Allen and Unwin, 1987), pp. 144-147; and Thierry Gontier, "Montaigne et la vieillesse: une philosophie des âges de la vie" [2004], available online at http://www.qc.ca/reftext.nsf/Documents/Vieillesse—Montaigne_et_la_vieillesse_une_philosophie_des_ages_de_la_vie_par_Thierry_Gontier (accessed 11 August, 2008).

[84] Sophocles; see Cicero, "On Old Age," section 14 *(Selected Works*, p. 232); cf. Plato, *The Republic*, 329b-329c *(The Republic of Plato*, trans. Allan Bloom [New York: Basic Books, 1968], p. 5).

[85] Montaigne, *Essais*, book 3, chapter 2, "On repenting," and book 3, chapter 5, "On some lines of Virgil"; *The Complete Essays*, pp. 919 and 948.

Looking back at himself, now that "my grey hair lends me credit," Montaigne reflects:

> What we call wisdom is the moroseness of our humours and our distaste for things as they are now. But in truth we do not so much give up our vices as change them—for the worse, if you ask me [...]; age sets more wrinkles on our minds than on our faces.

While looking at "those I know," he remarks, "what transformations do I daily see wrought by old age." Finally, however, Montaigne's reflections return to himself:

> [Old age] is a powerful illness which flows on naturally and imperceptibly. You must have a great store of study and fore-sight to avoid the imperfections which it loads upon us—or at least to weaken their progress. I know that, despite all my en-trenchments, it is gaining on me foot by foot. I put up such re-sistance as I can. But I do not know where it will take me in the end. Yet come what may, I should like people to know from what I shall have declined.[86]

Elsewhere, Montaigne argues that "philosophy has arguments for Man at birth as well as in senility,"[87] and in book 1, chapter 57, of his *Essais*, entitled "On the length of life," he writes that, by the age of twenty, "our souls are free from their bonds" and that "by then they show promise of all they are capable of," suggesting that the age of thirty marks the watershed sepa-rating decline from vigor. He counsels that "we should consider whatever age we have reached as an age reached by few" and that "since in the nor-mal course of events men never reach that far, it is a sign that we are get-ting on," concluding that, "considering the frailty of our life and the number of natural hazards to which it is exposed, we should not allow so large a place in it to being born, to leisure, and to our apprenticeship [*à la naissance, à l'oisiveté et à l'apprentissage*]."[88] Montaigne's reflections on old age thus issue in a call to action.

In his philosophy, Montaigne draws on classical and biblical (or, if one prefers, pagan and Christian) traditions alike. And both these tradi-tions, classical and biblical alike, feed into what is perhaps one of the

---

[86]Montaigne, *Essais*, book 3, chapter 2, "On repenting"; *The Complete Essays*, p. 921.

[87]Montaigne, *Essais*, book 1, chapter 26, "On educating children"; *The Complete Essays*, p. 183.

[88]Montaigne, *Essais*, book 1, chapter 57, "On the length of life"; *The Complete Essays*, pp. 366-369.

best-known passages that laments the process of ageing and divides life into seven stages. In Shakespeare's pastoral comedy, *As You Like It* (c. 1599), Jaques delivers the following famous speech:

> All the world's a stage,
> And all the men and women merely players.
> They have their exits and their entrances,
> And one man in his time plays many parts,
> His acts being seven ages. At first the infant,
> Mewling and puking in the nurse's arms.
> Then the whining school-boy, with his satchel
> And shining morning face, creeping like a snail
> Unwillingly to school. And then the lover,
> [...].
>> [...] Then a soldier,
>> [...] And then the justice,
>> [...] The sixth age shifts
> Into the mean and slippered pantaloon,
> With spectacles on nose and pouch on side,
> His youthful nose, well saved, a world too wide
> For his shrunk shank, and his big manly voice,
> Turning again toward childish treble, pipes
> And whistles in his sound. Last scene of all,
> That ends this strange, eventful history,
> Is second childishness and mere oblivion,
> Sans teeth, sans eyes, sans taste, sans everything.[89]

If this and other treatments of the motif of the stages of life place an emphasis on life as a slow decline and a long march to the end, other thinkers—notably, those in the German tradition—emphasize the rhythmic succession of different stages. For example, Goethe suggested there was a parallel between different philosophical stances and the stages of the individual's life. (For Goethe, the child is a Realist; the youth is an Idealist; the adult is a skeptic; while, so he concluded, the old man is always a mystic.[90]) Goethe's interest in the stages of life was shared by numerous Enlightenment and post-Enlightenment (or Romantic) thinkers.

In his *Anthropology from a Pragmatic Point of View* (*Anthropologie in*

[89]Shakespeare, *As You Like It*, Act II, Scene 7; *The Norton Shakespeare*, ed. Stephen Greenblatt et al. (New York and London: Norton, 1997), pp. 1622-1623.

[90]Goethe, *Maximen und Reflexionen*, no. 806; *Werke* [HA], vol. 12, pp. 540-541. For further discussion, see Eduard Spranger, "Goethe über die menschlichen Lebensalter" [1940], in *Goethe: Seine geistige Welt* (Tübingen: Wunderlich; Leins, 1967), pp. 74-107.

*pragmatischer Hinsicht*) (1798), Immanuel Kant (1724-1804) discussed the development of what he called "character" (*Charakter*). Somewhat abstractly, perhaps, he defines character as making "truthfulness one's supreme maxim, in the heart of one's confessions to oneself as well as in one's behavior toward everyone else," but we get a sense of what Kant really means when he writes that "to be able to simply say of a human being: 'he has a *character*' is not only to have *said* a great deal about him, but it is also to have *praised* him a great deal; for this is a rarity, which inspires profound respect and admiration toward him."[91] For Kant, the grounding of one's character is "like a kind of rebirth" (*gleich einer Art der Wiedergeburt*); it is, "like the beginning of a new epoch," something that cannot be brought about by "education, examples, and teaching" in a "gradual" way, but only "by an explosion." Moreover, he notes, only a few individuals attempt "this revolution" (*diese Revolution*) before the age of thirty, and fewer still establish it before they turn forty.[92]

Another figure in the German philosophical tradition, the philosopher Johann Gottlieb Fichte (1762-1814), argued for the fundamental interwovenness of birth and death, writing in *The Vocation of Man* (*Die Bestimmung des Menschen*) (1800):

> All death in nature is birth, and it is precisely in dying that the elevation of life appears visibly. There is no fatal principle in nature, for nature is all about life; it is not death that kills, but the more vital life [*das lebendigere Leben*] which, hidden behind the old, begins and develops. Death and rebirth—merely the struggle of life with itself, to show itself to be increasing transfigured, even more true to itself. And could *my* death be any different—of me, who am not simply a representation and depiction of life, but bear within me the original, the only true, and the essential life within me?[93]

By contrast, less abstract—and more practical—is the discussion of "The Ages of Life" offered by Arthur Schopenhauer (1788-1860) in the sixth chapter of his *Aphorisms on How to Live Well* (*Aphorismen zur Lebensweisheit*), one of the most successful parts of his *Parerga and Paralipomena* (1851).[94]

[91] Immanuel Kant, *Anthropology from a Pragmatic Point of View*, ed. and trans. Robert B. Louden (Cambridge: Cambridge University Press, 2006), pp. 195, 191.

[92] *Ibid.*, p. 194.

[93] Johann Gottlieb Fichte, *Die Bestimmung des Menschen*, ed. Theodor Ballauff and Ignaz Klein (Stuttgart: Reclam, 1962), p. 190.

[94] See Schopenhauer, *Counsels and Maxims*, trans. T. Bailey Saunders, eBooks@Adelaide, 2004;

In the conclusion to this essay, Schopenhauer draws on astrology—for its images, not because he believes in it—in order to divide life into seven stages. (This division applies to the life of the male individual, not the female.) First, at the age of ten, Mercury is in the ascendant, and the youth falls under the influence of this "crafty and eloquent" god; second, at the age of twenty, the sway of Venus begins, and man becomes "wholly given up to the love of woman"; third, at the age of thirty, Mars comes to the front—a man is now "all energy and strength"; fourth, at the age of forty, the rule of the four asteroids[95] begins—Ceres makes him favor what is useful, Vesta influences his home and hearth, Pallas teaches him what it is necessary to know, and Juno, a.k.a. his wife, rules as the mistress of the house…; fifth, at the age of fifty, the dominant influence is Jupiter—

> At that period a man has outlived most of his contemporaries, and he can feel himself superior to the generation about him. He is still in the full enjoyment of his strength, and rich in experience and knowledge; and if he has any power and position of his own, he is endowed with authority over all who stand in his immediate surroundings. He is no more inclined to receive orders from others; he wants to take command himself. The work most suitable to him now is to guide and rule within his own sphere. This is the point where Jupiter culminates, and where the man of fifty years is at his best[;]

—until, sixth, at the age of sixty, Saturn takes over ("unwieldy, slow, heavy and pale as lead," in the words of *Romeo and Juliet*); finally, Uranus, and "as the saying is, a man goes to heaven."

In a whimsical comment, Schopenhauer confesses that he has been unable to find a place for Neptune, as the planet discovered in orbit between Uranus and Pluto in 1846 is called. But Schopenhauer wants to call this planet "Eros" (for him, Eros is intimately connected with Death), to show—in a phrase that contains a distinctly Goethean echo—"how beginning and end meet together" (*wie sich an das Ende der Anfang knüpft*), or (in the phrase from "Permanence in Change" [*Dauer im*

---

available at http://etext.library.adelaide.edu.au/s/schopenhauer/arthur/counsels/complete.html (accessed August 20, 2007); Arthur Schopenhauer, *Werke in fünf Bänden*, ed. Ludger Lütkehaus, 5 + 1 vols. (Zurich: Haffmanns, 1988), vol. 4, pp. 467-483.

[95]The asteroids are "minor planets, the name meaning 'star-like'—the alternative (and now rare) 'planetoid' being etymologically better," discovered by astronomers in 1801 (Fred Gettings, *The Arkana Dictionary of Astrology* [London: Arkana, 1990], p. 46).

*Wechsel*, 1803]) "Let the start and end so fusing / Join in one and unify" (*Laß den Anfang mit dem Ende / Sich in eins zusammenziehn!*).[96] Eros, moreover, is the name of the penultimate stanza in Goethe's poem, "Primal Words. Orphic."

The rewards of Schopenhauer's essay are many. According to the German philosopher and phenomenologist Otto F. Bollnow (1903-1991), one of its key insights is into the relation between the stages of life and the perception of time.[97] To make this point, Schopenhauer uses the image of the inverted telescope:

> From the standpoint of youth, life seems to stretch away into an endless future; from the standpoint of old age, to go back a little way into the past; so that, at the beginning, life presents us with a picture in which the objects appear a great way off, as though we have reversed our telescope; while in the end everything seems so close. To see how short life is, a man must have grown old, that is to say, he must have lived long.

And according to Ludger Lütkehaus, "the centre of Schopenhauer's philosophy of old age" is to be found in "the reflection on the connection between time, age, knowledge, and happiness, that is: *relative* happiness."[98] In a sense, for Schopenhauer happiness is only attained in the recognition of its impossibility:

> A complete and adequate notion of life can never be attained by anyone who does not reach old age; for it is only the old man who sees life whole and knows its natural course; it is only he who is acquainted—and this is most important—not only with its entrance, like the rest of mankind, but with its exit too; so that he alone has a full sense of its utter vanity; whilst the others never cease to labor under the false notion that everything will come all right in the end.

Schopenhauer bears out this point with a nice example: "In my young days, I was always pleased to hear a ring at my door: ah! thought I, now for something pleasant. But in later life my feelings on such occasions were

---

[96]Goethe, *Selected Poems*, trans. John Whaley (London: Dent, 1998), p. 87; *Werke* [HA], vol. 1, p. 248.

[97]See Otto F. Bollnow, *Das Wesen der Stimmungen*, 3rd ed. (Frankfurt am Main: Klostermann, 1956), p. 173.

[98]Ludger Lütkehaus, "Das Alter ist die Stunde der Philosophie: Schopenhauers Philosophie des Alters," *Schopenhauer-Jahrbuch* 66 (1985): 195-200.

rather akin to dismay than to pleasure: heaven help me! thought I, what am I to do?" And growing old is compared to a piece of embroidery, crossing a hilltop, or burning a lamp. Schopenhauer is frank about the eradication of sexual desire: "When this passion is extinguished," he writes, "the true kernel of life is gone, and nothing remains but the hollow shell; or, from another point of view, life then becomes like a comedy, which, begun by real actors, is continued and brought to an end by automata dressed in their clothes."[99] Or as he pithily puts it: "Deserted by Venus, the old man likes to turn to Bacchus to make him merry." Yet the onset of old age brings, he argues, a special kind of knowledge—for "it is only towards the close of life that a man really recognizes and understands his own true self."

Other nineteenth-century thinkers in the German tradition offer reflections on life's stages as its "seasons." For example, in a collection of aphorisms entitled *Der Schriftsteller und der Mensch* (The Writer and the Man) (1834), the philosopher and anthropologist Ludwig Feuerbach (1804-1872) wrote:

> Life is the springtime of our thoughts and sensations; it is already late summer, indeed autumn, when they get written down. Of course the appeal of the blossom, the richness of the beautiful foliage, the bright green has now gone; but instead the early fruits that have yet to become perfect have been ripening in the light of truth.[100]

It is, however, probably to Solon's conception that the classicist turned philosopher-of-the-future Friedrich Nietzsche (1844-1900) refers when, in an aphorism entitled "The Ages of Life" in the second volume of *Human, All Too Human* (*Menschliches, Allzumenschliches*) (1879-1880/ 1886), he writes that "the comparison of the four seasons of the year with the four ages of life is a piece of worthy silliness."[101] Here, Nietzsche takes issues with the alleged correspondence between, on the one hand, the first twenty and the last twenty years of life and, on the other, a season of the

---

[99]Schopenhauer alludes to Socrates' reference at the beginning of *The Republic* to a remark attributed to Sophocles, who was asked if he could still have sex with a woman: "'Silence, man,' he said. 'Most joyfully did I escape it, as though I had run away from a sort of frenzied and savage master'" (*Republic*, 329c; Plato, *The Republic*, trans. Allan Bloom [New York: Basic Books, 1991], p. 5).

[100]Ludwig Feuerbach, *Sämtliche Werke*, ed. Wilhelm Bolin and Friedrich Jodl, 10 vols. (Stuttgart: Frommann-Holzboog, 1960), vol. 1, p. 271.

[101]"The Wanderer and his Shadow," §269; Friedrich Nietzsche, *Human, All-Too-Human*, trans. R. J. Hollingdale (Cambridge: Cambridge University Press, 1986), p. 375.

year. Between these years, however, does lie, Nietzsche claims, a period of
time susceptible to comparison, not with one, but with three seasons of
the year—for, according to Nietzsche, the three decades between the ages
of twenty and fifty correspond to summer, spring, and autumn respectively. "Human life does not have a winter, unless one wants to call those
cold recurring seasons of solitude, hopelessness and unfruitfulness, our
*periods of illness*, the winter seasons of man."

Winter is rejected by Nietzsche, for he associates it with the absence
of hope; and hope will, in *Thus Spoke Zarathustra* (*Also sprach Zarathustra*)
(written 1882-1884), come to lie at the core of Zarathustra's teaching; the
King, one of the Higher Men Zarathustra encounters in Part 4, tells him:
"All men possessed by great longing, great disgust, great satiety, / all who
do not want to live except they learn to *hope* again— except they learn
from you, O Zarathustra, the *great* hope!"[102] As, in the course of this aphorism, Nietzsche develops his own scheme, we learn that the twenties represent the "summer" of life; the thirties, its "spring"; while the forties are
"mysterious, like everything stationary; resembling a high, wide mountain plateau wafted by a fresh breeze; above it a clear, cloudless sky which
gazes down all day and into the night with the same unchanging gentle-
ness: the time of harvest and the heartiest cheerfulness—it is the *autumn*
of life." (When he wrote this aphorism, Nietzsche himself was in his late
thirties; in *Ecce Homo*, composed some eight years later, when he was in
his mid-forties, he would return to the autumnal motif in the *prooemium*
to this work.)

The absence of winter from Nietzsche's schema is significant; for
him, the autumn, the time of decline, is of great importance, not because
it presages winter and death, but because it is a necessary stage to the new
springtide beyond winter.[103] In another aphorism, Nietzsche claims that
"every philosophy is a philosophy of a certain stage of life," citing
Schopenhauer as an example of the philosophy of youth, while Plato, he
suggests, is more appropriate for one's mid-thirties:

> The stage of life at which a philosopher discovered his teach-
> ing is audible within it: he cannot prevent it, however exalted

---

[102]"The Greeting"; *Thus Spoke Zarathustra*, trans. R. J. Hollingdale (Harmondsworth: Penguin,
1961), p. 292. Elsewhere, we find evidence for a characteristically Nietzschean, ambivalent attitude
towards hope; see *Human, All-Too-Human*, vol. 1, §71; *Daybreak*, §38; and *The Antichrist*, §23.

[103]Equally significant, for example, is the absence of spring from the seasons in Stefan George's
cycle of poems *Das Jahr der Seele* (1897).

above time and the hour he may feel himself to be. Thus Schopenhauer's philosophy remains the reflected image of passionate and dejected *youth*—it is not a mode of thinking proper to men of older years; thus Plato's philosophy recalls the mid-thirties, when a cold and hot current are accustomed to buffet against one another, so that spray and delicate little clouds are thrown up and, under favouring circumstances and sunlight, the enchanting image of a rainbow.[104]

And in a note from Nietzsche's notebooks in this period, entitled "Short summer," he offered a variant on these reflections: "Some men's natures are blessed with summertime but for a moment: they had a late spring, and shall have a long autumn. They are more spiritual creatures [*Es sind die geistigern Geschöpfe*]."[105]

As Nietzsche approached his fortieth birthday, he wrote, in *The Gay Science* (*Die fröhliche Wissenschaft*) (1882; 1887), an aphorism entitled "in mid-life," *in media vita*. Here he announced that life had not "disappointed" him, but that, on the contrary, every year he found life "truer, more desirable, and more mysterious" (*wahrer, begehrenswerter und geheimnisvoller*); and he did so following his great liberation by "the idea that life could be an experiment of the seeker for knowledge," and, in turn, knowledge "a world of dangers and victories in which heroic feelings, too, find places to dance and play."[106] When Nietzsche had passed the midpoint of life, and was now forty-four, he maintained this stance in the passage that opens his autobiographical text, *Ecce Homo*:

> On this perfect day, when everything has become ripe and not only the grapes are growing brown, a ray of sunlight has fallen on to my life: I looked behind me, I looked before me, never have I seen so many and such good things together. Not in vain have I buried my forty-fourth year today, I was *entitled* to bury it—what there was of life in it is rescued, is immortal. [...] *How should I not be grateful to my whole life?*—And so I tell myself my life.[107]

[104]Nietzsche, "Assorted Opinions and Maxims," §271; *Human, All-Too-Human*, p. 277.

[105]Friedrich Nietzsche, *Sämtliche Werke: Kritische Studienausgabe*, ed. Giorgio Colli and Mazzino Montinari, 15 vols. (Berlin and New York: Walter de Gruyter; Munich: dtv, 1967-1977 and 1988), vol. 8, 46[3], p. 616.

[106]Friedrich Nietzsche, *The Gay Science*, trans. Walter Kaufmann (New York: Vintage, 1974), §324, p. 255.

[107]Friedrich Nietzsche, *Ecce Homo*, trans. R. J. Hollingdale (Harmondsworth: Penguin, 1979), p. 37.

Nietzsche's praise of this autumnal moment is entirely consistent with his claim to speak on behalf of "[the] party of life," for as Bertrand Vergely has written, as if commenting directly on this passage: "Let us live this autumnal moment when life detaches itself as the leaves detach themselves from the tree. One is no longer in a moment of death, but in a moment of life."[108]

In the twentieth century, the motif of the stages of life occurs in various followers of Nietzsche, including the German poet Stefan George (1868-1933), whose encounter in February 1902 with Maximilian Kronberger (or Maximin, as he called him)—an attractive thirteen-year-old boy, who would, tragically for George, die two years later, on Good Friday of 1904—would come to represent all that was beautiful, or even divine, on the earth. For George, the relationship with Maximin represented the resolution of his own midlife crisis: "We had just gone past the midday zenith of our life and we were afraid to look into our immediate future."[109] Equally, the same topos is used by George's erstwhile colleague and friend, the vitalist philosopher and graphologist Ludwig Klages (1872-1956), who wrote of his own life:

> Ever since ancient times it has been said that the human body tends to renew entirely its constituent material every seven (or, at most, nine) years, bringing about associated periodic transformations of one's soul and one's destiny. I can confirm this for three seven-year periods of my own life, but for no others. Against an external world that lacked any understanding and offered constant hindrances I was defended from my fourteenth to my twenty-first year by a blazing stream that surrounded my soul like Oceanus, on whose shores there grew poems that strike me today as of incomprehensible splendor; the subsequent seven-year period was one of fragmentation; with the next, I began to gather in, and at its end there was a long, indescribably laborious harvest.[110]

And among his early fragments dating back to 1900, published in the col-

---

[108]Nietzsche, *Ecce Homo*, "The Birth of Tragedy," §4; trans. Hollingdale, p. 51; Marie de Hennezel and Bertrand Vergely, *Une vie pour se mettre au monde* (Paris: Carnets Nord, 2010), p. 87.

[109]Stefan George, *Werke: Ausgabe in zwei Bänden* [1958] (Stuttgart: Klett-Cotta, 1984), vol. 1, p. 522; *"Wir hatten eben die mittägliche höhe unsres lebens überschritten und wir bangten beim blick in unsre nächste zukunft."*

[110]Ludwig Klages, "Einführung," in Alfred Schuler, *Fragmente und Vorträge aus dem Nachlaß*, ed. Ludwig Klages (Leipzig: Barth, 1940), p. 29.

lection *Rhythmen und Runen* (Rhythms and Runes) (1944), we find the following, tersely expressed aphorism entitled "Course of Life" (*Lebensgang*):

> After endless searching what one has tremblingly discovered: the colorful exterior of things, their meaning and essence. In magical transparency the *second world* as metaphysical reality. Forces and effects a puppet-show for the blindness of our thought—behind it the living universe, resounding from the wing-beat of the gods: this is what I *lived* in the storm of youth, what I *lost* in the age of temptation, what I *know* in the autumn of remembrance.[111]

For such writers as George and Klages, the motif of the stages of life is more than a literary topos: it provides a structural framework to understand their own emotional *and* intellectual development.

Finally, it will come as no surprise, given his close connections to Jung himself, to Jungian circles, and to the sources of Jung's thought, to discover that the idea of the stages of life plays an important role in *The Glass Bead Game* (*Das Glasperlenspiel*) (1943) by the novelist Hermann Hesse (1877-1962). In his last great work, arguably his masterpiece, Hesse conjures up an ultra-intellectual Utopia, the kingdom of Castilia, centered on a game of astonishing aesthetic complexity—the glass bead game of the novel's title.[112] One of its adepts, Josef Knecht, becomes chosen for the post of *Magister Ludi*, a position from which, however, he decides to resign. "My life, I resolved, ought to be a perpetual transcending," Knecht tells the President of the Order of the Glass Bead Game, "a progression from stage to stage [*von Stufe zu Stufe*]; I wanted to pass through one area after the next," and he explains further:

> In connection with the experiences of awakening, I had noticed that such stages and such areas exist, and that each successive period in one's life bears within itself, as it is approaching its end, a note of fading and eagerness for death. That in turn leads to a shifting to a new area, to awakening and new beginnings.[113]

---

[111]Ludwig Klages, *Rhythmen und Runen: Nachlass herausgegeben von ihm selbst* (Leipzig: Barth, 1944), p. 255.

[112]For further discussion of this work, see Paul Bishop, "Hermann Hesse, *Das Glasperlenspiel*: Beads of Glass, Shards of Culture, and the Art of Life," in *A Camden House Companion to Hermann Hesse*, ed. Ingo Cornils (Rochester, NY: Camden House, 2009), pp. 215-240.

[113]Hermann Hesse, *The Glass Bead Game*, trans. Richard and Clara Winston (Harmondsworth:

One of the poems attributed to Knecht's student-years is called precisely "Stages" (*Stufen*), and it constitutes a kind of *hommage* to the style of the late Goethe:

> As every flower fades and as all youth
> Departs, so life at every stage,
> So every virtue, so our grasp of truth,
> Blooms in its day and may not last forever.
> Since life may summon us at every age
> Be ready, heart, for parting, new endeavour,
> Be ready bravely and without remorse
> To find new light that old ties cannot give.
> In all beginnings dwells a magic force
> For guarding us and helping us to live.
>
> [...]
>
> Even the hour of our death may send
> Us speeding on to fresh and newer spaces,
> And life may summon us to newer races.
> So be it heart: bid farewell without end.
>
> [*Wie jede Blüte welkt und jede Jugend*
> *Dem Alter weicht, blüht jede Lebensstufe,*
> *Blüht jede Weisheit auch und jede Tugend*
> *Zu ihrer Zeit und darf nicht ewig dauern.*
> *Es muß das Herz bei jedem Lebensrufe*
> *Bereit zum Abschied sein und Neubeginne,*
> *Um sich in Tapferkeit und ohne Trauern*
> *In andre, neue Bindungen zu geben.*
> *Und jedem Anfang wohnt ein Zauber inne,*
> *Der uns beschützt und der uns hilft, zu leben.*
>
> [...]
>
> *Es wird vielleicht auch noch die Todesstunde*
> *Uns neuen Räumen jung entgegensenden,*
> *Des Lebens Ruf an uns wird niemals enden...*
> *Wohlan denn, Herz, nimm Abschied und gesunde!*][114]

---

Penguin, 1972), p. 371; *Gesammelte Werke*, 12 vols. (Frankfurt am Main: Suhrkamp, 1987), vol. 9, p. 439; "*Im Zusammenhang mit den Erlebnissen des Erwachens hatte ich gemerkt, daß es solche Stufen und Räume gibt und daß jeweils die letzte Zeit eines Lebensabschnittes eine Tönung von Welke und Sterbenwollen in sich trägt, welche dann zum Hinüberwechseln in einen neuen Raum, zum Erwachen, zu neuem Anfang führt.*"

[114]Hesse, *The Glass Bead Game*, p. 414; *Gesammelte Werke*, vol. 9, pp. 483-484.

When Knecht leaves his final stage on this earth and moves on to another, Hesse creates a scenario of pagan intensity: Knecht's charge, the young lad Tito, performs, against the light display of the early morning sunrise, "a ceremonial and sacrificial dance under the sign of Pan" (*dieser Fest- und Opfertanz des panisch Begeisterten*).[115]

## THE MIDLIFE CRISIS

If the course of the human life can be divided into a series of stages, how do we move from one stage to another? Is a smooth transition always possible, or can it turn into a bumpy ride? Above all, does life come to center on one major change, does it pivot around a central point? A crisis, even?

The first recorded use of the word *midlife* is in 1895, and thereafter it is nearly always associated with the word "crisis." In this respect, Elliott Jaques's paper of 1965 is the major reference, and it has sparked, as we shall see, a burgeoning secondary literature on the subject. But first, let us consider what the phrase "midlife crisis" itself might suggest. Despite the argument from the Chinese pictogram—that there is a fundamental ambivalence associated with the idea of crisis—there is a tendency for its connotations to be largely negative, and there appears to be a link between midlife crisis and depression. I am not qualified to make any clinical judgments, but two examples bear out this point. In the "Prelude" to his *Omens of Millennium* (1996), the literary critic Harold Bloom offers the following testimony:

> In the middle of the journey, at thirty-five, now thirty years ago, I got very wretched, and for almost a year was immersed in acute melancholia. Colors faded away, I could not read, and scarcely could look up at the sky. Teaching, my most characteristic activity, became impossible to perform. Whatever the immediate cause of my depression had been, that soon faded away in irrelevance, and I came to sense that my crisis was spiritual. An enormous vastation had removed the self, which until then had seemed strong in me.[116]

One wonders how Bloom, depressed at Yale in the 1970s, might fare today in a UK university, but his point is well taken; as is his next observa-

---

[115]Hesse, *The Glass Bead Game*, p. 392; *Gesammelte Werke*, vol. 9, pp. 466-467.

[116]Harold Bloom, *Omens of Millennium: The Gnosis of Angels, Dreams, and Resurrections* (London: Fourth Estate, 1997), pp. 24-25.

tion, that his "fury" with a London-based psychoanalyst led him to the real source of his cure (taking a second look at Hans Jonas's study of *The Gnostic Religion* in the light of reading Ralph Waldo Emerson).[117]

Another academic, this time one based in Britain, has a similar tale to tell. Lewis Wolpert offers a candid—at times, moving—account of his struggle with depression in *Malignant Sadness* (1999). His "Introduction" begins with the following sober confession:

> It was the worst experience of my life. More terrible even than watching my wife die of cancer. I am ashamed to admit that my depression felt worse than her death but it is true. I was in a state that bears no resemblance to anything I had experienced before. It was not just feeling very low, depressed in the commonly used sense of the word. I was seriously ill. I was totally self-involved, negative and thought about suicide most of the time. I could not think properly, let alone work, and wanted to remain curled up in bed all day. I could not ride my bicycle or go out on my own. I had panic attacks if left alone. And there were numerous physical symptoms [...]. The future was hopeless. I was convinced that I would never work again or recover. There was the strong fear that I might go mad.[118]

Like Bloom, Wolpert does not use the term "midlife crisis," but it is interesting that the book jacket says that "despite a happy marriage and a successful scientific career, he could think only of suicide." *Despite?* Many midlife crisis theories suggest, as we shall see, that success in personal and professional life is no protection against the midlife crisis; indeed, there is good evidence that success may well be an essential ingredient of it.

One of the merits of Wolpert's book is the link he makes between depression and melancholia—a condition which, as he suggests, is "probably as long as that of *Homo sapiens* itself," but is recognized in the Hippocratic writings of Greece in the fourth century BCE, discussed at length by Galen in the second century BCE, and analyzed by Aristotle. In the Middle Ages, the Church regarded "accidie," the "sin of sloth," as a cardinal sin, but during the fifteenth and sixteenth centuries accidie becomes increasingly associated with melancholia. In the late Elizabethan age the notion of melancholy returns to the fore with Robert Burton (1577-1640) and

---

[117]"What integrating Jonas and Emerson did for me was to find the context for my nihilistic depression" (*Omens of Millennium*, p. 26). For Bloom, that context turned out to be Gnosticism.

[118]Lewis Wolpert, *Malignant Sadness: The Anatomy of Depression* (London: Faber and Faber, 1999), p. vii.

his *Anatomy of Melancholy* (1621). As more recent examples, Wolpert cites accounts of depression offered by John Stuart Mill, Edgar Allan Poe, Gérard Nerval ("The Disinherited" [*El desdichado*]), and Gerard Manley Hopkins ("No worst, there is none. Pitched past pitch of grief..."). In Mill's case, however, the depression was not only overcome, but seemed to act as a motor-force for a new period of fresh creativity. If successfully resolved, can the midlife crisis be a good thing?

In what follows I offer a brief survey of the extensive literature on the midlife crisis—necessarily selective, but, it is hoped, representative. Writing in the second decade of the twentieth century, the phenomenologist and philosophical anthropologist Max Scheler (1874-1928) suggested that, "of the different *phases of life* (childhood, youth, maturity, old age)," not one "has retained its own particular value and its peculiar significance."[119] But the evidence collected below suggests that great significance (and, in some cases, great value) continues to be attached to the period of middle life, and the same may doubtless be said of the vast literature devoted to the period of early adult (im)maturity undergone by what are now called "teenagers."[120] Jung's paper of 1930 will be discussed in chapter 2, so the literature presented in these pages is intended to constitute an introduction to the issues in Jung's own exposition.

## WALTER B. PITKIN AND EDMUND BERGLER

A useful starting point is offered by Walter B. Pitkin's *Life Begins at Forty* (1932)—one of the first, one of the most famous, and surely one of the most wildly overoptimistic of books about the later years of life, and one that is very much a product of its time. Pitkin, a professor of journalism at Columbia University, reminds us of what it must have been like to have lived in a more innocent historical period: the first chapter is entitled "We Enter, Envying," and the final "We Exit, Envying." On the first page, Pitkin addresses the reader thus:

> You who are crossing forty may not know it, but you are the luckiest generation ever. The advantages you are about to enjoy will soon be recited, with a sincere undertone of envy. The

---

[119]Max Scheler, *Ressentiment* [*Das Ressentiment im Aufbau der Moralen*] [1915; based on *Über Ressentiment und moralisches Werturtheil*, 1912], trans. William W. Holdheim [1961]; cited in *German 20th Century Philosophical Writings*, ed. Wolfgang Schirmacher (New York and London: Continuum, 2003), p. 220.

[120]For the most recent discussion of this developmental period, see David Bainbridge, *Teenagers: A Natural History* (London: Portobello, 2009).

> whole world has been remodeled for your greater glory. An-
> cient philosophies and rituals are being demolished to clear
> the ground for whatever you choose to erect upon their sites.
> Every day brings forth some new thing that adds to the joy of
> life after forty. Work becomes easy and brief. Play grows
> richer and longer. Leisure lengthens. Life's afternoon is
> brighter, warmer, full of song; and long before the shadows
> stretch, every fruit grows ripe.[121]

With the First World War firmly behind him, and with no idea that, in
less than a decade, America and the world will be caught up in the toils of
the Second, Pitkin's cheerfulness knows no bounds:

> You, who have known barbarians and have been choked by
> the stench of diseased millions and have watched fifty million
> wretches die in a dirty brawl called war, under the lead of
> gangsters, will taste the full, tingling bouquet of a wine which,
> made of a million years of human vintage, is about to be
> tapped for the first time. Yes, you are the luckiest of all. Life
> begins at forty—now more richly than ever before, and per-
> haps as richly as never again.[122]

Nor were women exempt from this paradise. The seventh chapter, "Does
Woman's Life Begin at Forty?" opened with H. G. Wells's quip, "Is there,
after forty, any alternative to bridge?"—and answered both questions in
the affirmative.[123] He cites the example from *The Forum*, April 1932, of a
married woman called Jane Allan who decides to leave her well-paid job
and move with her family "into a cheap suburb where they found a pleasant house with a garden," where "she reads good books, entertains agree-
able people, plants flowers, and is conquering that first and last of all high
arts, cookery. After two years of this, she bears witness to its pleasant ade-
quacy" (although one can only wonder whether Jane continued to bear
witness in subsequent years).[124] Moreover, now that "housework is
becoming a joke," Pitkin asserts, "men and woman alike turn from the
ancient task of *making a living* to the strange new task of *living*."[125] To
help us carry out this task, Pitkin urges us to take Wordsworth or Thoreau

---

[121]Walter B. Pitkin, *Life Begins at Forty* (New York: McGraw-Hill, 1932), p. 3.

[122]*Ibid* ., p. 5.

[123]*Ibid.*, p. 112.

[124]*Ibid.*, pp. 117-118.

[125]*Ibid.*, p. 7.

as our model.[126] And he develops an energic conception of life—"life is activity, and its activity is a series of energy changes: nothing more and nothing less"[127]—distinguishing between five different levels of energy.[128] Although Pitkin acknowledges the limitations imposed by socioeconomic realities and class division—"the more fortunate millions in the upper income classes can double or treble their enjoyment [of their fourth, fifth, and sixth decades of life] merely by mastering a modern philosophy of life"[129]—he insists that his conception is not purely materialistic: "After forty, sensible people lead the simplified life. This must not be confused with the simple life, which seems to be a career of spinach and raw carrot, five miles from the nearest motion-picture theater."[130]

And yet: all is not entirely well in Pitkin's utopia. Every now and then, one passage or another betrays a deep disquiet, or anxiety, even. First, there is a certain melancholy of implicit underachievement: Wordsworth may be a good model to follow, but it is surely hard to do so—"How many of us have, in some form, done what the twenty-nine-year-old Wordsworth did, when, as he set forth from old Goslar, in Germany, he resolved to organize all his intelligence, energies, and poetical powers to the single end of creating a titanic philosophy [of] 'Man, Nature and Society'! And how many of us, again like Wordsworth, worked on and on for fifty years without finishing the task!"[131] Citing lines from *The Prelude*, Pitkin is surely right to reflect how "the annals of the great are filled with tales of dull youth blossoming late"[132]—but what of the annals of the not-so-great? Second, there is a nagging sense of flight, as in the following remarks from the third chapter, savagely entitled "Fools Die Young":

> So we come at length to a pleasant thought. One of the richest rewards of life after forty is the infrequency of fools. The silliest, the stupidest, the most vicious, and the most reckless of your generation have, ere this meridian is crossed, gone the way of the worm. Your company embraces a steadily growing

[126] *Ibid.*, pp. 39 and 60.

[127] *Ibid.*, p. 27.

[128] *Ibid.*, p. 45.

[129] *Ibid.*, p. 10.

[130] *Ibid.*, p. 49.

[131] *Ibid.*, p. 20.

[132] *Ibid.*, p. 39.

> majority of sensible, substantial, enterprising, shrewd, healthy, and generally prosperous people. So, if you are lucky enough to cross forty, you draw an extra dividend on the investment of your days in the form of more charming associates.[133]

Third, as far as the social sphere is concerned, certain phrases are extremely telling—"contacts with people, particularly with those whom we must persuade or order around, touch off potent endocrine reactions that burn us up in a bright flame," for example[134]—and occasionally a profound sense of dissatisfaction, sometimes even a deeply held contempt, bursts out, as when Pitkin urges us: "Well, contemplate American business in 1932; or American politics, or American taxes, or American cities, or American anything else you like. Across the baby face of each is written the word Vacant";[135] or when he writes that "a man has not learned to live until, among other accomplishments, he can say what he wants to say—or, having nothing to say, can keep quiet." With reference to the practice, then common, for telegraph companies to provide standard greeting messages for Christmas or New Year, Pitkin's disdain is palpable: "Look again at these sorry missives and shed one kindly tear over the stunted minds who send them," he writes. "Here we have, in its stark and ugly nakedness[,] the wordless[,] thoughtless adult," and he reflects that "so long as the species is absorbed with mere livelihood, it will be content to stumble along with crippled minds," wondering: "But after forty, when leisure and let-down come, what will such creatures do? So far as I can imagine their inwardness, they must feel like half-blinded animals in a trap."[136] Finally, Pitkin is skeptical of the benefits of psychoanalysis. While "all that Freud, Jung, Adler and the others record" about the weak and the neurotic as being slaves to their infancy is "only too accurate," their "theories about the mechanisms of regressions, suppressions, and dissociations" are, in his view, "much less reliable."[137]

Nevertheless, Pitkin pulls himself together, and on the final pages the reader is dismissed with the following stirring—and, in places, almost Mephistophelean—rhetoric:

[133] *Ibid.*, p. 43.
[134] *Ibid.*, p. 45.
[135] *Ibid.*, p. 64.
[136] *Ibid.*, pp. 67-69.
[137] *Ibid.*, p. 56.

So, we repeat, you of the Great Age which will soon begin anew are the luckiest of mortals. You first of all will taste the fruit of unlimited power. The core of the fruit is leisure, and the seed thereof is freedom. [...] Before you there will be no despair, behind you no vanity. From childhood to the coming of old age, you will expand serenely, ever learning, ever tasting new joys. At forty you will be wiser and happier than at thirty. At fifty you will be cleverer, steadier, and surer than at forty. At sixty you will be planning automobile trips to Mexico, a new sailboat, a fresh study of your village finances...[138]

I have cited Pitkin at such length because, reading between the lines, we can see, even if only in shadowy form, a good number of the problems with which the midlife crisis is associated. In the remaining years of the 1930s and the 1940s that followed, an awareness of the presence of death in this life will have become all too obvious. Global crisis replaces midlife crisis, and the topic disappears.

In the postwar years, however, with the return of economic prosperity, and with the development, thanks to technology, of a standard of living previously unimaginable (even to Walter Pitkin), the specter of midlife crisis also returned. One of the most subtle and intriguing discussions of it can be found in a book by the New York-based psychoanalyst Edmund Bergler (1899-1962), in his book entitled *The Revolt of the Middle-Aged Man* (1958).

Bergler's main thesis, drummed home on several occasions, is that man's "middle-age revolt" is really an "emotional second adolescence."[139] Who is the "middle-aged rebel" of whom Bergler speaks? He is, we are told, "a recognizable contemporary type: he lives in one of the great urban areas of the United States, and his income level is that of the upper middle class."[140] And what is his revolt? In the mythical terms used by one of Bergler's middle-aged men, it is "a descent into Hades," for "in this unpleasant locality the counterparts of many traditional mythological figures will be met with," one of the most important of whom is "Tantalus, who is represented in every human being."[141] Now Tantalus, along with such other great penitents in the mythical underworld as Sisyphus and

---

[138] *Ibid.*, p. 174.

[139] Edmund Bergler, *The Revolt of the Middle-Aged Man* (London: Hanison, 1958), p. 214; cf. pp. 4, 117, 165, 222, 285, and 303.

[140] *Ibid.*, p. vi, note.

[141] *Ibid.*, p. 29.

Prometheus, is a figure whom we shall meet again in Verena Kast's Jung-inspired approach to the midlife crisis, but Bergler's own method is far removed from anything archetypal, and is rather based on his own (in some respects, idiosyncratic) reading of Freud.

The central tenets of Bergler's method are that "what appears in consciousness is never an unconscious wish directly expressed, but only the inner defense against that wish,"[142] and that "the repetitiveness of infantile fantasies" are "the determining factor in neurotic adult behaviour."[143] The main mechanism that he uses to describes this middle-aged revolt is called "psychic masochism." Accordingly, the middle-aged rebel is "not a man who wants happiness in a hurry, but a man who is under the severest inner pressure, who is threatened with severest unconscious punishment, unless he makes good his inner promise of—happiness in a hurry."[144] Let us examine more closely this "masochistic pattern" of "pleasure-in-displeasure," and observe how *homo masochisticus* functions.

To the "genetic" picture of psychic masochism described by Freud, Bergler adds a detailed "clinical" picture.[145] Whereas, on the level of consciousness, *homo masochisticus* has "admirable" intentions and he aims to succeed, on the unconscious level he is, says Bergler, "a lover of defeat."[146] This is because of the adult's earlier identification, as a child, with his educators and their commands. The inner structure thus created is what Freud calls the "ego ideal"; for Bergler, it is "Department I," whose task is to supply "fictions designed to preserve as many vestiges as possible of the infantile fantasy of absolute power."[147] (In accordance with such fantasies, the ego abstains from bad acts, not because it has been told to, but because, so it deceives itself, it wants to.) At the same time, the "self-destructive elements of unconscious conscience" create "Department II"—a function of the child's unusable inward-flowing aggression,

---

[142]Edmund Bergler, *Divorce Won't Help* (New York and London: Harper, 1948), p. 15.

[143]Bergler, *The Revolt of the Middle-Aged Man*, p. 146.

[144]*Ibid.*, p. 77.

[145]*Ibid.*, p. 82.

[146]*Ibid.*, p. 80.

[147]*Ibid.*, p. 86. Elsewhere, Bergler cites an example from the first novel in Romain Rolland's ten-volume cycle *Jean-Christophe* (1904-1911) as an example of the fantasy of childhood omnipotence (*Divorce Won't Help*, p. 194). The small child looks up at the sky, and watches the clouds going from right to left. He commands them to go to the right; but still they move from right to left. He scolds them, and tells them again to go to the right; but they keep moving to the left. Upset, the child orders them again, only now to move from the right to the left. This time, the clouds obey his orders.

whose only purpose is to torture.[148] On this account, then, the superego consists of two parts: the ego ideal, and a "cruel slave-driver" that Bergler calls—borrowing a term from Plato, used to describe Socrates's inner spirit—*daimonion*.[149] Both Goethe and Jung use this term, too, but for Bergler, its connotations are exclusively negative. For this part of the superego is, according to Bergler, "obsessed with a lust to torture the ego," using as its weapon the ego ideal, so that "every time a discrepancy appears between the ego ideal and the ego"—as, inevitably, discrepancies will appear—"*daimonion* dictates feelings of guilt as penance."[150] And because "the conscious happiness of the individual depends on the countermeasures that he is able to take in order to checkmate his inner monster,"[151] the neurotic or the psychic masochist learn to "derive inner pleasure from external disappointment."[152] Thus he comes to believe that "the only pleasure one can derive from displeasure is to make displeasure a pleasure,"[153] and the psychic masochist goes even further, deriving "additional pleasure" from "outsmarting the stupid educator, and later from outsmarting the educator's inner successor, Department II of unconscious conscience," the "inner Frankenstein's monster."[154]

Bergler applies this complex, three-layered structure of (i) original aggression; (ii) resultant guilt; (iii) guilt changing into unconscious pleasure, which forms the core of the "pleasure-in-displeasure" pattern, to a variety of clinical cases, identifying two further characteristics which, when added to psychic masochism, result in the middle-age revolt. Despite the abstractness of his analysis, his examples are highly specific. First, this mechanism undergoes a quantitative increase as a defense against the unconscious conscience, which "uses the situation of aging" as a source of material for "ironic reproaches." The sight of two young people in love, for instance, leaves him "depressed and nostalgic, as though an

[148]Bergler, *The Revolt of the Middle-Aged Man*, p. 86.

[149]See Plato, *The Apology*, 31c-d: "You have often heard me say before on many occasions—that I am subject to a divine or supernatural experience [*daimonion*] […]. It began in my early childhood—a sort of voice which comes to me, and when it comes it always dissuades me from what I am proposing to do, and never urges me on" (*The Collected Dialogues*, ed. Edith Hamilton and Huntington Cairns [Princeton, NJ: Princeton University Press, 1963], p. 17).

[150]Bergler, *Divorce Won't Help*, p. 62.

[151]Bergler, *The Revolt of the Middle-Aged Man*, p. 88.

[152]*Ibid.*, p. 89.

[153]*Ibid.*

[154]*Ibid.*

inner voice had ironically commented, 'That's not for you any more, brother.'"[155] And second, there is what he calls the "subterfuge technique," a "desperate fight of the unconscious ego against the quantitative menace via the subterfuge of finding a witness, in the person of a new woman, whose very existence proves that the victim is still young"; in other words, "what appears to be a conscious attempt to improve one's lot by prolonging youth is in unconscious reality but an episode in the battle against psychic masochism."[156] Thus, when Goethe records in one of his aphorisms how, when "an elderly man was found fault with for continuing to trouble himself with young women," he retorted that it was the only way to rejuvenate oneself, "'and everyone wants to do that,'"[157] Bergler would not agree.

Whereas, in woman, "the unpleasantness—physical and mental—of the menopause" is sufficient to absorb her psychic masochism, and her change of life has a "biological substructure," the basis of the man's middle-aged rebellion is, says Bergler, "exclusively psychological"—nor can either be escaped.[158] "The long-drawn-out Jeremiad of the middle-aged rebel begins and ends," he writes, "with the stock formula: 'my wife doesn't understand me.'"[159] According to Bergler, there is "an amazing assortment of women, all different," that are classified by "these easy-to-satisfy rebels" as "understanding," and are classified by Bergler himself as follows: Miss Injustice Collector ("only the unconscious pleasure-in-displeasure pattern can explain why the girl exposes herself to a situation in which defeat is a ninety-per-cent predictable conclusion"),[160] Miss Mild Resignation, Miss Illusion, Miss Magic Gesture, Miss Revenge,[161] Miss Professional Troublemaker, Miss Rescue Fantasy,[162] Miss Gold Dig-

---

[155] *Ibid.*, p. 98.

[156] *Ibid.*

[157] *Maxims and Reflections*, ed. Hecker, no. 16, in Goethe, *"Maximen und Reflexionen": A Selection*, ed. and trans. R. H. Stephenson (Glasgow: Scottish Papers in Germanic Studies, 1986), pp. 75-76; *Werke* [HA], vol. 12, pp. 534-535.

[158] Bergler, *The Revolt of the Middle-Aged Man*, pp. 116 and 118.

[159] *Ibid.*, p. 121.

[160] *Ibid.*, p. 122.

[161] For further discussion of the complicated structure of the psychology of lesbianism as discerned by Bergler, see his *Neurotic Counterfeit-Sex: Impotence, Frigidity, "Mechanical" and Pseudosexuality, Homosexuality* (New York: Grune and Stratton, 1951), his triple monograph on homosexuality, frigidity, and impotence.

[162] See Edmund Bergler, *Unhappy Marriage and Divorce: A Study of Neurotic Choice of Marriage Partners* (New York: International Universities Press, 1946).

ger,[163] and Miss Promiscuous. So where, if anywhere, can a "normal—meaning not-too-neurotic—girl" be found? Bergler's answer is that "if a girl is halfway stable emotionally, she will automatically and unconsciously avoid the rebel's hopeless troubles and the problems arising from any relationship with him."[164] Instead, "so many of the young women attracted to middle-aged men are masochistic";[165] "the middle-aged rebel has no chance whatsoever of finding a new companion who is emotionally stable,"[166] and clearly the trouble begins when two neurotics get married—for the solution here, one should turn to Bergler's other writings, including *Conflict in Marriage: The Unhappy Undivorced* (1949), *Principles of Self-Damage* (1959), and *Tensions Can Be Reduced to Nuisances: A Technique for Not-Too-Neurotic People* (1960).

Two final points before we leave Edmund Bergler. First, one might object that, if psychic masochism is, in fact, a universal scourge, why does it manifest itself in middle-age revolt and not earlier? Bergler's answer is that psychic masochism is indeed a universal human problem, "deeply buried in the unconscious," but that "at certain times the latent tendency becomes acute," and one of these danger points is middle age. Middle age is a danger point because it brings us into a new relation to death; with the "death complex," a previously repressed fear "re-emerges."[167] According to Freud, death is not represented in the unconscious,[168] because death is beyond personal experience (which is not the case in, say, the fear of bodily damage). Behind the fear of death, Bergler claims, lies quite a different fear—"fear of one's own increased psychic masochism."[169]

And second, Bergler problematizes the idea of self-knowledge—a notion central to the project of psychoanalysis and analytical psychology alike. According to Bergler, the ego's aversion to self-scrutiny is related to the "humble beginnings" of mental self-observation in the phenomenon of *infantile peeping*. (On this account, the wish to be a "Peeping Tom" underlies, in fact, any and all attempts to know self or world.) For voyeur-

---

[163]See Edmund Bergler, *Money and Emotional Conflicts* (Garden City, NY: Doubleday, 1951).

[164]Bergler, *The Revolt of the Middle-Aged Man*, pp. 164-165.

[165]*Ibid.*, p. 165.

[166]*Ibid.*

[167]*Ibid.*, p. 224.

[168]See Sigmund Freud, *Thoughts for the Times on War and Death* (*Zeitgemäßes über Krieg und Tod*) (1915), §2, "Our Attitude Towards Death"; Freud, *SE*, vol. 14, pp. 273-302 (pp. 289-300).

[169]Bergler, *The Revolt of the Middle-Aged Man*, p. 226.

ism begins, according to Bergler, as a "deeply rooted wish to look at things *sexual*," being directed at first at the child's own person, but then shifting, later, to adult authority figures, to the "people with a halo." Because it is "forbidden" to understand these adults' sexuality, the child's curiosity becomes "diverted" to such nonsexual matters as objects, the world of nature, or the knowledge of external things in general. Bergler's contention is thus that this "buried connection" with "infantile peeping at one's own genitalia" (which is "intimately bound up with the taboo on infantile masturbation") sets up "unconscious barriers against introspection."[170]

Undeservedly (because the intricacy of his analysis is amazing, if not always convincing) forgotten, Bergler demonstrates the versatility of Freudian-inspired thinking. Yet in his social assumptions, he is just as much time-bound as Walter Pitkin. His choice of images is telling—such as when he compares the early stages of analysis to the "siege of a walled city"[171]—and he assumes that marriage is the only possible context for stable sexual relations. Given (and he may well be right) that "a non-ambivalent human relation does not exist,"[172] and his devastating analysis of the psychological mechanisms underlying "romantic love"—

> The cruel Superego holds up to the frightened unconscious Ego the self-created Ego-Ideal, like a mirror, and asks the eternal guilt-producing question: "Do you deny that you have not achieved your goals as set forth in your Ego-ideal?" But by projecting the Ego-Ideal onto the beloved, the Ego removes this discrepancy, for the beloved constantly attests that all the goals of the Ego-Ideal have been fulfilled. Therefore, no discrepancy—no guilt [...][173]

—not to mention the inevitable "neurotic love," in which the neurotic transfers both the Ego-Ideal *and* the *daimonion* onto the beloved,[174] Bergler's "tripartite compass" for matrimony—loving-kindness, compromise, and knowing one's place[175]—seems somewhat inadequate to the task at hand. And while denying the efficacy of the quasi-Goethean solution of "resignation"—dismissed as "a rather neurotic and unfavourable

---

[170] *Ibid.*, p. 177.

[171] *Ibid.*, p. 38.

[172] Bergler, *Conflict in Marriage: The Unhappy Undivorced* (New York: Harper, 1949), p. 162.

[173] Bergler, *Divorce Won't Help*, p. 58.

[174] *Ibid.*, p. 60.

[175] Bergler, *Conflict in Marriage*, p. 216.

outcome of the second formative period in man's infantile life"[176]—Bergler comes to the (Schopenhauerian) conclusion that "*relative* contentment and middle age are by no means mutually exclusive"; for, by using knowledge itself as "a weapon against the exaggeration of a conflict and the needless suffering of the affected individual and of his family," then "suffering with dignity, adaptation to reality without blaming it on the poor wife, making the best of life—short as it is—are difficult but not impossible."[177] So perhaps it is time to put Bergler's technique to the test, both in domestic and in workplace scenarios.

## ERIK H. ERIKSON AND ELLIOTT JAQUES

Another major contribution to the theory of the stages of life can be found in the work of Erik H. Erikson (1902-1994), one of the pioneering theorists of the life cycle. In this respect, his central text is the essay entitled "Growth and Crises of the Healthy Personality," published in a collection of papers called *Identity and the Life Cycle* (1959).[178] This work was followed a decade later by *Identity: Youth and Crisis* (1968), and towards the end of his life Erikson returned to the themes of these works in *The Life Cycle Completed: A Review* (1982).[179]

In "Ego Development and Historical Change: Clinical Notes," Erikson focused on the early stages of psycho-socio-sexual development. He compared "the coordinates of the moral burgher" as given in the conclusion to Kant's second Critique—"*the starry heavens above*" and "*the moral law within*"—with those of the early Freud, who "placed his fearful ego between the id within him and the mob around him."[180] Erikson emphasized that "in the experiences of the *pregenital stages*" the human infant "learns the basic variables of organismic-social existence, before his libido becomes free for its procreative task"—in other words, sexuality is always (already) subordinated to society.[181] According to Erikson, in his

---

[176]Bergler, *The Revolt of the Middle-Aged Man*, p. 308.

[177]*Ibid.*, p. 308.

[178]Erik H. Erikson, *Identity and the Life Cycle* [1959] (New York and London: Norton, 1980). For a comparison of what Erikson calls "psychosocial identity" with the Jungian notion of the "persona," see Murray Stein, *In Midlife: A Jungian Perspective* (Dallas, TX: Spring Publications, 1983), p. 26.

[179]Erik H. Erikson, *Identity: Youth and Crisis* (London: Faber, 1968); and *The Life Cycle Completed: A Review* [1982] (New York and London: Norton, 1985).

[180]Erikson, *Identity and the Life Cycle*, p. 19; cf. Immanuel Kant, *Practical Philosophy*, ed. and trans. Mary J. Gregor (Cambridge: Cambridge University Press, 1996), p. 269.

[181]Erikson, *Identity and the Life Cycle*, p. 37.

paper "On Narcissism" (1914) Freud identified three sources of human self-esteem—a residue of infantile narcissism, a fulfillment of the ego ideal in such infantile experiences as experience corroborates,[182] and the gratification of object libido.[183] From these three important infantile con- tributions to the individual's *ego identity* there emerges "a defined ego in a social reality."[184] For Erikson, "the self-esteem attached to the ego iden- tity" is based on "the rudiments of skills and social techniques which assure a gradual coincidence of functional pleasure and actual perfor- mance, of ego ideal and social role," thus containing "the recognition of a tangible future."[185]

Addressing himself to the theme of the relationship between (individ- ual) sexuality and (collective) responsibility—that is, as we shall see, tack- led by Goethe (albeit using a different vocabulary) in the stanza devoted to "Eros" in "Primal Words. Orphic"—Erikson argues that "if 'object libido' is to be satisfied, then genital love and orgastic potency must be assured of a cultural synthesis of economic safety and emotional security"; for "only such a synthesis gives unified meaning to the full functionality of genitality, which includes conception, childbearing, and child rear- ing."[186] Whereas "infatuation" projects the "incestuous childhood love" into "a present 'object,'" and "genital activity" helps two individuals "use one another as an anchor against regression," what Erikson calls *mutual genital love* "faces toward the future."[187] But if "a division of labour in that life task which only two of the opposite sex can fulfill together" consti- tutes "the synthesis of production, procreation, and recreation in the primary social unit of the family"—a conclusion, albeit a socially conser- vative one, that Goethe draws in "Primal Words. Orphic"—the modern world of the fifties posed the question, Erikson claimed, of "whether the problems of the machine age will be resolved by a mechanization of Man or by a humanization of industry."[188]

The starting-point of "Growth and Crises of the Healthy Personal-

---

[182]See Bergler's example taken from Romain Rolland (see footnote 147 above).

[183]Erikson, *Identity and the Life Cycle*, p. 38; cf. "On Narcissism: An Introduction" [1914], in Freud, *SE*, vol. 14, pp. 67-102.

[184]Erikson, *Identity and the Life Cycle*, p. 22.

[185]*Ibid.*, p. 39.

[186]*Ibid.*, p. 40.

[187]*Ibid.*

[188]*Ibid.*, pp. 46-47.

ity" is the distinction between Nature and Culture, exactly as we find it in Jung's paper on "The Stages of Life" (see chapter 2). "At birth," Erikson writes, "the baby leaves the chemical exchange of the womb for the social exchange system of his society, where his gradually increasing capacities meet the opportunities and limitations of his *culture*."[189] What Erikson called "personality," a concept analogous to, but not identical with, Jung's own notion, develops "according to steps predetermined"— archetypally? one feels bound to ask—"in the human organism's readiness to be driven toward, to be aware of, and to interact with, a widening social radius, beginning with the dim image of the mother and ending with Mankind."[190] In Erikson's diagram of epigenetic development, the individual moves (in three stages, from the first year to the third or fourth year) from a sense of basic trust, via a sense of autonomous will, to a sense of initiative.[191] What is significant about this account is its underlying pattern: as "each [component sense] comes to its ascendance," it "meets its crisis," and find its "lasting solution" toward the end of the stages mentioned.[192] Each stage, then, becomes a *crisis*, because "incipient growth and awareness in a significant part function goes together with a shift in instinctual energy and yet causes specific vulnerabilities in that part"; in short, each stage is a crisis "because of a radical *change of perspective*."[193] What Erikson says here about the earliest stages of ego development might well also be applied to one of its later stages, the midlife crisis.

Whereas the newborn infant "lives through, and loves with, his mouth," and the mother "lives through, and loves with, her breasts," the course of ego development involves various kinds of compensation during the same stage of development (what Erikson calls "horizontal" compensation), as opposed to those compensations that only emerge from later stages in the life cycle (or "longitudinal" compensations).[194] As an example of "the expression of *infantile urges* in *cultural patterns*," Erikson cites—just as "Primal Words. Orphic" contains a stanza devoted to *Tyche*—"the invigorating belief in 'chance,' that traditional prerogative of American trust in one's own resourcefulness and in Fate's store of good

[189] *Ibid.*, p. 53.
[190] *Ibid.*, p. 54.
[191] See *ibid.*, p. 55, diagram 2.
[192] *Ibid.*, p. 56.
[193] *Ibid.*
[194] *Ibid.*, pp. 58, 61.

intentions."[195] Yet, as a good psychologist, Erikson is too realistic (just as Goethe was) to rely exclusively on the power of *Tyche*, suggesting that "this belief, at times, can be seen to degenerate—in large-scale gambling, or in 'taking chances' in the form of an arbitrary and often suicidal provocation of Fate, or in the insistence that one has not only the right to an equal chance but also the privilege of being preferred over all other investors in the same general enterprise."[196]

The process of ego development is—much as described by the stanza devoted to *ananke* (Necessity) in "Primal Words. Orphic"—not without its moment of fear or anxiety: "besides irrational fears of losing one's autonomy—"don't fence me in" (cf. "It only seems we're free, years hem us in, / Constraining more than at our origin"[197])—there are "fears of being sabotaged in one's free will by inner enemies; of being restricted and constricted in one's autonomous initiative; and, paradoxically enough, at the same time of not being completely controlled enough; of not being told what to do."[198]

In summary, the early stages of ego development as laid out by Erikson involve five separate components: (1) basic trust versus basic mistrust; (2) autonomy versus shame and doubt; (3) initiative versus guilt; (4) industry versus inferiority; (5) identity versus identity diffusion, followed by the three stages of adulthood: (1) intimacy and distantiation versus self-absorption; (2) generativity versus stagnation; (3) integrity versus despair and disgust.[199] Yet Erikson is acutely alert to the cultural particularities that surround these stages, noting that "democracy in a country like America" poses "special problems," such as its insistence on "*self-made identities* ready to grasp many chances and ready to adjust to changing necessities of booms and busts, of peace and war, of migration and determined sedentary life."[200] In particular, Erikson emphasized the

---

[195] *Ibid.*, p. 64.

[196] *Ibid.*

[197] Or: "*So sind wir scheinfrei denn nach manchen Jahren / Nur enger dran, als wir am Anfang waren*" (see chapter 4).

[198] Erikson, *Identity and the Life Cycle*, p. 77. As Erikson warns, "while many such fears are, of course, based on the realistic appraisal of dangers inherent in complex social organizations"—as Erikson, working in the context of U.S. academia, will have been well aware—"and in the struggle for power, safety, and security, they seem to contribute to psychoneurotic and psychosomatic disturbances on the one hand, and, on the other, to the easy acceptance of slogans which seem to promise alleviation of conditions by excessive and irrational conformity" (p. 77).

[199] *Ibid.*, p. 100.

[200] *Ibid.*, pp. 98-99.

role of education—very much in the classical German sense of *Bildung*, as understood by Goethe—in correcting the one-sidedness of modern American culture:

> In a culture once pervaded with the value of the self-made man, a special danger ensues from the idea of a synthetic personality: as if you are what you can appear to be, or as if you are what you can buy. This can be counteracted only by a system of education that transmits values and goals which determinedly aspire beyond mere "functioning" and "making the grade."

For its part, analytical psychology can perform just such an educative task, by mediating knowledge of classical, medieval, and early modern culture to a contemporary audience of clients or readers.

Recalling Freud's response when he was once asked what a normal person should be able to do—*lieben und arbeiten*, "love and work," was Freud's answer (in Erikson's view, a "simple formula" which, however, "gets deeper as you think about it"[201])—Erikson introduces one of his main themes: integrity. "Only he who in some way has taken care of things and people and has adapted himself to the triumph and disappointments of being, by necessity, the originator of others and the generator of things and ideas," Erikson argues, "only he may gradually grow the fruit of the seven stages" and achieve the eighth.[202] For Erikson, integrity

---

[201] Erik H. Erikson, "Growth and Crises of the Healthy Personality" [1950], in *Identity and the Life Cycle*, pp. 51-107 (p. 102).

[202] Erikson, *Identity and the Life Cycle*, p. 104. In his correspondence with Oskar Pfister, Freud had already remarked in his letter of 6 March 1910 that he was unable to contemplate with equanimity a "life without work": "to fantasize and to work are the same thing for me, there is nothing else that I enjoy" [*Phantasieren und Arbeiten fällt für mich zusammen, ich amüsiere mich bei nichts anderem*] (Sigmund Freud and Oskar Pfister, *Briefe 1909-1939*, ed. Ernst L. Freud and Heinrich Meng [Frankfurt am Main: Fischer, 1963], p. 32). Likewise, the theme of work—its necessity, as well as (dare one say it?) its pleasures—is central to Goethe and Freud. Goethe's activist ethic is well summarized in *Wilhelm Meister's Journeyman Years* (*Wilhelm Meisters Wanderjahre*) (1821/1829), in which one of the characters of the novel—the educated aristocrat and major turned mineralogist and mining engineer, Jarno, now called Montan—insists on the reciprocity of "thinking" and "doing," delivering the celebrated maxim, "thought and action, action and thought, that is the sum of all wisdom" [*Denken und Tun, Tun und Denken, das ist die Summe aller Weisheit*] (*GE* 10, 280). The central tenet of this injunction is found in numerous reflections, such as this one: "There is nothing more miserable than a decent man without work; the most beautiful of gifts becomes disgusting to him" [*Elender ist nichts als der behagliche Mensch ohne Arbeit, das schönste der Gaben wird ihm eckel*] (*Tagebuch*, 13 January 1779; Goethe, *Werke* [WA], vol. III.1, p. 77). Of course, this emphasis on work is not restricted to Goethe and Freud. Kant, for example, believed that "work is the best way of enjoying one's life" [*Arbeit* [*ist*] *die beste Art sein Leben zu genießen*] (Kant, *Anthropologie*, book 2, §260; *Gesammelte Schriften* [Prussian Academy Edition], 29 vols. [Berlin: Reimer; Walter de Gruyter, 1902-1980], vol. 7, 232; *Anthropology*

resides in "the significance of one's own and only life cycle and of the people who have become significant for it as something that had to be and that, by necessity, permitted of no substitutions."[203] Indeed, such a goal could be described as the outcome of the Jungian process of individuation, or (in the precise Goethean sense) as an expression of *resignation*.[204] Such resignation is best understood as a form of "acceptance," in line with Bertrand Vergely's distinction between *se résigner* and *accepter*: for "whoever resigns himself says yes to life despite himself, in not ceasing to refuse it," while "whoever accepts says yes to life, because he wants to."[205]

---

*from a Pragmatic Point of View*, trans. Mary J. Gregor [The Hague: Nijhoff, 1974], p. 101); compare with Kant's advice to a young person: "get fond of work: deny yourself enjoyments, not to *renounce* them but to keep them, as much as possible, only in prospect" [*gewinne die Arbeit lieb; versage dir Vergnügen, nicht um ihnen zu **entsagen**, sondern so viel als möglich immer nur im Prospect zu behalten!*] (*Anthropology*, book 2, §63; *Gesammelte Schriften*, vol. 7, 237; trans. Gregor, p. 105), and the emphasis on work constitutes part of the legacy of German Idealism in psychoanalysis. Given his reputation, it might be surprising to learn that the psychoanalyst Wilhelm Reich (1897-1957) was attached to the idea of "work democracy," believing that—in the words of his motto—"love, work, and knowledge are the wellspring of our life" [*Liebe, Arbeit und Wissen sind die Quellen unseres Lebens*], and so "they should also govern it" [*sie sollen es auch regieren*]. Reich's message was, as one of his commentators has put it, of "extraordinary simplicity": "You don't have to do anything special or new. All you have to do is to continue what you are doing: plough your fields, wield your hammer, examine your patients, take your children to the school or to the playground, report on the events of the day, penetrate ever more deeply into the secrets of nature" (Wilhelm Reich, *Listen, Little Man* [London: Souvenir Press, 1972], p. 116; cited in David Boadella, *Wilhelm Reich: The Evolution of his Work* [London: Arkana, 1985], p. 236).

[203] Erikson, *Identity and the Life Cycle*, p. 104. Failure to achieve "integrity" results in a condition that Erikson describes as *despair*, accompanied by an unconscious *fear of death*, and to which he applies the (Nietzschean) label, *disgust*: "The lack or loss of this accrued ego integration is signified by *despair* and an often unconscious *fear of death*: the one and only life cycle is not accepted as the ultimate of life. Despair expresses the feeling that the time is too short, too short for the attempt to start another life and to try out alternate roads to integrity. Such a despair is often hidden behind a show of disgust, a misanthropy, or a chronic contemptuous displeasure with particular institutions and particular people—a disgust and a displeasure which (not allied with constructive ideas and a life of cooperation) only signify the individual's contempt of himself" (pp. 104-105).

[204] On the theme of resignation (*Entsagung*) in Goethe there has accumulated a massive literature, including Wilhelm Flitner, *Goethe im Spätwerk: Glaube, Weltsicht, Ethos* (Hamburg: Claassen und Goverts, 1947); Arthur Henkel, *Entsagung: Eine Studie zu Goethes Altersroman* (Tübingen: Niemeyer, 1954); Bernd Peschken, *Entsagung in "Wilhelm Meisters Wanderjahren"* (Bonn: Bouvier, 1968); William Meads, "Goethe's Concept of *Entsagung*," *Pacific Coast Philology* 8 (1973): 34-41; Melitte Gerhard, "Ursache und Bedeutung von Goethes 'Entsagung,'" *Jahrbuch des Freien Deutschen Hochstifts* (1981): 110-115; Mauro Ponzi, "Zur Entstehung des Goetheschen Motivs der 'Entsagung,'" *Zeitschrift für Germanistik* 7 (1986): 150-159; and, for an attempt to relate the Stoic sources of "resignation" to the novel *Elective Affinities* (*Die Wahlverwandtschaften*) (1809), see Paul Bishop, *The World of Stoical Discourse in Goethe's Novel "Die Wahlverwandtschaften"* (Lewiston, NY: Mellen, 1999).

[205] De Hennezel and Vergely, *Une vie pour se mettre au monde*, p. 80. For Vergely, "acceptance of old age and death" is related to the Full (p. 104), and "wisdom" resides in "acceptance" (or consent), as the Ancients teach us (p. 109).

Although the phenomenon was known to earlier thinkers and analysts, the actual phrase "midlife crisis" was coined, in his groundbreaking paper published in 1965,[206] by the Canadian psychologist Elliott Jaques (1917-2003).[207] Through Jung's work, the expression then entered the discourse of popular culture. For Jaques, the midlife crisis takes place in one's middle thirties, a time of transition. This transition, he noted, is "often obscured" in women because of the onset of the menopause, while in men "the change has from time to time been referred to as the male climacteric, because of the reduction in the intensity of sexual behaviour which often occurs at that time."[208] Jaques became aware of middle age as a critical stage in development, he says, when reading *The Voyage Home* (1964), the autobiography of the English poet and critic Richard Church (1893-1972), and being struck by the death rate among creative artists in their late thirties. He noticed—just as Goethe did in his conversation with Johann Peter Eckermann of 11 March 1828[209]—the disproportionately large number of creative individuals who die between 35 and 39, or who, surviving this period, show a sudden burst of creativity after it. According to Jaques, Bach, Rossini, Racine, Goldsmith, Constable, Goya, Ben Jonson, Gauguin, and Donatello are all examples, as is Goethe, who, "between the ages of 37 and 39, underwent a profound change in outlook, associated with his trip to Italy."[210]

In the opening words of *The Divine Comedy*—Dante's masterpiece, begun when he was banished from Florence at the age of 37— Jaques finds "great power and tremendous psychological depth":

[206]See Jaques, "Death and the Mid-Life Crisis." *Nomen est omen?* Jaques's surname is indeed identical to the name of the character in Shakespeare's *As You Like It*. For further discussion of the elective function of names, see René Major, *De l'élection: Freud face aux idéologies américaine, allemande et soviétique* (Paris: Aubier, 1988), esp. pp. 19-20 and 57-58.

[207]On the basis of his work for the U.S. Army and various corporations, Jaques developed a theory of social behavior and organization design, reflected in a series of books, including *A General Theory of Bureaucracy* (Aldershott: Gregg Revivals, 1976) and *Requisite Organization: A Total System for Effective Managerial Organization and Managerial Leadership for the 21st Century* (Arlington: Cason Hall, 1997). Having qualified as analyst in London under Melanie Klein (1882-1960), Jaques developed such concepts as time span of discretion and felt fair pay, and although his ideas have fallen out of favor with some management theorists, his work is continued by the Requisite Organization International Institute in Florida, USA.

[208]Jaques, "Death and the Mid-Life Crisis," p. 502.

[209]See Johann Peter Eckermann, *Conversations of Goethe*, ed. J. K. Moorhead, trans. John Oxenford [1930] (New York: Da Capo, 1998), p. 252. This conversation will be discussed in greater detail in chapter 3.

[210]Jaques, "Death and the Mid-Life Crisis," p. 503.

> Midway this way of life we're bound upon,
>     I woke to find myself in a dark wood,
>     Where the right road was wholly lost and gone.
>
> Ay me! how hard to speak of it—that rude
>     And rough and stubborn forest! the mere breath
>     Of memory stirs the old fear in the blood;
>
> It is so bitter, it goes nigh to death [...].[211]

At a deep level, Jaques argues, these words can be interpreted as "the opening scene of a vivid and perfect description of the emotional crisis of the mid-life phase," and he finds evidence for this view in the fact that, in the years preceding his exile (i.e., in his early thirties), Dante's outlook had already begun to undergo a transformation, from the idyllic view of the *La Vita Nuova* (c. 1290)—written when he was between the ages of 27 and 29—to the "philosophy" he presented in allegorical form in the *Convivio*, written between the ages of 36 and 38.

As Jaques carefully argues, the "crisis" of midlife is closely bound up with the awareness of personal death, a fact that many people seek to deny or the consciousness of which they try to evade. He draws on Klein's work on how the individual can "work through" the "infantile-depressive position," and his paper concludes with the notion, echoing Plotinus, of "sculpted creativity":[212]

> Out of the working through of the depressive position, there
> is further strengthening of the capacity to accept and tolerate

---

[211] *Hell*, Canto I, ll. 1-7; Dante, *The Divine Comedy*, vol. 1, *Hell*, trans. Dorothy L. Sayers (Harmondsworth: Penguin Books, 1949), p. 71. Compare with Jung's comments in a lecture given at the ETH on 14 June 1935: "A point exists at about the thirty-fifth year when things begin to change, it is the first moment of the shadow side of life, of the going down to death. It is clear that Dante found this point and those who have read *Zarathustra* will know that Nietzsche also discovered it. When this turning point comes people meet it in several ways: some turn away from it; others plunge into it; and something important happens to yet others from the outside. If we do not see a thing Fate does it to us" (in *Modern Psychology Vol. 1 and 2: Notes on Lectures given at the Eidgenössische Technische Hochschule, Zürich, by Prof. Dr. C. G. Jung, October 1933–July 1935*, ed. Barbara Hannah, 2nd ed. [Zurich: privately printed, 1959], p. 223; cited in Jung, *The Red Book*, p. 232, n. 32).

[212] "Withdraw into yourself and look. And if you do not find yourself beautiful yet, act as does the creator of a statue that is to be made beautiful; he cuts away here, he smoothes there, he makes this line lighter, this other purer, until a lovely face has grown upon his work. So do you also: cut away all that is excessive, straighten all that is crooked, bring light to all that is overcast, labour to make all one glow of beauty and never cease chiselling your statue, until there shall shine out on you from it the godlike splendour of virtue" (Plotinus, *Enneads*, 1.6.9; in Plotinus, *The Enneads*, trans. Stephen MacKenna, 4th ed, rev. B. S. Page [London: Faber and Faber, 1969], p. 63). For further discussion, see Michel Onfray, *La Sculpture de soi: La morale esthétique* (Paris: Grasset, 1993), pp. 77-90.

conflict and ambivalence. One's work need no longer be experienced as perfect. It can be worked and re-worked, but it will be accepted as having shortcomings. The sculpting process can be carried on far enough so that the work is good enough. There is no need for obsessional attempts at perfection, because inevitable imperfection is no longer felt as bitter persecuting failure. Out of this mature resignation comes the serenity in the work of genius, true serenity, serenity which transcends imperfection by accepting it.[213]

As far as the denial of death is concerned, Jaques could well have cited the case of Goethe, whose attitude toward death is known to have been complicated, not to say fraught.[214] In his paper, Jaques also comes extremely close to articulating the concept of *harmony* or *totality* at the heart of German classicism, which aims at the construction of the singular, unique—even if, inevitably, imperfect—individual personality. With good reason, Jaques describes "the positive creativeness and the tone of serenity which accompany the successful endurance of this frustration" as "characteristic of the mature production" of Goethe, Beethoven, Virgil —and Dante, the final words of whose *Paradiso*—

> Yet, as a wheel moves smoothly, free from jars,
> My will and my desire were turned by love,
>
> The love that moves the sun and the other stars[215]

—bring Jaques's paper to its end. In their "strong and quiet confidence," these words express the spirit that, Jaques concludes, "overcomes the crisis of middle life, and lives through to the enjoyment of mature creativeness and work in full awareness of death which lies beyond—resigned but not defeated."[216] Once again, the (Goethean) notion of resignation defines the successful negotiation of the midlife crisis.

---

[213]Jaques, "Death and the Mid-Life Crisis," p. 513.

[214]As evidence of Goethe's "death neurosis," critics point to Goethe's horror of death and his avoidance of funerals, yet his depiction of death in so many works (*Götz von Berlichingen, Die Leiden des jungen Werthers, Die Wahlverwandtschaften, Faust*, etc.); see Bernd Lutz's entry under "Tod" in *Metzler Goethe Lexikon*, ed. Benedikt Jeßing, Bernd Lutz, and Inge Wild (Stuttgart and Weimar: Metzler, 1999), pp. 488-489.

[215]*Paradiso*, canto 33, ll. 143-145; Dante, *The Divine Comedy*, vol. 3, *Paradise*, trans. Dorothy L. Sayers and Barbara Reynolds (Harmondsworth: Penguin, 1962), p. 347.

[216]Jaques, "Death and the Mid-Life Crisis," p. 513.

## GAIL SHEEHY AND DANIEL J. LEVINSON

Of the many subsequent discussions of the stages of life in the wake of Elliott Jaques's paper, two have become particularly famous. The first of these is Gail Sheehy's *Passages: Predictable Crises of Adult Life* (1976),[217] which discerned six developmental moments in the unfolding life of the adult, from "Pulling Up Roots" in the period from 18 to 22 years, then experiencing "The Trying Twenties" (from 22 to 28), undergoing the "Passage to the Thirties" (28 to 32); next comes to the stage of "Rooting and Extending" (32 to 39), followed by the "Deadline Decade" in the years 35 to 45; finally, after the age of 45, comes the choice of "Renewal or Resignation" (the latter in a non-Goethean sense).[218] And second, there is Daniel J. Levinson's popular bestseller, *The Seasons of a Man's Life* (1978), the classic study of adult development that identified four overlapping eras in the "life cycle."[219] Let us glance briefly at each of these studies in turn.

In her "road map of adult life," Gail Sheehy—formerly a reporter who had covered events on Bloody Sunday in Northern Ireland, and subsequently a popular writer on psychological themes, a contributor to *Vanity Fair*, and a biographer of Hillary Clinton—redefines what Jung called "individuation" (analogous to what Abraham H. Maslow [1908-1970] termed "self-actualization," and others "integration" or "autonomy") as "gaining our authenticity," a goal described as "the arrival at that felicitous state of inner expansion in which we know of all our potentialities and possess the ego strength to direct their full reach."[220] She credits Jung with being "the first major analytic thinker" to have viewed "middle life" as being "the time of maximum potential for personality growth," as being precisely the moment when "we yearn [...] for the undividedness of self that has always been lacking."[221] In particular, Sheehy emphasizes Jung's insights into the complementaristic gendering of the psyche, and into the opportunity midlife provides for "many of our archetypal images of 'feminine' and 'masculine,' images we unconsciously project upon a mate," to be withdrawn.[222] She cites Jung's paper on "Marriage as a Psy-

[217] Gail Sheehy, *Passages: Predictable Crises of Adult Life* (New York: Dutton, 1976).
[218] *Ibid.*, pp. 29-46.
[219] Daniel J. Levinson et al., *The Seasons of a Man's Life* (New York: Ballantine, 1978), p. 317.
[220] Sheehy, *Passages*, p. 34.
[221] *Ibid.*, p. 119.
[222] *Ibid.*

chological Relationship" (*Die Ehe als eine psychologische Beziehung*) (1925), in which he speaks of the necessity of "confronting our own contrasexual aspect" and integrating it, thereby making possible "an extraordinary enrichment of experience."[223] Drawing on the famous study written by Jolande Jacobi (1890-1973), Sheehy notes Jung's warning that "when middle-aged men become effeminate and women belligerent, it is an indication of these persons having failed to accord their inner life due recognition."[224] And she also cites a paper by Levinson in which he lists "the acceptance of the feminine" as one of the major tasks for a man in midlife transition.[225]

When preparing *Passages*, Sheehy had had access to data being gathered by Daniel J. Levinson (1920-1994), one of the founding psychologists in the field of Positive Adult Development, and his colleagues at Yale. In *The Seasons of a Man's Life*—whose title echoes a motif we have already encountered in Pythagoras, Ovid, Feuerbach, Nietzsche, and Klages—Levinson acknowledged, as "the father of the modern study of adult development," the figure of Jung, as well as the work of Erikson.[226] Levinson and his colleagues identified four overlapping periods in the life cycle, structured around a series of transitions: first, the early adult transition from childhood and adolescence to early adulthood; second, the midlife transition from early to middle adulthood; and third, the late adult transition from middle to late adulthood.[227] Among the case studies discussed by Levinson is the example of the British philosopher Bertrand Russell (1872-1970), who introduces the second volume of his autobiography by referring to the period from 1910 (i.e., when Russell was 38) to 1914 (i.e., when he was 42) as "a time of transition," characterized in the following—and highly telling—way:

> My life before 1910 and my life after 1914 were as sharply separated as Faust's life before and after he met Mephistopheles. I underwent a process of rejuvenation, inaugurated by Ottoline Morrell and continued by the War. It may seem cu-

[223] *Ibid.*, p. 119; see Jung, *CW* 17, §324-345.

[224] Sheehy, *Passages*, p. 120.

[225] *Ibid.*, p. 120; cf. p. 364, note 3, where Sheehy cites Levinson's paper at the Menninger Foundation symposium "Normal Crises of the Middle Years" in 1973, in which "overcoming the 'masculine-feminine polarity,' acknowledging the feminine in himself, and seeing the loved woman as a true peer," are counted among the seven tasks of "midlife transition" for a man.

[226] Levinson, *The Season's of a Man's Life*, pp. 4-5; cf. p. 33.

[227] *Ibid.*, pp. 57 and 317.

rious that the War should rejuvenate anybody, but in fact it
shook me out of my prejudices and made me think afresh on a
number of fundamental questions. [...] I have therefore got
into the habit of thinking of myself as a non-supernatural
Faust for whom Mephistopheles was represented by the Great
War.[228]

Levinson places great emphasis on the life cycle as an "organic whole" and
on "the coexistence and interpenetration" of its constituent periods or
stages. Citing a passage from *À la recherche du temps perdu* (1913-1927)
by Marcel Proust (1871-1922), in which the narrator describes the
human being as "a creature without any fixed age," yet nevertheless governed by the "epochs" of life—

> For man is a creature without any fixed age, who has the fac-
> ulty of becoming, in a few seconds, many years younger, and
> who, surrounded by the walls of time through which he has
> lived, floats within them but as though in a basin the surface
> level of which is constantly changing, so as to bring him into
> the range now of one epoch, now of another
>
> [*Car l'homme est cet être sans âge fixé, cet être qui a la faculté de
> redevenir en quelques secondes de beaucoup d'années plus jeune,
> et qui entouré des parois du temps où il a vécu, y flotte, mais
> comme dans un bassin dont le niveau changerait constamment et
> le mettrait à la portée tantôt d'une époque, tantôt d'une
> autre*[;]*[229]

—Levinson remarks that "only after we understand the profound significance of the epochs in our lives," as Proust did, can we "understand the
ways in which one is, at a single time, a child, a youth, a middle-aged and
an elderly person."[230] For we are, Levinson continues, "never ageless," and
"as we gain a greater sense of our own biographies [...] we can begin to
exist at multiple ages"; in this process, he concludes, "we do not fragment
ourselves; rather, we become more integrated and whole."[231] (We should
note here again that the goal of synthesis or wholeness is not something
unique to analytical psychology.)

---

[228]*Ibid.*, p. 31; cf. Bertrand Russell, *The Autobiography of Bertrand Russell*, vol. 2, *1914-1944*
(New York: Little, Brown, 1968), p. 1.

[229]Marcel Proust, *À la recherche du temps perdu*, vol. 3 (Paris: Gallimard, 1954), "La fugitive," pp.
613-614; translated by C. K. Scott Moncrieff, cited in Levinson, *The Seasons of a Man's Life*, p. 321.

[230]Levinson, *The Seasons of a Man's Life*, p. 321.

[231]*Ibid.*, p. 321.

OTHER APPROACHES, INCLUDING THE RETURN
OF THE NOONDAY DEMON

Taken together, Levinson's and Sheehy's studies defined the midlife crisis
as a popular psychological concept in ways that profoundly influenced the
literature on the subject for the following decades.

For example, *Men in Mid-Life Crisis* (1978) is a classic example of the
late-seventies literature on the midlife crisis, written by Jim Conway, a
Baptist minister who was an associate professor and director of the Doctor
of Ministry program at Talbot Theological Seminary. The front cover of
the UK edition of *Men in Mid-Life Crisis* features what has virtually
become a modern emblem of the condition: a photograph of a man in a
brown raincoat, sitting alone outside, hunched and reading a newspaper,
with his back to the viewer. As Conway succinctly, if understatedly, puts
it, "the man in mid-life crisis is an unhappy man."[232] With admirable
frankness Conway outlines his own experience of the midlife crisis, an
account that is comparable to Harold Bloom's quasi-Gnostic experiences
at Yale around the same time, confirms the link with depression, and uses
the archetypal motif of descent:

> My depression had grown all through the spring, summer,
> and autumn. By October it had reached giant proportions. I
> would often stare out of the window or simply sit in a chair,
> gazing into space. Several times I had gone for long drives in
> the car, on bike rides, or on long walks. I had reached
> rock-bottom. I was ready to chuck everything. Repeatedly I
> had fantasies of getting on a dinghy and sailing off to some
> unknown destination where no one knew me and where I car-
> ried no responsibility for anyone in my church or family.[233]

Interestingly, Conway does not suggest that religious faith can prevent
the midlife crisis (although he believes, one suspects, it is part of the solution to it). In Conway's book, as in much of the literature on midlife,
other motifs occur that we shall encounter later in our discussion of Goethe's poem "Primal Words. Orphic." For instance, the topos of the
*daimonic* is related by Conway to what is, as we shall see, a central idea in
Goethe's poem, namely, "hope," when he writes that "the mid-life crisis

---

[232] Jim Conway, *Men in Mid-Life Crisis* [1978] (Exeter: Paternoster, 1983), p. 68. Conway finds
precursors of the midlife crisis in the biblical period, citing David's midlife affair with Bathsheba and
the experiences of Elijah as examples (pp. 67, 176).

[233] *Ibid.*, p. 9.

demon loses its terror as we understand the normal developmental stages of life, and our understanding gives good reason for hope."[234] Central here to this notion of the *daimon* is its manifestation as the "midday demon"[235]—or, as the French call it, *le démon de midi* (on which there is an equally vast Francophone literature).[236] Peter Chew defines this phenomenon as "the 'devil' that gets into men at the 'noonday' of their lives when their wives have perhaps grown matronly," relating the *démon de midi* to the German expression, *Torschlusspanik* ("closed-door panic"), or "the pursuit of young women by middle-aged men seeking a final fling 'before the gates close.'"[237] The term itself is based on a verse from the Psalms, "Thou shalt not be afraid for [...] the destruction that wasteth at noonday" (Psalm 91:5-6), and can be found in Patristic literature and in the work of the Desert Fathers in particular (including Evagrius of Pontus, John Cassian, and Basil of Caesarea).[238] The topos returned to popularity in the second decade of the twentieth century, not least because of Paul Bourget's influential (and entertaining) two-volume novel, *Le démon de midi* (1914).[239] One of its most recent revivals was the French comedy film *Le Démon de midi* (2005), directed by Marie-Pascale Osterrieth and starring Michèle Bernier and Simon Abkarian, based on the *bande dessinée* entitled *Le Démon de midi* by Florence Cestac (1996).

What most readers today will undoubtedly find problematic about Conway's discussion is not simply its male-oriented focus, but its

[234]*Ibid.*, p. 91.

[235]*Ibid.*, p. 66.

[236]See, with an emphasis on psychoanalytical interpretations, Roger Callois, "Les démons de midi," *Revue d'histoire des religions* 115 (1937): 142-173, and 116 (1937): 54-83 and 143-186, reprinted as *Les démons de midi* (Paris: Fata Morgana, 1991); Serge Cottet, "Démon de midi et poussée constant," *Ornicar? Digital*, No. 167, 11 May 2001; online at http://www.lacanian.net/Ornicar % 20online/Archive%20Od/ornicar/articles167cot.htm (accessed 21 April 2010); and Paul-Laurent Assoun, *Le démon de midi* (Paris: Éditions de l'Olivier, 2008).

[237]Peter Chew, *The Inner World of the Middle-Aged Man* (New York: Macmillan, 1976), p. 58.

[238]For discussion of the *daemonium meridianum* in its Patristic interpretation as form of *acedia*, see Dietrich Grau, *Das Mittagsgespenst (daemonium meridianum): Untersuchungen über seine Herkunft, Verbreitung und seine Erforschung in der europäischen Volkskunde*, Quellen und Studien zur Volkskunde, vol. 9 (Siegburg: F. Schmitt, 1966); Rudolph Arbesmann, "The 'Daemonium Meridianum' and Greek and Latin Patristic Exegesis," *Traditio* 14 (1968): 17-31; Reinhard Kuhn, *The Demon of Noontide: Ennui in Western Literature* (Princeton, NJ: Princeton University Press, 1976); and Andrew Crislip, "The Sin of Sloth or the Illness of the Demons? The Demon of Acedia in Early Christian Monasticism," *Harvard Theological Review* 98 (2005): 143-169.

[239]Paul Bourget, *Le démon de midi*, 2 vols. (Paris: Plon, 1914).

male-oriented—some might call it patriarchal—angle or approach, perhaps most neutrally described as its traditionalist bias towards the male's
point of view. Here, for example, is Conway's advice to a woman (i.e.,
wife) whose partner (i.e., husband) is undergoing the midlife crisis:

> It is important for a woman during her husband's crisis to
> work on her own physical attractiveness, including weight
> and muscle tone; improve her wardrobe; and alter her
> life-style a little in order to fit more nearly the changing needs
> her husband is feeling. Perhaps at no other time in their mar-
> ried life is she so likely to be in competition with other
> women. So, even though the quality of caring is going to be
> the characteristic a man wants long-range, she must be attrac-
> tive to him during the short-range crisis period. A wife who
> can cope with all this and remain sane is likely to emerge on
> the other side with her marriage not only intact but im-
> proved.[240]

Well, that's alright, then. As if in recognition of this deficit, two years later
Sally Conway, an adjunct instructor at Talbot Theological Seminary (and
Jim Conway's spouse), wrote *You and Your Husband's Mid-Life Crisis*
(1980); while, in acknowledgment of the existence of a female midlife cri-
sis, too, the husband-and-wife team subsequently coauthored *Women in
Mid-Life Crisis* (1983). Indeed, the Conways have gone on to bring
midlife issues into the electronic age, using such media as radio and the
Internet. In the eighties, they could be heard on the radio program
*Mid-Life Dimensions*, broadcast on numerous stations across the United
States; they are founders of Christian Living Resources; and they estab-
lished the website www.midlife.com, one of a burgeoning number of
Internet sites about the midlife crisis.[241]

Yet there persists in the literature a sense that midlife is more a problem for men than it is for women, perhaps because the female menopause
constitutes a more clearly identifiable development in the stages of a
woman's life. (As Conway points out, there is vast disagreement over
*when* exactly the midlife crisis takes place:[242] between 30 and 39?[243]

---

[240]Conway, *Men in Mid-Life Crisis*, pp. 167-168.

[241]See, for example, http://lifetwo.com (which also offers a podcast), http://www.happiness
-after-midlife.com, and the website of The John D. and Catherine T. MacArthur Foundation Research Network on Successful Midlife Development, http://midmac.med.harvard.edu.

[242]Conway, *Men in Mid-Life Crisis*, p. 20.

[243]Kenn Rogers, "Mid-Career Crisis," *Saturday Review of Society*, February 1973, pp. 37-38.

between 35 and 45?[244] between 40 and 50?[245]) Reading between the lines of another book that appeared in the same year as Conway's, Homer R. Figler's *Overcoming Executive Mid-Life Crisis* (1978), the gender, class, *and* the national cultural contours of this particular psychological condition become clear.[246] The midlife crisis—"a real, existing phenomenon," Figler insists—is defined as "nothing more nor less than a problem brought about by the ageing process," but it is a problem aggravated (in a way that Goethe, from what he writes in his commentary on "Primal Words. Orphic," would entirely have understood) by "an interaction of the person's personality and the world in which he lives."[247]

Figler's book is constructed, perhaps to make it more understandable by the crisis-stricken executives to whom it is addressed, as more or less a series of lists. The setting for the midlife crisis, for instance, is said to consist of (a) technological and cultural lag (i.e., the consequences of the pace of technological change); (b) communication overload; (c) social upheaval; (d) social value systems (including "an ever-lowering quality of goods and services," of the kind that Walter Pitkin could never have envisaged, but that may be more familiar to us); and (e) loss of religious faith (an item which reflects more U.S. than European cultural expectations).[248] The list of symptoms of the midlife crisis is comprehensive—dividing them into (a) personality-oriented symptoms, i.e., (i) unhappiness (as Conway, too, had noted); (ii) insecurity; (iii) depression; (iv) indecision; (v) fear and anxiety (very Kierkegaardian...); (vi) conflict; (vii) nervousness; (viii) restlessness; (ix) a feeling of being trapped; and (x) an obsession with death, illness, and old age; and (b) behavioral symptoms, i.e., (i) irrational job changes; (ii) reduction in productivity; (iii) resentment (very Nietzschean...); (iv) a retreat from responsibility; (v) alcohol; (vi) infidelity; (vii) inconsistency of behavior; and (viii) divorce (the area that Edmund Bergler had treated at such length)—just as the list of causes of midlife problems is exhaustive,[249] divided as they are into

[244]These are the dates favored by Daniel Levinson ("The Normal Crises of the Middle Years," symposium sponsored by the Menninger Foundation at Hunter College, New York City, 1 March 1973 [transcript, p. 9] and Gail Sheehy *(Passages*, see above).

[245]See Barbara R. Fried, *The Middle -Age Crisis* (New York: Harper & Row, 1967); Joel and Lois Davitz, *Making It from Forty to Fifty* (New York: Random House, 1976).

[246]Homer R. Figler, *Overcoming Executive Mid-Life Crisis* (New York: John Wiley & Sons, 1978).

[247]*Ibid.*, pp. xi and 2.

[248]*Ibid.*, pp. 12-18.

[249]*Ibid.*, pp. 20-36.

(a) physical causes, i.e., (i) specific psychological changes with old age; (ii) knowledge of the aging process; (b) environmental causes, i.e., (i) job pressures; (ii) changes in society; (iii) expectations of others; and (c) emotional causes, i.e., (i) personal adjustment; (ii) the lack of a meaningful personal philosophy ("unfortunately," Figler remarks, "knowing that 'IF YOU ARE NICE TO PEOPLE THEY WILL BE NICE TO YOU' doesn't help very much as a guide for your life when the doctor tells you that you have cancer and have only a 50-50 chance of surviving surgery"[250]); (iii) life's options; (iv) illness; (v) frustration (resulting in stress); (vi) a feeling of being trapped; (vii) an emphasis on "youth" in advertising, mass media, etc. ("it would not be too much of an overstatement," Figler observes, "to say that Madison Avenue has created a mass inferiority complex for that portion of the population that is over 35"[251]); (viii) the concept of age; (ix) grouping ("misery loves company" leads to "well, everyone has these troubles, so I guess I can just live with them"); (x) depth of personal relationships; and (xi) fears. This final category subdivides even further, into a list that definitively repudiates the pre-World War II optimism of Pitkin's *Life Begins at Forty*, and constitutes a crushing indictment of modern American life, viz.: (i) fear related to the pressure of deadlines; (ii) fear born out of living in a rat race; (iii) fear brought on by giving up of ourselves; (iv) fear of failure; (v) fear of illness; (vi) fear of the end coming too soon; (vii) fear of being honest and standing up for what one believes; (viii) fear of old age; (ix) fear of being tired; (x) fear born out of pressure—all of which amount to an overwhelming sensation of fear, anger, and frustration at "a constant stream of little rip-offs and no way to obtain justice or simple satisfaction," after which there can only remain one more fear: (xii) fear of death.

Against this tidal wave of midlife negativity, which is imbued with a deeply pessimistic cultural outlook, a veritable *decline of the West*, Figler offers the brisk advice that part of the solution is to "set up a flexible game plan for the rest of your life" and to develop a series of "action plans."[252] Yet anyone burdened—indeed, crushed—with the multiplicity of problems, personal and social, outlined in Figler's previous pages, would surely be unable to find the energy to "set up a follow-up program," and would find in his glib-sounding conclusion—"with the necessary commitment

[250] *Ibid.*, p. 59.
[251] *Ibid.*, p. 69.
[252] *Ibid.*, pp. 104 and 111.

and effort, the mid-life crisis need never occur. It is all up to you!"²⁵³—a
fresh source of despair.

### JUNGIAN APPROACHES TO MIDLIFE

Perhaps the sense of a dead end being reached in offering solutions to the
midlife crisis—a crisis within the literature on the midlife crisis, as it
were—helps explain why there was a growth in interest in the problems of
midlife crisis from a specifically Jungian angle. Already in 1971 a conference held in Ascona, Switzerland, under the auspices of Eranos Foundation, had discussed, with contributions from Ernst Benz (1907-1978),
Aniela Jaffé (1903-1991), Gilles Quispel (1916-2006), Henry Corbin
(1903-1978), James Hillman (b. 1926), and Adolf Portmann (1897-
1982), the theme of "the stages of life" in the "creative process,"²⁵⁴ but in
the eighties, three major studies by Murray Stein, Verena Kast, and Daryl
Sharp were published.

   To begin with, Murray Stein's *In Midlife: A Jungian Perspective*
(1983) takes as its material "the stories and images that cluster around the
Greek god Hermes and around some other mythic figures, various
anthropological studies on initiation and rites of passage, and the experience of midlife among individuals in contemporary Western society as
studied and commented on by social scientists and as encountered in [...]
analytical practice."²⁵⁵ In his study, Stein takes the Greek god Hermes,
"the guide of souls through liminality," as the central figure in the psychological drama of the stages of life.²⁵⁶ "The presence, and the role, of the
archetypal unconscious within transitional periods is a central theme" of
his book, Stein writes, "and Hermes is a figure who represents this presence," so that "as Dante had his Virgil, we will have Hermes as our guide
into and out of the experience of the midlife transition and its Inferno of
liminal existence."²⁵⁷

---

²⁵³*Ibid.*, pp. 151 and 161.

²⁵⁴Adolf Portmann and Rudolf Ritsema, eds., *The Stages of Life in Creative Process; Die
Lebensalter im schöpferischen Prozess; Les moments créateurs dans les saisons de la vie* [*Eranos Jahrbuch*,
vol. 40 – 1971] (Leiden: Brill, 1973).

²⁵⁵Murray Stein, *In Midlife: A Jungian Perspective* [1983] (Putnam, CT: Spring Publications,
2003), pp. 110-111.

²⁵⁶Stein defines "psychological liminality" as a state in which "a person's sense of identity is hung
in suspension," created "whenever the ego is unable any longer to identify fully with a former self-im-
age" (*In Midlife*, pp. 8 and 11).

²⁵⁷Stein, *In Midlife*, p. 7. For further discussion of the archetypal significance of Hermes, see

Defining midlife as "a time when persons are going through a fundamental shift in their alignment with life and with the world," Stein argues that "this shift has psychological and religious meaning beyond the interpersonal and social dimensions"; midlife, then, is "a crisis of the spirit"—a crisis in which "old selves are lost and new ones come into being," or "a travail of psyche," into and through which Stein offers "a way of involvement, a Hermetic pathway."[258] To the process of psychological change occurring at midlife, when the individual shifts from an orientation around the persona to an orientation around the Self, Stein applies the threefold schema used by Arnold van Gennep to describe rites of passage—separation, liminality, and reintegration.[259]

In the course of detailed readings of the opening of the *Iliad*, Book 24, as "a classic expression of a liminal period" (p. 10); of "Hektor's resignation in the face of what he calls 'fate' [cf. *Iliad*, Book 6]" as a "recognition that he cannot develop past the *persona*" (p. 32); of the descent of the suitors to Hades in the *Odyssey*, Book 24, as "a radical experience of liminality" (p. 57); of the Circe episode in the *Odyssey* as "a classic picture of midlife individuation"—"confrontations with the anima (Circe), leading to a consciously worked-out relationship with this figure, followed by a further descent into liminality (Hades) and a meeting with the figure of a wise old man (Teiresias)" (p. 86; cf. p. 121)—and the *Odyssey*, Book 11, as analogous to Jung's own mission to honor Poseidon, the god of the collective unconscious (pp. 124-126), Stein suggests that, in these and other situations, Hermes "induces contact with a remote, unconscious content," for he is "a messenger, the go-between, for an unconscious complex that is a combination of wishes, desires, impulses, thoughts, and images clustered around an archetypal core" (p. 77).

For Stein, "the realm of the gods" represents "the unconscious in its archetypal depths" (p. 11), and when, in mythical terms, "the gods are

Walter F. Otto, *The Homeric Gods: The Spiritual Significance of Greek Religion* [*Die Götter Griechenlandes*], trans. Moses Hadas [1955] (London: Thames and Hudson, 1979), pp. 104-124; Norman O. Brown, *Hermes the Thief: The Evolution of a Myth* (New York: Vintage, 1969); Karl Kerényi, *Hermes: Guide of Souls: The Mythologem of the Masculine Source of Life* (Zurich: Spring Publications, 1976); Rafael López-Pedraza, *Hermes and His Children* (Zurich: Spring Publications, 1977); and Ginette Paris, *Pagan Grace: Dionysus, Hermes, and Goddess Memory in Daily Life* (Dallas, TX: Spring Publications, 1990).

[258] Stein, *In Midlife*, pp. 3, 5.

[259] *Ibid.*, pp. 24-27, 42, 51-52; cf. Arnold van Gennep, *The Rites of Passage*, trans. Monika B. Vizedom and Gabrielle L. Caffee (Chicago: University of Chicago Press, 1960). Following page references in the text are to Stein, *In Midlife*.

upset," then, in psychological terms, "archetypal figures of the unconscious are disturbed by the situation developing in consciousness, and so
they set into motion a compensating chain of events" (pp. 15-16). His
central conclusion is that "building the bridge between ego-consciousness
and the unconscious" is "both the central psychological task of midlife
and its greatest opportunity for individuation" (p. 81)—in Jungian
terms, "developing the 'transcendent function'" or "living the 'symbolic
life'" means developing a "dialectical relationship between structure and
liminality," and "sensing the archetypal dimensions within the patterns,
actions, and choices of everyday life" (p. 145). Ultimately, Stein claims,
"the key value that can be derived from this period of crisis and turmoil" is
a "religious attitude": namely, "the continuing consciousness—once the
midlife transition has been completed—of Hermes' presence in a person's
life" (p. 129).

As the title of *Sisyphos: Der alte Stein—der neue Weg* (1986) suggests,
Verena Kast seeks to use a particular myth to discuss the specificities of the
midlife crisis from a Jungian perspective.[260] The most immediate literary
reference point is Albert Camus's famous essay, *The Myth of Sisyphus* (*Le
Mythe de Sisyphe*) (1942), but the topos can be found in Goethe, too. In
his conversation with Johann Peter Eckermann of 27 January 1824, Goethe is recorded as saying:

> I have ever been esteemed one of Fortune's chiefest favourites;
> nor will I ever complain or find fault with the course my life
> has taken. Yet, truly, there has been nothing but toil and
> care; and I may say that, in all my seventy-five years, I have
> never had a month of genuine comfort [*keine vier Wochen
> eigentliches Behagen*]. *It has been the perpetual rolling of a stone,
> which I have always had to raise anew.* [*Es war das ewige Wälzen
> eines Steines, der immer von neuem gehoben sein wollte.*] My an-
> nals will render clear what I say now. The claims upon my ac-
> tivity, from both within and without, were too numerous.[261]

And in a section entitled "Of Great Concern" (*Bedenklichstes*) published
in vol. 2, no. 3, of *Art and Antiquity* (*Kunst und Altertum*) (1820), and
reprinted in his *Maxims and Reflections*, Goethe associates the myth of Sisyphus, cursed by the gods with the task of ceaselessly pushing the boulder

---

[260]Verena Kast, *Sisyphus: The Old Stone—A New Way, A Jungian Approach to Midlife Crisis*
[1986], trans. Norman M. Brown (Einsiedeln: Daimon, 1991).

[261]Eckermann, *Conversations of Goethe*, p. 38; my emphasis.

up the hill, with the story of Tantalus, whose punishment in the underworld consists in the sight of fruits and water that forever elude his grasp,
to suggest that, if the attainment of the self during one's lifetime is a real
possibility, so is one's failure to do so:

> The most wonderful error is the one that relates to ourselves
> and to our faculties: namely that we are dedicated to a worthy
> task, an honorable enterprise, to which we are not equal, that
> we are striving after a goal that we shall never be able to reach.
> The Tantalus-like, Sisyphus-like suffering that results is expe-
> rienced the more keenly, the more honest one is about it. And
> yet very often, when we see ourselves separated for ever from
> what is intended, we have already found on the way some-
> thing else desirable, something suited to us, to be content with
> which we were in fact born.[262]

For Kast, "the myth of Sisyphus expresses a fundamental experience of
human existence, an essential aspect of life and human nature,"[263] but it
presents itself, she argues, "above all in midlife."[264]

Pointing out that, in ancient Greece, an unsculpted stone was considered a symbol for Hermes or Apollo,[265] Kast suggests that the labors of Sisyphus represent "an exertion which ultimately facilitates the breakthrough
of something divine in a human being."[266] Kast concentrates on the trick-
ster aspects of Hermes, also discussed (see above) by Stein,[267] and she
reminds us that, in the *Phaedrus*, Plato claims that each person, by virtue
of imitating this god or that god in actual life, belongs to the retinue of the
particular god concerned.[268]

Significantly, in her discussion of the myth of Sisyphus Kast introduces the category of hope, noting that that "hope implies a view toward
the future, toward change, and therefore toward creative transformation."
For "hope"—Kast continues, as if alluding to the final stanza of Goethe's
"Primal Words. Orphic" (see chapter 4)—"gives us wings," it "consoles
us"; although, she adds, hope sometimes also "distracts us and hinders us

---

[262]Goethe, *Maxims and Reflections*, ed. Hecker, no. 68; in *Werke* [HA], vol. 12, p. 516.

[263]Kast, *Sisyphus*, p. 19.

[264]*Ibid.*, p. 24; cf. p. 26.

[265]*Ibid.*, p. 49.

[266]*Ibid.*, p. 50.

[267]*Ibid.*, p. 57.

[268]*Ibid*. See Plato, *Phaedrus*, 252c–253a, in Plato, *The Collected Dialogues*, ed. Edith Hamilton
and Huntington Cairns (Princeton, NJ: Princeton University Press, 1963), pp. 498-499.

in actually achieving what is possible," since we may "hope for future transformation" instead of "tackling what needs to be changed in the present," which sometimes gives hope a "bad reputation."[269] Moreover, Kast's conclusions are, in a sense, preeminently Goethean when she writes that "the existential themes that are addressed in the myth of Sisyphus are the polarities of autonomy and independence, of expansion and moderation, and of insistence on one's own will and acceptance of limits," and that ultimately the myth of Sisyphus is about "the necessity of creating a life in the face of death, whose presence has always been felt in the form of life changes," and hence "the necessity to live as intensely as possible in the face of death while accepting inevitable changes."[270] As Kast shrewdly highlights, Goethe in his conversation with Eckermann describes the "rolling of the stone" as "an issue of demand, from within as well as from without."[271] Addressing "The Myth in Midlife," Kast concludes that "the challenge presented by aging" consists above all in the task of learning "to accept repetitions as a way of structuring the passing of time in relationship to the death which is entering our lives."[272]

In *The Survival Papers: Anatomy of a Midlife Crisis* (1988), the Canadian analyst Daryl Sharp presents a fictional(ized) case history of a midlife crisis, involving a patient called Norman; his wife, Nancy; the analyst-narrator; his friend, Arnold; and his anima figure, Rachel. As a case history, *The Survival Papers* seeks to illustrate how "a midlife crisis is marked by the sudden appearance of atypical moods and behavior patterns," when "those in their middle years, male and female in more or less equal numbers, who have always managed quite well, have held down a job, perhaps married and had children," suddenly one day find that "nothing works any more."[273] Yet the central conceit behind *The Survival Papers* is to demonstrate that while "the particular circumstances that bring a person to a midlife crisis are as multitudinous as grains of sand on a beach," they could not, however, "be called unique [...] any more than one grain of sand differs from another." For although such particularities are "always related to the person's individual psychology and life situa-

---

[269] Kast, *Sisyphus*, p. 42.

[270] *Ibid.*, pp. 77-78.

[271] *Ibid.*, p. 83.

[272] *Ibid.*, p. 88.

[273] Daryl Sharp, *The Survival Papers: Anatomy of a Midlife Crisis* (Toronto: Inner City Books, 1988), p. 13.

tion," behind them lie "the general patterns of thought and behavior that have been universally experienced, and expressed, since the beginning of mankind"—in other words, the archetypes.[274]

In his introduction, Sharp discusses how "those who have a midlife crisis are caught in the grip of an inner necessity—a psychological imperative to embark on the journey of self-discovery," with reference to a passage, cited by Jung, from Goethe's *Faust*, Part One. In the Witch's Kitchen, Mephistopheles (ironically) offers Faust, who is "sick of this crazy magic stuff," an alternative, non-magic solution to his problems in the form of the following advice:

> Very well;
> You'll need no fee, no doctor and no spell.
> Go out onto the land at once, begin
> To dig and delve, be primitive
> In body and mind, be bound within
> Some altogether narrower sphere;
> Eat food that's plain and simple, live
> Like cattle with the cattle, humbly reap
> The fields you have manured with your own dung.

> [*Gut! Ein Mittel, ohne Geld*
> *Und Arzt und Zauberei zu haben:*
> *Begib dich gleich hinaus aufs Feld,*
> *Fang an zu hacken und zu graben,*
> *Erhalte dich und deinen Sinn*
> *In einem ganz beschränkten Kreise,*
> *Ernähre dich mit ungemischter Speise,*
> *Leb mit dem Vieh als Vieh, und acht es nicht für Raub,*
> *Den Acker, den du erntest, selbst zu düngen.*][275]

(No wonder that, instead, Faust prefers to rejuvenate himself using the Witch's magic elixir!) On this passage, where Mephisto mocks the idea of withdrawing to a "simple life," Jung offers the following sharp—indeed, scathing—remarks: "There is of course nothing to stop [someone] from taking a two-room cottage in the country, or from pottering about in a garden and eating raw turnips. But his soul laughs at the deception."[276] As

---

[274] *Ibid.*, p. 141.

[275] *Faust* I, ll. 2351-2359; Johann Wolfgang von Goethe, *Faust: Part One*, trans. David Luke (Oxford and New York: Oxford University Press, 1987), pp. 72-73.

[276] Jung, "The Relations between the Ego and the Unconscious" (1928), *CW* 7 §258. Compare with Jung's later remarks in the Swiss magazine *DU: Schweizerische Monatsschrift* (May 1941), pub-

Sharp interprets these comments, "the simple life is an option only for those tied to it by outer necessity" (which, by implication, neglects to take into account the rôle of *inner* necessity), as a result of which "the rest of us really have only two choices: to be a willing and conscious participant in our own individuation process or a hapless victim."[277] The ambition of Jungian psychology, of course, is to promote and enable the former option.

Subsequently, work from a Jungian perspective on the midlife crisis continued into the early nineties. In *The Middle Passage: From Misery to Meaning in Midlife* (1993), James Hollis rebaptized the midlife crisis as "the Middle Passage," which he interprets as "a wonderful, though often painful, opportunity to revision our sense of self" (p. 7).[278] Hollis distinguishes four phases of life, which he defines as childhood, first adulthood (from the ages of twelve to forty), second adulthood (launched by the midlife crisis), and mortality—four identities that can be characterized by their corresponding axes: the parent-child relationship; the axis between ego and world; the axis between ego and Self; and the Self-Cosmos (or Self-God) axis (pp. 23-27). In childhood, we develop a "provisional personality"—"a series of strategies, chosen by the fragile child to manage existential angst" (p. 10). But, as we "live out, unconsciously, reflexes assembled from the past," it becomes clear that the process of socialization is, in fact, "a progressive estrangement from the natural sense of self with which we are born" (p. 14). For Hollis, what is attained in first adulthood is equally as provisional as the previous stage, for it is "full of blunders, shyness, inhibitions, mistaken assumptions, and always, the silent rolling of the tapes of childhood" (p. 20). Over time, and certainly by midlife, a "disparity" opens up between "the inner sense of self and the acquired personality," which becomes so great that "the suffering can no longer be suppressed or compensated," and so "decompensation" occurs (p. 15). Thus "the transit of the Middle Passage occurs in the fearsome clash

---

lished under the title "Return to the Simple Life" (*Rückkehr zum einfachen Leben*), where Jung argues that "the spirit is another world within this world," but that "to find happiness in the spirit one must be possessed of a 'spirit' to find happiness in," or in other words—"an attainable sausage is as a rule more illuminating than a devotional exercise" [*der Geist ist aber ein Jenseits in diesem Diesseit*s; *um im Geist ein Glück zu finden, muß man schon dementsprechenden "Geist" haben; ein erreichbarer Schinken ist meist einleuchtender als eine Andachtsübung*] (*CW* 18 §1343-§1356 [§1347, §1346]).

[277] Sharp, *The Survival Papers*, p. 15.

[278] James Hollis, *The Middle Passage: From Misery to Meaning in Midlife* (Toronto: Inner City, 1993). Page references in the text refer to this edition.

between the acquired personality and the demands of the Self," and the Middle Passage represents "a summons from within to move from the provisional life to true adulthood, from the false self to authenticity" (p. 15).

When "the acquired sense of self, with its assembled perceptions and complexes, its defense of the child within, begins to grate and grind against the greater Self which seeks its own realization" (p. 17), we have reached the stage of the Middle Passage, "less a chronological event than a psychological experience" (p. 18). To his analysis of the midlife crisis Hollis brings an insistence on the importance of Jung's typological theories:

> At midlife we feel a lot of distress, much of it outer, much inner. Part of the inner distress originates from the fact that we, and our society, have colluded in neglecting the whole person. We have coasted on what was easy for us; we were rewarded for productivity, not wholeness. In our dreams we live out the other side of the personality, for the inferior function is the trapdoor to the unconscious. If we are going to develop as individuals, and if we are going to enhance our relationships, we have to take seriously the issue of typology. (p. 76)

What Hollis terms "the turn within" thus involves a dialogue between the persona and the shadow—in typological terms, the emergence of the inferior function—that provides the psychological context for the relationship problems, midlife affairs, reconstructing the parent-child relationship (and dealing with the parent complex), and reestablishing one's sense of job versus vocation: all characteristics of the Middle Passage. For, as Hollis argues, "if the meaning of life is directly related to the scope of consciousness and personal development, then the invasions of the shadow at midlife are necessary and potentially healing" (p. 79).

As the first of several case studies of the Middle Passage in literature, Hollis examines Goethe's *Faust*, a text that he reads as "the dialogue of the ego at midlife with its split-off parts" (p. 81). In the Gretchen story of Part One in particular, Hollis suggests, we can see Faust as "a person who has developed the dominant function, his intellect, at the expense of his shadow and his anima." When the penumbra of the shadow crosses the anima, the results are "disastrous, as midlife affairs often are." Because what we do not know can "hurt us, and others," Hollis argues that "Faust is not unethical, but in his unconsciousness he is destructive" (p. 82). Thus the function of the Middle Passage is to contribute to individuation, and hence to an increase in consciousness: by (re)connecting with the "lost child" within (p. 104), and leading a "passionate life" (p. 106), we can, Hollis believes, find an exit from the "swamplands of the soul," whose denizens are "loneliness, loss, grief, doubt, depression, despair, anxiety, guilt, and betrayal" (p. 107).

Finally, as an example of the penetration of Jungian ideas into the public arena, mention should be made of a PBS television program, *The Midlife Survival Guide* (1996), which accompanied a book, *Awakening at Midlife*, by the Virginia-based Jungian therapist Kathleen A. Brehony.[279] Alluding in the course of her "guide" to Dante, T. S. Eliot, Virginia Woolf, Virgil, Rainer Maria Rilke, Pierre Teilhard de Chardin, and Walt Whitman, Brehony brings her book to a close by narrating an anecdote about the Sufi poet and mystic Jalāl ad-Dīn Muhammad Rumī (1207-1273), and his friend, a wandering ecstatic called Shams-e-Tabrīzī (d. 1248). Shams, it is said, took Rumi's mystical books and threw them into a pond. "Now," he told him, "you must live what you know."[280] Some readers may feel inspired to look for a nearby pond to dispose of the seemingly innumerable studies of the midlife crisis that continue to appear, but they provide evidence of a continuing discourse, or even a persistence of a myth (in the Jungian sense), surrounding the notion of the stages of life.

## LITERATURE OF THE NINETIES

From the ever-expanding literature of the nineties from a non-Jungian perspective, I shall consider just nine titles. First, in *Fulfillment in Adulthood: Paths to the Pinnacle of Life* (1994), Calvin A. Colarusso argues that "death awareness" constitutes the "quintessential midlife experience."[281] Noting "a shift in perspective from Victorian preoccupations with sex and morality to a current-day preoccupation with absurd death and annihilation," Colarusso writes that, "confronted with death and violence at every

[279]Kathleen A. Brehony, *Awakening at Midlife: A Guide to Reviving Your Spirit, Recreating Your Life, and Returning to Your Truest Self* (New York: Riverhead Books, 1996).

[280]*Ibid.*, p. 335. Other versions of this anecdote exist. See *Me and Rumi: The Autobiography of Shams-I Tabrizi*, trans. William C. Chittick (Louisville, KY: Fons Vitae, 2004).

[281]Calvin A. Colarusso, *Fulfillment in Adulthood: Paths to the Pinnacle of Life* (New York and London: Plenum Press, 1994), p. 239. For further discussion, see Robert J. Lifton, *History and Human Survival* (New York: Random House, 1970); *Home from the War* (New York: Simon & Schuster, 1973); *Death in Life* (New York: Touchstone Books, 1976); *The Life of the Self* (New York: Simon & Schuster, 1976); and *The Broken Connection* (New York: Simon & Schuster, 1979).

turn, on our street corners and television screens," we have "lost the ability to recognize the psychological connection between the phenomenon of death and the flow of life."[282] Colarusso draws on Erikson's idea that the acceptance in midlife of the notion of our personal death can pave the way for a mystic union with the cosmos, warding off despair in old age: such acceptance, in Erikson's words, is "a post-narcissistic love of the human ego—not of the self—as an experience which conveys some world order and spiritual sense"; such an "acceptance of one's one and only life cycle as something that has to be" constitutes "a comradeship with the ordering ways of distant times and different periods."[283]

Second, in their booklet *The Stages of Life* (1995), Ralph Rowbottom (an industrialist turned personal counselor) and Nicholas Spicer (a city worker turned Jungian analyst, who trained in Zurich with Marie-Louise von Franz and Dieter Baumann) proposed replacing Shakespeare's seven Ages of Man; Freud's division of early development into oral, anal, phallic, and genital stages; Jung's "powerful image" of the rising sun of the early years, coming to its zenith in one's late thirties, and its gradual setting in the years thereafter (see chapter 2); and Erikson's extension of the Freudian scheme into a comprehensive lifelong system in eight stages, with their own eight-part schema: (1) babe-in-arms (from birth); (2) toddler (about one); (3) infant (about two); (4) schoolchild (about five); (5) adolescent (about 11); (6) young adult (about 20); (7) mature adult (late twenties); and (8) ageing adult (about 60). Perhaps most important about their short work, however, is their recognition of "the many helpful paths" towards the state of enlightenment of the final stage "that have been discovered through the ages—the various forms of prayer, meditation, study, spiritual exercise and the like."[284] As we shall see, Goethe's poem "Primal Words. Orphic" draws on the tradition of *exercices spirituels*, as Pierre Hadot calls them,[285] and seeks to make the insight of the ancient traditions available to his—and our—age.

---

[282]Colarusso, *Fulfillment in Adulthood*, p. 239.

[283]*Ibid.*, p. 241; cf. Erik Erikson, *Childhood and Society*, 2nd ed. (New York: Norton, 1963), p. 268.

[284]Ralph Rowbottom and Nicholas Spicer, *The Stages of Life: A New Look* (Bath: R. W. Rowbottom, 1995), p. 20.

[285]See Pierre Hadot, *What is Ancient Philosophy?* [*Qu'est-ce que la philosophie antique?*] [1996] (Cambridge, MA: Harvard University Press, 2002); and *Philosophy as a Way of Life: Spiritual Exercises from Socrates to Foucault*, ed. Arnold I. Davidson, trans. Michael Chase (Malden, MA: Blackwell, 1995).

Third, one of the most explicitly Christianized versions of the stages of life appeared in Patrick Morley's *The Seven Seasons of a Man's Life* (1995), which identified the seven seasons as reflection, building, crisis, renewal, rebuilding, suffering, and success.[286] Entirely overlooking the cultural discrepancies between the biblical world and modern life, Morley resolutely equates contemporary psychological problems with spiritual episodes: the book of Psalms, for example, is called "The Burnout Book" and described as an "immediate crisis management tool."

Fourth, the link between midlife crisis and ageing came into particular focus at the end of the last century, as in *Beyond Mid-Life Crisis: A Psychodynamic Approach to Ageing* (1995) suggests. Already Jim Conway had suggested that the five emotional stages of preparation for one's death as outlined by Elisabeth Kübler-Ross (1926-2004)—(1) denial; (2) anger; (3) bargaining; (4) depression; and (5) acceptance—could, "with only minor modifications," be "adapted to the man going through mid-life."[287] But in this work Peter Hildebrand, a member of the Independent Group of the British Psychoanalytic Society, whose work is based on the ideas of Donald Winnicott (1896-1971), Michael Balint (1896-1970), and other Object Relations theorists, and who has conducted a workshop on problems of the second half of life in the Tavistock Clinic for some twenty years, discusses "the ways in which people come to terms with such challenges—the need to accept and optimize their own life and achievements, consider them as meaningful, and continue to develop their own skills and capacities within their actual physical capacities."[288] Hildebrand adopts from Colarusso and from Robert A. Nemiroff the seven-stage schema of the individual and marital stages of development, namely: (1) pulling up roots (18-21 years); (2) provisional adulthood (22-28); (3) transition at age 30 (29-31); (4) settling down (32-39); (5) midlife transition (40-42 years); (6) middle adulthood (43-59); and (7) older age (60 years and over), with their corresponding individual and marital tasks, particularly in respect of conflict, intimacy, power, and boundaries.[289]

[286]Patrick M. Morley, *The Seven Seasons of a Man's Life* (Grand Rapids, MI: Zondervan, 1997).

[287]Conway, *Men in Mid-Life Crisis*, p. 92; cf. Elisabeth Kübler-Ross, *On Death and Dying* (New York: Macmillan, 1969), pp. 38-137.

[288]Peter Hildebrand, *Beyond Mid-Life Crisis: A Psychodynamic Approach to Ageing* (London: Sheldon Press [SPCK], 1995), p. 6.

[289]*Ibid.*, pp. 9ff.; cf. Robert A. Nemiroff and Calvin A. Colarusso, *The Race Against Time: Psychotherapy and Psychoanalysis in the Second Half of Life* (New York: Plenum, 1985).

Hildebrand's "hopeful" conclusion is that "as people age they can accept conflict as inevitable, and recognize the needs and capacities of others as well as their own," but some might find that his afterword, in which he envisages "the need for the creation and recreation of smaller communities within which the men and women of the next [i.e., the present] millennium will live and work," foresees "a very important role for the older person here, since they [*sic*] will become the guarantor and provider of many services in such small communities," and suggests that "some form of training which will provide older people with models for the work which will be available in the new dispersed small communities would be of help"—for example, double-entry book-keeping—disappointing, to say the least.[290] Again, one cannot help but feel our general social and cultural expectations have come a long way (down) since Walter Pitkin's visionary depiction of the future in *Life Begins at Forty*.

Fifth, Angela Neustatter's *Look the Demon in the Eye: The Challenge of Mid-Life* (1996), a work cited in a pamphlet published by Mind, a mental health charity in England and Wales,[291] represents a return to the motif of the *démon de midi*. The exact source of her title is a remark attributed to David Lyons—we need to "look the demon in the eye and stay put, absorbing its state and understanding what it means rather than running scared."[292] Neustatter provides a survey of the literature on midlife crisis to date, both clinical and literary, and cites Jung on the subject on a number of occasions.[293] Her work emphasizes the physiological aspects of the midlife crisis—"almost every argument I have heard making a positive or even sanguine case for the loss of youthful looks," she says, "sounds at best *faute de mieux* and more often like the hollow howl of defiant rationalization"[294]—on one occasion discussing the decline in sexual potency accompanying the midlife crisis in men over fifty in a remarkable passage that stands out for its brutal clarity (or perhaps its clear brutality):

> The fact that sexual failure, contrasting with the early days
> when an erection all too often bloomed at the slightest provo-

---

[290]Hildebrand, *Beyond Mid-Life Crisis*, p. 108.

[291]Janet Gorman, *How to survive midlife crisis* ([GB:] Mind Publications, 1996), a booklet published by Mind (National Association for Mental Health).

[292]Angela Neustatter, *Look the Demon in the Eye: The Challenge of Mid-Life* (London: Michael Joseph, 1996), p. 139.

[293]*Ibid.*, pp. 21, 92, 182.

[294]*Ibid.*, p. 28.

cation, tends to occur along with other signs of ageing, compounds the sense of having reached a plateau for many. It is at
this time that they may, as Deidre Sanders, agony aunt for the
*Sun* newspaper says, feel a deep regret and resentment at having missed out on the sexual revolution. They see what looks
like adventurous and promiscuous sex on offer to younger
men and then they look at their own thinning hair turning salt
and pepper, the bags under the eyes, the too-large gut and feel
anger at having been born too soon to experience what looks
like the feast of uninhibited sex which later generations had.
Then their son brings home a ravishing girlfriend and beats
them at tennis, and the despair hits home with profound
physical repercussions.[295]

Jointly, if unwittingly, Angela Neustatter and the *Sun*'s agony aunt have
invoked a powerful suburban version of what Kristeva would call *the
abject.*

Finally, the nineties saw a return to the debate on midlife by Gail
Sheehy and by Daniel Levinson. Correcting an earlier bias, and com-
pleted (following Daniel Levinson's death in 1994) by his wife, Judy
Levinson, there appeared in 1996 a study entitled *Seasons of a Woman's
Life*.[296] And in *New Passages: Mapping Your Life Across Time* (1995),
Sheehy undertook a considerable revision of her earlier developmental
model.[297] Within an overarching framework of three main periods,
labeled "Provisional Adulthood" (from 18 to 30 years), followed by "First
Adulthood" (from 30 to 45), and finally the "Second Adulthood" (from
45 to 85+), she devises a set of descriptors for each decade of the male life,
beginning with the "Tryout Twenties" (including "Catch 30," or the "Passage to First Adulthood"), followed by the "Turbulent Thirties" (with its
"Age 35 Inventory"). From the "Old Territory" of "Middlescence,"
involving the "Early Midlife Crisis" and the "'Little Death' of First Manhood," the individual moves in the "Flourishing Forties" via the "Passage
to the Age of Mastery" to the "Flaming Fifties" and the beginning of the
"New Territory," where the map of life includes such episodes as the
"Birth of Second Adulthood," the "Pits to Peak" experience of the "Optimism Surge," but also the "Mortality Crisis," the "Meaning Crisis," and

---

[295] *Ibid.*, p. 217.

[296] Daniel J. Levinson, with Judy D. Levinson, *Seasons of a Woman's Life* (New York: Knopf, 1996).

[297] Gail Sheehy, *New Passages: Mapping Your Life Across Time* (New York: Random House, 1995).

the "Male 'Menopause.'" The bridge of the "Passage to the Age of Integrity" brings us to the "Serene Sixties," a landscape whose notable sights include "Growing the Brain," and sailing on the lake of "Coalescence" in the boat of "Mature Love" to the island of the "Sexual Diamond," while "Active Risk-Taking" and the experience of being "Grand Dads" take us, via the "Sage Seventies" and the "Uninhibited Eighties," into the "Nobility of the Nineties" and the final stage of being "Celebratory Centenarians."

Three years later, in *Passages in Men's Lives: New Directions for Men at Midlife* (1998), not only is the specifically male focus of her study explicitly recognized, but the map of men's lives receives even further fine-tuning.[298] Now recategorized as simply "The 20s," the "Turbulent 30s," the "Flourishing 40s," the "Fearless 50s," the "Influential 60s," and finally "The 70s," this framework corresponds to a schema moving from "Catch 30," to "Early Midlife Crisis," "Age of Mastery," "Male Menopause," "Age of Integrity," and "Age of Influence"; likewise to the progression from "Racing Car Sex," to "Dutiful Sex," "Masters Tournament Sex," "Surfing Sex," and "Snuggling Sex"; similarly, to an elaborate sequence of episodes including the transition from an "Idealized Youthful Self" to being a "Marathon Man"; the "Vanity Crisis," "Flagrant Freedom," and "First Fatality Jitters," not to mention the experiences of "Father-Son Power Struggles" and "The Trouble with Wives"; then in the 50s, the moment of "MANopause," the attitude of "Take This Job and Shove It," experiencing "Gender Rivalry" and "Gender Crossover," as well as "Opening the Spiritual Dimension," moving "From Competing to Connecting," and discovering "Post-Nesting Zest"; while "Growing the Brain," obeying the imperative "Don't Retire! Redirect!" and undergoing the "Black Tempest" finally brings us to "Lusty Winter."

All in all, an extraordinary voyage, yet underlying this immense complexity, the same Dante-esque topos can still be clearly detected: "Midway this way of life we're bound upon, / I woke to find myself in a dark wood, / Where the right road was wholly lost and gone."

---

[298]Gail Sheehy, *Passages in Men's Lives: New Directions for Men at Midlife* (New York: Random House, 1998), originally (and awkwardly) entitled *Understanding Men's Passages: Discovering the New Map of Men's Lives* (New York: Random House, 1998).

## Recent French Approaches:
### Éric Deschavanne and Pierre-Henri Tavoillot, Marie de Hennezel and Bertrand Vergely

Amid the plethora of recent studies and articles on the midlife crisis (or, as it is now called, "midlife change" or "midlife development"[299]), we shall bring our survey of literature on the stages of life to a close with two books (written in French) from philosophical and psychoanalytical perspectives. First, the French philosophers Éric Deschavanne and Pierre-Henri Tavoillot have devoted a major study to the Philosophy of the Ages of Life (*Philosophie des âges de la vie*) (2007).[300] Structured around two questions—"Why grow up?" and "Why grow old?"—Deschavanne and Tavoillot examine the entire cultural history of the (st)ages of life, and examine current social shifts underway in Western societies: their fascinating account brings an intellectual-historical and sociological apparatus to bear on the problem of the midlife crisis. They take as their starting point the sociocultural observation that "what is happening right in front of us is neither the twilight of the [st]ages of life nor the dawn of their ceaseless struggle, but their slow and difficult reconfiguration," which means that "we are still living the [st]ages [of life], but we still do not really know how to think about the new way in which we are living them" (p. 17). Their central hypothesis is that *le jeunisme* (as they call it, or "the cult of youth," as it may be translated), which "consigns the adult to the garbage heap, puts the handing down [of tradition] out for scrap and leaves the communal world out of the picture, does not necessarily constitute the essence of democratic individualism," but on the contrary, "the various ages and the ideal of adult maturity are being reconfigured today within the ambit of the problem of the construction of individuality" (pp. 61-62). Not only, they argue, does the current confusion over the status of children, adolescents, adults, and in particular older adults, mask this reconfiguration (p. 258), but "the question of the [st]ages [of life] is being reformulated within the framework of the problem of *personal identity*,"

---

[299] For example, see Richard A. Friedman, "Crisis? Maybe He's a Narcissistic Jerk," *The New York Times*, 15 January 2008; Carlo Strenger and Arie Ruttenberg, "The Existential Necessity of Midlife Change," *Harvard Business Review*, February 2008, pp. 82-93; and David G. Blanchflower and Andrew J. Oswald, "Is well-being U-shaped over the life cycle?" *Social Science and Medicine* 66 (2008): 1733-1749.

[300] Éric Deschavanne and Pierre-Henri Tavoillot, *Philosophie des âges de la vie: Pourqui grandir? Pourquoi veillir?* (Paris: Grasset, 2007). Subsequent page references in the text are to this volume.

and that "at the heart of an *individual identity* the [st]ages [of life] can recover their visibility and their normativity beneath the fog that disguises them" (p. 260). The work of Jung in particular is recognized (p. 285), although it is not fully related to the intellectual-historical context that, elsewhere, they describe in such detail. To the questions of the book's subtitle and the corresponding questions, Deschavanne and Tavoillot reply, albeit somewhat abstractly, as follows: "What is a child? A being that wants to grow up. Why grow up? To become an adult. What is an adult? A being that enters the universe of experience, responsibility, and authenticity. Why grow old? To try to deepen these three infinite tasks."[301]

Arguably the most powerful part of their superb study is the page where they cite the Italian philosopher Norberto Bobbio (1909-2004), who once claimed to have learned more from his visits to an old people's home than from any philosophical treatise. Some of the remarks of these inhabitants are quoted verbatim:

> Life is always an error. I wouldn't live it again for anything in the world.
>
> > (An eighty-five-year-old widow
> > whose son died in an accident)
>
> You think you are attached to objects, to memories, to things. It takes a life to build one's own home, one's snug corner, one's armchairs. And then one day, nothing matters any more. Absolutely nothing.
>
> > (An eighty-one-year-old architect
> > who had lost his wife)
>
> I mustn't begin to cry, that's all so terrible [...]. You can't imagine what it's like to wait for nothing. You can't imagine. I can't explain it. Immediately I begin to cry.
>
> > (An eighty-five-year-old widow who had "stopped
> > living" after the death of her husband)
>
> Our life is as if it had never existed, and as for me, bit by bit, I'm forgetting everything, and when I have forgotten everything, I'll die and there'll be nothing more to say.[302]

---

[301] *Ibid.*, p. 415; cf. pp. 508-509.

[302] Norberto Bobbio, "Au ralenti: Vieillesse, mémoire, mort" [2000], in *Le sage et la politique: Ecrits moraux sur la vieillesse et la douceur*, trans. Pierre-Emmanuel Dauzat and Denis Trierweiler (Paris: Albin Michel, 2004), pp. 114-115; cited in Deschavanne et Tavoillot, *Philosophie des âges de la vie*, p. 410.

Such bleakness is powerfully and persuasively combatted by the French psychoanalyst Marie de Hennezel and the philosopher and theologian Bertrand Vergely in a jointly-authored book with the programmatic title: *Une vie pour se mettre au monde* (A Life to Find One's Place in the World).[303]

Acknowledging such explicitly Jungian notions as the "process of individuation" (*Individuationsprozeß*) (p. 147), the teleological goal of vital energy (p. 149), and the Shadow (p. 150), and accepting the general thesis of *la crise du mitan de la vie* (p. 8), de Hennezel and Vergely revive the Plotinian image of sculpture, inviting us to think of our life as a work of art—a work of art gradually reaching its fulfillment (pp. 9, 76-77, 140, 157, 159, 186, 217). Saturated with the idea of eternal youthfulness and rejuvenation (pp. 10, 20, 28, 78, 84, 163), their book proposes the project of "growing old without being old" (*vieillir sans être vieux*) (pp. 21, 162). In her contribution, Marie de Hennezel identifies seven fears associated with growing old, and—in opposition to the campaign for voluntary euthanasia and assisted suicide—she vigorously champions, in contrast to its contemporary expression as a problematic kind of narcissism, a more fundamental, Kantian conception of individual autonomy (p. 73).

For his part, Vergely discerns four stages as the individual approaches the end of his or her life: denial, revolt, despair, and acceptance (p. 81). For Vergely, acceptance is key: it is the fulfillment of the process of maturation (p. 80), a process that takes the individual from birth, through adolescence and adulthood, to old age and ultimately death (p. 85). Rejecting the figure of Faust, who sells his soul to the devil in order to remain young (pp. 99, 131-132), Vergely urges us to embrace age, ageing, and death— as a means of discovering new life. His message? One should give form to one's life, and he distinguishes between three different ways of doing so: creating a human form, an artistic or creative form, and a spiritual form, each in its turn associated with dignity, with style, and with hope (p. 161). (In chapter 4, we shall argue, along with Goethe, that hope is more properly associated with the artistic or the creative.) In two respects, Vergely's argument anticipates points we shall examine about Goethe. First, as if echoing the conclusion to Goethe's "Permanence in Change" (*Dauer im Wechsel*), "Let the start and end so fusing / Join in one and unify" (*Laß den Anfang mit dem Ende / Sich in **eins** zusammenziehn!*; see above),

---

[303]See note 108, above. Subsequent page references in the text are to this volume.

Vergely speaks of a "strange alchemy" whereby one "allows life to flourish on its own," thus "joining up" the "two extremes of time, the end and the beginning, the origin and the destination" (p. 162). Second, although he does not mention Orpheus (and, indeed, is a practicing Orthodox Christian), Vergely speaks repeatedly of the "mystery of life," the "mystery of existence," and the "mystery of Being" (pp. 85 and 119, 118 and 140, 138). And, as if echoing Goethe's engagement in "'Primal Words. Orphic" with the categories of chance and fate, of *tyche* and *fatum*, he discovers in the concept of destination a means of mediating between them: "In bringing together chance [*le hasard*] and fate [*le destin*], in somehow turning chance into the destiny of fate [*le destin du destin*]," the discovery of our destination reveals "the profundity of existence" (p. 179).

Although each of us is destined to die, our destiny is something we make for ourselves: this is the collective wisdom that emerges from the acres of print about the midlife crisis, it is the ancient wisdom of the Orphic mysteries, and it is the message we shall find in Goethe's poem, "Primal Words. Orphic," read through the prism of Jung's analytical psychology.

CHAPTER 2

# The Turning Point of Life: What Conflict the Sun Must Experience at Midday!

Jung's paper "The Stages of Life" (*Die Lebenswende*) was originally delivered as a lecture,[1] and subsequently published as two articles under the title "The Psychic Problems of the Stages of Human Life" (*Die seelischen Probleme der menschlichen Altersstufen*) in the *Neue Zürcher Zeitung* on 14 and 16 March 1930.[2] In a substantially revised form, it was republished as *Die Lebenswende* (literally, "The Turning-Point of Life") in the collection of papers entitled *Seelenprobleme der*

[1]According to a note accompanying the version published in the *Neue Zürcher Zeitung* (see note 2 below), the lecture was held in Munich. However, we know that Jung spoke on "Probleme der Lebensalter und Generationen" at the Deutsche Akademie für Soziale und Pädagogische Frauenarbeit in Berlin on 15 January 1930 (followed a week later by Leopold von Wiese und Kaiserswaldau on the same topic); the lecture was held in the *Bürgersaal* of the Schöneberger Rathaus, beginning at eight o'clock in the evening. Jung may well, of course, have given the same lecture on two occasions, or the location of the lecture has been confused. For the poster containing information about the Berlin lecture, see [Hs 1055: 650a] in the C. G. Jung-Archiv, ETH-Bibliothek, Zurich.

[2]The two extracts, published in the *Neue Zürcher Zeitung* on Friday, 14 March 1930 (*NZZ*, vol. 151, no. 476) and on Sunday, 16 March 1930 (*NZZ*, vol. 151, no. 492), consist of the following paragraphs or sections from the text as published in the *Gesammelte Werke*: part I = §759, §§760-761, §762, §764, §765, §766, §§768-769, §770, §771, §772, §§773-774, §§776-777, §778, §779; part II = §780, §782, §783, §784, §785, §786, §790, §792, §793, §794. For the original handwritten manuscript of "Die seelischen Probleme der menschlichen Altersstufen," see [Hs 1055: 66] in the C. G. Jung-Archiv, ETH-Bibliothek, Zurich. There are only very few, minor variations between the manuscript and published version(s).

*Gegenwart*, volume 3 of the series *Psychologische Abhandlungen*, published
by the Rascher Verlag in 1931.[3]

Jung begins his paper with the topos of modesty, telling us that "to
discuss the problems connected with the stages of human development" is
"an exacting task" (*eine überaus anspruchsvolle Aufgabe*).[4] For to do so, he
claims, means "nothing less than unfolding a picture of psychic life in its
entirety from the cradle to the grave."[5] To examine the stages of life, then,
is to examine the development of the life of the psyche. Jung insists on the
"problematic" nature of his subject, describing the issues involved as
"things that are difficult, questionable, or ambiguous" (*Schwierigkeiten,
Fragwürdigkeiten, Zweideutigkeiten*); concluding that, as a consequence,
"there will be much to which we must add a question-mark in our
thoughts" and that, "worse still, there will be some things we must accept
on faith, while now and then we must even indulge in speculations
(*spekulieren*)."[6] As imbued with Goethe's *Faust* as Jung was, he must have
recalled Mephistopheles' description of someone who speculates—

> Take it from me: the slave of introspection
> Is like a beast on arid waste
> By some foul fiend led round and round,
> While, all about, green meadowlands abound
>
> [*Ich sag' es dir: ein Kerl, der spekuliert,
> Ist wie ein Tier, auf dürrer Heide
> Von einem bösen Geist im Kreis herumgeführt,
> Und rings umher liegt schöne grüne Weide*][7]

—and a few paragraphs on, Jung returns to his concerns about the problematic nature of his subject. Here, despite this caveat about speculation—indeed, because of it—Jung emphasizes the interdisciplinary
nature of his work:

> In treating the problems of psychic life, we perpetually stum-
> ble upon questions of principle belonging to the private do-
> mains of the most heterogeneous branches of knowledge. We

---

[3]Jung, *CW* 19, pp. 22-23. See "Die Lebenswende" in: C. G. Jung, *Seelenprobleme der Gegenwart*,
vol. 3 of *Psychologische Abhandlungen* (Zurich: Rascher, 1931), pp. 248-274.

[4]Jung, *CW* 8 §749.

[5]Jung, *CW* 8 §749.

[6]Jung, *CW* 8 §749.

[7]*Faust* I, ll. 1830-1833; Johann Wolfgang von Goethe, *Faust: A Tragedy*, trans. Walter Arndt, ed.
Cyrus Hamlin (New York and London: Norton, 1976), pp. 43-44.

disturb and anger the theologian no less than the philosopher, the physician no less than the educator; we even grope about in the field of the biologist and of the historian. This extravagant behaviour [*Diese Extravaganzen*] is due, not to arrogance, but to the circumstances that the human psyche is a unique combination of factors [*ein absonderliches Gemisch von Faktoren*] which are, at the same time, the special subjects of far-reaching lines of research.[8]

Similarly, in Sigmund Freud's writings we find a similar acknowledgment of the cross-disciplinary nature of psychoanalysis, when he writes in the posthumously published *Outline of Psychoanalysis* (*Abriß der Psychoanalyse*) (1938) that "the phenomena with which we are dealing do not belong to psychology alone; they have an organic and biological side as well" (*Die Phänomene, die wir bearbeiten, gehören nicht nur der Psychologie an, sie haben auch eine organisch-biologische Seite*).[9]

Right at the beginning of his paper, Jung introduces a central distinction between two major categories—nature and culture. "The psychic life of the civilized human being" (*Das seelische Leben des Kulturmenschen*) is, like the subject of Jung's paper, "full of problems" (*voll Problematik*); indeed, he says, "we cannot even think of it except in terms of problems."[10] By using the term *Kulturmensch*, Jung (again, like Freud) does not operate with the distinction between *Kultur* ("culture") and the logical, rational values of *Zivilisation* ("civilization")—a topos developed and problematized by Nietzsche.[11] The problems of our lives as human beings in civilization are said, however, to have one common root—consciousness:

> Our psychic processes are made up to a large extent of reflections, doubts, experiments [*Überlegungen, Zweifel, Experimente*], all of which are almost completely foreign to the unconscious, instinctive mind of primitive man. It is the growth of consciousness which we must thank for the existence of problems; they are the Danäan gift of civilization.[12]

[8]Jung, *CW* 8 §752.

[9]Freud, *SE* 23, pp. 139-207 (here: §8, p. 195).

[10]Jung, *CW* 8 §750.

[11]See Nietzsche, *The Will to Power* (*Der Wille zur Macht*), §121 and §122, in Friedrich Nietzsche, *The Will to Power*, ed. Walter Kaufmann, trans. R. J. Hollingdale and Walter Kaufmann (New York: Vintage, 1968), p. 75.

[12]Jung, *CW* 8 §750.

Jung's critique of consciousness echoes Nietzsche's; and again, the problematic nature of culture/civilization is an issue of equal concern to Freudian psychoanalysis. In 1930 Freud devoted a major essay to *Civilization and Its Discontents* (*Das Unbehagen in der Kultur*),[13] whose argument could be summed up in the following words from the *Outline of Psychoanalysis*: "It is easy for a barbarian to be healthy; for a civilized human being, the task is hard" (*Der Barbar, erkennen wir, hat es leicht gesund zu sein, für den Kulturmenschen ist es eine schwere Aufgabe*).[14] In turn, Nietzsche, Freud, and Jung alike are building on the earlier Enlightenment tradition of *Kulturkritik* that can be found, for example, in Friedrich Schiller's *On the Aesthetic Education of Humankind* (*Über die ästhetische Erziehung des Menschen*) (1795), in which Schiller argues:

> Civilization, far from setting us free, in fact creates some new need with every power it develops in us. [*Die Kultur, weit entfernt, uns in Freiheit zu setzen, entwickelt mit jeder Kraft, die sie in uns ausbildet, nur ein neues Bedürfnis*]. [...] Thus do we see the spirit of the age wavering between perversity and brutality, between unnaturalness and mere nature, between superstition and moral unbelief; and it is only through an equilibrium of evils that it is still sometimes kept within bounds.[15]

For Jung, consciousness involves a distancing from instinct, which is associated with nature. As he dynamically expresses it, "the turning-away from and placing-oneself-in-opposition to instinct creates consciousness" (*das Abweichen vom und das Sich-in-Gegensatz-Setzen zum Instinkt schafft Bewußtsein*).[16] By equating instinct with nature, and consciousness with culture, Jung rejects any simplistic "return to nature" *à la* Rousseau.[17]

---

[13] Freud, *SE* 21, pp. 57-145.

[14] Freud, *SE* 23, p. 185. Freud's claim here echoes the view of, for example, Johann Gottfried Herder in *On Cognition and Sensation in the Human Soul* (*Über Erkennen und Empfinden in der menschlichen Seele*) (1774) and Immanuel Kant in *Essay on the Diseases of the Head* (*Versuch über die Krankheiten des Kopfes*) (1764) that it is almost impossible for a savage to become insane.

[15] Letter 5, §5, in Friedrich Schiller, *On the Aesthetic Education of Man, in a Series of Letters*, ed. and trans. Elizabeth M. Wilkinson and L. A. Willoughby, 2nd ed. (Oxford: Clarendon Press, 1982), pp. 27-29.

[16] Jung, *CW* 8 §750 [translation modified].

[17] Cf. "Analytical Psychology and 'Weltanschauung'" (1927): "Hemmed round by rationalistic walls, we are cut off from the eternity of nature. Analytical psychology seeks to break through these walls by digging up again the fantasy-images of the unconscious which our rationalism has rejected. These images lie beyond the walls; they are part of the nature *in us*, which apparently lies buried in our

"Instinct," he writes, "is nature and seeks to perpetuate nature, whereas consciousness can only seek culture or its negation," so that "whenever, inspired by a Rousseau-esque yearning, it strives to return to nature, it 'cultivates' nature."[18] The problem with which Jung is grappling here is the same as the one explored by Schiller in his famous essay, "On Naïve and Sentimental Poetry" (*Über naïve und sentimentalische Dichtung*) (1796): in Schillerian terms, the modern consciousness can only be a "sentimental," not a "naïve," one.[19]

This opposition between nature and culture structures Jung's theory of the stages of life as he sets it out in his paper. The first half of life, he will argue, is directed towards the concerns of nature, while the aim of the second half, he will more tentatively suggest, is cultural:

> The significance of the morning undoubtedly lies in the development of the individual, our entrenchment in the outer world, the propagation of our kind, and the care of our children. This is the obvious purpose of nature. [...] Culture lies outside the purpose of nature [*Kultur liegt jenseits des Naturzweckes*]. Could by any chance culture be the meaning and purpose of the second half of life?[20]

Now, in order to characterize this difference between the first and the second halves of life, between life oriented towards nature and life oriented towards culture, Jung uses one of the most ancient images known to anthropology, the passage of the sun across the sky. He develops this image at length in an arresting passage:

> Imagine a sun that is endowed with human feeling and the momentary human consciousness of time [*eine Sonne, von menschlichem Gefühl und menschlichem Augenblick beseelt*]. In the morning it rises from the nocturnal sea of unconsciousness and looks upon the wide, bright world which lies before it in an expanse that steadily widens the higher it climbs in the firmament. In this extension of its field of action caused by its

---

past and against which we have barricaded ourselves behind the walls of reason. Analytical psychology tries to resolve the resultant conflict not by going 'back to nature' with Rousseau, but by holding on to the level of reason we have successfully reached, and by enriching consciousness with a knowledge of humankind's psychic foundations" (*CW* 8 §739).

[18] Jung, *CW* 8 §750 [translation modified].

[19] See Friedrich Schiller, *On the Naïve and Sentimental in Literature*, trans. Helen Watanabe-O'Kelly (Manchester: Carcanet New Press, 1981).

[20] Jung, *CW* 8 §787.

own rising, the sun will discover its significance; it will see the attainment of the greatest possible height, and the widest possible dissemination of its blessings, as its goal. In this conviction the sun pursues its course to the unforeseen zenith— unforeseen, because its unique, individual existence could not know in advance its point of culmination.[21]

The sun of human consciousness is limited in a number of respects: it knows only a time punctuated by moments (*Augenblicksbewußtsein*), and it cannot foresee exactly when it will have reached the highest point of its journey. As it pursues that journey, so the phenomenal world in all its richness and variety is illuminated by consciousness. Inevitably, however, a turning point is reached:

> At the stroke of noon the descent begins. And the descent means the reversal of all the ideals and values that were cherished in the morning [*der Untergang ist die Umkehrung aller Werte und Ideale des Morgens*]. The sun falls into contradiction with itself. It is as though it should draw in its rays instead of emitting them. Light and warmth decline and are at last extinguished.[22]

In the original manuscript and in the version published in the *Neue Zürcher Zeitung*, Jung at this point added the exclamation: "What conflict the sun must experience at midday!" (*Welchen Zwiespalt muß die Sonne am Mittag erleben!*).[23]

Now, in its inspiration this solar imagery is obviously mythic. It had informed in considerable detail Jung's fantasies in *The Red Book*, where the rising of the sun to the East is a powerful and constantly recurring image.[24] A few years after his articles in the *Neue Zürcher Zeitung*, Jung will argue in his paper "On the Archetypes of the Collective Unconscious" (*Über die Archetypen des kollektiven Unbewußten*) (1934) that

---

[21]Jung, *CW* 8 §778 [translation modified].

[22]Jung, *CW* 8 §778.

[23]See [Hs 1055: 66], C. G. Jung-Archiv, ETH-Bibliothek, Zurich (p. 18); *NZZ*, 14 March 1930 [Hs 1055: 650]. For the positive sense that Jung gives to conflict, see his letter to Olga Fröbe-Kapteyn of 20 August 1945, where he writes that, although "conflicts of duty" make "endurance and action" so "difficult," this "apparently unendurable conflict is proof of the rightness of [one's] life," for "a life without inner contradiction is either only half a life or else a life in the Beyond"—which is "destined only for angels" (Jung, *L* 1, p. 375).

[24]See, for example, C. G. Jung, *The Red Book: Liber Novus*, ed. Sonu Shamdasani, trans. Mark Kyburz, John Peck, and Sonu Shamdasani (New York and London: Norton, 2009), pp. 286-288, 291, 299, and 309-310).

myths themselves are nothing other than assimilations of sensory experiences to psychic processes:

> It is not enough for the primitive to see the sun rise and set; this external observation must at the same time be a psychic happening: the sun in its course must represent the fate of a god or hero who, in the last analysis, dwells nowhere except in the soul of man. All the mythologized processes of nature, such as summer and winter, the phases of the moon, the rainy seasons, and so forth, are in no sense allegories of these objective occurrences; rather they are symbolic expressions of the inner, unconscious drama of the psyche [*symbolische Ausdrücke für das innere und unbewußte Drama der Seele*] which becomes accessible to human consciousness by way of projection—that is, mirrored in the events of nature.[25]

In his philosophy of symbolic forms, Ernst Cassirer (1874-1945) offers a similar argument. He explains the function of "mythical intuition" (*mythische Vorstellung*) in terms of its opposition to "metaphysical consciousness" (*metaphysisches Bewußtsein*). Whereas "for the highly developed *metaphysical* consciousness the certainty of immortality rests above all on a sharp analytical distinction between body and soul, between the physical-natural world and the spiritual world" (*die scharfe, analytische Scheidung, die dieses Bewußtsein zwischen "Körper" und "Seele", zwischen der Welt des physisch-natürlichen und des "geistigen" Seins vollzieht*), by contrast "the original mythical consciousness knows nothing of any such division or dualism":[26]

> Here the certainty of survival is rooted in the reverse view: here it is continuously reinforced by the intuition of nature as a cycle of new births. For all things that grow are interrelated and magically intertwined. In the festive rituals with which man accompanies certain decisive phases of the year, above all the descent of the sun from the autumnal equinox or its rising and the return of light and life, it is everywhere evident that this is no mere reflection, no analogical copy of an outward event, but that human action and the cosmic process are here directly interwoven [*daß es sich dabei nicht um die bloße Spiegelung, um eine analogische Abbildung eines äußeren*

---

[25]Jung, *CW* 9/i §7.

[26]Ernst Cassirer, *Mythical Thought* [1925], vol. 2 of *The Philosophy of Symbolic Forms*, trans. Ralph Manheim (New Haven and London: Yale University Press, 1955), pp. 189-190.

*Geschehens handelt, sondern daß hier das menschliche Tun und*
*das kosmische Werden sich unmittelbar ineinanderschlingen].*[27]

According to such nineteenth- and twentieth-century anthropologists as
Max Müller (1823-1900) and Leo Frobenius (1873-1938), solar mythology underlay all forms of religion.[28] But while the motif of the rising and
setting sun is undoubtedly ancient, its use here has two more immediate
predecessors, with both of whom Jung was certainly familiar. First, there
is Goethe, who beautifully evokes the rising of the sun as "the most solemn hour" (*die feierlichste Stunde*) at the beginning of *Faust*, Part Two:

> Let me look up!—Each giant summit-height
> Proclaims already this most solemn hour:
> They are the first to taste the eternal light,
> As we shall, when its downward course is ended.
> Now the green-slanting meadow-slopes are bright
> Again, each detail new and clear and splendid,
> And day spreads stepwise with the dark's downsinking:
> See, the sun rises!—But my eyes offended
> Turn away dazzled, from this great sight shrinking.
>
> [*Hinaufgeschaut!—Der Berge Gipfelriesen*
> *Verkünden schon die feierlichste Stunde;*
> *Sie dürfen früh des ewigen Lichts genießen,*
> *Das später sich zu uns hernieder wendet.*
> *Jetzt zu der Alpe grüngesenkten Wiesen*
> *Wird neuer Glanz und Deutlichkeit gespendet,*
> *Und stufenweis herab ist es gelungen;—*
> *Sie tritt hervor!—und leider schon geblendet,*
> *Kehr' ich mich weg, vom Augenschmerz durchdrungen.*][29]

---

[27] *Ibid.*, pp. 189-190.

[28] Certainly, some of the most ancient religious texts, such as the Sanskrit hymns of the Rig Veda
(c. 1200-900 BCE) feature solar gods (see *The Rig Veda*, ed. and trans. Wendy Doniger O'Flaherty
[Harmondsworth: Penguin, 1981], pp. 177-200). Equally, solar mythology underlay the worship of
Mithras, a pagan cult in which both Nietzsche and Jung took an interest. For Nietzsche's remarks on
Mithraism, see his notes in the *Nachlass* for Spring-Summer 1878 (Nietzsche, *Kritische Studienausgabe*
[= *KSA*], ed. Giorgio Colli and Mazzino Montinari, 14 vols. [Munich: dtv; Berlin and New York: Wal-
ter de Gruyter, 1998], vol. 8, 28[17], 28[22], 28[24], 28[34], pp. 506-508), following his visit to the
grotto of Mithras on Capri in 1887 (see vol. 14, pp. 610-611); Jung's interest in Mithras is extensively
documented and discussed in Richard Noll, *The Jung Cult: Origins of a Charismatic Movement*
(Princeton, NJ: Princeton University Press, 1994).

[29] *Faust II*, ll. 4695-4703; Johann Wolfgang von Goethe, *Faust: Part Two*, trans. David Luke
(Oxford and New York: Oxford University Press, 1994), p. 5.

In the rising of the sun in the natural world, Faust himself is not slow to see a symbol of experiences on the psychological level:

> And thus, when with our heart's whole hope for guide
> Towards our goal we have struggled on unthinking,
> And find fulfilment's portals open wide—
> From those unfathomed depths a sudden mass
> Of life bursts forth, we stand amazed: we tried
> To set the torch of life alight—alas,
> A sea of flame engulfs us, ah what flame
> Of love or hate, burning, consuming us
> With pain and joy, which strangely seem the same! [...]

> [*So ist es also, wenn ein sehnend Hoffen*
> *Dem höchsten Wunsch sich traulich zugerungen,*
> *Erfüllungspforten findet flügeloffen;*
> *Nun aber bricht aus jenen ewigen Gründen*
> *Ein Flammenübermaß, wir stehn betroffen;*
> *Des Lebens Fackel wollten wir entzünden,*
> *Ein Feuermeer umschlingt uns, welch ein Feuer!*
> *Ist's Lieb'? ist's Haß? die glühend uns umwinden,*
> *Mit Schmerz und Freuden wechselnd ungeheur*] [...].[30]

Other poems—such as "Ganymede" (*Ganymed*) (1774), "Dedication" (*Zueignung*) (1784), and "Testament of Old Persian Faith" (*Vermächtnis altpersischen Glaubens*) from the "Book of the Parsee" (*Buch des Parsen*) of the *West-Eastern Divan* (*West-Östlicher Divan*) (1819)[31]—also take the sun as their central motif, so it is not surprising that Karl Justus Obenauer (1888-1973) could write that "the rising sun is one of Goethe's great primordial experiences" (*eines der großen Urerlebnisse Goethes*).[32] On a famous occasion, returning from a coach ride with Eckermann in the countryside around Weimar on 2 May 1824, Goethe contemplated the setting sun as they turned by Tiefurt into the road leading back, quoted a line attributed to Nonnus of Panopolis—"Still it continues the self-same sun, e'en while it is sinking" (*Untergehend sogar ists immer dieselbige Sonne*)[33]—and mused to Eckermann:

---

[30] *Faust II*, ll. 4704-4712; Goethe, *Faust: Part Two*, trans. Luke, p. 5.

[31] Goethe, *GE* 1, 30-33; *GE* 1, 88-95; and Johann Wolfgang von Goethe, *Poems of the West and East: West-Eastern Divan—West-Östlicher Divan: Bi-Lingual Edition of the Complete Poems*, trans. John Whaley (Berne, Berlin, Frankfurt am Main: Lang, 1998), pp. 418-423.

[32] Karl Justus Obenauer, *Der faustische Mensch: Vierzehn Studien zum zweiten Teil von Goethe's "Faust"* (Jena: Diederichs, 1922), p. 34.

[33] This attribution has been contested by, for example, Eduard von Welz, who suggests instead as

"At seventy-five," continued he, with much cheerfulness [*mit großer Heiterkeit*], "one must of course sometimes think of death. But this thought never gives me uneasiness; for I am convinced that our spirit is indestructible, and that its activity continues from eternity to eternity [*es ist ein fortwirkendes von Ewigkeit zu Ewigkeit*]. It is like the sun, which seems to set only to our earthly eyes, but which in reality never sets but shines on unceasingly [*Es ist der Sonne ähnlich, die aber eigentlich nie untergeht, sondern unaufhörlich fortleuchtet*]."[34]

And on 11 March 1832, in one of his most important conversations with Eckermann (and from which we will extract several important themes), he is recorded as having said:

"If I am asked whether it is in my nature to pay [Jesus Christ] devout reverence, I say—certainly! I bow before Him as the divine manifestation of the highest principle of morality. If I am asked whether it is in my nature to revere the Sun, I again say—certainly! For he is likewise a manifestation of the highest Being, and indeed the most powerful that we children of earth are allowed to behold. I adore in him the light and productive power of God; by which we all live, move, and have our being—we, and all the plants and animals with us [*das Licht und die zeugende Kraft Gottes, wodurch allein wir leben, weben und sind, und alle Pflanzen und Tiere mit uns*]."[35]

In several of Goethe's late poems, including "Testament" (*Vermächtnis*) (1829) and a text that will be central to our discussion, "Primal Words. Orphic" (*Urworte. Orphisch*) (1817-1818), the image of the sun is used to invert the ethical coordinates of Kant's second critique, "the starry sky above me" and "the moral law within."[36] In "Testament," it is the inner sun that supplies the moral law to the autonomous individual; in the first

---

a source Straton of Sardis (see *The Greek Anthology*, Book 12, §178) ("'Untergehend sogar ist's immer dieselbige Sonne': Ein kleiner Fund im Goethejahr," *Jahrbuch der Goethe-Gesellschaft* 19 [1933]: 85-93 [p. 92]).

[34] Johann Peter Eckermann, *Conversations of Goethe with Johann Peter Eckermann*, ed. J. K. Moorhead, trans. John Oxenford [1930] (New York: Da Capo, 1998), p. 60.

[35] Eckermann, *Conversations of Goethe*, p. 422; alluding to Acts of the Apostles 17:28.

[36] "Two things fill the mind with ever new and increasing admiration and reverence, the more often and the more steadily one reflects on them: *the starry heavens above me and the moral law within me*" (*Critique of Practical Reason*, Part 2, "Doctrine of Method of Pure, Practical Reason," Conclusion; Immanuel Kant, *Practical Philosophy*, ed. and trans. Mary J. Gregor [Cambridge: Cambridge University Press, 1996], p. 269).

stanza of "Primal Words. Orphic," the astrological sun represents the daimonic "law" of the individual.[37]

Second, we find the motif of the rising and setting sun in another text with which Jung was profoundly well acquainted, Nietzsche's *Thus Spoke Zarathustra* (*Also sprach Zarathustra*) (1882-1884). At the end of Part One, Zarathustra commands his disciples to abandon him and find themselves, promising at that stage to return "to celebrate the great noontide":

> And this is the great noontide: it is when Man stands at the middle of his course between animal and Superman and celebrates his journey to the evening as his highest hope: for it is the journey to a new morning.
>
> Then Man, going under, will bless himself; for he will be going over to Superman; and the sun of his knowledge will stand at noontide.
>
> "*All gods are dead: now we want the Superman to live*"—let this be our last will one day at the great noontide!
>
> [*Und das ist der grosse Mittag, da der Mensch auf der Mitte seiner Bahn steht zwischen Tier und Übermensch und seinen Weg zum Abende als seine höchste Hoffnung feiert: denn es ist der Weg zu einem neuen Morgen.*
>
> *Alsda wird sich der Untergehende selber segnen, dass er ein Hinübergehender sei; und die Sonne seiner Erkenntnis wird ihm im Mittage stehn.*
>
> "*Todt sind alle Götter: nun wollen wir, dass der Übermensch lebe*"—*diess sei einst am grossen Mittage unser letzter Wille!*][38]

---

[37]Goethe, *GE* 1, 266-269; *GE* 1, 230-233. For further discussion, see chapter 4.

[38]"Of the Bestowing Virtue" (*Von der schenkenden Tugend*), §3, in *Thus Spoke Zarathustra*, trans. R. J. Hollingdale (Harmondsworth: Penguin, 1969), pp. 103-104; *KSA* 4, 102. In his turn, Nietzsche may have been prompted to use this image because of its occurrence in Schopenhauer's *The World as Will and Representation* (*Die Welt als Wille und Vorstellung*) (1818). In book 1, §54, Schopenhauer writes: "The form of the present is essential to the objectification of the will. As an extensionless point, it cuts time which extends infinitely in both directions, and stands firm and immovable, like an ever-lasting midday without a cool evening, just as the actual sun burns without intermission, while only apparently does it sink into the bosom of the night. If, therefore, a person fears death as his annihilation, it is just as if he were to think that the sun can lament in the evening and say: 'Woe is me! I am going down into eternal night.' [...] The earth rolls on from day into night; the individual dies; but the sun itself burns without intermission, an eternal noon [*Die Erde wälzt sich vom Tage in die Nacht; das Individuum stirbt: aber die Sonne selbst brennt ohne Unterlaß ewigen Mittag*]" (Arthur Schopenhauer, *The World as Will and Representation*, trans. E. F. J. Payne, 2 vols. [New York: Dover Publications, 1969], vol. 1, pp. 280-281). Earlier on in this work, in §23, Schopenhauer writes that, "just as the first morning dawn shares the name of sunlight with the rays of the full midday sun," so all the various

In his seminars on Nietzsche's *Zarathustra*, Jung relates this passage to the opening of Dante's *Divine Comedy*, to a psychological event that happens "to certain people, if not consciously, then at least unconsciously," which he calls feeling "the touch of the self."[39] The theme of the Great Noontide is one of the great structuring ideas of *Zarathustra*, not least because, in the words of Otto Friedrich Bollnow (1903-1991), at midday "the dimension of temporality is abandoned and an experience, otherwise inaccessible to human beings, is opened up";[40] in the case of Zarathustra's own midday experience, in the chapter entitled "At Noontide" (*Mittags*), time "flies away," humankind falls into "the well of eternity," and Zarathustra drinks "an ancient brown drop of happiness";[41] for at midday, as Nietzsche wrote in *Human, All Too Human* (1886), "the human being is happy, but it is a heavy, heavy happiness."[42]

*These intertexts powerfully condition our reading of Jung's paper: via Goethe, the image of the sun is assimilated to the pattern of a successful life; via Nietzsche, it is redolent of a moment of unforeseen and transformative change. And we should allow them to condition our reading, for they informed the very genesis of Jung's thinking.*[43]

---

forms of striving must bear the name of *will*, "which indicates that which is the being-in-itself of every thing in the world, and is the sole kernel of every phenomenon" (p. 118).

[39] C. G. Jung, *Nietzsche's "Zarathustra": Notes of the Seminar given in 1934-1939*, ed. James L. Jarrett (London: Routledge, 1989), vol. 2, p. 838. According to Jung, "the animal is the unconscious existence, the merely biological, personal ego existence, and the evening is the problem of individuation, the becoming of the self or the Superman; and this is not the going down to the evening, but is the advance to a new morning, which means the idea of rebirth in the self or to the self" (*ibid.*, vol. 2, p. 839). In the "Liber secundus" in his *Red Book*, the chapter entitled "The Castle in the Forest" begins: "[...] I am walking alone in a dark forest and I notice that I have lost my way" [*In der zweiten Nacht danach gehe ich einsam in finsterem Walde und ich merke, dass ich mich verirrt habe*] (Jung, *The Red Book*, p. 261; C. G. Jung, *Das Rote Buch: Liber Novus* [Düsseldorf: Patmos, 2009], p. 261), and an editorial note points out that, in his copy of the *Inferno*, Jung had marked its opening with a slip of paper.

[40] Otto Friedrich Bollnow, *Unruhe und Geborgenheit im Weltbild neuerer Dichter*, 3rd ed. (Stuttgart, Berlin, Cologne: Kohlhammer, 1953), p. 145; cf. pp. 157-160. For discussion of the proximity between the theme of the Great Noontide and the chapter "At Midday," see Otto Friedrich Bollnow, *Das Wesen der Stimmungen*, 3rd ed. (Frankfurt am Main: Klostermann, 1956), pp. 219-221.

[41] Nietzsche, *Thus Spoke Zarathustra*, trans. Hollingdale, p. 288.

[42] Nietzsche, *Human, All Too Human*, vol. 2, "The Wanderer and His Shadow," §308: "At Noon"; Friedrich Nietzsche, *Human All Too Human: A Book for Free Spirits*, trans. R. J. Hollingdale (Cambridge: Cambridge University Press, 1986), p. 387.

[43] Nor are these texts the only possible sources for Jung's imagery. In *The Adornment of the Spiritual Marriage*, the Flemish mystic Jan van Ruysbroeck (1293-1381) compares the fourfold manner of the first coming of Christ in the believer's heart (1) to the rising sun upon the mountains—"We wish to compare the powerful shining of the sun which, from the moment of its rising, gives light to the entire world and pervades it with its radiance and warmth. In the same way Christ, the eternal sun who

For all his preference for primitive imagery, Jung is sophisticated enough to know both the limitations of metaphor—as well as the power of the one he has chosen. "All comparisons are lame," he acknowledges, "but this simile is at least no lamer than others."[44] Moreover, such metaphors of morning/evening, or spring/autumn, he contends, correspond in their pattern to a profound physiological, as well as psychological, truth:

> Fortunately we humans are not rising and setting suns, for then it would fare badly with our cultural values. But there is something sunlike within us [*Aber etwas ist sonnenhaft in uns*], and talk of the morning and spring, and the evening and autumn of life, is not just sentimental chatter, but to indicate psychological truths; indeed, even more, physiological facts, for the reversal of the sun at noon changes even bodily characteristics [*Morgen und Frühling und Abend und Herbst des Lebens sind bloß sentimentales Gerede, sondern psychologische Wahrheiten, ja noch mehr, es sind sogar physiologische Tatsache, denn der Mittagsumsturz verkehrt sogar körperliche Eigenschaften*].[45]

The phrase "something sunlike in us" echoes Goethe's poetic text in the introduction to his *Doctrine of Color* (*Zur Farbenlehre*) (1810), "Were the eye not of the sun, / How could we behold the light? / If God's might and ours were not as one, / How could His work enchant our sight?"[46] And

---

dwells in the highest part of the spirit, sends forth his beams and radiance and light"—(2) to the sun in the sign of Gemini, and (3) to the sun in the sign of Cancer and then in the sign of Leo; the fourth mode—the withdrawal of Christ and human forsakenness—is compared to the sun in the sign of Virgo and then in the sign Libra (Book 2, Parts Two and Three, chapters 8 to 13; John Ruusbroec, *The Spiritual Espousals and Other Works*, trans. James A. Wiseman [New York, Mahwah, Toronto: Paulist Press, 1985], pp. 76-98 [pp. 77-78]). Jung cites a passage from this work by Ruysbroeck in his "Foreword" to Suzuki's *Introduction to Zen Buddhism* (1939) (*CW* 11 §890) and in *Mysterium Coniunctionis* (*CW* 14 §158, n. 210); cf. *The Spiritual Espousals*, Book 1, Part One, chapter 26 (pp. 69-70).

[44]Jung, *CW* 8 §779. Compare with Goethe's observation in his *Doctrine of Color* (*Zur Farbenlehre*) (1810) that "language is, in fact, merely symbolic, merely figurative, never a direct expression of the objective world, but only a reflection of it" (§751; *GE* 12, 277); and his comments on metaphor in the "History of the Doctrine of Color" where, in a section on "Intentional Colors," he writes that "poetry has, in terms of parables [*Gleichnisreden*] and indirect expression [*uneigentlichen Ausdruck*], huge advantages over other forms of language, for it can make use of each and every image, each and every relation according to how it wishes to do so"; thus poetry is able "to compare the spiritual with the physical, and vice versa; the thought with the flash of lightning, the lightning flash with the thought, and in this way the reciprocal life of objects in the world is best expressed" (Goethe, *Werke* [HA], vol. 14, pp. 105-106). For further discussion, see Max Black, *Models and Metaphors: Studies in Language and Philosophy* (Ithaca, NY: Cornell University Press, 1962).

[45]Jung, *CW* 8 §780 [translation modified].

[46]Goethe, *GE* 12, 164. The "mystic in antiquity," to whose words *neque vero oculus unquam videret solem, nisi factus solaris esset* Goethe here alludes, is Plotinus: "To any vision must be brought an

Jung's entire vocabulary here is highly suggestive of the catastrophic change that takes place halfway through life: *der Mittagsumsturz* implies not just the reversal, but the collapse that takes place at noon, or the collapse even of noontide itself.

So far, Jung's scheme has been dualistic, dividing life into two phases, morning and evening phases. For Jung this division brings with it consequences for our behavior, even existential implications. "We cannot live," he says, "the afternoon of life according to the programme of life's morning; for what was great in the morning will be little in the evening, and what in the morning was true will, in the evening, have become a lie."[47] Between the morning of life and the evening, between the challenges and promises of the first half of life and those of the second, lies a moment of stasis, when everything pauses before it begins to turn in a new direction—a moment we might (for reasons that will become clear) call an "Orphic moment."

In his account of the development of the ego, Jung goes on to develop a three-stage theory of ego formation. On this account, the first stage of consciousness ("mere recognition") is an anarchic/chaotic state; the second stage (the developed ego-complex) is "monarchic" or "monistic"; while the third stage (the awareness of dualism, that is, "self-consciousness") is a dualistic state.[48] Yet this threefold process is immediately subsumed as the first stage of a larger, fourfold schema, at the heart of which lies precisely this Orphic moment.

According to Jung, the first stage of life is childhood, a period in which he shows no further interest here. The second stage of life, youth, extends from the period of puberty to middle life (that is, between 35 and 40).[49] This stage consists essentially in adaptation to the outer world, in the construction of an ego in social and financial, as well as psychological, terms. In his earlier, and seminal, paper on "The Relations between the

---

eye adapted to what is to be seen, and having some likeness to it. Never did an eye see the sun unless it had first become sunlike, and never can the Soul have a vision of the First Beauty unless it itself be beautiful" (Plotinus, *Enneads*, 1.6 [9]; Plotinus, *The Enneads*, trans. Stephen MacKenna, abridged John Dillon [Harmondsworth: Penguin, 1991], p. 55). Compare with Goethe's comments on the reciprocity of inner and outer worlds in his conversation with Eckermann of 26 February 1824 (*Conversations of Goethe*, pp. 47-48).

[47] Jung, *CW* 8 §784; Compare with Hegel's comments on the time-related nature of truth in the chapter on "sense certainty" (*Die sinnliche Gewißheit*) in his *Phenomenology of Spirit*; see G. W. F. Hegel, *Phenomenology of Spirit* [1807], trans. A. V. Miller (Oxford: Clarendon Press, 1977), "Sense-Certainty: or the 'This' and 'Meaning,'" pp. 58-66.

[48] Jung, *CW* 8 §758.

[49] Jung, *CW* 8 §759.

Ego and the Unconscious" (*Die Beziehungen zwischen dem Ich und dem Unbewußten*) (1928), Jung had spoken of the need to adopt a *persona*, a social mask that the individual must wear, in order to function properly in society, but with which (s)he should not identify.[50] (The sociologist Erving Goffman [1922-1982] later made use of a similar idea of the mask, in his famous discussion of the presentation of the self in everyday life. More recently, some have begun to talk about the individual's need for "impression management."[51])

In his discussion of the stages of life, Jung does not minimize the difficulties this stage of life entails. He says that "to win for oneself a place in society and to transform one's nature so that it is more or less fitted to this kind of existence is, in all cases, a considerable achievement," describing it in agonistic terms as "a fight waged within oneself as well as outside, comparable to the struggle in childhood for the existence of an ego" (*ein Kampf nach innen und außen, vergleichbar dem Kampfe des Kindesalters um die Existenz des Ich*).[52] Jung's agonistic conception finds a resonance in Freud, who writes in the *Outline of Psychoanalysis* that "the ego fights on two fronts: it has to defend its existence against an external world which threatens it with annihilation as well as against an internal world that makes excessive demands" (*das Ich kämpft also auf zwei Fronten, es hat sich seiner Existenz zu wehren gegen eine mit Vernichtung drohende Aussenwelt wie gegen eine allzu anspruchsvolle Innenwelt*).[53]

[50]*CW* 7 §237, §245-246. In a note to "Ego Development and Historical Change," Erikson offered a stringent critique of Jung, arguing that in his concept of the *persona* one sees "a weak ego sell out to a compelling social prototype," so that "a fake ego identity is established which suppresses rather than synthesizes those experiences and functions which endanger the 'front'" (*Identity and the Life Cycle* [New York and London: Norton, 1980], p. 180). According to Erikson's own view of ego development, "the synthesizing function of the ego constantly works on subsuming in fewer and fewer images and personified *Gestalten* the fragments and loose ends of all the infantile identifications" and, in so doing, "it not only uses existing historical prototypes; it also employs individually methods of condensation and of pictorial representation which characterize the products of collective imagery." Yet while this argument gradually turns into a personal critique of Jung himself—as someone who "could find a sense of identity in psychoanalytic work only by a juxtaposition of his ancestors' mystical space-time and whatever he sensed in Freud's ancestry," so that "his scientific rebellion thus led to ideological repression and (weakly denied) political reaction"—it remains in part a defense of Jung at the hand of his (Freudian) detractors, when Erikson adds that "this phenomenon [...] had its group-psychological counterpart in reaction within the psychoanalytic movement: as if in fear of endangering a common group identity based on common scientific gains, psychoanalytic observers chose to ignore not only Jung's interpretations but the facts he observed" (p. 180).

[51]See Erving Goffman, *The Presentation of the Self in Everyday Life* (Garden City, NY: Doubleday and Company, 1959).

[52]Jung, *CW* 8 §771.

[53]Freud, *SE* 23, 200.

In psychological (or "inner") terms, the stage of youth involves an abandonment of childhood attachments, an embrace of the world,[54] and a coming to terms with the psychological Other, a recognition and acceptance of "what is different and strange as part of his own life, as a kind of 'also-I'" (*das andere, das Fremde* [...] *als sein Leben und als ein Auch-Ich*).[55]

[54] Compare with Goethe's remark in "Significant Help Given by an Ingenious Turn of Phrase" (*Bedeutendes Fördernis durch ein einziges geistreiches Wort*) (1825) that "human beings know themselves only insofar as they know the world; we perceive the world only in ourselves, and ourselves only in the world" [*der Mensch kennt nur sich selbst, insofern er die Welt kennt, die er nur in sich und sich nur in ihr gewahr wird*] (Goethe, *GE* 12, 39).

[55] Jung, *CW* 8 §764. A meditation on the concept of the Other constitutes an important, and often overlooked, element of Jung's late work. In an Eranos lecture later published as "Concerning Rebirth" (*Über Wiedergeburt*) (1940/1950), Jung takes the example of the friendship between Mithras and the sun-god as the starting-point for his discussion of the relationship between the individual and the inner Other—"a certain other one, within" (*aliquem alium internum*—Martin Ruland), an "inner voice"—that the alchemists and the *Exercitia spiritualia* of St. Ignatius sought to develop (Jung, *CW* 9/i §235-§236): "The 'Other' may be just as one-sided in one way as the ego is in another," and yet "the conflict between them may give rise to truth and meaning—but only if the ego is willing to grant the Other its rightful personality" [*Der Andere ist wohl so einseitig in seiner Art wie das Ich in einer anderen. Aus dem Konflikt der beiden kann Wahrheit und Sinn hervorgehen, aber allerdings nur dann, wenn das Ich gewillt ist, dem anderen gerechterweise Persönlichkeit zuzubilligen*] (Jung, *CW* 9/i §237). In *The Psychology of the Transference* (*Die Psychologie der Übertragung*) (1946), he writes that "the underlying idea of the psyche proves it to be a half bodily, half spiritual substance, an *anima media natura*, as the alchemists call it, an hermaphroditic being capable of uniting the opposites, but who is never complete in the individual *unless related to another individual*" (Jung, *CW* 16 §454; my emphasis). According to Jung, "the unrelated human being lacks wholeness, for he can achieve wholeness only through the soul, and the soul cannot exist without its other side, which is always found in a 'You' [*im 'Du'* ]" (*CW* 16 §454). For Jung, "wholeness is a combination of I and You [*Die Ganzheit besteht aus der Zusammensetzung von Ich und Du*], and these show themselves to be parts of a transcendent unity [*transzendentale Einheit*] whose nature can only be grasped symbolically, as in the symbols of the *rotundum*, the rose, the wheel, or the *coniunctio Solis et Lunae*" (*CW* 16 §454). Whilst Jung cites the alchemical view that refers the threefold nature of the individual (*corpus, anima, spiritus*) back to a primal Oneness, he enunciates in a footnote the following three principles: (1) "wholeness is the product of an intrapsychic process which depends essentially on the relation of one individual to another"; (2) "relationship paves the way for individuation and makes it possible, but is itself no proof of wholeness"; (3) "the projection upon the feminine partner contains the anima"—see Jung's theory of interpersonal relations, articulated in *The Relation between the Ego and the Unconscious* and *Psychological Types* (1921)—"and sometimes the self" (*CW* 16 §454, n. 16). In "On the Nature of the Psyche" (1947/1954), Jung writes that the goal of individuation, "the self" (*das Selbst*), includes—"as symbolism has shown from old"—"infinitely more than just the ego," for the Self is, as Jung puts it, "just as much the Other(s) as the 'I' [*ebenso der oder die anderen wie das Ich*]" (*CW* 8 §432). In *Mysterium Coniunctionis* (1955-1956), Jung interpreted the lines "Life I seek through all the ages / Which for death in flames is yearning" [*Das Lebend'ge will ich preisen / Das nach Flammentod sich sehnet*] in Goethe's poem "Sacred Yearning" (*Selige Sehnsucht*) from the *West-Östlicher Divan* (*Poems of the West and East*, trans. Whaley, pp. 46-47) in terms of the "demand" of the unconscious for "an interest in it for itself," as a call for it "to be accepted above all for what it is," although he went on to insist on the essential alterity of the unconscious, the Other which I also am: "Once the existence of the opposite is asserted, then the ego not only may, but should, come to terms with the demand that thus arises," for "without the recognition of the content given one by the unconscious, its compensatory effect is not

In outer terms, the goals of the first half of life are "money-making, social achievement, family and posterity," as he says at one point, or "expansion of life, usefulness, efficiency, the cutting of a figure in society, the shrewd steering of offspring into suitable marriages and good positions," as he elaborates a few lines later.[56] (As Jung remarks: that's quite enough goals!) Although these lists betray a bourgeois, even conservative, outlook on the part of Jung, he assigns these goals to the realm of nature, not culture.[57] Moreover, these goals, both inner and outer, bring with them their own *values*; but their validity is temporary, and applies only to this particular stage of life in which the individual finds himself or herself—whatever she or he might like to think:

> The nearer we approach to the middle of life, and the better we have succeeded in entrenching ourselves in our personal attitudes and social positions, the more it appears as if we had discovered the right course and the right ideals and principles of behaviour. For this reason we suppose them to be eternally valid, and make a virtue of unchangeably clinging to them.[58]

The point of Jung's theory of the stages of life, however, is that the midlife

---

only impossible, it actually changes into its opposite" (*CW* 14 §192). Further on in this work, in the course of discussing the therapeutic technique of "active imagination," Jung writes that the analyst should encourage the analysand to turn the inner drama experienced in the course of analysis into "a real getting-to-grips with the alter ego" [*eine wirkliche Auseinandersetzung mit seinem eigenen Gegenüber*]: "For nothing in us ever remains quite uncontradicted, and consciousness can take up no position which will not call up, somewhere in the dark corners of the psyche, a negation or compensatory effect, approval or resentment. This process of coming-to-terms with the Other in us is well worth while [*Die Auseinandersetzung mit dem anderen in uns lohnt sich*], because in this way we get to know aspects of our nature which we would not allow anybody else to show us and which we ourselves would never have admitted" (*CW* 14 §706). Finally, a complex paragraph in *Memories, Dreams, Reflections* develops a sophisticated psychological dialectic of self and other, limitation and limitlessness: "The consciousness of my strictest limitation in the self [*Begrenzung im Selbst*] is linked to the limitlessness of the unconscious [*die Unbegrenztheit des Unbewußten*]. In this consciousness I experience myself both as limited [*begrenzt*] and as eternal [*ewig*], as the One and the Other [*als das Eine und das Andere*]" (*MDR*, 357). For a groundbreaking discussion of this problem, which sets the agenda for further research on this difficult area of Jung's thought, see Lucy Huskinson, "The Self as Violent Other: The Problem of Defining the Self," *Journal of Analytical Psychology* 47 (2002): 437-458.

[56] *CW* 8 §787; and §789.

[57] Jung, *CW* 8 §787. Jung has been accused of an inclination toward an "ultra-conservativism" (Frank McLynn, *Carl Gustav Jung: A Biography* [London: Bantam, 1996], pp. 347-354). He also made occasional attempts at political intervention, such as calling in 1939 for the mobilization of all Swiss males, or being willing for his name to go forward as a candidate to the Swiss parliament for the Landesring der Unabhängigen (National Group of Independents); Jung was not elected (McLynn, *Carl Gustav Jung*, p. 442; Ronald Hayman, *A Life of Jung* [London: Bloomsbury, 1999], p. 365). Need, however, this alleged conservatism invalidate Jung's insights into social behavior?

[58] Jung, *CW* 8 §772.

crisis (as an Orphic moment) throws the permanency of these values into doubt.[59]

Just as Jung emphasizes the importance of ego development and developing a social persona, yet warns against ego "inflation,"[60] as well as against overidentification with the social mask,[61] so he asks that "when the obvious purpose of nature has been attained—and more than attained— shall the earning of money, the extension of conquests, and the expansion of life go steadily on beyond the bounds of all reason and sense?"[62] Clearly, no; and Jung warns of the consequences of failing to adapt to the later stages of life: "Whoever carries over into the afternoon the law of the morning, or the natural aim, must pay for it with damage to his soul, just as surely as a growing adult must pay for this mistake with social failure."[63] Or in other words, for these *social* achievements there is a *psychological* cost to pay.

> We overlook the essential fact that the social goal is attained only at the cost of a diminution of personality. Many—far too many—aspects of life which should also have been experienced lie in the lumber-room among dusty memories [*in den Rumpelkammern verstaubter Erinnerung*]; but sometimes, too, they are glowing coals under grey ashes [*glühende Kohlen unter grauer Asche*].[64]

Following the resolution of the midlife crisis—and, assuming it is successful, the subsequent reorientation—in the third stage of life the individual continues to fight, only it is now a different kind of battle; and continues

---

[59]In this respect the midlife crisis is indeed a "crisis" (*Krise*) in the sense that Otto Friedrich Bollnow defines the term—as "not simply a kind of small mishap, which happens from time to time and could have been avoided through greater care, but which has the important function of confronting the individual with a test of authenticity—an authenticity in fact achieved by going through the crisis" (Hans-Peter Göbbeler and Hans-Ulrich Lessing, *Otto Friedrich Bollnow im Gespräch* [Freiburg im Breisgau and Munich: Alber, 1983], p. 79). According to Bollnow, a crisis involves two moments: an act of purification, and a decision (*Existenzphilosophie und Pädagogik: Versuch über unstetige Formen der Erziehung* [Stuttgart: Kohlhammer, 1959], p. 28); for Jung, the second of these two elements is the more important.

[60]"The Relationship between the Ego and the Unconscious"; Jung, *CW* 7 §227.

[61]Jung, *CW* 7 §305-308.

[62]Jung, *CW* 8 §787.

[63]*CW* 8 §787; "*wer solchermaßen das Gesetz des Morgens, also den Naturzweck, in den Lebensnachmittag ohne Not hinüberschleppt, muß es mit seelischen Einbußen bezahlen, genau wie ein Junger, der seinen kindischen Egoismus ins erwachsene Alter hinüberretten will, seinen Irrtum mit sozialen Mißerfolgen begleichen muß.*"

[64]Jung, *CW* 8 §772.

to struggle, only with problems of a different kind. Instead of adapting to the outer world, now it is the task of the individual to adapt to the inner world, to re-member the "totality of the personality" (*Totalität der Persönlichkeit*), and to construct, not the ego, but the Self (*das Selbst*). "For a young person it is almost a sin, or at least a danger, to be too preoccupied with himself or herself," Jung claims, "but for the ageing person it is a duty and a necessity to devote serious attention to his or her self."[65] In many respects, Jung's core distinction between the ego and the Self reflects the difference between the ego(t)istic subjectivity of the *Sturm und Drang* and the organic development of the personality in classicism, between *Egoismus* and (what Goethe called) "pure selfhood" (*reine Selbstheit*).[66]

Instead of being concerned with "the attachments of the ego," in the second half of life we should listen for "the call of the self." In his lecture on "The Inner Voice" (*Die Stimme des Innern*), delivered at the Kulturbund in Vienna in November 1932 and published in revised form as "The Development of the Personality" (*Vom Werden der Persönlichkeit*) (1934), Jung described the personality in holistic terms as "a well-rounded psychic whole that is capable of resistance and abounding in energy" (*eine bestimmte, widerstandsfähige und kraftbegabte seelische Ganzheit*):[67]

> Personality is the supreme realization of the innate idiosyncrasy of a living being. It is an act of high courage flung in the face of life, the absolute affirmation of all that constitutes the individual, the most successful adaptation of the universal conditions of existence coupled with the greatest possible freedom for self-determination.[68]

This concept of "personality" has its roots, as I have suggested elsewhere,[69] in a classical conception of personal totality, expressed by Goethe in the following lines from his *West-Eastern Divan* (*West-Östlicher Divan*):

---

[65] Jung, *CW* 8 §785 [translation modified].

[66] Letter to Carl Friedrich Zelter of 27 January 1832; Goethe, *Briefe* [HA], vol. 4, p. 469.

[67] Jung, *CW* 17 §286.

[68] Jung, *CW* 17 §289; "*Persönlichkeit ist die Tat des höchsten Lebensmutes, der absoluten Bejahung des individuell Seienden und der erfolgreichsten Anpassung an das universal Gegebene bei größtmöglicher Freiheit der eigenen Entscheidung.*"

[69] See Paul Bishop, *Analytical Psychology and German Classical Aesthetics: Goethe, Schiller, and Jung*, volume 1, *The Development of the Personality* (London and New York: Routledge, 2007), chapter 5.

Nations, rulers, slaves subjected,
All on this one point agree:
Joy of earthlings is perfected
In the personality.

Every life is worth the choosing
If oneself one does not miss;
Everything is worth the losing
To continue as one is.

[*Volk und Knecht und Überwinder,*
*Sie gestehn, zu jeder Zeit:*
*Höchstes Glück der Erdenkinder*
*Sei nur die Persönlichkeit.*

*Jedes Leben sei zu führen,*
*Wenn man sich nicht selbst vermißt;*
*Alles können man verlieren,*
*Wenn man bliebe, was man ist.*][70]

The outcome of what Jung in his lecture to the Kulturbund called, following Goethe, "the development of personality," is what, in "The Stages of Life," is termed, in a beautiful phrase, *die Erleuchtung des Selbst*—"the illumination of the self."[71]

Such illumination is intimately bound up with the fourth and final stage, old age—and the preparation for death. According to Jung, in one sense this stage brings the life of the individual full circle, inasmuch as childhood and extreme old age are completely different, yet have something in common: "submersion in unconscious psychic happenings."[72] In "The Stages of Life," Jung dismisses the suggestion that the fear of death is the prime reason for the midlife crisis.[73] Yet in the opening paragraph of a paper published in the *Europäische Revue* in 1934, entitled "The Soul and Death" (*Seele und Tod*), he succeeds in capturing the essence of precisely this fear:

> When one is alone and it is night and so dark and still that one
> hears nothing and sees nothing but the thoughts which add
> and subtract the years, and the long row of those disagreeable

---

[70]Goethe, *Poems of the West and East*, trans. Whaley, p. 281. The ambiguous concluding lines could also be translated as "Everything is for the losing, / If one remains just as one is"—in other words, the syntax deliberately combines the two elements of Being (*Sein*) and Becoming (*Werden*).

[71]Jung, *CW* 8 §785.

[72]Jung, *CW* 8 §795.

[73]Jung, *CW* 8 §778.

facts which remorselessly indicate how far the hand of the clock has moved forward, and the slow, irresistible approach of the wall of darkness which will eventually engulf everything I love, possess, wish for, hope for, and strive for, then all our profundities about life slink off to some undiscoverable hiding-place, and fear envelops the sleepless one like a smothering blanket.[74]

Can this fear really be discounted so easily? According to Hegel, "death [...] is what is most terrible," yet "not the life that shrinks from death and keeps itself undefiled by devastation, but the life that endures, and preserves itself through, death is the life of the spirit."[75] For Edmund Bergler, the fear of death is "one of the most important repositories" of an "inner scourge," the scourge of psychic masochism and its pattern of "pleasure-in-displeasure."[76] But surely death, which Jung describes as "that unproblematic ending of individual existence,"[77] is every bit as problematic as the stages of life? Or is Jung thinking of Epicurus's argument that death is, in fact, nothing that concerns us?[78]

[74]Jung, *CW* 8 §796. An extract from this article appeared in the *Berliner Tageblatt* of 17 April 1934, and in an abridged form it was published under the title "Von der Psychologie des Sterbens" in the *Münchener Neueste Nachrichten* on 2 October 1935; the entire paper was included in *Wirklichkeit der Seele: Anwendungen und Fortschritte der neueren Psychologie*, volume 4 in the series of *Psychologische Abhandlungen*, published in Zurich by the Rascher Verlag in 1934 (Jung, *CW* 19, pp. 27 and 29).

[75]Hegel, *Phenomenology of Spirit*, preface, §34; Hegel, *Texts and Commentary: Hegel's Preface to His System in a New Translation*, ed. and trans. Walter Kaufmann (Notre Dame, IN: University of Notre Dame Press, 1977), p. 50. We cannot, so Hegel grimly argues, dispense with "seriousness, pain, and the patience and work of the negative" (§21; p. 30).

[76]Edmund Bergler, *The Revolt of the Middle-Aged Man* (London: Bernard Hanison, 1958), p. 226. According to Bergler, there exists a "complicated substructure" of fear when we react to the news that a friend or a relative has died. For there is not only the fear that pertains to self-preservation ("I hope nothing happens to me"), there is also a fear that grows out of the pleasure-in-displeasure pattern. Accordingly, there is an unconscious identification of the danger of death with the danger of a "masochistic fiesta," in response to which the unconscious ego gives a "warning signal" of fear. The "unexpected conflict" of the individual with his "inner conscience" thus creates "unconscious defense mechanisms," with the "paradoxical result" that the only unconscious defense to counter an "unconscious trend from the arsenal of masochistic derivatives" is the "mobilization of the opposite tendency," that is—aggression. "Because a defense against the inner masochistic danger must be organized, conscious aggression appears, directed against the poor sick friend," but in reality this conflict between pity (or commiseration) and aggression is an expression of "the unconscious fight against that greatest of inner dangers, the masochistic pleasure-in-displeasure pattern." Such "defensive pseudo-aggression" can manifest itself, Bergler claims, in various other ways, such as dreams, our general attitude, or our approach to money matters (pp. 227-228). For further discussion, see Bergler's *Money and Emotional Conflicts* (New York: Doubleday, 1951).

[77]Jung, *CW* 8 §796.

[78]See Epicurus, *Letters, Principal Doctrines, and Vatican Sayings*, trans. Russel M. Geer (New York and London: Macmillan, 1964), p. 60: "Death is nothing to us"; cf. his *Letter to Menoeceus*:

In his essay on "The Soul and Death," Jung defines life as "an energic process, just like any other,"[79] and in line with this approach, he even defines the goal of life as, in fact, death. For, "like every energic process, it is, in principle, irreversible, and is therefore directed towards a goal"; and this goal is "a state of rest."[80] In these words we hear an echo of one of Freud's most controversial ideas. In *Beyond the Pleasure Principle* (*Jenseits des Lustprinzips*) (1920), Freud had argued, from the evidence of the compulsion to repeat, for the existence of an instinctual principle of regression, by means of which the living organism seeks to return to an earlier, inorganic state—that is, death. In the context of his discussion of the biological experiments on unicellular and multicellular organisms by the biologist August Weismann (1834-1914),[81] Freud wrote that *Thanatos*, or the "death drive," seeks to "dissolve" living units and to "bring them back to their primaeval, inorganic state."[82]

A century and a half earlier, Schiller wrote in a letter of October 1785 to Ludwig Ferdinand Huber that "you will see the fate of all human plans" suggested by the symbol of the arc created by a ball thrown into the air. "We all strive and aim to reach the zenith, like a rocket," Schiller wrote, "but we all make the same arc and fall back to Mother Earth. Still, this arc is so beautiful!! [*Doch auch dieser Bogen ist ja so schön!!*]."[83] Jung effectively fuses Schiller's and Freud's thinking when, in a mathematical version of his "mythic-natural" model of the journey of the sun, he depicts "the curve of life" as being "like the parabola of a projectile which, disturbed from its initial state of rest, rises and then returns to a state of repose."[84] For Jung, death *is* the ultimate goal of life:

> In the long run everything that happens is, as it were, no more
> than the initial disturbance of a perpetual state of rest which
> forever attempts to re-establish itself. [...] With the attain-

---

"Death, the most dreaded of evils, is [...] of no concern to us; for while we exist death is not present, and when death is present we no longer exist" (*ibid.*, p. 54).

[79] Jung, *CW* 8 §798 [translation modified].

[80] Jung, *CW* 8 §798 [translation modified].

[81] August Weismann, *The Germ-Plasm: A Theory of Heredity*, trans. William Newton Parker and Harriet Rönnfeldt (London: W. Scott, 1893); translated from *Das Keimplasma: Eine Theorie der Vererbung* (Jena: Fischer, 1892).

[82] Freud, *SE* 21, 118-119.

[83] Schiller, *Werke: Nationalausgabe*, ed. on behalf of the Goethe-und-Schiller-Archiv, the Schiller-Nationalmuseum, and the Deutsche Akademie, 43 vols. (Weimar: Böhlau, 1943 - ), vol. 24, p. 26; translated in Frederick Beiser, *Schiller as Philosopher: A Re-Examination* (Oxford: Clarendon Press, 2005), p. 32.

[84] Jung, *CW* 8 §798.

ment of maturity and the zenith of biological life, which coincides roughly with middle age, life's drive toward a goal by no means stops. With the same intensity and irresistibility with which it strove upward before middle age, life now descends; for the goal no longer lies on the summit, but in the valley where the ascent began [*das Ziel liegt nicht auf dem Gipfel, sondern im Tale, wo der Aufstieg begann*].[85]

Moreover, the midlife crisis, the top point of the parabolic curve of life, turns out to be nothing less than, as he puts it, the "birth of death":

> What happens in the secret hour of life's midday is the reversal of the parabola, *the birth of death* [*die Geburt des Todes*]. The second half of life does not signify ascent, unfolding, increase, exuberance, but death, since its goal is the end. Not-wanting-the-fulfilment-of-life is the same as Not-wanting-its-end. Both mean: Not-wanting-to-live. Not-wanting-to-live is identical with Not-wanting-to-die. [*Seine-Lebenshöhe-nicht-Wollen ist dasselbe wie Sein-Ende-nicht-Wollen. Beides ist: Nicht-leben-Wollen. Nicht-leben-Wollen ist gleichbedeutend mit Nicht-sterben-Wollen.*] Waxing and waning make the same curve [*Werden und Vergehen ist dieselbe Kurve*].[86]

The medieval saying, *media vita in morte sumus* ("in the midst of life we are in death"), retains its truthfulness, and may be restated as "in the middle of life, we are in death."[87]

In "The Soul and Death," Jung states with even greater clarity (and even greater urgency) than he does in "The Stages of Life," that—*in order to further life*—it is important to accept the necessity of death. In "Stages" he writes that "it is more hygienic to discover in death a goal toward which one can strive, and resisting it is something unhealthy and abnormal, for it robs the second half of life of its purpose."[88] One should "strive" (*streben*) toward death, then, not "struggle" (*sich sträuben*) against it. Here Jung's argument reflects the view of Goethe, expressed aphoristically in conversation with Friedrich Wilhelm Riemer on 24 May 1811: "The whole art of life consists in giving up our existence, in order that we may

---

[85]Jung, *CW* 8 §798 [translation modified].

[86]Jung, *CW* 8 §800 [translation modified].

[87]Friedrich Hiebel, *Goethe: Die Erhöhung des Menschen: Perspektiven einer morphologischen Lebensschau* (Berne and Munich: Francke, 1961), p. 54. Compare with the medieval antiphon used as the basis of Luther's hymn, "Mitten wir im Leben sind, / Mit dem Tod umfangen" (*Evangelisches Gesangbuch*, #309); cf. Nietzsche's letter to Heinrich Köselitz, 11 September 1879.

[88]Jung, *CW* 8 §792 [translation modified].

exist" (*Unser ganzes Kunststück besteht darin, daß wir unsere Existenz aufgeben, um zu existieren*).[89] In his later paper Jung radicalizes his earlier formulation, deploying a similar rhetorical structure to Goethe's,[90] when he writes: "From the middle of life onward, only he remains vitally alive, who is ready to die with life" (*Von der Lebensmitte bleibt nur der lebendig, der mit dem Leben sterben will*).[91] This vocabulary of "the living," or "what is alive," or *das Lebendige*, as well as the ideas of death and renewal, recalls the language of Goethe's famous poem, "Sacred Yearning" (*Selige Sehnsucht*) and its iconic message, "Die and become!" (*Stirb und werde!*).[92] Ultimately Jung, like Goethe, regards life as an "art," which does not exclude the recognition that "only a very few people are artists in life [*Lebenskünstler*], and the art of life [*die Lebenskunst*] is the most distinguished and rarest of all the arts [*die vornehmste und seltenste aller Künste*]," for "who ever succeeded in draining the whole cup with 'grace' [literally, 'with beauty']? [*daß die wenigsten Menschen Lebenskünstler sind und daß zudem die sind—den ganzen Becher in Schönheit zu leeren, wem gelänge das?*]."[93]

Thus in "The Stages of Life" Jung recognizes the reluctance that many, if not all, individuals experience when faced with the task of changing their life goals and psychological attitudes in response to the midlife crisis. This reluctance, he claims, recapitulates the earlier resistance of the child to growing up and becoming an adult:

> Just as the childlike human being shrinks back in fear from what is unknown about the world and life, so the adult shrinks back from the second half of life, as if unknown, dangerous tasks await him there, or as if he were threatened with sacrifices and losses which he does not wish to accept, or as if his life up to now seemed to him so fair and precious [*so schön und so teuer*] that he could not relinquish it.[94]

---

[89]Cf. *Maxims and Reflections*, ed. Hecker, # 302; *Goethe's "Maximen und Reflexionen": A Selection*, ed. and trans. R. H. Stephenson (Glasgow: Scottish Papers in Germanic Studies, 1986), p. 130.

[90]See R. H. Stephenson, "The Poem as Presentational Symbol: Poetic Wisdom in Goethe's *Maximen und Reflexionen*," in *Poetic Knowledge: Circumference and Centre: Papers from the Wuppertal Symposium 1978*, ed. Roland Hagenbüchle and Joseph T. Swann (Bonn: Bouvier, 1980), pp. 114-121 (p. 117).

[91]Jung, *CW* 8 §800.

[92]Goethe, *Poems of the West and East*, trans. Whaley, pp. 46-47.

[93]Jung, *CW* 8 §789. For further discussion, see Sonu Shamdasani, "'The boundless expanse': Jung's Reflections on Life and Death," *Quadrant: Journal of the C. G. Jung Foundation for Analytical Psychology* 38 (2008): 9-32, in which he suggests that, for Jung, analysis became a modern form of the *ars moriendi* (p. 24).

[94]Jung, *CW* 8 §777.

In his first great work, *Transformations and Symbols of the Libido* (*Wandlungen und Symbole der Libido*) (1911-1912), Jung had already understood the need for sacrifice to enable future (psychological) development, and had used the image of the sun to express this insight:

> The sun, victoriously arising, tears itself away from the embrace and clasp, from the enveloping womb of the sea [*Aus der Umarmung und Umschlingung, dem einhüllenden Schoße des Meeres, entreißt sich die Sonne, siegreich emporsteigend*], and sinks again into the maternal sea, into night, the all-enveloping and the all-reproducing, leaving behind it the heights of midday, and all its glorious works [*und sinkt, die Mittagshöhe und all ihr glorreiches Werk hinter sich lassend, wieder ins mütterliche Meer, in die alles verhüllende und alles wiedergebärende Nacht*]. This image was the first, and was profoundly entitled to become the symbolic carrier of human destiny; in the morning of life man painfully tears himself loose from the mother, from the domestic hearth, to rise through battle to his heights, not seeing his worst enemy in front of him, but bearing him within himself as a deadly longing for the depths within, for drowning in his own source, for becoming absorbed into the mother. His life is a constant struggle with death, a violent and transitory delivery from the always lurking night [*Sein Leben ist ein beständiges Ringen mit dem Tode, eine gewaltsame und vorübergehende Befreiung von der stets lauernden Nacht.*][95]

Already, in 1911-1912, Jung had recognized that death was not so much an external threat, as an internal tendency to return to the "state of rest," to attain *nirvana*, to achieve self-extinction:

> This death is no external enemy, but a deep personal longing for quiet and for the profound peace of non-existence, for a dreamless sleep in the ebb and flow of the sea of life [*Dieser Tod ist kein äußerer Feind, sondern ein eigenes und inneres Sehnen nach der Stille und der tiefen Ruhe des Nichtseins, dem traumlosen Schlafe im Meere des Werdens und Vergehens*]. Even in his highest endeavour for harmony and equilibrium, for philosophic[al] depths and artistic enthusiasm, he seeks death, immobility, satiety and rest [*Selbst in seinem höchsten Streben nach Harmonie und Ausgeglichenheit, nach philosophischer*

---

[95] Jung, *PU* §566. For the revised version of this passage in *Symbols of Transformation* (1952), see Jung, *CW* 5 §553.

*Vertiefung und künstlerischer "Ergriffenheit" sucht er den Tod, die Bewegungslosigkeit, die Sättigung und die Ruhe].*[96]

As Jung explains in "The Stages of Life," this resistance to (psychological) change is nothing new, and can be found at an earlier stage of "the widening of the horizon of life,"[97] namely, during the period of ego formation in the period of childhood. This expansion, Jung writes, begins already at birth, "when the child leaves the narrow confinement of the mother's body," and from that point on it steadily increases, "until it reaches its climax in the problematic state, when the individual starts to struggle against it."[98]

In this paper, Jung warns repeatedly of the dangers of "looking back" (*zurückschauen, den Blick rückwärts lenken, zurückblicken*),[99] urging us instead, in the second half of life, to "look forward." The basis of this advice is, Jung adds, his own clinical experience: "I have observed," he claims, "that a life directed to an aim is in general better, richer and healthier than an aimless one, and that it is better to go forwards with the stream of time than backwards against it" (*daß ein zielgerichtetes Leben im allgemeinen ein besseres, reicheres, gesünderes ist als ein zielloses, und daß es besser ist, mit der Zeit vorwärts als gegen die Zeit rückwärts zu gehen*).[100] To describe this "widening" or "expansion" of life, Jung uses the term "*diastole*," expressly noting its use by Goethe.[101]

Now, in Goethe's writings the terms *diastole* and *systole* are used in his dynamic conception of life, according to which, as one commentator has written, "processes, qualities, powers of mind or body, are not good or bad in themselves; their value depends on the way they function in relation to the other tendencies of the organism, whose life is endangered if any one of them gets out of hand, if it is not kept in check by its regulative counterpart, if the natural rhythm of polarity is not maintained."[102] Goe-

---

[96]Jung, *PU* §566.

[97]Jung, *CW* 8 §765.

[98]Jung, *CW* 8 §765.

[99]Jung, *CW* 8 §777, §789, §790.

[100]Jung, *CW* 8 §792.

[101]Jung, *CW* 8 §765.

[102]Elizabeth M. Wilkinson, "'Tasso—ein gesteigerter Werther' in the Light of Goethe's Principle of 'Steigerung,'" in Elizabeth M. Wilkinson and L. A. Willoughby, *Goethe: Poet and Thinker* (London: Arnold, 1962), pp. 185-213 (p. 200). For further discussion, see Gero von Wilpert, *Goethe-Lexikon* (Stuttgart: Kröner, 1998), p. 1039; and Andrew Jaszi, *Entzweiung und Vereinigung: Goethes symbolische Weltanschauung* (Heidelberg: Stiehm, 1973).

the's texts refer variously to systole and diastole, synkresis and diakresis, attraction and repulsion, inhalation and exhalation,[103] thinking and action,[104] and "en-selfing" and "un-selfing" (*Verselbstung* and *Entselbstung*).[105] The concepts of systole and diastole come most explicitly to the fore in Goethe's *Doctrine of Color*, where he calls the way "inhaling presupposes exhaling," "each systole its diastole," the "eternal rule of life":[106]

> To divide the united, to unite the divided, is the life of nature; this is the eternal systole and diastole, the eternal collapsion and expansion, the inspiration and expiration of the world in which we live, weave, and exist.[107]

In his second great work, *Psychological Types* (*Psychologische Typen*) (1921), Jung refers to "the all-embracing principle of systole and diastole," which he reinterprets in terms of the psychological mechanisms of introversion and extraversion.[108] And in a later essay, Jung talks of the power of psyche to achieve greater integration precisely by means of disintegration, claiming that "a dissociation is not healed by being split off, but by a more complete disintegration":

> All the powers that strive for unity, all healthy desire for selfhood, will resist the disintegration, and in this way [the individual] will become conscious of the possibility of an inner integration, which before he or she had always sought outside

---

[103]"In all our breathing are two kinds of blessing" [*Im Atemholen sind zweierlei Gnaden*]; Goethe, *Poems of the West and East*, trans. Whaley, p. 17.

[104]"Thought and action, action and thought, that is the sum of all wisdom, known from time immemorial, practiced from time immemorial, not realized by all. Both must always alternate in life, like breathing out and breathing in. Like question and answer, neither should occur without the other" (*Wilhelm Meister's Journeyman Years*, Book Two, chapter 9; Goethe, *GE* 10, 280).

[105]"It suffices if we will just recognize that our condition, even though seeming to drag us down and oppress us, is such that we are still left with the opportunity, nay, the duty of raising ourselves up and fulfilling the plans of the deity. This is what we do when, while compelled on the one hand to concentrate into ourselves, we do neglect, on the other hand, to expand, in regular pulsations, away from ourselves [*daß wir, indem wir von einer Seite uns zu verselbsten genötiget sind, von der andern in regelmäßigen Pulsen uns zu entselbstigen nicht versäumen*]" (*From My Life: Poetry and Truth* [*Aus meinem Leben: Dichtung und Wahrheit*], Part Two, book 8; Goethe, *GE* 4, 263; *Werke* [HA], vol. 9, p. 353). For further discussion, see Andreas B. Wachsmuth, "'Sich verselbsten' und 'entselbstigen' —Goethes Altersformel für die rechte Lebensführung," *Goethe: Neue Folge des Jahrbuchs der Goethe-Gesellschaft* 11 (1949): 263–292.

[106]*Doctrine of Color, §38; Goethe, GE* 12, 173.

[107]*Doctrine of Color*, §739; Goethe, *GE* 12, 274 [translation modified]; cf. Johann Wolfgang von Goethe, *Theory of Colours*, trans. Charles Lock Eastlake [1840] (Cambridge, MA, and London: MIT Press, 1970), p. 294. Again, note the allusion to St. Paul's speech in the Areopagus.

[108]Jung, *CW* 6 §4; cf. §6, §356, §428.

himself or herself. We will then find our reward in an undivided self.[109]

(Moreover, Jung notes, such is what happens "very frequently about the midday of life, and in this wise our miraculous human nature enforces the transition that leads from the first half of life to the second.")[110]

Now, this common terminological use points to a far greater and more important set of affinities between Goethe and Jung. Chief among these affinities is the importance both Goethe and Jung attach to the symbol and to its effect. In "Toward a Theory of Weather" (*Versuch einer Witterungslehre*) (1825), Goethe wrote: "We can never see directly what is true, i.e., identical with what is divine; we look at it only in reflection, in example, in the symbol [*wir schauen es nur im Abglanz, im Beispiel, Symbol*], in individual and related phenomena. We perceive it as a life beyond our grasp [*unbegreifliches Leben*], yet we cannot deny our need to grasp it."[111] And in an aphorism Goethe defined "true symbolism" as being "where the particular represents the general, not as dream and shadow, but as the living-momentary revelation of what cannot be explored [*lebendig-augenblickliche Offenbarung des Unerforschlichen*].[112] The symbol, he said, is "the thing, without being the thing, and yet it is the thing"; it is "an image that has come together in the mental mirror, and yet identical with the object."[113] Symbol, in Goethe's thought, is thus contrasted

---

[109]Jung, "Marriage as a Psychological Relationship" (*Die Ehe als psychologische Beziehung*) (1925/1969), *CW* 17 §334; "*Alle Kräfte, die nach Einheit streben, alles gesunde Sichselberwollen wird sich gegen die Zerreißung auflehnen, und dadurch wird ihm die Möglichkeit einer inneren Vereinigung, die er früher immer außen suchte, bewußt. Er findet als sein Gut das Ungeteiltsein in sich selber.*"

[110]Jung, *CW* 17 §335; "*Dies ist, was zur Zeit des Lebensmittags überaus häufig geschieht; und auf diese Weise erzwingt die merkwürdige Natur des Menschen jenen Übergang aus der ersten in die zweite Lebenshälfte.*" In line with his remarks in "The Stages of Life," Jung describes this transition as "a transformation of nature into culture, of instinct into spirit" [*eine Wandlung von Natur in Kultur, von Trieb in Geist*].

[111]Goethe, *GE* 12, 145; *Werke* [HA], vol. 13, p. 305.

[112]*Maxims and Reflections*, ed. Hecker, # 314; Goethe, *Werke* [HA], vol. 12, p. 471; "*Das ist die wahre Symbolik, wo das Besondere das Allgemeine repräsentiert, nicht als Traum und Schatten, sondern als lebendig-augenblickliche Offenbarung des Unerforschlichen.*"

[113]Goethe, *Werke* [WA], vol. I.49, p. 142; "*Das Symbol* [...] *ist die Sache, ohne die Sache zu sein, und doch die Sache; ein im geistigen Spiegel zusammengezogenes Bild, und doch mit dem Gegenstand identisch.*" In 1818, Goethe published an essay entitled *Philostrats Gemälde*, an analysis of the pictures described in his *Eikones* (*Imagines*) by the third-century Greek orator Flavius Philostratus, to which he added the essay *Antik und modern* and, in 1820, a further essay, later given by Eckermann the title *Nachträgliches zu Philostrats Gemälden*, from which the remarks quoted here are taken (Goethe, *Werke* [WA], vol. I.49, pp. 136-148 [p. 142]). For further discussion, see Christoph Michel, "Goethe und Philostrats 'Bilder': Wirkungen einer antiken Gemäldegalerie," *Jahrbuch des Freien Deutschen Hochstifts*, 1973, pp. 117-156.

with allegory, for "symbolism transforms the phenomenon into an idea, the idea into an image, and in such a way that the idea-in-the-image remains infinitely effective and unattainable—and though it be expressed in every language, it will remain inexpressible."[114] And Goethe's concept of the symbol has eminently existential implications, for "everything that happens is a symbol, and, inasmuch as it represents itself perfectly, refers to everything else."[115]

For Jung, of course, the dream and, in a sense, its associated "shadows" (visions, religious trances, mystical experiences, alchemical imagery, ecclesiastical symbolism) revealed precisely the symbol, of whose beneficial and reconciling effects he spoke so eloquently in *Psychological Types*.[116] And in "The Stages of Life" Jung sets next to the work of the "intellect" (*Intellekt*) another kind of thinking, "a thinking in primordial images, in symbols [*ein Denken in urtümlichen Bildern, in Symbolen*], which are older than the historical human being, which are inborn in him since primordial times and outlast all generations—eternally living, they fill the depths of our psyche."[117] Indeed, for Jung, "the full life [*volles Leben*] is only possible in harmony with [these symbols]," and so "wisdom [*Weisheit*] is a return to them."[118]

This wisdom of the symbol is the belief of both men that the hope of new life lies in listening to "the call of the self."[119] And this symbolic wisdom is the subject of Goethe's poem "Primal Words. Orphic" (*Urworte. Orphisch*), which explores, in a way that is astonishingly consistent with the tenets of Jungian psychology, what this "call of the self" consists of, and is structured around the great symbols of the ancient Orphic religion.

---

[114]*Maxims and Reflections*, ed. Hecker, #1113; Goethe, *Werke* [HA], vol. 12, p. 470; "*Die Symbolik verwandelt die Erscheinung in Idee, die Idee in ein Bild, und so, daß die Idee im Bild immer unendlich wirksam und unerreichbar bleibt und, selbst in allen Sprachen ausgesprochen, doch unaussprechlich bliebe.*"

[115]Letter to Carl Ernst Schubarth (1796-1861) of 2 April 1818; Goethe, *Briefe* [HA], vol. 3, p. 426.

[116]Jung, *CW* 6 §828.

[117]Jung, *CW* 8 §794.

[118]Jung, *CW* 8 §794.

[119]This phrase is now widespread in psychoanalytic literature, particularly the psychosynthesis school of Roberto Assagioli and the transpersonal psychology school of Stanislav Grof.

# PART TWO

Nowhere are we closer to the sublime secret of all origination than in the recognition of our own selves, whom we always think we know already. Yet we know the immensities of space better than we know our own depths, where—even though we do not understand it—we can listen directly to the throb of creation itself.

—Jung, "Analytical Psychology and 'Weltanschauung'"

In the meantime I had gained the insight that the greatest and most important problems of life are fundamentally insoluble. [...] They can never be solved, but only outgrown.

—Jung, "The Secret of the Golden Flower"

CHAPTER 3

# Goethe's Orphism

Goethe's influence on Jung was profound and far-reaching. For as well as the conceptual connections between Goethe's outlook and Jung's, which are numerous and substantial, Goethe exercised a more subtle, almost subterranean, influence on Jung's writing, on the stylistic level of expression and formulation. One is reminded of a phrase that has been used to describe Ernst Cassirer's relation to Goethe, and might think of Jung's writing as a kind of "eavesdropping" on Goethe.[1]

Consider, for example—from Jung's paper, originally delivered as an Eranos lecture, on the "Psychological Aspects of the Mother Archetype" (*Die psychologischen Aspekte des Mutter-Archetypus*) (1939/1954)—the following passage:

> I am far from wishing to belittle the divine gift of reason, man's highest faculty. But in the role of absolute tyrant it has no meaning—no more than light would have in a world where its counterpart, darkness, was absent. Man would do well to heed the wise counsel of the mother and obey the inexorable law of nature which sets limits to every being [*Den weisen Ratschlag der Mutter und ihr unerbittliches Gesetz der natürlichen Beschränkung sollte der Mensch wohl in acht*

---

[1] Compare with Barbara Naumann's comment on the intellectual relationship between Ernst Cassirer and Goethe (see *Philosophie und Poetik des Symbols: Cassirer und Goethe* [Munich: Fink, 1998], p. 14).

*nehmen*]. He ought never to forget that the world exists only because opposing forces are held in equilibrium. So, too, the rational is counterbalanced by the irrational, and what is planned and purposed by what *is* [*Nie sollte er vergessen, daß die Welt darum besteht, weil sich ihre Gegensätze die Waage halten. So ist auch das Rationale durch das Irrationale, und das Bezweckte durch das Gegebene aufgewogen*].[2]

On examination, such a passage reveals itself to be rich in Goethean ideas. First, there is its overarching idea, the acknowledgment of the limitation of reason. In his essay entitled "Doubt and Resignation" (*Bedenken und Ergebung*) (1818/1820), for instance, Goethe drew attention to the so-called "epistemological gap" between idea and experience. Here Goethe wrote that "the real difficulty, one we do not always see clearly," is that "between idea and experience there inevitably yawns a chasm which we struggle to cross with all our might, but in vain"; and that, "in spite of this, we are forever in search of a way to overcome this gap with reason, intellect, imagination, faith, feeling, delusion [*Vernunft, Verstand, Einbildungskraft, Glauben, Gefühl, Wahn*], and—when all else fails— folly [*Albernheit*]."[3] Likewise, in his conversation with Johann Peter Eckermann of 13 February 1829, Goethe spoke of the restrictions of reason, and of the concomitant need for a "highest reason" (*höchste Vernunft*) in order to understand nature. "The understanding will not reach nature," Goethe told Eckermann, "Man must be capable of elevating himself to the highest reason, to come into contact with the divinity, which manifests itself in the primitive phenomena [*Urphänomenen*], behind which she hides and which proceed from her."[4] In an echo of this phrase, in "The Stages of Life" (*Die Lebenswende*), Jung speaks of the need for a "wider and higher consciousness" to provide us with "certainty and clarity" about our life.[5]

Second, there is the imagery of light and darkness, of *Licht* and *Dunkel*. Jung's complementaristic approach in these lines chimes well with Goethe's, as expressed in his remark in "On Shakespeare's Day" (*Zum Shakespears Tag*) (1771) that "what noble philosophers have said

[2]Jung, *CW* 9/i §174.

[3]Goethe, *GE* 12, 33.

[4]Johann Peter Eckermann, *Conversations of Goethe*, trans. John Oxenford, ed. J. K. Moorhead [1930] (New York: Da Capo, 1998), pp. 293–294 [translation modified].

[5]Jung, *CW* 8 §751.

about the world applies to Shakespeare too," namely: "What we call evil is only the other side of good; evil is necessary for good to exist and is part of the whole, just as the tropics must be torrid and Lapland frigid for there to be a temperate zone,"[6] or his dictum in his review of Sulzer's *The Fine Arts* in 1772 that, in nature, "beautiful and ugly, good and evil, all exist side by side with equal rights."[7]

Third, both Goethe and Jung follow Virgil's injunction, *antiquam exquirite matrem!*[8] In his letter to Friedrich Leopold zu Stolberg of 2 February 1789, we find Goethe relating, in the context of a confession of his adherence to Lucretius, how it "always pleases and gladdens" him to see that "all-maternal nature [*die allmütterliche Natur*] also allows delicate sounds and tones to resonate gently for delicate souls amid the undulations of her harmonies, and thus permits the finite human being to enjoy a feeling of empathy with the eternal and the infinite."[9] And the maternal aspect of nature underpins his famous poem, "On the Lake" (*Auf dem See*), written on Lake Zurich in 1775 during a boating expedition with the same Stolberg:

> And fresh nourishment, new blood
> I suck from a world so free;
> Nature, how gracious and how good,
> Her breast she gives to me. [...]
>
> [*Und frische Nahrung, neues Blut*
> *Saug ich aus freier Welt;*
> *Wie ist Natur so hold und gut,*
> *Die mich am Busen hält!* [...]][10]

For Hans Eggert Schröder (1905-1985), such texts, as well as Goethe's reference to Plutarch in his remarks to Eckermann about those mysterious figures, the Mothers, in *Faust*, Part Two, made during their conversation of 10 January 1830,[11] mark Goethe out as one of the earliest (re)discover-

---

[6]Goethe, *GE* 3, 165.

[7]Goethe, *Werke* [HA], vol. 12, p. 18.

[8]"Seek out, then, your first mother" (Virgil, *The Aeneid*, Book Three, l. 96; *The Aeneid*, trans. C. Day Lewis [Oxford: Oxford University Press, 1986], p. 66).

[9]Goethe, *Briefe* [HA], vol. 2, p. 109. For a later use of this auditory metaphor, see *Doctrine of Color*, "Preface" (Goethe, *GE* 12, 158).

[10]Goethe, *GE* 1, 41; trans. Christopher Middleton.

[11]Eckermann, *Conversations of Goethe*, p. 342. See Plutarch, "Life of Marcellus," §20 (Plutarch, *Lives*, trans. Bernadotte Perrin, 11 vols. [London: Heinemann; New York: Putnam, 1914-1926], vol. 5, p. 489); but compare also Plutarch, "The Obsolescence of Oracles," §22 (Plutarch, *Moralia*, trans.

ers of matriarchy, in whose wake there followed, among others, Joseph Görres (1776-1848), Georg Friedrich Daumer (1800-1875), Johann Jakob Bachofen (1815-1887), and Ludwig Klages (1872-1956).[12] And to this list we should surely add the name of Jung, too.

Fourth, moving from the maternal-matriarchal to the metaphysical, there is the notion of *polarity*. In his letter to Friedrich von Müller of 24 May 1828, Goethe spoke of "the two great driving-wheels of nature,"[13] namely, polarity (*Polarität*), and specification (*Spezifikation*). Polarity is, Goethe says, "a state of constant attraction and repulsion," "a property of matter insofar as we think of it as material"; this dynamic, polaristic conception of nature is even more vividly expressed in one of his *Maxims and Reflections*, in which Goethe writes that the "basic characteristic of an individual organism" is "to divide, to unite, to merge into the universal, to abide in the particular, to transform itself, to define itself, and, as living things tend to appear under a thousand conditions, to arise and vanish, to solidify and melt, to freeze and flow, to expand and contract."[14] "Specification"—a property of matter "insofar as we think of it as spiritual"—is defined by Goethe as "the drive for specific character, the stubborn persistence of things which have finally attained reality [*zur Wirklichkeit gekommen*]."[15] Or, in the words of one commentator, specification is "the differentiation of what is vague and inchoate [...] into something of a clearly defined form and function."[16]

Elsewhere, Goethe expresses his fundamentally energic conception of life when he formulates as an aphorism the idea that "tension is the apparently indifferent state of an energetic entity that is on the brink of manifesting itself, differentiating itself, and entering into polarity."[17] Such an

---

Frank Cole Babbitt, 14 vols. [London: Heinemann; Cambridge, MA: Harvard University Press, 1927-1976], vol. 5, pp. 415-417).

[12]Hans Eggert Schröder, "'Der alten Mutter forschet nach'" [1971], in *Schiller–Nietzsche–Klages: Abhandlungen und Essays zur Geistesgeschichte der Gegenwart* (Bonn: Bouvier Verlag Herbert Grundmann, 1974), pp. 444-453.

[13]Goethe, "A Commentary on the Aphoristic Essay 'Nature' (Goethe to Chancellor von Müller)" (1828); Goethe, *GE* 12, 6-7.

[14]Goethe, *Maxims and Reflections*, ed. Hecker, #571; Goethe, *GE* 12, 303-304.

[15]Goethe, "Problems" (1823); Goethe, *GE* 12, 43.

[16]Elizabeth M. Wilkinson, "'Tasso—ein gesteigerter Werther' in the Light of Goethe's Principle of 'Steigerung,'" in Elizabeth M. Wilkinson and L. A. Willoughby, *Goethe: Poet and Thinker* (London: Arnold, 1962), pp. 185-213 (p. 189).

[17]Goethe, *Maxims and Reflections*, ed. Hecker, #1255; *Goethe's "Maximen und Reflexionen": A Selection*, ed. and trans. R. H. Stephenson (Glasgow: Scottish Papers in Germanic Studies, 1986), p. 123.

approach is clearly compatible with Jung's principle that, "both theoretically and practically, polarity is inherent in all living things," a principle that in *Memories, Dreams, Reflections* (*Erinnerungen, Träume, Gedanken*) (1963) is traced back to Heraclitus: "Just as all energy proceeds from opposition, so the psyche too possesses its inner polarity, this being the indisputable prerequisite for its aliveness, as Heraclitus realised long ago."[18] In "The Stages of Life," Jung rejects any neurotic flight from the past—or from the future—that reinforces a "narrow range of consciousness" instead of "shattering it in the tension of opposites and building up a state of wider and higher consciousness."[19] Thus Jung's model of synthesis is, in contrast to Hegel's, fundamentally polaristic—or rather, binary—in conception.[20] And, like Goethe's synthetic thought, Jung's seeks to retain the energic tension between the opposites, to refine them (*steigern*), and to elevate them to a higher level of specification. The psycho-existential implications of this outlook are expressed by Jung in his paper on the midlife crisis as follows:

> The serious problems in life, however, are never fully solved. If ever they should appear to be so it is a sure sign that something has been lost [*ein Verlust*]. The meaning and purpose of a problem seem to lie not in its solution but in working at it incessantly. This alone preserves us from stultification and petrification [*Verdummung und Versteinerung*].[21]

Or as Goethe expressed the same idea, in admittedly more rhetorically sophisticated terms: "People say that between two opposed opinions truth lies in the middle. Not at all! A problem lies in-between: invisible, eternally active life, contemplated in peace."[22]

Finally, the very notion of the midlife crisis can be found in Goethe's conversations with Eckermann. On 11 March 1828—the conversation is one of Goethe's most important, for in it he also addresses himself, as we shall see, to the concepts of the *daimon* and the *entelechy*—Goethe is recorded by Eckermann as saying that "natural geniuses" experience "a

---

[18]Jung, *MDR*, p. 379.

[19]Jung, *CW* 8 §767.

[20]For a definition of "binary synthesis," see Elizabeth M. Wilkinson and L. A. Willoughby, "Appendix III: Visual Aids," in Friedrich Schiller, *On the Aesthetic Education of Man*, 2nd ed. (Oxford: Clarendon Press, 1982), pp. 349-350.

[21]Jung, *CW* 8 §771.

[22]Goethe, *Maxims and Reflections*, ed. Hecker, #616; *Goethe's Maximen und Reflexionen*, trans. Stephenson, p. 83.

renewed puberty" (*eine wiederholte Pubertät*),[23] citing Byron as a case in point: "You will find that in middle age a man frequently experiences a change [*eine Wendung*]; and that, while in his youth everything has favoured him, and has prospered with him, all is now completely reversed, and misfortunes and disasters are heaped up one upon another."[24] From this example, and from the lives of Napoleon, Mozart, and Raphael, Goethe drew the dark conclusion that "the individual must be ruined":

> "But do you know what I think about it? Man must be ruined again! [*Der Mensch muß wieder ruiniert werden!*] Every extraordinary man has a certain mission to accomplish. If he has fulfilled it, he is no longer needed upon earth in the same form, and Providence uses him for something else. But as everything here below happens in a natural way, the daimons keep tripping him up till he falls at last. Thus it was with Napoleon and many others. Mozart died in his six-and-thirtieth year. Raphael at the same age. Byron only a little older. But all these had perfectly fulfilled their missions; and it was time for them to depart, that other people might still have something to do in a world made to last a long while."[25]

"Renewed puberty" thus constitutes, in Goethe's terms, a "primordial phenomenon" (or *Urphänomen*) of human development: in the midst of the ageing of *physis*, a renewing of spirit is announced, a new step on the path to integration.[26]

Jung's theory of the midlife crisis can thus be seen as an elaboration of Goethe's original *aperçu*, but the conversation with Eckermann is not the only text of Goethe's that Jung may have had in mind. For in one of Goethe's major poems, "Primal Words. Orphic" (*Urworte. Orphisch*), we can find further parallels with Jung's theory of the midlife crisis, the fear of death, and the hope for change. But first, what is the significance of the adjective "Orphic" in the title of this poem?

---

[23]Eckermann, *Conversations of Goethe*, p. 249.

[24]Eckermann, *Conversations of Goethe*, p. 249.

[25]Eckermann, *Conversations of Goethe*, p. 252.

[26]Friedrich Hiebel, *Goethe: Die Erhöhung des Menschen: Perspektiven einer morphologischen Lebensschau* (Munich and Berne: Francke, 1961), p. 50.

## THE CULT OF ORPHEUS

The main stories of the legend of Orpheus are well known: his journey to the underworld to rescue, only to lose, his wife, Eurydice; his journey with Jason and the Argonauts, where his music drowned out the song of the Sirens; and his death, in the wilderness of Thrace, at the hands of the Maenads.[27] Even after his death, his head continued to sing as it and his lyre floated to the island of Lesbos, where only Apollo could silence his singing, while Zeus turned his lyre into a constellation in the sky. In book four of his *Georgics*,[28] Virgil relates how Aristaeus—responsible for Eurydice's death in the first place—offered sacrifice to Orpheus: which reminds us that, in addition to being a figure in Greek mythology, Orpheus was at the center of an important ancient mystery school or cult.[29]

In comparison with the world conjured up in ancient Greek epic, "with its enlightened traits, with its delight—at times, its frivolous delight—in the pleasures of this world," the religion and morality of post-Homeric Greece wear, in the words of Theodor Gomperz, "a thoroughly altered aspect," as "solemn, gloomy, and dismal features begin to predominate."[30] For the first time we begin to hear of "the expiation of murder, the worship of souls, and the sacrifices to the dead"—and of a cult centered on the figure of a mysterious minstrel, a lyre-player from Thrace, whose music delights and charms everyone—even wild animals—even the birds...[31] For Pindar, Orpheus is the "father of song,"

[27] For a comprehensive account, see Robert Graves, *The Greek Myths: Combined Edition* (London: Penguin, 1992), pp. 111-115.

[28] Virgil, *Georgics*, book 4, ll. 541-558, in *Eclogues; Georgics; Aeneid I-VI*, trans. H. Rushton Fairclough (Cambridge, MA: Harvard University Press, 1999), pp. 257-259. For further discussion, see M. Owen Lee, *Virgil as Orpheus: A Study of the "Georgics"* (Albany, NY: SUNY Press, 1996).

[29] For major discussions of the cult of Orpheus, see the entries by F. Münzer, "Orpheus," in *Pauls Real-Encylopädie der classischen Altertumswissenschaft*, ed. Wilhelm Kroll, 24 vols. (Stuttgart: Metzler, 1894-1919), vol. 18.1, cols. 1200-1316; by Konrat Ziegler, "Orphische Dichtung," *Pauls Real-Encylopädie der classischen Altertumswissenschaft*, vol. 18.2, cols. 1321-1417; and by O. Gruppe, "Orpheus," in W. H. Roscher, *Ausführliches Lexikon der griechischen und römischen Mythologie*, 6 vols. (Leipzig: Teubner, 1897-1902), vol. 3.1, cols. 1058-1207; as well as Ivan M. Linforth, *The Arts of Orpheus* [1941] (New York: Arno Press, 1973); W. H. C. Guthrie, *Orpheus and Greek Religion: A Study of the Orphic Movement* [1952] (Princeton: Princeton University Press, 1993); Robert Böhme, *Orpheus: Der Sänger und seine Zeit* (Berne and Munich: Francke, 1970); M. L. West, *The Orphic Poems* (Oxford: Clarendon Press, 1983); and Elisabeth Henry, *Orpheus with His Lute: Poetry and the Renewal of Life* (London: Bristol Classical Press, 1992).

[30] Theodor Gomperz, *Greek Thinkers: A History of Ancient Greece*, trans. Laurie Magnus, 4 vols. (London: Murray, 1906-1912), vol. 1, p. 80.

[31] See Mircea Eliade, *A History of Religious Ideas*, trans. Willard R. Trask, 3 vols. (Chicago and London: University of Chicago Press, 1982), vol. 2, *From Gautama Buddha to the Triumph of Chris-*

whom Apollo had taught to play the lyre;[32] for Aeschylus, his "voice of
rapture dragged all creatures in his train";[33] the fact he is depicted on a
metope at Delphi shows his proximity to Apollo. According to one tradition, Orpheus was the son of a Thracian king, Oeagrus, and the muse of
epic poetry, Calliope, whilst another regarded him as the offspring of
Apollo and Calliope. Orpheus's very name has been derived etymologically (if hypothetically) from a number of roots, including the archaic
verb *orbhao-* ("to be deprived of," "to long for"), *orphe* ("darkness"), and
*orphanos* ("fatherless"). The most famous literary accounts of Orpheus—
of how he rescues Eurydice, dead from a serpent's bite, from Hades, but
against the advice of Persephone looks back and so loses her forever; of
how he meets his own bloody death at the hands of the maenads, in a
Dionysos-like *sparagmos*—are given by Virgil in his *Georgics* and by Ovid
in his *Metamorphoses*.[34] From there, the figure of Orpheus recurs time and
again in philosophical, theological, and literary texts throughout the
ages.[35] In addition to literary texts (Pindar, Ovid, Virgil, Apollonius of
Tyana), numerous artists, sculptors and painters—from a third-century
mosaic in the Archaeological Museum in Palermo and fourth-century
sculpture in the Byzantine and Christian Museum in Athens, to the
French neoclassicist and proto-Impressionist Jean-Baptiste-Camille
Corot (*Orphée*, 1861), the pre-Raphaelite John William Waterhouse
(*Nymphs Finding the Head of Orpheus*, 1905), and the French Symbolist
Gustav Moreau (*Orphée*, 1865)—not to mention composers of operas—
from Angelo Poliziano (whose *Orfeo* has not survived), via Claudio
Monteverdi (*Orfeo*, 1607), Telemann (*Orpheus*, 1726), and Gluck (*Orfeo*

*tianity*, pp. 180-209; the entries by Christoph Auffarth, Gabrielle Sed-Rajina, and Arwed Arnulf, "Orpheus," and Christoph Auffarth, Irina Wandrey, and Fritz Graf, "Orphiker/Orphik" in *Religion in
Geschichte und Gegenwart: Handbuch für Theologie und Religionswissenschaft*, ed. Hans Dieter Betz, 4th
ed., 8 vols. (Tübingen: Mohr Siebeck, 2008), vol. 6, cols. 670-674.

    [32]Pindar, *Pythian Ode*, no. 4, l. 177; Pindar, *The Odes*, trans. John Sandys (London: Heinemann;
New York: Putnam, 1927), p. 217.

    [33]Aeschylus, *Agamemnon*, l. 1630; *Greek Tragedies*, ed. David Grene and Richmond Lattimore, 2
vols. (Chicago and London: University of Chicago Press, 1960), vol. 1, p. 58.

    [34]Virgil, *Georgics*, book 4, ll. 453-525, in Virgil, *Eclogues; Georgics; Aeneid I-VI*, trans. H.
Rushton Fairclough, pp. 250-257 (for an analysis of the literary qualities of this passage, see Victor Davis Hanson and John Heath, *Who Killed Homer? The Demise of Classical Education and the Recovery of
Greek Wisdom* [New York: Encounter, 2001], p. 185-186); and Ovid, *Metamorphoses*, book 10, ll.
1-107; book 11, ll. 1-99, in Ovid, *Metamorphoses*, trans. A. D. Melville (Oxford and New York: Oxford University Press, 1987), pp. 225-228 and 249-252.

    [35]For a collection of relevant texts, see Wolfgang Storch, ed., *Mythos Orpheus: Texte von Vergil bis
Ingeborg Bachmann* (Leipzig: Reclam, 1997).

ed Euridice, 1762), as well as Jacques Offenbach (*Orphée aux Enfers*, 1858), to Stravinsky (*Orpheus*, 1948), Harrison Birtwhistle (*The Mask of Orpheus*, 1986), and Philip Glass (*Orphée*, 1993)—have invested the figure of Orpheus with religious or artistic significance. All that remains of the actual Orphic writings themselves, however, is fragmentary: portions of text have survived,[36] as have some of the hymns allegedly associated with the cult.[37] (In fact, the doctrinal content of these hymnic texts is, it has been argued, only marginally Orphic.[38])

These hymns address various divinities (such as Hecate, Pan, Proteus, or Apollo, Mercury, Bacchus), astrological bodies (the heaven, the ether, the stars, the sun, the moon), natural forces or phenomena (the clouds, the seasons, the night) and, indeed, Nature herself.[39] The precise nature of their original function, liturgical or otherwise, and their relation to the famous mystery cult based at Eleusis remain obscure, and indeed must do so; for the Orphic mysteries were precisely that—mysterious. Most probably, however, they involved the ritual death and dismemberment, followed by the incubation and reconstitution, of the cultic initiate.[40] (Hence the link between Orphic theology and the myth of Dionysos,[41] a central topos in the thought of Nietzsche and Jung alike.) Perhaps one can apply to the Orphic mysteries what Aristotle said of the initiates of Eleusis—namely, that they learned nothing, but that they "experienced," that they "suffered."[42]

[36]Otto Kern, *Orphicorum Fragmenta* (Berlin: Weidmann, 1922; reprinted Zurich: Weidmann, 1972).

[37]Wilhelm Quandt, *Orphei Hymni* (Berlin: Weidmann, 1941; 2nd ed., 1955); *The Orphic Hymns*, trans. Apostolos N. Athanassakis, Society of Biblical Literature: Texts and Translations, 12; Graeco-Roman Religion Series, 4 (London: Scholars Press, 1977). Whilst out of date, the following edition offers an extensive introduction that reflects the view of Orpheus that had formed in the eighteenth and nineteenth centuries: see *The Mystical Hymns of Orpheus: Translated from the Greek, and demonstrated to be the Invocations which were used in the Eleusinian Mysteries* [1787], trans. Thomas Taylor, 2nd ed. (London: Dobell; Reeves and Turner, 1896). See also M. L. West, *The Orphic Hymns* (Oxford: Clarendon Press, 1983).

[38]Ziegler, "Orphische Dichtung," p. 1327.

[39]The interchangeability of divinities and nature in Orphic thought is a point noted by Thomas Taylor in his translation of *Commentaries of Proclus in the "Timaeus" of Plato in Five Books: Containing a Treasury of Pythagoric and Platonic Physiology*, 2 vols. (London: Taylor, 1820), vol. 2, p. 282.

[40]Sara Rappe, *Reading Neoplatonism: Non-discursive Thinking in the Texts of Plotinus, Proclus, and Damascius* (Cambridge: Cambridge University Press, 2000), p. 143.

[41]See Jean Pépin, "Plotin et le miroir de Dionysos (*Enn.* IV, 3 [27], 12, 1-2)," *Revue internationale de Philosophie* 24 (1970): 304-320.

[42]See Synesius, *Dio*, 10.48a, citing Aristotle: "As Aristotle claims that those who are being initiated into the mysteries are to be expected not to learn anything but to suffer some change, to be put

Now, Mircea Eliade (1907-1986), the comparatist and historian of religion,[43] remarks that Orpheus's powers and the central episodes in his biography are "strangely reminiscent of shamanic practices."[44] His relations with Dionysos and Apollo, he notes, "confirm his fame as 'founder of Mysteries,'" and the claim in one of the Orphic fragments that Orpheus "has shown us the most sacred initiations" suggests a proximity to the Eleusinian Mysteries,[45] which centered on the myth of Persephone in Hades, but about which we know little more.[46] The rite of initiation associated with his cult, Eliade tells us, involved vegetarianism, asceticism, purification, and religious instruction (*hieroi logoi*, sacred books),[47] and Plato records that "the rule known as Orphic" included "universal insistence on vegetarianism, and entire abstention from all that is ani-

---

into a certain condition, i.e., to be fitted for some purpose" (*The Works of Aristotle*, ed. Sir David Ross, vol. 12, *Select Fragments* [Oxford: Clarendon Press, 1952], "Fragments on Philosophy," no. 15, p. 87; cf. Synesius of Cyrene, *The Essays and Hymns*, trans. Augustine Fitzgerald, 2 vols. [Oxford: Oxford University Press; London: Humphrey Milford, 1930], vol. 1, p. 163). For further discussion, see Walter Burkert, *Greek Religion: Archaic and Classical* [*Griechische Religion der archaischen und klassischen Epoche*] [1977], trans. John Raffan (Oxford: Basil Blackwell, 1985), p. 286: "Aristotle states, however, that the important thing was not to learn anything but to suffer or experience (*pathein*) and to be brought into the appropriate state of mind through the proceedings."

[43]For a discussion of Eliade in relation to Jungian circles, see Steven M. Wasserstrom, *Religion after Religion: Gershom Scholem, Mircea Eliade, and Henry Corbin at Eranos* (Princeton, NJ: Princeton University Press, 1999).

[44]Eliade, *History of Religious Ideas*, vol. 2, p. 181: "Like the shamans, he is both healer and musician; he charms and masters wild animals; he goes down to the underworld to bring back the dead; his head is preserved and serves as an oracle, just as the skulls of Yukagir shamans did even as late as the nineteenth century." For further discussion, see Mircea Eliade, *Shamanism: Archaic Techniques of Ecstasy* [1964], trans. Willard R. Trask (Princeton, NJ: Princeton University Press, 1972), pp. 391-392. On Goethe's interest in shamanism, see Gloria Flaherty, "Goethe and Shamanism," *Modern Language Notes* 104 (1989): 580-596.

[45]West, *The Orphic Poems*, pp. 23-24; Eliade, *History of Religious Ideas*, vol. 2, p. 182. For contemporary scholarship on the Eleusinian and other Greek mystery cults, see Michael B. Cosmopoulos, ed., *Greek Mysteries: The Archaeology and Ritual of Ancient Greek Secret Cults* (London and New York: Routledge, 2003), esp. pp. 1-78; Jennifer Larson, *Ancient Greek Cults: A Guide* (New York and London: Routledge, 2007), esp. pp. 69-85; and Hugh Bowden, *Mystery Cults in the Ancient World* (London: Thames and Hudson, 2010), esp. pp. 26-48.

[46]Eliade, *History of Religious Ideas*, vol. 1, *From the Stone Age to the Eleusinian Mysteries*, pp. 290-301. Interest in the Eleusinian Mysteries resurfaces at the time of Romanticism, as discussed in Manfred Frank, *Der kommende Gott: Vorlesungen über die Neue Mythologie, 1. Teil* (Frankfurt am Main: Suhrkamp, 1982), pp. 245-278; and see Hegel's early poem, "Eleusis" (1796) (G. W. F. Hegel, *Werke*, ed. Eva Moldenhauer and Karl Markus Michel, 20 vols. [Frankfurt am Main: Suhrkamp, 1971], vol. 1, *Frühe Schriften*, pp. 230-233); and for discussion, see H. S. Harris, *Hegel's Development: Toward the Sunlight, 1770-1801* (Oxford: Clarendon Press, 1972), pp. 244-248. On the persistence of "mysteries" associated with the town of Eleusis, see the second section entitled "The bus that stops at Eleusis" in Eliade, *History of Religious Ideas*, vol. 2, pp. 414-416.

[47]Eliade, *History of Religious Ideas*, vol. 2, p. 184.

mal."[48] The cult's beliefs included the transmigration of the soul, and hence the belief in its immortality;[49] and for all that Plato—in the form of Phaedrus's remarks in the *Symposium* about how Orpheus "seemed, like the mere minstrel that he was, to be a lukewarm lover, lacking the courage to die as Alcestis died for love, and choosing rather to scheme his way, living, into Hades"[50]—sought to distance himself from them, major Orphic doctrines, especially that of the immortality of the soul, are reflected in his teachings on the body as the "jail" or "prison" of the soul,[51] philosophy as "a preparation for death,"[52] and his "mythology of the soul."[53] The allusions to Orphic cosmology in Plato and their persistence in Neoplatonic thinkers suggest that, as one commentator puts it, Orpheus changes "from the enchanted visionary of the earlier tradition" into "a metaphysically astute theologian for the later Neoplatonists."[54]

Moreover, one of these thinkers, Proclus, intimates there is a connection between an important source of Platonism—namely, the philosophy of Pythagoras—and the doctrines of the ancient Orphic cult. According to Proclus in his *Commentary on Plato's "Timaeus,"* what Orpheus "delivered mystically through arcane narrations" was learned by Pythagoras "when he celebrated orgies in the Thracian Libethra, being initiated by Aglaophemus in the mystic wisdom which Orpheus derived from his mother Calliope, in the mountain Pangaeus."[55] Here lies the link between Orphism, Pythagoreanism, and the mystery cult at Eleusis, centered on the notion of a *katabasis* or descent—the journey of Orpheus to the underworld, the purificatory rituals of Pythagoreanism, and Persephone's descent to Hades and return to Demeter in the Lesser and Greater Mysteries celebrated at Eleusis[56]

---

[48]Plato, *Laws*, book 6, 782c; Plato, *Collected Dialogues*, p. 1358. For further discussion, see E. R. Dodds, *The Greeks and the Irrational* [1951] (Berkeley, Los Angeles, London: University of California Press, 1997), pp. 147-150.

[49]Eliade, *History of Religious Ideas*, vol. 2, p. 184.

[50]Plato, *Symposium*, 179d; Plato, *Collected Dialogues*, p. 534.

[51]Plato, *Cratylus*, 400c (Plato, *Collected Dialogues*, pp. 437-438); *Phaedo*, 62b (Plato, *Collected Dialogues*, p. 45).

[52]Plato, *Phaedo*, 64a-c; Plato, *Collected Dialogues*, pp. 46-47.

[53]Plato, *Gorgias* 493; *Phaedo* 107e; *Republic*, book 7 (the myth of the cave); and *Phaedrus*, 246b ff.

[54]See Rappe, *Reading Neoplatonism*, chap. 7, "Transmigrations of a Myth: Orphic Texts and Platonic Contexts," pp. 143-166 (p. 143).

[55]Proclus, *Life of Pythagoras*, cited in *The Mystical Hymns of Orpheus*, "Introduction," p. viii. Compare Rappe, *Reading Neoplatonism*, "Proclus Reads Orpheus," pp. 157-166 (cf. p. 118).

[56]See the Homeric Hymn "To Demeter," in *Hesiod, The Homeric Hymns and Homerica*, trans. Hugh G. Evelyn-White (Cambridge, MA: Harvard University Press; London: Heinemann, 1914), pp. 289-325.

(a narrative so compelling that, centuries after the decline of the cult, Schiller attempted to reimagine it in a long poem called "The Festival of Eleusis" [*Das Eleusische Fest*] [1798]).[57] This descent is followed by the initiate's reascent or rebirth, so that the central (one might say, archetypal) idea of the ancient mystery cults is: descent and rebirth, dying and becoming, *stirb und werde*...

In the late nineteenth and early twentieth centuries there was a renaissance of interest in the Orphism of antiquity;[58] particularly so, it turns out, among scholars and thinkers who were influential for Jung. Let us briefly consider here three such figures. First, there is the Swiss cultural historian and anthropologist J. J. Bachofen, one of the great scholars in nineteenth-century Basel. In "The Three Mystery Eggs," one of the sections in his *Essay on Ancient Mortuary Symbolism* (*Versuch über die Gräbersymbolik der Alten*) (1859), Bachofen discusses a tomb painting found in the columbarium of the Villa Pamphili in Rome. For Bachofen, the depiction of five young men sitting around a table with three eggs on it referred to "the Orphic primordial egg," an object that represented "the material source of things, which brings forth all life from out of itself," comprising "both becoming and passing away" and encompassing "both the bright and the dark side of nature," and hence was "half white and half black or red" in color:

> These colors [i.e., white and black/red] flow into one another as unremittingly as life and death, day and night, becoming and passing away. They do not exist merely in proximity but also within one another. Death is the precondition of life, and only in the same measure as destruction proceeds can the creative power be effective. In every moment becoming and passing away operate side by side.[59]

Even if Bachofen believed in the superiority of the symbol over the myth,[60]

---

[57]See Friedrich Schiller, *The Minor Poems*, trans. John Herman Merivale (London: Pickering, 1844), pp. 293-302; Schiller, *Sämtliche Gedichte und Balladen*, ed. Georg Kurscheidt (Frankfurt am Main: Insel, 2004), pp. 35-40.

[58]For a discussion of the background to developments in German philology in the early twentieth century, see Ingo Gildenhard and Martin Ruehl, eds., *Out of Arcadia: Classics and Politics in Germany in the Age of Burckhardt, Nietzsche and Wilamowitz* (London: Institute of Classical Studies, 2003), esp. Suzanne Marchand, "From Liberalism to Neoromanticism: Albrecht Dieterich, Richard Reitzenstein, and the Religious Turn in *fin-de-siècle* German Classical Studies," pp. 129-160.

[59]Johann Jakob Bachofen, *Myth, Religion, and Mother Right: Selected Writings of J. J. Bachofen*, trans. Ralph Manheim (Princeton, NJ: Princeton University Press, 1973), pp. 25-26.

[60]Bachofen, *Myth, Religion, and Mother Right*, p. 48: "Myth is the exegesis of the symbol"; cf.

he understood, from his study of this Pamphilian grave painting, that "the myth restores the ancient dignity of the Orphic symbolism," and that since "to expound the mystery doctrine in words would be a sacrilege against the supreme law," it "can only be represented in terms of myth," and "that is why mythology is the language of the tomb."[61]

Second, writing in the wake of Bachofen, the German classical philologist Albrecht Dieterich (1866-1908) devoted his *Habilitationsschrift*, entitled *De hymnis Orphicis capitula quinque*, to a study of the Orphic hymns, publishing his results in 1891.[62] And third, the Hungarian-born classicist Karl Kerényi (1897-1973) undertook an intensive study of Orpheus. He emphasized that, seen in its context, the origin of Orphism, or "the appearance of the Orphic cosmogony in its written form," was not "a typical [...] religious 'movement,' a new 'mysticism,'" but "a complicated historical phenomenon," albeit one that had persisted in two forms—as fragmentary papyri detailing sacred rites that had survived the centuries, and under the guise of all true forms of initiation in the Western world, but most noticeably in "the books of the poets, rich in imagery and full of music."[63]

Nor was the proto-Jungian tradition alone in its fascination with the cult of Orpheus. For example, the German vitalist philosopher Ludwig Klages conjured up the world of the Orphic Greece as follows:

> Everything is in motion and wanders, announces itself, unfolds and floats away, and thus it is *alive*; drives and wishes, desire for satiation or copulation, war and fraternization conglomerate the airy, dissolve the solid, draw the celestial fire into the embrace of the swamps, send as mist the nourishing waters into the glowing flames of the sun. The belief in universal liveliness, in panmixia and incessant change is the life-blood of myth and the systems of the earliest thinkers.[64]

---

"The sublime dignity and richness of the symbol reside precisely in the fact that it not only allows of but even encourages different levels of interpretation, and leads us from truths of physical life to those of a higher spiritual order" (p. 25).

[61]Bachofen, *Myth, Religion, and Mother Right*, p. 48.

[62]Dieterich's *Habilitationsschrift*, *De hymnis orphicis capitula quinque* (Marburg, 1891), is republished as "De hymnis Orphicis," in Albrecht Dieterich, *Kleine Schriften*, ed. Richard Wünsch (Leipzig and Berlin: Teubner, 1911), pp. 69-110. For a brief discussion of Dieterich's study of Orphism, see Wünsch, "Albrecht Dieterich," in Dieterich, *Kleine Schriften*, pp. ix-xlii (esp. pp. xiv-xv).

[63]Karl Kerényi, "Die orphische Kosmogonie und der Ursprung der Orphik: Ein Rekonstruktionsversuch" [1949], in *Humanistische Seelenforschung* (Wiesbaden: VMA-Verlag, 1978), pp. 323-339 (pp. 324, 339).

[64]Ludwig Klages, *Vom kosmogonischen Eros*, 2nd ed. (Jena: Diederichs, 1926), p. 131; cited by Ernst Bloch in *Erbschaft dieser Zeit: Erweiterte Ausgabe* [1962] [*Werkausgabe*, vol. 4] (Frankfurt am

But with the later collapse of the outlook of antiquity, in Klages's view, Orphism "fled from this inner *breach* into the ascetic delusion of the body as the tomb of the soul," and out of Orphic theology developed the Platonic doctrine of the Ideas.[65]

## ORPHEUS IN THE AGE OF ROMANTICISM

Thus, historically speaking, the doctrine of the cult of Orpheus represented a transitional stage from the naïve polytheism of the Homeric world, whatever form that belief might actually have taken,[66] to the more philosophical speculation of the fourth and fifth centuries B.C.E.[67] Whilst rooted in the mother cults of the neolithic period and in the orgiastic cult traditions of the Middle East, Orphism initiated the process of moving away from nature by reflecting on nature that results in the flowering of pre-Socratic thought.[68] And the Orphic hymns—dating from second- to third-century Greece, and addressed to various divine entities—represent the last lyrical expression of ancient Greece, bridging age-old tradition and the ethical values of the new epoch.[69]

That new epoch was characterized by the destruction of paganism and the triumph of Christianity;[70] in this period, the Orphic cult disappeared along with the suppression of the pagan sites, but its doctrines resurfaced in the teachings of the Gnostics.[71] Indeed, the iconography of Orphism is still alive and well in the paintings on the walls of the catacombs, where Christ is depicted as the "good shepherd" but with facial

---

Main: Suhrkamp, 1985), p. 339; translated in Bloch, *Heritage of Our Times*, trans. Nevill and Stephen Plaice (Cambridge: Polity Press, 1991), p. 308. Klages paid close attention to the Orphic cosmogonies, particularly as preserved in the work of Hesiod, as a source of information about what he called "cosmogonic Eros" (see *Vom kosmogonischen Eros*, pp. 36, 108); see, too, Baal Müller, *Kosmik: Prozeßontologie und temporale Poetik bei Ludwig Klages und Alfred Schuler: Zur Philosophie und Dichtung der Schwabinger Kosmischen Runde* (Munich: Telesma-Verlag, 2007), pp. 149-151.

[65]Klages, *Vom kosmogonischen Eros*, pp. 190 and 195.

[66]See Paul Veyne, *Les Grecs ont-ils cru à leurs mythes?* (Paris: Seuil, 1983).

[67]Johannes Hoffmeister, "Goethes 'Urworte. Orphisch': Eine Interpretation," *Logos* 19 (1930): 173-212 (p. 174).

[68]Karl A. Wipf, *Elpis: Betrachtungen zum Begriff der Hoffnung in Goethes Spätwerk* (Berne and Munich: Francke Verlag, 1974), p. 130.

[69]Thus the commentary in *Griechische Lyrik*, trans. Dietrich Ebener (Berlin and Weimar: Aufbau-Verlag, 1976), p. 596.

[70]For discussion of this period, see Robin Lane Fox, *Pagans and Christians* (London: Viking, 1986; 2nd ed., 2006); and Charles Freeman, *The Closing of the Western Mind: The Rise of Faith and the Fall of Reason* (London: Heinemann, 2002).

[71]Eliade, *History of Religious Ideas*, vol. 2, p. 371; Hiebel, *Goethe: Die Erhöhung des Menschen*, p. 35.

characteristics typical of representations of Orpheus.[72] This persistence of the pagan under a veneer of the Christian perhaps explains the great revival of interest in Orphism that took place in the late eighteenth and early nineteenth century in the circles of German Romanticism. In the writings of Novalis (1772-1801),[73] for instance, the figure of the poet acquires distinctly Orpheus-like features; in the fifth of the *Hymns to the Night* (*Hymnen an die Nacht*) (1799), whose title echoes one of the texts in the Orphic hymnary (no. 3, "To Night"), an itinerant singer brings a message from Greece to Palestine, and thence to India: "In death was announced eternal life, / You are death—and you make us healthy" (*Im Tode ward das ewge Leben kund, / Du bist der Tod und machst uns erst gesund*).[74] The conclusion to Novalis's unfinished novel, *Heinrich von Ofterdingen* (1802), was to involve, according to Ludwig Tieck, a reconciliation of Christianity and paganism—including the story of Orpheus.[75] In one of his aphorisms, Novalis declared that "only when the philosopher appears as Orpheus will the whole [i.e., of history] order itself in regular-general and higher-educated, significant masses—in true *sciences*."[76] And, inasmuch as he regarded the content of drama as "a process of transformation, purification, and reduction" (*eine Verwandlung—eine Läuterungs, Reduktionsproceß*),[77] Novalis has been regarded as a predecessor of Nietzsche in his *The Birth of Tragedy* (*Die Geburt der Tragödie*) (1872).

Equally, the synthesis of paganism and Christianity is a recurring theme in the poetry of Friedrich Hölderlin (1770-1843). In his "Hymn to the Genius of Greece" (*Hymne an den Genius Griechenlands*) (c. 1790), for instance, he proclaimed the excellence of the spirit of the country, the glories of whose ancient culture he sought elsewhere to capture in complicated, haunting verse—

[72]Hiebel, *Goethe: Die Erhöhung des Menschen*, p. 35.

[73]See Walter A. Strauss, *Descent and Return: The Orphic Theme in Modern Literature* (Cambridge, MA: Harvard University Press, 1971), pp. 27-49.

[74]Novalis, *Schriften*, ed. Richard Samuel and Paul Kluckhohn, 5 vols. (Stuttgart: Kohlhammer, 1960-1968), vol. 1, p. 147.

[75]Novalis, *Schriften*, vol. 1, p. 368.

[76]Novalis, *Schriften*, vol. 3, p. 335; "*Erst dann, wenn der Philosoph, als Orpheus erscheint, ordnet sich das Ganze in regelmäßige gemeine und höhere gebildete, bedeutende Massen—in ächte* Wissenschaften *zusammen.*"

[77]Novalis, "Poësie," §44 ["Logologische Fragmente," II], in Novalis, *Schriften*, vol. 2, p. 535. See Frederick Hiebel, "Goethe's *Maerchen* in the Light of Novalis," *Publications of the Modern Language Association* 63 (1948): 918-934.

You come, and Orpheus' love
Floats up to the eye of the world,
And Orpheus' love
Swirls down to the Acheron,
You swing the magic wand,
And Aphrodite's belt espies

The drunken Maeonides.

[*Du kommst und Orpheus' Liebe*
*Schwebet empor zum Auge der Welt,*
*Und Orpheus' Liebe*
*Wallet nieder zum Acheron.*
*Du schwingest den Zauberstab,*
*Und Aphrodites Gürtel ersieht*

*Der trunkene Mäonide.*][78]

—while in other poems he pursued an overtly syncretistic goal, such as in "The Only One" (*Der Einzige*) (c. 1801-1802/1803), where Christ is addressed as "Heracles' brother," in other words, as Dionysos.[79]

As well as identifying poetry with mythology—"The core, the center of poetry is to be found in mythology, and in the mysteries of the ancients"[80]—Friedrich Schlegel (1772-1829) may be considered the discoverer of the "primordial Orphic past" (*orphische Vorzeit*)—thus the title of a major section in his *History of the Poetry of the Greeks and Romans* (*Geschichte der Poesie der Griechen und Römer*) (1798).[81] Schlegel's call for a "new mythology" rooted in Greece, his aphoristic style, and his irony anticipate significant aspects of Nietzsche's thought—until, that is, Schlegel's conversion to Catholicism in 1808 and his move into administration for the Austrian government in his later life.[82]

As Schlegel's approach to Orpheus in his writings on classical antiquity

[78]Hölderlin, "Hymne an den Genius Griechenlands," in Friedrich Hölderlin, *Sämtliche Gedichte*, ed. Jochen Schmidt (Frankfurt am Main: Deutscher Klassiker Verlag, 2005), pp. 107-108 (p. 108). By Maeonides (i.e., the son of Maeon), Hölderlin is referring to Homer who, in *The Iliad*, book 14, describes the alluring girdle of Aphrodite.

[79]Hölderlin, "Der Einzige," 2nd version, in *Sämtliche Gedichte*, pp. 347-350 (p. 348). For further discussion, see Frank, *Der kommende Gott*, pp. 269-270, 287-290.

[80]Friedrich Schlegel, *Athenäum*, III, 18, 96; cited in Strauss, *Descent and Return*, p. 20.

[81]Friedrich Schlegel, *Kritische Friedrich-Schlegel-Ausgabe*, ed. Ernst Behler et al., 15 vols. (Paderborn, Munich, Vienna: Schöningh; Zurich: Thomas-Verlag, 1958-2006), vol. 1, pp. 399-428. See Frank, *Der kommende Gott*, p. 93.

[82]See McGahey, *The Orphic Moment*, p. 53.

suggests, the figure of Orpheus and the meaning of the Orphic cult also came to the forefront of philological concerns. In 1810-1812 Friedrich Creuzer (1771-1858), a classical philologist in Heidelberg, published the first edition of his massive, four-volume study, *Symbolik und Mythologie der alten Völker* (Symbols and Mythology of the Ancient Peoples) (1810-1812),[83] which stimulated a major debate on the meaning of myth.[84] Creuzer came under attack from numerous quarters: from Johann Heinrich Voss (1751-1826), who published an *Antisymbolik*;[85] from Christian August Lobeck (1781-1860) in his *Aglaophamus* (1829);[86] from the Göttingen philologist Karl Otfried Müller (1797-1840), in two extensive reviews in the *Göttinger Gelehrte Anzeigen*;[87] and from the Leipzig philologist Johann Gottfried Hermann (1772-1848), in *Ueber das Wesen und die Behandlung der Mythologie: Ein Brief an Herrn Hofrat Creuzer* (On the Nature and Treatment of Mythology: A Letter to Creuzer) (1819).[88] Later, as we shall see, Creuzer and Hermann would cross swords again in another debate, which concerns itself more specifically with the significance of Orphism. But what was it about Creuzer's work that provoked such controversy?[89]

[83]Friedrich Creuzer, *Symbolik und Mythologie der alten Völker, besonders der Griechen*, 4 vols. (Leipzig: Leske; Heyer und Leske, 1810-1812); second edition, 4 vols. (Leipzig and Darmstadt: Heyer und Leske, 1819-1821), expanded with two additional volumes by Franz Joseph Mone (1796-1871); third edition (Leipzig and Darmstadt: Leske, 1837-1842).

[84]See Ernst Howald, *Der Kampf um Creuzers Symbolik: Eine Auswahl von Dokumenten* (Tübingen: Mohr, 1926).

[85]Johann Heinrich Voss, *Antisymbolik*, 2 vols. (Stuttgart: J. B. Metzler, 1824); republished, 2 vols. (Eschborn: Klotz, 1994).

[86]Christian August Lobeck, *Aglaophamus; sive, De theologiae mysticae Graecorum causis libri tres*, 2 vols. (Königsberg: Borntraeger, 1829); republished as *Aglaophamus: Drei Bücher über die Grundlagen der Mysterienreligion der Griechen mit einer Sammlung der Fragmente der orphischen Dichter* (Darmstadt: Wissenschaftliche Buchgesellschaft, 1968).

[87]"Friedrich Creuzer's Symbolik und Mythologie" (1821), and "Symbolik und Mythologie der alten Völker besonders der Griechen, von Dr. Friedrich Creuzer" (1825), in Karl Otfried Müller, *Kleine deutsche Schriften über Religion, Kunst, Sprache und Literatur, Leben und Geschichte des Althertums, nebst Erinnerungen aus dem Leben des Verfassers*, ed. Eduard Müller, 2 vols. (Breslau: Max, 1847-1848), vol. 2, pp. 3-20 and 25-30.

[88]Gottfried Hermann, *Ueber das Wesen und die Behandlung der Mythologie, ein Brief an Herrn Hofrat Creuzer* (Leipzig: G. Fleischer, 1819); extracted in Karl Kerényi, *Die Eröffnung des Zugangs zum Mythos: Ein Lesebuch*, Wege der Forschung, vol. 20 (Darmstadt: Wissenschaftliche Buchgesellschaft, 1967), pp. 59-61.

[89]For further discussion, see the extremely helpful background information in Josine H. Blok, "Quests for a Scientific Mythology: F. Creuzer and K. O. Müller on History and Myth," *History and Theory* 33/3 [Theme Issue 33: Proof and Persuasion in History] (December 1994): 26-52; and "'Romantische Poesie, Naturphilosophie, Construction der Geschichte': K. O. Müller's Understand-

Leaving aside the fact that Creuzer's notorious relationship with Karoline von Günderode (1780-1806), the Romantic poetess, ended tragically with her suicide in the Rhine—a scandal of the age—it has been argued that his fundamental shift toward an "idealist" interpretation took place during his relationship with her.[90] On Creuzer's account, myth was subordinated to the symbol, to the embodiment of thought and sense perception.[91] This symbolic core expanded, through time, into the diversity of myths, reflecting different cultures. Thus behind the multiplicity of myth lay "a universal natural symbolism and a mythic, poetic, and at times ecstatic religion."[92] Whereas, for Creuzer, the work of myth lay in the transposition of "what has been thought" into "what has happened" (*das Gedachte in ein Geschehen umzusetzen*),[93] one of his opponents in Göttingen, K. O. Müller, argued that myth contains "what has been thought *and* what has happened,"[94] thereby altering the preeminence accorded by Creuzer to the symbol. For along with that preeminence, so Müller (and Creuzer's other opponents) felt, went an unwarranted emphasis on the irrational, on the religious—on the "mystical." (In fact, shortly after his appointment to Göttingen, Müller wrote in a letter to his parents that "one has to be very careful here not to be deemed a mystic, for the old bunch of Göttingen professors mixes every possible *Naturphilosophie*, romantic poetry, new theology, higher historical analysis, symbolic mythology etc. in one bowl and then pours it all right down the sink."[95]) Unwarranted, that is, as far as these critics were concerned: by

---

ing of History and Myth," in *Zwischen Rationalismus und Romantik: Karl Otfried Müller und die antike Kultur*, ed. William M. Calder, III, and Renate Schlesier (Hildesheim: Weidmann, 1998), pp. 55-97; as well as Frank, *Der kommende Gott*, pp. 83-104; and Christoph Jamme, "'Göttersymbole': Friedrich Creuzer als Mythologe und seine philosophische Wirkung," in *200 Jahre Heidelberger Romantik*, ed. Friedrich Strack [*Heidelberger Jahrbücher*, vol. 51] (Berlin: Springer, 2008), pp. 487-498.

[90]Blok, "Quests for a Scientific Mythology," p. 29; "'Romantische Poesie, Naturphilosophie, Construktion der Geschichte,'" p. 76. As Ernst Cassirer explains, Creuzer "looked on myth as an allegorical, symbolic language concealing a secret meaning, a purely ideal content which can be glimpsed behind its images" (*The Philosophy of Symbolic Forms* [1923-1929], vol. 2, *Mythical Thought* [1925], trans. Ralph Manheim [New Haven and London: Yale University Press, 1955], p. 38).

[91]See Frank, *Der kommende Gott*, p. 91.

[92]Blok, "Quests for a Scientific Mythology," p. 30; "'Romantische Poesie, Naturphilosophie, Construktion der Geschichte,'" p. 77.

[93]Creuzer, *Symbolik* (2nd ed.), vol. 1, p. 99.

[94]Karl Otfried Müller, *Prolegomena zu einer wissenschaftlichen Mythologie: Mit einer antikritischen Zugabe* (Göttingen: Vandenhoeck und Ruprecht, 1825), p. 70; cf. Blok, "Quests for a Scientific Mythology," p. 39.

[95]Letter of 21 November 1819; Carl Otfried Müller, *Lebensbild in Briefen an seine Eltern, mit*

contrast, F. W. J. Schelling (1775-1854) welcomed Creuzer's approach to myth.[96]

A further disagreement on the nature of myth took place between Creuzer and Hermann, which led to the publication of their correspondence on the issue in question: the works of Hesiod and Homer.[97] Yet however much Hermann may have disagreed with Creuzer, he shared his fascination with Orpheus, editing a collection of fragmentary texts relating to his cult under the title *Orphica*.[98] Creuzer's and Hermann's *Letters*, together with a collection of treatises on classical archaeology by the Danish archaeologist Jörgen Zoega (1755-1809), translated from Latin into German by Friedrich Gottlieb Welcker (1784-1868), professor of archeology at Göttingen,[99] constituted Goethe's chief source for his knowledge of Orphism, and he was well aware of the controversy surrounding Creuzer, whom he met on several occasions during his visit to Heidelberg in 1815.

Later, Creuzer's *Symbolik* was a major source for inspiration for Bachofen,[100] who adopted a distinctly Creuzerian position on the relation between myth and symbol. "Myth," he wrote, is "the exegesis of the symbol," for "it unfolds in a series of outwardly connected actions what the symbol embodies in a unity."[101] For Bachofen, the tenets of Orphism

---

*dem Tagebuch seiner italienisch-griechischen Reise*, ed. Otto and Else Kern (Berlin: Weidmann, 1908), pp. 54-55; cited in Blok, "Quests for a Scientific Mythology," p. 33. A similar kind of concern is expressed by Jung in *Transformations and Symbols of the Libido*, in a footnote where he proposes "psychosynthesis" as a complementary approach to "psychoanalysis": "This time I shall hardly be spared the reproach of mysticism," he complains (*PU* §99, n. 17). Tellingly, Fichte defended his teaching *in extenso* against the charge of mysticism in *Die Anweisung zum seligen Leben* (1806), particularly in the second lecture, whereas in "Vorlesungen über die Methode des akademischen Studiums" and in "Über das Verhältnis der Naturphilosophie zur Philosophie überhaupt" Schelling was prepared to describe his *Naturphilosophie* as *Mystizismus*.

[96]See Walter Burkert, "Griechische Mythologie und die Geistesgeschichte der Moderne," in *Les études classiques aux XIXe et XXe siècles: Leur place dans l'histoire des idées*, ed. Olivier Reverdin and Bernard Grange (Geneva: Fondation Hardt, 1980), pp. 159-199 (p. 163); Cassirer, *Mythical Thought*, p. 15.

[97]Gottfried Hermann and Friedrich Creuzer, *Briefe über Homer und Hesodius vorzüglich über die Theogonie* (Heidelberg: Oswald, 1818). Although the book was predated to 1818, it was actually published in 1817. The text is available from the Göttinger Digitalisierungszentrum at the following url: http://www.gdz.sub.uni-goettingen.de/cgi-bin/digbib.cgi?PPN50536459X.

[98]Gottfried Hermann, ed., *Orphica* (Leipzig: Fritsch, 1805; reprinted Hildesheim: Olms, 1971).

[99]Georg Zoëga, *Abhandlungen*, ed. Friedrich Gottlieb Welcker (Göttingen: Dieterich, 1817). For further discussion of Zoega and Welcker, see Walter Dietze, "Urworte, nicht sonderlich orphisch," *Goethe-Jahrbuch* 94 (1977): 11-37 (p. 25, n. 29).

[100]Blok, "Quests for a Scientific Mythology," p. 28; Frank, *Der kommende Gott*, pp. 93-96.

[101]Bachofen, *Myth, Religion, and Mother Right*, p. 48.

belonged to "the oldest theology"—that is, the belief that "matter develops from chaos to form, from imperfection to perfection, from crude disorder to increasingly more refined articulation and organization; the beautiful first originates in a formative progression from the lower to the higher" (*und in der immer größern Vollkommenheit des Geschaffenen kommt auch das schaffende Prinzip in stets wachsender Schönheit zur Offenbarung*).[102]

In Bachofen's discussion of the relationship between Dionysos and Apollo, Orpheus becomes a mediating figure between the solar and the chthonic, between the uranian and the telluric, in fact, between the opposites: "Now Dionysos is recognized as the ruler of the telluric sphere, and the uranian half is conceded to Apollo, so that the highest domain of light relinquished by Apollo is restored to that god which the oldest form of Orphism had worshipped in its purer form."[103] Thus, by virtue of a kind of binary synthesis, Dionysos becomes "the sun of the lower hemisphere" (or in Macrobius's words: *sol in infero hemisphaerio*), "the solar principle of the dark earth, which, far removed from its home, illuminates the closed depths of matter."[104] In the wake of Romanticism, both Orphic motifs in general—as the extensive secondary literature on the subject demonstrates[105]—and the work of Creuzer in particular remained a significant force within Modernism.[106]

As far as Jung is concerned, both Creuzer and Bachofen are the major sources of his knowledge of the Orphic cult.[107] Given the richness of the themes of *katabasis*, life-through-death, and artistic creativity in the leg-

---

[102]Bachofen, "Ocnus the Rope Plaiter," in "An Essay on Mortuary Symbolism" (1859); *Myth, Religion, and Mother Right*, pp. 21-65 (p. 58); *Mutterrecht und Religion*, ed. Hans G. Kippenberg, 6th ed. (Stuttgart: Kröner, 1984), p. 72.

[103]Bachofen, *Der Mythus von Orient und Occident: Eine Metaphysik der alten Welt*, ed. Manfred Schroeter, introd. Alfred Baumler (Munich: Beck, 1926), p. 396; cf. Strauss, *Descent and Return*, p. 18.

[104]Bachofen, *Der Mythus von Orient und Occident*, p. 397.

[105]For further discussion, see Walter Rehm, *Orpheus: Der Dichter und die Toten* (Düsseldorf: L. Schwann, 1950); Eva Kushner, *Le Mythe d'Orphée dans la littérature français contemporaine* (Paris: Nizet, 1961); Gwendolyn M. Bays, *The Orphic Vision: Seer Poets from Novalis to Rimbaud* (Lincoln, NE: University of Nebraska Press, 1964); and Georges Cattaui, *Orphisme et prophétie chez les poètes français* (Paris: Plon, 1965).

[106]See Leon Surette, *The Birth of Modernism: Ezra Pound, T. S. Eliot, W. B. Yeats and the Occult* (Montreal: McGill-Queen's University Press, 1993); and George S. Williamson, *The Longing for Myth in Germany: Religion and Aesthetic Culture from Romanticism to Nietzsche* (Chicago and London: University of Chicago Press, 2004), chap. 3, "Olympus under Siege: Creuzer's *Symbolik* and the Politics of the Restoration," pp. 121-150.

[107]Jung's library contains, for instance, Creuzer's *Symbolik und Mythologie der alten Völker, besonders der Griechen* (1810-1821), and volumes 1 and 4 of Bachofen's *Gesammelte Werke* (1943-1954): *Das Mutterrecht* (1897), *Der Mythos von Orient und Occident* (1926), and *Versuch über*

end of Orpheus, Jung's specific references to the cult are surprisingly
sparse. In *Symbols of Transformation* he refers to the forty-sixth and
fifty-second Orphic hymns,[108] and there is a passing reference in *Mysterium Coniunctionis*;[109] while in *Aion* he mentions Robert Eisler's comparative study of Orphic and early Christian symbolism.[110] Yet Orphic
ideas clearly structure Jung's thought, which explains the persistent interest taken by Jungian circles in Eleusinian, Orphic, and related mysteries,
as witnessed by various lectures organized by the Eranos Foundation and
by a recent issue of *Spring Journal* on the topic of Orpheus.[111]

### GOETHE'S RELATION TO THE ORPHIC MYSTERIES

As the Austrian Germanist and anthroposophist Friedrich Hiebel
(1903-1989) has pointed out, there exist in the popular imagination two
entirely different images of Goethe.[112] On the one hand, there is the
Olympian Goethe, the "great pagan," as Heine recalled his contemporaries knew him,[113] the Apollonian Goethe, the man of the Weimar court,
the state minister, the admirer of Greco-Roman classicism. We might call
this, if somewhat simplistically, the "classical" Goethe or, more critically,
the "bourgeois" Goethe. This is the image of Goethe in the engraving on
the mantelpiece in the professor's house that so disturbs Harry Haller in
*The Steppenwolf* (1927).[114] On the other hand, another image enjoys a
certain currency, in particular among anthroposophists and some analytical psychologists: this is the "mystic" Goethe, the esoteric Goethe—Goethe as Orphic magician, as alchemist, as Gnostic, as Neoplatonist, as
*Naturphilosoph*, as the wise prophet.[115] Similarly, there exist two com-

---

*die Gräbersymbolik der Alten* (1859) (*C. G. Jung Bibliothek: Katalog*, privately published
Küsnacht-Zürich, 1967).

[108] Jung, *CW* 5 §528, n. 61, and §530.

[109] Jung, *CW* 14 §734.

[110] Jung, *CW* 9/ii §162. See Robert Eisler, *Orpheus—The Fisher* (London: Watkins, 1921).

[111] See *The Mysteries: Papers from the Eranos Yearbooks* (London: Routledge and Kegan Paul,
1955); and *Spring: A Journal of Archetype and Culture* 71 (Fall 2004), entitled *Orpheus*.

[112] Hiebel, *Goethe: Die Erhöhung des Menschen*, p. 20.

[113] See *The Romantic School*, book 1; Heinrich Heine, *Die romantische Schule* [1833; 1835], ed.
Helga Weidmann (Stuttgart: Reclam, 1976), p. 48.

[114] Hermann Hesse, *Steppenwolf*, trans. Basil Creighton, rev. Walter Sorrell (Harmondsworth:
Penguin, 1965), pp. 95-99.

[115] Compare with Müller's account of the 69-year-old Goethe using his role as a Merlin-like figure to excuse himself from a picnic: "'Let me go, my children,' he said, suddenly rising from his seat,
'let me hasten in solitude to my stones down there; for after such conversations it befits the old Merlin

pletely opposite images of Jung: the scientist, the clinician, the experi-
menter in word-association, the founder of a modern psychology; and
Jung the occultist, the astrologer, the mystic, the wizard of Küsnacht... In
the case of Goethe and Jung alike, there is something to be said for both
sets of images; to discern the truth, however, we have to distinguish substance from rhetoric, and genuine argumentation from techniques of
self-presentation.

Goethe's attitude to the Orphic cults is a complex one, and is bound
up with the preoccupations of his cultural politics.[116] The debate over the
understanding of ancient Greece in Germany was—in the eighteenth
century[117] as it was in the twentieth[118]—in part a means to discuss other
issues of contemporary relevance. Thus the background to Goethe's
image of the ancient Greeks is formed by the rationalism of the Enlightenment. During his youth there appeared rationalizing accounts of Greek
mythology, written by Benjamin Hederich (1675-1748) and l'abbé
Antoine Banier (1673-1741),[119] and a skeptical approach to philology was
pioneered by Christian Gottlob Heyne (1729-1812) and Friedrich
August Wolf (1759-1824). Their view of the ancient Greeks culminated
in the major canonical text of German Enlightenment classicism,

---

to re-acquaint himself with the primordial elements [*mit den Urelementen*].' We watched him for a
long time, while he, robed in his light-gray coat, descended solemnly into the valley, studying this
rock, or this plant, as he went, testing the former with his mineralogical hammer. Already the hills
threw longer shadows, in which, like a ghostly apparition, he gradually disappeared" (Flodoard von
Biedermann, ed., *Goethes Gespräche*, 5 vols. [Leipzig: Biedermann, 1909-1911], vol. 2, p. 420). Un-
kind critics have spoken of the "creation of an aura" (*Auratisierung*) of the person of Goethe; see
Christa Bürger, *Der Ursprung der bürgerlichen Institution Kunst im höfischen Weimar* (Frankfurt:
Suhrkamp, 1977), but for a more sympathetic presentation of the elderly Goethe, see Eduard
Spranger, "Goethe als Greis" [1932], in *Goethe: Seine geistige Welt* (Tübingen: Wunderlich; Leins,
1967), pp. 318-349.

[116]For further discussion, see Ernst Grumach, *Goethe und die Antike*, 2 vols. (Berlin: Walter de
Gruyter, 1949); Ernst-Richard Schwinge, *Goethe und die Poesie der Griechen* [*Abhandlungen der geistes-
und sozialwissenschaftlichen Klasse*, vol. 5] (Stuttgart: Steiner, 1986); and Jochen Schmidt,
*Metamorphosen der Antike in Goethes Werk* [*Schriften der philosophisch-historischen Klasse der
Heidelberger Akademie der Wissenschaften*, vol. 26] (Heidelberg: Winter, 2002).

[117]For further discussion, see E. M. Butler, *The Tyranny of Greece over Germany: A Study of the Influence exercised by Greek Art and Poetry over the Great German Writers of the Eighteenth, Nineteenth and
Twentieth Centuries* (Cambridge: Cambridge University Press, 1935); and Humphry Trevelyan, *Goethe and the Greeks* [1941] (New York: Octagon Books, 1972).

[118]For further discussion, see the articles collected in Ingo Gildenhard and Martin Ruehl, eds.,
*Out of Arcadia: Classics and Politics in Germany in the Age of Burckhardt, Nietzsche and Wilamowitz*
(London: Institute of Classical Studies, 2003).

[119]Benjamin Hederich, *Gründliches Lexikon mythologicum* (1724; revised 1770); Antoine Banier,
*Mythologie et les fables expliquées par l'histoire* (1738-1740).

*Geschichte der Kunst des Altertums* (History of the Art of Antiquity) (1764), by Johann Joachim Winckelmann (1717-1768). From Winckelmann, Goethe took over the emphasis on the Homeric world of the Olympian gods, a mixture of (in Nietzsche's terms) the Apollonian and the Dionysian, "a noble simplicity and a silent grandeur" (*eine edle Einfalt und eine stille Grösse*).

In his study of "Winckelmann and His Age" (1805), Goethe expressed the ideal of human being as embodied in the work of the classicist as follows: "When our nature functions soundly as a whole, when we feel that the world of which we are a part is a huge, beautiful, admirable and worthy whole, when this harmony gives us a pure and uninhibited delight, then the universe, if it were capable of emotion, would rejoice at having reached its goal and admire the crowning glory of its own evolution."[120] In turn, this poses *the* aesthetic question: "What purpose would those countless suns and planets and moons serve, those stars and milky ways, comets and nebulae, those created and evolving worlds"—what purpose would there be at all, "if a happy human being did not ultimately emerge to enjoy existence?"[121] For Goethe, "the ultimate goal of evolving nature is the beautiful human being" (*das letzte Produkt der sich immer steigernden Natur ist der schöne Mensch*),[122] but surely such beauty is only transitory? "At this point," however, "art enters," and—

> —since human beings represent the pinnacle of nature, they see themselves as complete beings, who in turn have to produce a pinnacle. To that end, human beings strive upwards [*steigert sich*], imbuing themselves with all perfection and virtue, calling to their aid their ability to choose, to create order and harmony, to lend significance, until finally they reach the level of the production of art, which occupies a preeminent place next to their other deeds and works. Once produced, the work of art stands before the world in its ideal reality [*in seiner idealen Wirklichkeit*], producing a last effect, indeed the ultimate one: for by means of developing spiritually [*geistig*] from a totality of strengths, it absorbs all that is magnificent, admirable, and agreeable, and elevates, by means of endowing soul to the human figure [*die menschliche Gestalt beseelt*], the human being above himself or herself, rounds off the circle of life

[120]Goethe, *GE* 3, 101 [translation modified]; *Werke* [HA], vol. 12, p. 98.

[121]Goethe, *GE* 3, 101; *Werke* [HA], vol 12, p. 98.

[122]Goethe, *GE* 3, 103; *Werke* [HA], vol. 12, p. 102.

and deeds, and deifies him or her for the present, in which the past and future are contained [*die Gegenwart, in der das Vergangene und Künftige begriffen ist*].[123]

The reference point for Goethe's comments in this passage is the statue, made of gold and ivory for the Temple of Zeus in Olympia, by Phidias, the Athenian sculptor of the fifth century B.C.E.; and such feelings as these, Goethe assures us, seized all those who saw Phidias's statue of the Olympian Zeus: "A god had become a human being in order to make a human being into a god" (*Der Gott war zum Menschen geworden, um den Menschen zum Gott zu erheben*).[124]

This is the world of the ancient Greeks as embodied in the nine-teenth-century museum display in Basel, into which Jung once wandered as a child. "We had to go [...] through the gallery of antiquities," as the account in *Memories, Dreams, Reflections* records this episode, and "sud-denly I was standing before these marvellous figures! Utterly over-whelmed, I opened my eyes wide, for I had never seen anything so beautiful [*etwas derart Schönes*]."[125] Likewise, when he had completed his medical examinations, Jung traveled to Munich, and admired the classical art collections there.[126] Yet, just as that world contained something shock-ing (too shocking, in the eyes of Jung's aunt, for a child to see: "My aunt pulled me by the hand to exit—I trailing always a step behind her—cry-ing out, 'Disgusting boy, shut your eyes; disgusting boy, shut your eyes!' Only then did I see that the figures were naked and wore fig leaves,"[127] and in Munich, Jung would have seen an exhibition in the Neue Pinakothek of the paintings of Franz Stuck, including the famous painting "Sin"[128]), so Goethe, in the wake of his study of Winckelmann, and following the death of Schiller, had begun to become aware of something he found uncomfortable in the world of the ancient Greeks.

Thanks to a meeting with Friedrich Creuzer (see below), Goethe encountered the new vision of the Greeks that was beginning to evolve in

---

[123]Goethe, *GE* 3, 104 [translation modified]; *Werke* [HA], vol. 12, p. 103.

[124]Goethe, *GE* 3, 104 [translation modified]; *Werke* [HA], vol. 12, p. 103.

[125]Jung, *MDR*, 22.

[126]Jung, *MDR*, 132.

[127]Jung, *MDR*, 31.

[128]See Jung, *PU* §9; cf. §196, n. 80. For a discussion of the likely impact of Stuck's work on Jung, see Richard Noll, *The Aryan Christ: The Secret Life of Carl Jung* (New York: Random House, 1997), pp. 44-45.

Romantic circles. In 1810, the same year that saw the publication of the first volume of Creuzer's *Symbolik und Mythologie*, Goethe published his *Farbenlehre* (*Doctrine of Color*). In the introduction to this work, he discussed optics (and the functioning of the eye) in relation to the physical phenomenon of light:

> The eye owes its existence to light. From among the less ancillary organs of the animals, light has called forth one organ to become its like, and thus the eye is formed by light, for light, so that the inner light may emerge to meet the outer light.[129]

At this juncture in his argument, Goethe evokes the pre-Socratic philosopher Empedocles: "Here we are reminded of the ancient Ionian school, which always placed a strong emphasis on the principle that only things of like nature may recognize one another." And he went on to refer to the words of "an old mystic"—in fact, the Neoplatonic philosopher Plotinus[130]—citing the famous lines *neque vero oculus unquam videret solem, nisi factus solaris esset* from the sixth tractate of the first *Ennead*, which he presented in poetic form as follows:

> Were the eye not of the sun,
> How could we behold the light?

[129]Goethe, *GE* 12, 164; *Werke* [HA], vol. 13, p. 323.

[130]In a paralipomenon to *Dichtung und Wahrheit*, Goethe recalled how, in 1764, he became fascinated with Plotinus: "As if by inspiration Plotinus gave me especial pleasure, so that I borrowed his works and spent my days and evenings, much to the displeasure of my room-mate, poring over them. For his part, he kept on telling me that these writings were completely incomprehensible and it was precisely their incomprehensibility that made them so irresistibly attractive to young, impressionable [*schwärmerischen*] people. [...] For a while I was gripped by Plotinus: for this way of thinking was rooted in Christianity (in turn rooted in Judaism), to which I was indebted for the greater part of my education; but the difficulties kept on mounting up, and I lost patience with slogging through obscure passages, secretly admitting that perhaps my friend might have been right after all" (*Werke* [WA], vol. I.27, p. 382). On the encouragement of F. A. Wolf, Goethe returned in 1805 to his interest in Plotinus (see Goethe's letter to F. A. Wolf of 30 August 1805; *Briefe* [HA], vol. 3, p. 14). For further discussion, see P. F. Reiff, "Plotin und die deutsche Romantik," *Euphorion* 19 (1912): 602-612; H. F. Müller, "Goethe und Plotinos," *Germanisch-romanische Monatsschrift* 7 (1915-1919): 45-60; Franz Koch, *Goethe und Plotin* (Leipzig: Weber, 1925); Franz Koch, "Plotins Schönheitsbegriff und Goethes Kunstschaffen," *Euphorion* 26 (1925): 50-74; Grumach, *Goethe und die Antike*, vol. 2, pp. 815-821; Hermann Schmitz, *Goethes Altersdenken im problemgeschichtlichen Zusammenhang* (Bonn: Bouvier, 1959), pp. 50-104; and Volkmar Hansen, "'Gleichsam zum erstenmal im Plato gelesen'—Goethes Platonismus," in *Platonismus im Orient und Okzident: Neuplatonische Denkstrukturen im Judentum, Christentum und Islam*, ed. Raif Georges Khoury, Jens Halfwassen, and Frederik Musall (Heidelberg: Winter, 2005), pp. 233-245. For Jung's interest in Plotinus and the relationship of analytical psychology to Neoplatonism, see Hans-Rudolf Schwyzer, "Archetyp und absoluter Geist: C. G. Jung und Plotin," in *Neue Zürcher Zeitung*, 25-26 July 1975, "Literatur und Kunst," p. 38; and Hazel E. Barnes, "Neo-Platonism and Analytical Psychology," *The Philosophical Review* 54/6 (November 1945): 558-577.

If God's might and ours were not as one,
How could His work enchant our sight?

[*Wär nicht das Auge sonnenhaft,*
*Wie könnten wir das Licht erblicken?*
*Lebt' nicht in uns des Gottes eigne Kraft,*
*Wie könnt' uns Göttliches entzücken?*][131]

Here the word "sunlike" (in German, *sonnenhaft*) renders the Greek word *helioeides*, or "sun-like." That is, there is something divine within each of us; there is something "sunlike" in the individual, there is an internal sun, around which the individual is oriented. As we shall see (in chapter 4), the image of the sun turns out to be central, not just in Jung's paper on "The Stages of Life," but also in the first stanza of Goethe's "Primal Words. Orphic" (and in other late poems).

Now in 1805, after the publication of his study of Winckelmann and following the death of Schiller, Goethe had turned his attention to Plotinus again. He translated maxims from Plotinus's *Enneads*, sending them to his friend, the musician Carl Friedrich Zelter. At the same time, in one of *Maxims and Reflections* from precisely this period, Goethe explicitly mentions the figure of Orpheus in the context of the debate, initiated by Schelling, on the relation between architecture and music:

> One should think of Orpheus who, when he was sent to a large, desolate building space, wisely sat down in the choicest spot and, through the enlivening tones of his lyre, created the spacious market-place around him. The boulders, torn from their massive entirety and quickly seized by the powerfully commanding, amicably enticing notes, had to shape themselves according to the dictates of art and craftmanship, by enthusiastically moving along and obediently organising themselves into rhymic layers and walls.[132]

Here the achievement of Amphion, one of the sons of Zeus and, together with Zethus, the founder of the seven-gated city of Thebes, is applied to Orpheus, to underscore his creative, artistic potential.[133]

---

[131]Goethe, *GE* 12, 164; *Werke* [HA], vol. 13, p. 324.

[132]Goethe, *Maxims and Reflections*, ed. Hecker, #1133; *Werke* [HA], vol. 12, p. 474.

[133]According to the myth, Amphion "walk[ed] around the site of Thebes playing his lyre and charming the stones into a wall" (Simon Hornblower and Antony Spawforth, eds., *The Oxford Classical Dictionary*, 3rd ed. [Oxford and New York: Oxford University Press, 1996], p. 75). See Horace, *Art of Poetry*, ll. 392-395: "While men still roamed the forests, they were restrained from bloodshed and a bestial way of life by Orpheus, the sacred prophet and interpreter of the divine will—that is why

During his second Rhine journey in 1815, Goethe met Creuzer in person in Heidelberg, and had "a long and interesting discussion" with him about "the symbolic interpretation and deep meaning of the persons and legends of Greek mythology," and about how—in Creuzer's view—every Greek figure had a double significance, its "mere reality" hiding a "higher symbol."[134] In his autobiography, Creuzer himself records having a conversation with Goethe in 1815 about an essay he had published, in which he touched on an esoteric reading of Pythagoras and the Orphics, as well as discussing at length a marble relief, displayed in the Louvre and allegedly depicting a scene from a Dionysian cult, showing old Silenus and a younger faun bringing fruit as an offering to a goddess.[135] This conversation could, according to Creuzer, "assist in understanding a poem better" (*kann zum näheren Verständnis eines Gedichtes dienen*)—the poem in question, of course, being "Gingo Biloba," a text in the *West-Eastern Divan* (*West-Östlicher Divan*) (1819) about the oriental tree with a characteristic dual leaf structure, which concludes with the lines: "Because I am One and Double" (*Weil ich eins und doppelt bin*).[136] (Goethe is one and double, because he is Goethe, while speaking, in the *West-Eastern Divan*, in the voice of Hafiz. Yet applying Creuzer's own principle to Goethe's state-

---

he is said to have tamed tigers and savage lions. Amphion, too, the founder of Thebes, is credited with having moved stones by the strains of his lyre, and led them where he would with this sweet blandishment" (Aristotle/Horace/Longinus, *Classical Literary Criticism*, trans. T. S. Dorsch [Harmondsworth: Penguin, 1965], p. 92).

[134]See the account given by Gustav F. K. Parthey (1798-1872), based on Creuzer's recollections (Biedermann, *Goethes Gespräche*, vol. 2, pp. 355-356).

[135]Friedrich Creuzer, *Aus dem Leben eines alten Professors* [*Deutsche Schriften: neue und verbesserte*, part 5, vol. 1] (Leipzig and Darmstadt: Leske, 1848), p. 110; see "Idee und Probe alter Symbolik," in Carl Daub and Friedrich Creuzer, eds., *Studien*, 6 vols. (Frankfurt and Heidelberg: Mohr und Zimmer, 1805-1811), vol. 2 (1806), pp. 224-324. For further discussion, see Hiebel, *Goethe: Die Erhöhung des Menschen*, p. 208; Ernst Beutler, "Die Boisserée-Gespräche von 1815 und die Entstehung des Gingo-Biloba-Gedichtes," in *Essays um Goethe: Erweiterte Frankfurter Ausgabe*, ed. Christian Beutler (Frankfurt am Main and Leipzig: Insel, 1995), pp. 389-422; and Barbara Becker-Cantarino, "Mythos und Symbolik bei Karoline von Günderrode und Friedrich Creuzer," in *200 Jahre Heidelberger Romantik*, ed. Friedrich Strack (Berlin: Springer, 2008), pp. 281-298.

[136]Johann Wolfgang von Goethe, *Poems of the West and East: West-Eastern Divan—West-Östlicher Divan: Bi-Lingual Edition of the Complete Poems*, trans. John Whaley (Berne, Berlin, Frankfurt am Main: Lang, 1998), pp. 260-261. For further discussion, see the commentary in Johann Wolfgang Goethe, *Gedichte*, ed. Bernd Witte (Stuttgart: Reclam, 2001), pp. 915-919. By contrast, Goethe's letter to Rosine Städel of 27 September 1815 suggests another biographical context: his erotic attachment to Marianne von Willemer; see Goethe, *Briefe* [HA], vol. 3, pp. 321-322. For further discussion, see Detlef Kremer, "Ein allegorisches Lesezeichen des *West-östlichen Divan*," in *Interpretationen: Gedichte von Johann Wolfgang Goethe*, ed. Bernd Witte (Stuttgart: Reclam, 1998), pp. 217-230. Truly, the "secret meaning" (*geheimen Sinn*) of which the third line of the poem speaks can be interpreted in many different ways!

ment, it alludes to a bigger question: Is reality simply reality? Or does it have another double—symbolic, or archetypal—meaning?) And so, as Hiebel puts it, into the "garden" of Greek humanism, built on the foundations of Winckelmann's classicism, there now came, via recent research into myth and oriental mystery cults, a "taste" for the "secret" meaning of ancient Greece, for its night-side, for its "Orphic, Dionysian darknesses" (*die Orphischen dionysische Finsternisse*), as Goethe called them in a letter to Carl Ludwig von Knebel (1744-1834) (see below).[137] This development on Goethe's part towards a more complex understanding of ancient Greece took yet another step forward in 1817, when Creuzer sent Goethe a copy of his recently published correspondence with Gottfried Hermann about Hesiod and Homer.

## CREUZER AND HERMANN, ZOEGA AND WELCKER

"As an ethical-aesthetic mathematician," Goethe wrote of himself in 1826, "I must in my late years still work towards final, ultimate formulae, by means of which alone the world is still comprehensible and bearable for me."[138] One such formula took the form of the five stanzas of the poem "Primal Words. Orphic," which Goethe wrote at the age of sixty-eight on 7 and 8 October 1817.[139] Their composition was preceded by a couple of weeks' intensive reflection on Orphic themes, for which the immediate occasion had been the copy, sent to Goethe in mid-September by Creuzer, of the debate in the form of his correspondence with Hermann (who, as we have seen, had edited the *Orphica*, a collection of fragmentary texts containing all that remained in written form of the Orphic religion).

Goethe's first encounter with the *Orphica* had probably taken place about half a century earlier, when Johann Gottfried Herder's *Versuch einer Geschichte der lyrischen Dichtkunst* (Attempt at a History of Lyric Poetry) (1766) drew Goethe's attention to Georg Christoph Hamberger's edition (1764), extensively annotated by Andreas Christian Eschenbach and Johann Matthias Gesner.[140] Thanks also to Herder, Goethe would have been aware of Eschenbach's study, *Epigenes de poesi orphica* (1702)

---

[137]Hiebel, *Goethe: Die Erhöhung des Menschen*, p. 209.

[138]Letter to Sulpiz Boisserée of 3 November 1826; Goethe, *Briefe* [HA], vol. 4, p. 208.

[139]On the genesis of "Primal Words. Orphic," see Karl Borinski, "Goethes 'Urworte. Orphisch,'" *Philologus* 69 (1910): 1-9; and Theo Buck, *Goethes "Urworte. Orphisch" interpretiert und mit einer Dokumentation versehen* (Frankfurt am Main, Berlin, Berne: Peter Lang, 1996), pp. 21-29.

[140]See Ralph Häfner's entry on "Orphik" in *Goethe Handbuch in vier Bänden*, ed. Bernd Witte et al., 4 vols. in 5 (Stuttgart: Metzler, 1996-1998), vol. 4/2, *Personen – Sachen – Begriffe L-Z*, pp. 821-822. See also Franz Dornseiff and Friedrich John, "Goethe und Orpheus," *Forschungen und*

and Thomas Blackwell's *Letters concerning Mythology* (1771), which had also been translated into French. But if from no other source, Goethe would have been able to read about the Orphics in the popular encyclopedic compendium known as the *Kleiner Brucker*, which contained an article on the Orphic hymns.[141] Looking back in *Dichtung und Wahrheit*, Goethe suggested that his belief that poetry, religion, and philosophy are essentially the same thing had been nourished by his reading of the Bible (the Book of Job, the Song of Solomon, and the Book of Proverbs), as well as the Orphic Hymns and the Hymns of Hesiod. Goethe's friendship with the theologian Georg Christoph Tobler (1757-1812), who translated the *Argonautica* of Apollonius and the Orphic Hymns in 1784, constituted another encounter with Orphic literature which, it has been argued, influenced the hymnic, not to say oracular, style and quasi-mystical content of a text from this time, "On Nature," later attributed by Goethe to Tobler.[142] Certainly, the parallels between this text and the Orphic hymn "To Nature" were convincing enough for Ernst Robert Curtius,[143] and both this text and Hermetic thought, such as the *Asclepius*, inform the portrayal of the *Erdgeist* (Earth Spirit) in *Faust*, Part One.[144] But it was the

---

*Fortschritte* 26 (1950): 178-181. Häfner speaks of three phases in Goethe's reception of Orphic literature, but it might be more accurate to say that Goethe's awareness of the existence of Orphic texts reflected his general (high) level of education, before he took a particular interest in them in 1817.

[141] See Goethe, *Dichtung und Wahrheit*, Part Two, Book 6, in *GE* 4, 172; *Werke* [HA], vol. 9, p. 221. Johannes Jakob Brucker's *Institutiones historiae philosophiae, usui academicae iuventutis adornatae* [Introduction to the History of Philosophy for the Use of Young Academics] (1747; Goethe owned the 1756 edition, originally in his father's library) was a one-volume abbreviation of the much larger *Historia critica philosophiae a mundi incunabulis* [Critical History of Philosophy from the Beginning of the World] (1742-1744; 1766-1767); see Trunz's notes in *Werke* [HA], vol. 6, p. 678.

[142] See Franz Schulz, "Der pseudogoethische Hymnus an die Natur," in Herbert Cysarz et al., *Internationale Forschungen zur deutschen Literaturgeschichte: Julius Petersen zum 60. Geburtstag dargebracht* (Leipzig: Quelle & Meyer, 1938), pp. 79-100; and Franz Dornseiff, "Die antike Quelle von Goethe-Tobler's Aufsatz 'Die Natur,'" *Die Antike* 15 (1939): 274-276. Dornseiff highlights notable similarities between the tenth Orphic Hymn, addressed to *physis*, with the text of "On Nature." According to Humphry Trevelyan, Goethe's interest in the Orphic hymns, translated in 1765 by Johann Matthias Gesner, may have been mediated by Johann Gottfried Herder (*Goethe and the Greeks*, pp. 63-64), and Mark O. Kistler has suggested that this interest in Orphism was shared by Shaftesbury ("The Sources of the Goethe-Tobler Fragment 'Die Natur,'" *Monatshefte* 46 (1954): 383-389). For Freud's interest in this text, see Imre Hermann, "Goethes Aufsatz *Die Natur* und Freuds weitere philosophisch-psychologische Lektüre aus den Jahren 1880-1900," *Jahrbuch der Psychoanalyse* 7 (1974): 77-100; and for its further impact, see Henry F. Fullenwider, "The Goethean Fragment 'Die Natur' in English Translation," *Comparative Literature Studies* 23 (1986): 170-177.

[143] Ernst Robert Curtius, *European Literature and the Latin Middle Ages* [1948], trans. Willard R. Trask (London and Henley: Routledge & Kegan Paul, 1953), p. 107.

[144] See Frederick Amrine, "The Unconscious of Nature: Analyzing Disenchantment in *Faust I*," *Goethe Yearbook* 17 (2010): 117-132 (pp. 127-128).

controversy between Hermann and Creuzer in the second decade of the nineteenth century that sparked Goethe's real interest.

Hermann's and Creuzer's co-authored book, *Briefe über Homer und Hesiodus vorzüglich über die Theogonie* (Letters on Homer and Hesiod, Especially on His "Theogony") (1818), was concerned with the relation of the Orphic religion to mythology. At the core of their dispute lay the so-called "Homeric Hymns"—a collection of texts, traditionally attributed to Homer or to Hesiod, and dedicated (like the Orphic hymns) to a variety of deities, although (unlike the Orphic hymns) it is doubtful whether their function was devotional or liturgical. The question was: Were these texts evidence of a later, mystical tradition or of an ancient, primordial religion that predated even Homer?[145] In turn, this question raised another: Was the ancient world a source of rational order and beauty, or should it be understood irrationally—theologically, even mystically?

In his letter to Creuzer of 1 October 1817, Goethe thanked him for, as he wrote, "having forced me to look down into a region, against which I otherwise tend nervously to be on my guard."[146] In these words, one critic has written, there lies real fear;[147] for another commentator, the source of this fear is nothing less than the irrational itself.[148] Later in this letter to Creuzer, Goethe tried to contain (or to relativize) this fear; to shed some light, as it were, on the Orphic darkness. "We other, latter-day poets must revere our ancestors'—Homer's, Hesiod's, etc.—legacy as the original canonical texts," he wrote, and whilst he was prepared to assume the existence of "an old popular faith," its value lay for today lay in "pure, characteristic personification, without ambush or allegory"; for, he continued, "what later the priests brought out of the darkness, and the philosophers into the light, we may ignore"—such, at any rate, was his "creed."[149] And yet: Goethe's interest in the Orphics had been stirred. Within a week or

---

[145]Dietze, "Urworte, nicht sonderlich orphisch," p. 24.

[146]Goethe, *Briefe* [HA], vol. 3, p. 401; *"Sie haben mich genötigt in eine Region hineinzuschauen, vor der ich mich sonst ängstlich zu hüten pflege."*

[147]Werner Kraft, "Urworte. Orphisch," in *Goethe: Wiederholte Spiegelungen aus fünf Jahrzehnten* (Munich: edition text + kritik, 1986), pp. 193-292, p. 194.

[148]Buck, *Goethe's "Urworte. Orphisch,"* p. 28. For further discussion of Goethe's attitude towards the rational and the irrational, see Eugen Wolf, "Irrationales und Rationales in Goethes Lebensgefühl," *Deutsche Vierteljahresschrift für Literaturwissenschaft und Geistegeschichte* 4 (1926): 491-507.

[149]Goethe, *Briefe* [HA], vol. 3, p. 402; *"Wir andern Nachpoeten müssen unserer Altvordern, Homers, Hesiods uam., Verlassenschaft als urkanonische Bücher verehren. […] Einen alten Volksglauben*

so, he was reading Welcker's edition of Zoega's treatises (the entry in Goethe's diary for 7 October 1817 records this fact, noting Zoega's interest in "Orphic concepts.")[150]

According to Zoega (who cited the authority of Necepsos, the ancient Egyptian king who invented astrology, and Ambrosius Theodosius Macrobius [395-423 B.C.E.], a Neoplatonic philosopher), in the Orphic tradition four "holy words" depicted the four deities that attend the birth of the individual: Δαιμων (*daimon*), Τυχη (*tyche*), Ερως (*eros*), and Αναγκη (*ananke*). To these, Zoega noted, there should be added a fifth word, a fifth deity—Ελπις (*elpis*).[151] This information had a direct impact on Goethe and on the composition of "Primal Words. Orphic,"[152] and so we reproduce the relevant passage from Macrobius here:

> The Egyptians also maintain that the attributes of the caduceus illustrate the generation, or "genesis" as it is called, of mankind; for they say that four deities are present to preside over a man's birth: his Genius [*daimon*], Fortune [*tyche*], Love [*eros*], and Necessity [*ananke*]. By the first two they understand the sun and the moon; for the sun, as the source of the breath of life and of heat and of light, is the creator and the guardian of a man's life and is therefore believed to be the Genius, or god [*daimon*], of a newborn child; the moon is Fortune [*tyche*], since she has charge of the body, and the body is at the mercy of the fickleness of change; the kiss of the serpents is the symbol of Love [*eros*]; and the knot is the symbol of Necessity [*ananke*].[153]

Arguably, however, the impact on Goethe of Hermann's and Creuzer's debate over Hesiod and Homer was even greater.

---

*setzen wir gern voraus, doch ist uns die reine charakteristische Personifikation ohne Hinterhalt und Allegorie alles wert; was nachher die Priester aus dem Dunklen, die Philosophen ins Helle getan, dürfen wir nicht beachten. So lautet unser Glaubensbekenntnis."*

[150]Goethe, *Werke* [WA], vol. III.6, p. 119; *"Orphische Begriffe."*

[151]Georg Zoega, "ΑΓΑΘΗΙ ΤΥΧΗΙ: Tyche und Nemesis," in *Abhandlungen*, pp. 32-55 (pp. 34-40, 46, and 52); see Macrobius, *Saturnalia*, book 1, chapter 19, §§16-18; cited in Borinski, "Goethes 'Urworte. Orphisch,'" pp. 2 and 7.

[152]Pierre Hadot describes Macrobius's *Saturnalia*, mediated by Zoega, as nothing less than "the source of Goethe's poem" (*N'oublie pas de vivre: Goethe et la tradition des exercices spirituels* [Paris: Albin Michel, 2008], p. 174).

[153]Macrobius, *Saturnalia*, book 1, chapter 19, §§17-18; in Macrobius, *The Saturnalia*, trans. Percival Vaughan Davies (New York and London: Columbia University Press, 1969), pp. 135-136. This passage is cited in Welcker's edition of Zoega's *Abhandlungen*, "ΑΓΑΘΗΙ ΤΥΧΗΙ: Tyche und Nemesis," pp. 39-40.

In the wake of his reading of their correspondence, Goethe drew up a schematic historical outline, under the title "Epochs of the Spirit" (*Geistes-Epochen*). This short text, published in *Über Kunst und Alterthum* (vol. 1, no. 3) in 1817, divides intellectual history into six epochs: the Primordial Age (*Urzeit*), the Age of Poetry, the Age of Theology, the Age of Philosophy, the Age of Prose, and finally—and pessimistically—the Age of Dissolution.[154] In the words of the German literary critic Werner Danckert (1900-1970), "Epochs of the Spirit" elaborates "an outline of the fate of culture, it traces the biomorphic curve of cultural organisms in their most general, typical characteristics."[155] And according to the historian Friedrich Meinecke (1862-1954) in The Rise of Historicism (*Die Entstehung des Historismus*) (1936), this "grandiose sketch" shows "how every stage of development brings forth elements that, in turn, seek to overcome it";[156] while, long before Meinecke, Bachofen had argued in the introduction to *Mother Right* (*Das Mutterrecht: Eine Untersuchung über die Gynaikokratie in der alten Welt*) (1861), that "the earliest phenomena in the lives of peoples tend to reappear at the end of their development," so that "the cycle of life returns to its beginning."[157]

What was Goethe really thinking? We might reconstruct his thoughts as follows. Everywhere he looked—in nature, in history, in everyday life—he saw change. "Everything is metamorphosis in life, in plants and

[154] Goethe, *Werke* [HA], vol. 12, pp. 298-300. For further discussion of this text, see Arnold Bergstraesser, "Die Epochen der Geistesgechichte in Goethes Denken," *Monatshefte für deutschen Unterricht, deutsche Sprache und Literatur* 40 (1948): 127-136. The historical pessimism informing this periodization is reflected in his conversation of 29 January 1826, in which he shared with Eckermann this secret: "All eras in a state of decline and dissolution are subjective; on the other hand, all progressive eras have an objective tendency. Our present time is retrograde, for it is subjective: we see this not merely in poetry, but also in painting, and much besides" (*Conversations of Goethe*, p. 126). This aspect of Goethe's *Weltbild* is discussed by Werner Deubel in "Goethe als Begründer eines neuen Weltbildes: Eine Skizze" [1931], in *Im Kampf um die Seele: Wider den Geist der Zeit: Essays und Aufsätze, Aphorismen und Gedichte*, ed. Felicitas Deubel (Bonn: Bouvier, 1997), pp. 118-162 (pp. 133-137).

[155] Werner Danckert, *Goethe: Der mythische Urgrund seiner Weltschau* (Berlin: Walter de Gruyter, 1951), p. 192; cf. pp. 584-585, nn. 57 and 59.

[156] Friedrich Meinecke, *Die Entstehung des Historismus*, 2 vols. (Munich and Berlin: Oldenbourg, 1936), vol. 2, pp. 603-604.

[157] "Introduction" [to *Mother Right*], in Bachofen, *Myth, Religion, and Mother Right*, pp. 69-120 (p. 103); "Vorrede zum Mutterrecht," in *Der Mythus von Orient und Occident*, pp. 1-59 (pp. 41-42); "[d]aß die frühesten Zustände der Völker am Schlusse ihrer Entwicklung wiederum nach der Oberfläche drängen. Der Kreislauf des Lebens führt das Ende von neuem in den Anfang zurück." Bachofen's historiographical principles are set out in more detail in "Die Grundgesetze der Völkerentwicklung und der Historiographie," in *Gesammelte Werke*, ed. Karl Meuli, 10 vols. (Basel: Schwabe, 1943-1967), vol. 6, pp. 409-441.

animals, up to human beings, and in them, too," he declared in conversation with Sulpiz Boisserée on 3 August 1815.[158] Goethe's view of historical metamorphosis returned to the level of the individual, and coincided with his intense interest in the Orphic tradition, reflected in the poem "Primal Words. Orphic"; his diary entry for 8 October 1817 records that Goethe had "written out five stanzas."[159] And in a letter to Knebel on 9 October 1817, Goethe wrote that, "via Hermann, Creuzer, Zoega, and Welcker,"[160] he had become "caught up in Greek mythology, in fact, in the Orphic dark realms [*Orphische Finsternisse*]."[161] From receiving Creuzer's letter to writing "Primal Words. Orphic" had thus been a matter of no more than two weeks or so.[162] Yet into these stanzas Goethe packed his entire outlook about the forces of change (or metamorphosis) in human lives and about the (self) realization of the individual's *entelechy*.[163]

For Goethe, there was an important issue at stake in the debate between Hermann and Creuzer. In the view of one commentator, the cult of Orpheus—as the most ancient Greek religion on record, with its roots in pre-classical times—represented a potential threat to "the light and clarity of [Goethe's] preferred image of Homeric Greece, because of its association with more ancient Egyptian and Indian cults."[164] For Goethe, Greek mythology revealed "what was paradigmatically human,"[165] and what worried Goethe about Orphism, we have already surmised, was what it revealed about the potentially overwhelming power of the irrational.[166] As Goethe once remarked about primordial phenomena, the

---

[158]Biedermann, *Goethes Gespräche*, vol. 2, p. 314.

[159]Goethe, *Werke* [WA], vol. III.6, p. 119; *"Fünf Stanzen in's Reine geschrieben."*

[160]Or, in other words, the historians who inaugurate the tradition of Schelling's treatise *On the Deities of Samothrace* [*Über die Gottheiten von Samothrake*] [1815], Bachofen's *Mother Right*, Nietzsche's *The Birth of Tragedy*, Erwin Rohde's *Psyche: The Cult of Souls and the Belief in Immortality among the Greeks* [*Psyche: Seelencult und Unsterblichkeitsglaube der Griechen*] [1890-1894], and Jacob Burckhardt's posthumously published *The Greeks and Greek Civilization* [*Griechische Kulturgeschichte*] [1898-1902] (Hoffmeister, "Goethes 'Urworte. Orphisch,'" p. 173; cf. Hans Pyritz, *Goethe-Studien*, ed. Ilse Pyritz [Cologne and Graz: Böhlau, 1962], p. 220; cited in Dietze, "Urworte, nicht sonderlich orphisch," p. 31, n. 42).

[161]Goethe, *Werke* [WA], vol. IV.28, p. 272.

[162]Buck, *Goethe's "Urworte. Orphisch,"* p. 25.

[163]Hiebel, *Goethe: Die Erhöhung des Menschen*, p. 36.

[164]M[ichael] R. Minden, "'Urworte. Orphisch,'" *German Life and Letters* 36 (1982/1983): 77-86 (p. 77).

[165]Jochen Schmidt, *Goethes Altersgedicht "Urworte. Orphisch": Grenzerfahrung und Entgrenzung* (Heidelberg: Winter, 2006), p. 10.

[166]Buck, *Goethes "Urworte. Orphisch,"* p. 28; cf. Werner Kraft, "Urworte. Orphisch," p. 194.

*Urphänomene*, when they "stand unveiled before our senses we become nervous, even anxious. Sensuous individuals seek salvation in astonishment, but soon that busy matchmaker, the understanding, arrives with her efforts to marry the highest to the lowest."[167] Not surprisingly, perhaps, Goethe was not overly impressed with what the editors of the *Weimarer Ausgabe* call Creuzer's "symbolic-allegorical-mystical" approach to myth—which he dismissed in a note as "Creuzers's overinterpretation" (*Creuzers Überdeuteley*)—inclining instead toward Hermann's more "poetic-personificatory" approach.[168]

Does, then, "Primal Words. Orphic" represent Goethe's abandonment of the classical-Enlightenment-rational version of the ancient Greek ideal? Does Goethe, in this work, distance himself from classicism and embrace Romanticism? Does the poem even reveal Goethe to be an Orphic mystic? To make such claims would be to exaggerate—and to miss the point. A few months after completing "Primal Words. Orphic," in an important letter written to Sulpiz Boisserée on 16 January 1818, Goethe was to lament how, in his view, the approach to antiquity pioneered by Winckelmann had been abandoned. This abandonment was, he believed, a matter for great regret, because "Winckelmann's path to reach the artistic concept" had been "entirely the right one."[169] Instead, he went on to complain, "contemplation turned into interpretation, and eventually lost itself in misinterpretation; whoever did not know how to look properly, began to delude himself, and so one became lost in the distances of Egypt and India, when one had the best right at hand in front of one"—in other words, in classical Greece.[170] Already Zoega, he continued, "began to wobble," and from that point on, "one had to suffer the unholy Dionysian mysteries"; until, in turn, Creuzer, and then Welcker, "deprive us daily more and more of the great advantages of the delightful multiplicity of the Greeks and the dignified unity of the Israelites."[171] (It

---

[167]Goethe, *Maxims and Reflections*, ed. Hecker, #412; *GE* 12, 303 [translation modified]; "*Vor den Urphänomenen, wenn sie unseren Sinnen enthüllt erscheinen, fühlen wir eine Art von Scheu, bis zur Angst. Die sinnlichen Menschen retten sich ins Erstaunen; geschwind aber kommt der tätige Kuppler Verstand und will auf seine Weise das Edelste mit dem Gemeinsten vermitteln.*"

[168]Goethe, *Werke* [WA], vol. I.53, p. 428; cf. *Werke* [WA], vol. I.53, p. 429.

[169]Goethe, *Briefe* [HA], vol. 3, p. 413; "*Winckelmanns Weg, zum Kunstbegriff zu gelangen, war durchaus der rechte.*"

[170]Goethe, *Briefe* [HA], vol. 3, p. 413; "*sehr bald aber zog sich die Betrachtung in Deutung über und verlor sich zuletzt in Deuteleien; wer nicht zu schauen wußte fing an zu wähnen und so verlor man sich in ägyptische und indische Fernen, da man das Beste im Vordergrunde ganz nahe hatte.*"

[171]Goethe, *Briefe* [HA], vol. 3, p. 413; "*Zoega fing schon an zu schwanken* [...] *und man hatte nun*

was, surely, such comments as these that prompted Nietzsche once to remark that "Goethe did not understand the Greeks."[172]) By contrast, Hermann in Leipzig was, he maintained, "our real champion" (*unser eigenster Vorfechter*), praising in particular the fifth letter in his exchange with Creuzer, and Hermann's treatise *De mythologia Graecorum antiquissima* (On the Mythology of Ancient Greece) (1817).[173] In a sense, Goethe was uninterested in who—Creuzer or Hermann—was, historically speaking, right about Orphism. What mattered, rather, was which interpretation—Creuzer's theological, or Hermann's rationalistic approach—was, as he put it, "critically-Hellenically patriotic," and it turned out to be Hermann's, because "from his development and from his hypothesis there is so infinitely more to be learnt than I have rarely found in so few pages to be the case."[174] Goethe once expressed this skepticism about the fruitfulness of historico-philological investigation in a short satirical poem in book 6 of his *Gentle Epigrams* (*Zahme Xenien*):

> Those historical symbols—
> Only a fool would think they matter,
> Searching amid the emptiness,
> And missing the world out there.
>
> [*Die geschichtlichen Symbole—*
> *Thörig, wer sie wichtig hält,*
> *Immer forschet er in's Hohle*
> *Und versäumt die reiche Welt.*][175]

And in another epigram—entitled, in one manuscript, "To the Symbolist" (*Dem Symboliker*) and included, in another, among three poems written as a poetic commentary on a symbolic representation, based on a sketch by the Danish sculptor Bertel Thorvaldsen (1770-1844), of Apollo

---

*immerfort an den unseligen dionysischen Mysterien zu leiden. Creuzer [...] und nun auch Welcker entziehen uns täglich mehr die großen Vorteile der griechischen lieblichen Mannigfaltigkeit und der würdigen israelitischen Einheit."*

[172]Friedrich Nietzsche, *Twilight of the Idols*, "What I Owe to the Ancients," §4; *Twilight of the Idols; The Anti-Christ*, trans. R. J. Hollingdale (Harmondsworth: Penguin, 1968), p. 109.

[173]Hermann and Creuzer, *Briefe über Homer und Hesiodus*, Letter 5, pp. 56-87; Gottfried Hermann, *Dissertatio de mythologia Graecorum antiquissima* (Leipzig: Staritz, 1817).

[174]Goethe, *Briefe* [HA], vol. 3, p. 413; *"denn mir ist es ganz einerlei, ob die Hypothese philologisch-kritisch haltbar sei, genug, sie ist kritisch-hellenisch patriotisch und aus seiner Entwickelung und an derselben ist so unendlich viel zu lernen als mir nicht leicht in so wenigen Blättern zu Nutzen gekommen ist."*

[175]Goethe, *Werke* [WA], vol. I.3, p. 354; cited in Hoffmeister, "Goethes 'Urworte. Orphisch': Eine Interpretation," p. 175.

unveiling a bust of Isis or Artemis as a personification of Nature—Goethe
took a thinly disguised shot at Creuzer himself:

> Don't look for hidden cults!
> Beneath the veil, leave what stands!
> If you want to live, o fool,
> Look behind you, in the open.
>
> [*Suche nicht verborgne Weihe!*
> *Unterm Schleier laß das Starre!*
> *Willst du leben, guter Narre,*
> *Sieh nur hinter dich in's Freie.*][176]

So the real question was: Whose version of antiquity, Creuzer's or Hermann's,
promoted the aesthetic ideal that Goethe believed to be the true one? His
rejection of Creuzer can make Goethe sound all very Apollonian.

And yet there is another side to Goethe's interest, too. For Goethe, it
is true, realized that one had to abandon the rationalist, Enlightenment
version of the ancient Greeks, as formulated by Winckelmann, which had
downplayed and neglected the role of the mystery cults. But he refused
simply to adopt from Creuzer, and from like-minded Romantics, an
interpretation of those mystery cults which made them central to their
understanding of the ancient world. No, one can read the situation as follows: Goethe decided to go his own way, developing, in the quarter of a
century or so following his study of Winckelmann and the death of
Schiller, his own individual path of Orphic mysticism.[177] There is no
doubt he rejected the abstraction and, worse, the intellectual obscuran-
tism of Creuzer and the Romantics, and "Primal Words. Orphic" can be
read as representing, albeit in an understated way, an anti-Romantic
polemic.[178] That polemical intent emerges more clearly in another short
poem, directed against Creuzer and against the arts editor of the
*Stuttgarter Morgenblatt*, Ludwig Schorn:

---

[176]Goethe, *Werke* [WA], vol. I.3, p. 354; cf. *Werke* [WA], vol. I.4, p. 137. For further discussion
of these two texts with particular reference to their historical background and the iconographical context, see Peter M. Daly, "'Genius, die Büste der Natur enthüllend'—Emblem, Occasional Poetry and
Philosophical Statement in the Poetry of the Older Goethe," *Seminar: A Journal of Germanic Studies*
20/1 (February 1984): 27-52 (esp. 38-44); and Pierre Hadot, *The Veil of Isis: An Essay on the History of
the Idea of Nature*, trans. Michael Chase (Cambridge, MA; London: Belknap Press, 2006), pp.
247-252.

[177]Hiebel, *Goethe: Die Erhöhung des Menschen*, p. 214.

[178]For further discussion of the anti-Romantic aspect to "Primal Words. Orphic," and in Goethe's work in general, see Schmidt, *Goethes Altersgedicht "Urworte. Orphisch,"* pp. 11, 13, 15 and 29.

I'm tired of all the contradiction,
The seemingly endless argumentation.
In the end, I *have* to quit the battle,
So improve your temper, now I'm gone!
The dream of life, just let me dream it,
Just not with Creuzer, nor with Schorn!

[*Müde bin ich des Widersprechens,*
*Des ew'gen Lanzenbrechens,*
*Muß doch das Feld am Ende räumen.*
*Nur besänft'ge deinen Zorn!—*
*Laß mich den Traum des Lebens träumen,*
*Nur nicht mit Creuzer und Schorn!*][179]

And in the Cabiri scene of *Faust,* Part Two, Goethe would satirize Creuzer's *Symbolik und Mythologie,* as well as Schelling's treatise *On the Deities of Samothrace* (*Über die Gottheiten von Samothrake*) (1815),[180] in the lines spoken by Homunculus.[181]

Although, in his view, another researcher in this area, the poet, playwright, and architect of German classicism Christoph Martin Wieland (1733-1813), had been right to flee "those dark secrets" of the ancient mystery cults, he also believed Wieland had been equally right to recognize that "precisely under these, perhaps rather strange, covers, higher concepts had been introduced for the first time to crude, sensuous human beings, and, by means of *intuitive symbols,* powerful, illuminating ideas had been awoken."[182] As we have already noted (see chapter 2), Goethe, like Jung, attached great significance to the symbol as a vehicle of knowledge. And the writings of Hermann, Creuzer, and Welcker had, as he put it to Johann Heinrich Meyer on 28 October 1817, "made him think" about ancient art and mythology.[183]

---

[179]Goethe, *Werke* [WA], vol. I.5, p. 186. The art historian Ludwig Schorn (1793-1842) was the editor of the "Kunstblatt," originally published as a supplement to the "Morgenblatt," published in Stuttgart.

[180]See F. W. J. von Schelling, *Treatise on "The Deities of Samothrace,"* ed. and trans. Robert F. Brown (Missoula, MT: Scholars Press for the American Academy of Religion, 1976). For discussion of the significance of this text, see Edward Allen Beach, *The Potencies of God(s): Schelling's Philosophy of Mythology* (Albany, NY: State University of New York Press, 1994), pp. 36-37.

[181]See *Faust,* Part Two, ll. 8219-8222; Johann Wolfgang von Goethe, *Faust: Part Two,* trans. David Luke (Oxford and New York: Oxford University Press, 1994), p. 115.

[182]Goethe, *Werke* [WA], vol. I.36, p. 344; "Zu brüderlichem Andenken Wielands" (1813), Goethe's commemorative speech on Wieland, was delivered to members of the Anna Amalia Masonic Lodge on 18 February 1813.

[183]Goethe, *Werke* [WA], vol. IV.28, p. 291; "*Schriften von Hermann, Creuzer, Welcker haben*

In his study of the history of Nature—her allegorical personification as Isis or Artemis, and the notion of "unveiling" or discovering her "secrets"—the French intellectual historian Pierre Hadot (1922-2010) sets up a distinction between a "Promethean" attitude to Nature and an "Orphic" attitude,[184] the former characterized by a violent, intrusive, and aggressive approach, and by "audacity, boundless curiosity, the will to power, and the search for utility;"[185] the latter, in contrast, by a more thoughtful, respectful, even seductive approach.[186] If Prometheus represents the methods of science and technology, Orpheus represents the methods of aesthetic contemplation;[187] methods, moreover, that Hadot finds are preeminent in Goethe's scientific studies.[188] That what, at first sight, appears in Goethe to be mystical might, in fact, be aesthetic, is something that Carl Gustav Carus (1789-1869)—a writer familiar to Jung— seems to have understood. In his *Neun Briefe über Landschaftsmalerei* (Nine Letters on Landscape Painting) (1831), he wrote (with reference to Goethe's poem "In Honor of Howard" [*Zu Howards Ehrengedächtnis*]): "Art appears as the very peak of science, it becomes—as it clearly perceives and gracefully veils the secrets of science—in the true sense *mystical* or, as Goethe also called it: *orphic.*"[189] In this precise sense, then, Goethe is indeed an Orphic writer.

Like Jung, who saw in mythology a repository of timeless, archetypal motifs, Goethe believed that mythology offers an "inexhaustible treasury of divine and human symbols."[190] Now, one such human-divine symbol is precisely the symbol of Orpheus, and in the Classical Walpurgisnacht

---

*mich über alte Kunst und Mythologie denken machen.*" A few years later, in a letter to J. H. Meyer of 25 August 1819, Goethe would be much less appreciative about Creuzer and his "dark-poetic-philosoph-ical-holier-than-thou blind alley" (*den dunkel-poetisch-philosophisch-pfäffischen Irrgang*) (Goethe, *Briefe* [HA], vol. 3, p. 462).

[184]Hadot, *The Veil of Isis*, pp. 95-96.

[185]*Ibid.*, pp. 101-151; p. 96.

[186]*Ibid.*, pp. 155-210.

[187]*Ibid.*, p. 211.

[188]See chapter 18, entitled "Aesthetic Perception and the Genesis of Forms," and chapter 20, en-titled "Isis Has No Veils," in Hadot, *The Veil of Isis*, pp. 211-229 and 247-261. In Nietzsche, Hadot finds a similar (implied) contrast between the Promethean and the Orphic in *The Gay Science*, Preface to the Second Edition, §4; and *The Birth of Tragedy*, §15 (*The Veil of Isis*, p. 292).

[189]C. G. Carus, *Neun Briefe über Landschaftsmalerei* (Villingen/Schwarzwald: Reichelt, [n.d.]), p. 52.

[190]Goethe, *Dichtung und Wahrheit*, Part Three, book 15; *GE* 4, 470; *Werke* [HA], vol. 10, p. 49; "*einen unerschöpflichen Reichum göttlicher und menschlicher Symbole.*"

scene of *Faust II*, Goethe sought to reinvest this symbol with fresh significance.[191] In his search for the beauty of classical Greece—represented in
personified form by Helena—Faust is brought by Chiron the centaur to
Manto, an aged prophetess and the daughter of Tiresias (in Goethe's text,
she is the daughter of Asclepius, the god of healing).[192] According to Virgil, the Sibyl of Cumae had guided Aeneas on his visit to the underworld
(*Aeneid*, book 6), and Goethe here transfers this story to the legend of
Orpheus: Manto will thus send Faust where Orpheus once went before.
Whereas Chiron regards Faust's quest for classical beauty as insane—"My
dear sir, as a man you are entranced; / As spirits, we should call it an
advanced / State of derangement"[193]—Manto, by contrast, sees in Faust
someone who "desires the impossible":

> On the impossible he sets his heart;
> Such men I love. So enter with good cheer,
> Rash wooer! Down through this dark passage here,
> In Olympus' deep core, Persephone
> Waits for forbidden greetings secretly.
> I smuggled Orpheus in once this way too;
> Use your chance better. Come now, down with you!
>
> [*Den lieb' ich, der Unmögliches begehrt.*
> *Tritt ein, Verwegner, sollst dich freuen!*
> *Der dunkle Gang führt zu Persephoneien.*
> *In des Olympus hohlem Fuß*
> *Lauscht sie geheim verbotnem Gruß.*
> *Hier hab' ich einst den Orpheus eingeschwärzt;*
> *Benutz es besser! frisch! beherzt!*][194]

What is "impossible" to be desired is art, which conjures up timeless, primordial beauty in a material appearance. For art, as Karl Justus Obenauer
put it, "completes in appearance what nature is incapable of doing: it
makes the human being divine in the present, in which the past and the
future are likewise embraced."[195]

---

[191] Hiebel, *Goethe: Die Erhöhung des Menschen*, pp. 212-213; Strauss, *Descent and Return*, p. 25.

[192] Chiron belongs to the legend of Orpheus for, thanks to Chiron, Jason learned that only with
the help of Orpheus would he and his companions be able to pass by the Sirens, and so Orpheus joined
the expedition of the Argonauts.

[193] *Faust II*, ll. 7446-7447; Goethe, *Faust: Part Two*, trans. Luke, p. 92; "*Mein fremder Mann! als
Mensch bist du entzückt; / Doch unter Geistern scheinst du wohl verrückt.*"

[194] *Faust II*, ll. 7488-7494; Goethe, *Faust: Part Two*, trans. Luke, p. 93.

[195] Karl Justus Obenauer, *Der faustische Mensch: Vierzehn Studien zum zweiten Teil von Goethes
"Faust"* (Jena: Diederichs, 1922), p. 106.

To help attain this "impossible desire," Manto sends Faust on his journey to the Underworld, his initiation into the mysteries of Persephone, his descent to the Mothers. Faust must confront his Orphic moment; he must become the new Orpheus![196] And as the new Orpheus, he will learn from the mistakes of the previous Orpheus. On that occasion, Persephone had agreed to release Eurydice from Hades, on the condition that Orpheus not look back at Eurydice as she followed him. But Orpheus did look—and so he lost her. As the "second Orpheus,"[197] Faust must do better; he must achieve the sacred union, and not succumb to the tragedy of separation and death.[198]

## FAUST AS ORPHEUS

When Eckermann, in his conversation with Goethe on 10 January 1830, asked about the meaning of the Mothers scene, the sage of Weimar (as T. S. Eliot called him) famously "wrapped himself up in mystery," looking at Eckermann "with wide-open eyes" and repeating the words: "'The Mothers! Mothers! Nay, it sounds so strange.'"[199] If, in this conversation, Goethe's references to Plutarch help locate the historical source of these maternal figures,[200] it is only close attention to the actual text of *Faust* that can help elucidate their real meaning.[201]

---

[196]On one occasion Goethe, who tended toward a skeptical attitude towards musical setting of his texts, applied to Faust's monologues (such as the one that opens the first "Study" scene) in *Faust*, Part One, the following words of Coleridge: "An orphic tale indeed, / A tale divine of high and passionate thoughts, / To their own music chaunted" (account by Friedrich Förster of meetings with Goethe in 1821; Biedermann, *Goethes Gespräche*, vol. 2, p. 517); cf. Samuel Taylor Coleridge, *Biographia Literaria, or Biographical Sketches of My Literary Life and Opinions* [1817], ed. George Watson (London: Dent; New York: Dutton, 1965), chapter 13, p. 165; citing "To William Wordsworth" [1807], ll. 45-47, in *The Portable Coleridge*, ed. I. A. Richards (New York: Penguin, 1978), p. 191.

[197]See *Faust*-Paralipomenon 123C; Johann Wolfgang Goethe, *Faust: Texte*, ed. Albrecht Schöne (Frankfurt am Main: Deutscher Klassiker Verlag, 2005) = *Werke* [Frankfurter Ausgabe], vol. 7/1, p. 643. See also Johann Wolfgang Goethe, *Faust: Kommentare*, ed. Albrecht Schöne (Frankfurt am Main: Deutscher Klassiker Verlag, 2005) = *Werke* [Frankfurter Ausgabe], vol. 7/2, p. 527.

[198]Hiebel, *Goethe: Die Erhöhung des Menschen*, p. 213. For further discussion, see Obenauer, *Der faustische Mensch*, pp. 104-106.

[199]Eckermann, *Conversations of Goethe*, p. 342.

[200]*Ibid.* See Plutarch, "Life of Marcellus," §20 (Plutarch, *Lives*, trans. Bernadotte Perrin, 11 vols. [London: Heinemann; New York: Putnam, 1914-1926], vol. 5, p. 489); but compare also Plutarch, "The Obsolescence of Oracles," §22 (Plutarch, *Moralia*, trans. Frank Cole Babbitt, 14 vols. [London: Heinemann; Cambridge, MA: Harvard University Press, 1927-1976], vol. 5, pp. 415-417).

[201]Another possible source of the Faustian Mothers is the German Hermetic tradition. In cabbalistic thought, three letters of the alphabet are known as "mothers" and identified with the elements of fire, water, and earth (cf. Agrippa, *Magische Werke*, vol. 1, p. 343); while in his *Von der Menschwerdung* [1620] (part 2, chapter 2, §4), Jacob Böhme speaks of God, as the original creator,

Within the overall architecture of Goethe's text, this scene refers back
to and develops earlier expressions of the theme of creation and destruction in *Faust*, Part One. In the opening "Night" scene, Faust turns to his
mystical books, and conjures up the Earth Spirit (*Erdgeist*), who describes
himself to the presumptuous scholar as follows:

> In tides of living, in doing's storm,
> Up, down, I wave,
> Waft to and fro,
> Birth and grave,
> An endless flow,
> A changeful plaiting,
> Fiery begetting.
> Thus at Time's scurrying loom I weave and warp
> And broider at the Godhead's living garb.

> [*In Lebensfluten, im Tatensturm*
> *Wall' ich auf und ab,*
> *Webe hin und her!*
> *Geburt und Grab,*
> *Ein ewiges Meer,*
> *Ein wechselnd Weben,*
> *Ein glühend Leben*
> *So schaff' ich am sausenden Webstuhl der Zeit*
> *Und wirke der Gottheit lebendiges Kleid.*][202]

For his part, Faust repeatedly tells us—in those monologues Jung apparently found so tedious[203]—how he is prepared to embrace both creation
and destruction, joy and terror, pleasure and pain.[204] After he has signed
the pact with Mephistopheles, he sets out his ambitions more precisely.[205]

---

bearing within him seven mothers, out of which the *prima materia* arises (cf. Friedrich Christoph
Oetinger, *Swedenborgs irdische und himmlische Philosophie* [1858], p. 12; cited in Goethe,
*Faust-Dichtungen*, ed. Ulrich Gaier, 3 vols. [Stuttgart: Reclam, 1999], vol. 2, *Kommentar* I, p. 640).

[202] *Faust I*, ll. 501-509; Johann Wolfgang von Goethe, *Faust: A Tragedy*, trans. Walter Arndt, ed.
Cyrus Hamlin (New York and London: Norton, 1976), pp. 16-17. For Goethe's use of motifs belonging
to the Orphic conception of nature and to such Hermetic texts as the *Asclepius* (especially §34, "If you
consider the whole, you will learn that the sensible world itself and all it contains are in truth covered over
by that higher world as if by a garment"; Brian P. Copenhaver, ed., *Hermetica: The Greek "Corpus
Hermeticum" and the Latin "Asclepius" in a New English Translation with Notes and Introduction* [Cam-
bridge: Cambridge University Press, 1992], pp. 88-89), see Amrine, "The Unconscious of Nature," pp.
127-128).

[203] See Jung, *MDR*, 78.

[204] *Faust I*, ll. 464-467; Goethe, *Faust*, trans. Arndt, pp. 14-15.

[205] *Faust I*, ll. 1766-1775; Goethe, *Faust*, trans. Arndt, p. 47.

This creative drive to experience the universal will involve, tragically, the destruction of the particular, symbolized by Gretchen, whose demise— because of (the consequences of) his own actions—Faust prophetically foretells in the scene "Forest and Cave" (*Wald und Höhle*).[206] How the destruction of Gretchen, awaiting execution for matricide and infanticide at the end of Part One—an event as terrible in human terms as the murder, towards the end of Part Two, of Philemon and Baucis—fits in with Lynceus's view of the-world-as-beauty (and in what sense Gretchen, who appears in the final scene of Part Two as a penitent,[207] is, in the words of the Voice from Above, "saved" or "redeemed" [*gerettet*]),[208] are the kinds of questions that must have worried Jung and made him think that Goethe had "rendered evil innocuous."[209]

In the palace of the Holy Roman Emperor where Faust and Mephistopheles turn up in Act 1 of Part Two, Faust is placed in charge of the imperial entertainments. At the command of the emperor, who maintains an astrologer at his court, Faust must conjure up the spirits of Helen of Troy and Paris, the cultural ideal of the female and the male (ll. 6183-6186), and Faust turns for help to Mephisto, taking him into a dark gallery to speak with him. Here, Mephisto tells Faust about the Mothers;[210] and about the path to the Mothers, that is no path;[211] and about the sheer nothingness that surrounds them.[212] In turn, Faust responds to what he learns from Mephisto with terror and amazement;[213] then with skepticism;[214] and finally with enthusiasm.[215] It would be too simplistic to say that Mephisto sends Faust to the Mothers; rather, he is reluctant, yet excited to see whether Faust will make it there—and back again. Mephisto provides the means of access to the realm of the Mothers: he gives Faust a small key, which glows and expands in his hand, that will enable him to enter this mysterious realm, and Faust, stamping his feet, disappears from sight.

[206] *Faust I*, ll. 3348-3360; Goethe, *Faust*, trans. Arndt, p. 93.

[207] See *Faust II*, stage direction before l. 12068; Goethe, *Faust*, trans. Arndt, p. 343.

[208] *Faust I*, l. 4611; Goethe, *Faust*, trans. Arndt, p. 133.

[209] Jung, *MDR*, 79.

[210] *Faust II*, ll. 6212-6216; Goethe, *Faust*, trans. Arndt, pp. 176-177.

[211] *Faust II*, ll. 6222-6224; Goethe, *Faust*, trans. Arndt, p. 177.

[212] *Faust II*, ll. 6225-6227 and 6246-6248; Goethe, *Faust*, trans. Arndt, p. 177.

[213] *Faust II*, l. 6127; Goethe, *Faust*, trans. Arndt, p. 177.

[214] *Faust II*, ll. 6228-6232; Goethe, *Faust*, trans. Arndt, p. 177.

[215] *Faust II*, ll. 6255-6256; Goethe, *Faust*, trans. Arndt, pp. 177-178.

There is much to be said about this scene, both about its deliberate, even parodic, mystification, as well as its influence—as much stylistic as anything else—on Jung's thinking about the pleroma in his *Septem Sermones ad Mortuos*, a work whose context is provided by *The Red Book*.[216] In a sense, the Mothers Scene functions as a key to understanding the concept of the collective unconscious, as Jung himself suggested in his letter to Freud of 23 June 1911, in which he comments that "unconscious fantasy is an amazing witches' kitchen" (*die unbewußte Phantasie ist eine unglaubliche Hexenküche*), citing the following lines from *Faust*, Part Two—

> Formation, transformation,
> The eternal mind's eternal recreation.
> Enswathed in likenesses of manifold entity;
> They see you not, for only wraiths they see.

> [*Gestaltung, Umgestaltung,*
> *Des ewigen Sinnes ewige Unterhaltung,*
> *Umschwebt von Bildern aller Kreatur,*
> *Sie sehn dich nicht, denn Schemen sehn sie nur.*][217]

In his letter, Jung comments that "this is the matrix of the mind, as the little great-grandfather correctly saw" (*hier ist die Gebärmutter des Geistes, wie der Herr Urgroßvater richtig erkannt hat*),[218] and in the work that is regarded as marking his break with Freud, *Transformations and Symbols of the Libido* (1911-1912), Jung makes constant—one might almost say, insistent—references to *Faust*. These references structure his argument, so that it is no exaggeration to say, as John Kerr has done, that "the central motif" of this work is "clearly Faustian."[219]

At the same time, however, the satirical flavor of the text resists any such interpretation, because of the extremity of Mephisto's high-flown,

---

[216] For further discussion, see Christine Maillard, *Les Sept Sermons aux Morts de Carl Gustav Jung* (Nancy: Presses universitaires de Nancy, 1993).

[217] *Faust II*, ll. 6287-6290; Goethe, *Faust*, trans. Arndt, p. 178.

[218] Sigmund Freud and C. G. Jung, *The Freud-Jung Letters: The Correspondence between Sigmund Freud and C. G. Jung*, ed. William McGuire, trans. Ralph Manheim and R. F. C. Hull (Cambridge, MA: Harvard University Press, 1988), p. 341. For further discussion of the significance of this scene for Jung, see Paul Bishop, *Analytical Psychology and German Classical Aesthetics*, vol. 1, *The Development of the Personality* (London and New York: Routledge, 2007), pp. 63-70.

[219] John Kerr, *A Most Dangerous Method: The Story of Jung, Freud, and Sabina Spielrein* (London: Sinclair-Stevenson, 1994), p. 326. For further discussion, see Bishop, *Analytical Psychology and German Classical Aesthetics*, vol. 1, *The Development of the Personality*, pp. 58-62.

pompous rhetoric. (In the following scene set in the "Great Hall," in which the spirits of Paris and Helena appear, Faust's own portentous-ness and pathos, contrasting with the gossip and the back-chat of the ladies of the court, has a similar function, making it impossible to take the action at face value,[220] yet many commentators—Jung and Rudolf Steiner included—seem to overlook the irony and satire, even the comedy-within-tragedy at work in Goethe's text, particularly in this scene.)

Yet surely the main point is that Goethe never actually depicts the Mothers—we only hear about them from Mephisto; indeed, they are essentially *beyond depiction*, which may or may not cast a doubt over the seriousness with which the scene is to be treated. So perhaps Jung was right: the location of the Mothers is not a place, since it is beyond space and time, but *a state of mind*—and it is the affective quality of the vast, aching emptiness and nothingness of the realm of the Mothers that Mephisto chooses to emphasize. Even if Faust were to be abandoned at sea, there would still, even in such utter isolation and desolation, be more than in the Mothers' realm, for—"There you see Nothing—vacant gaping farness" (*Nichts wirst du sehn in ewig leerer Ferne*).[221] Thus the realm of the Mothers is best understood as a psychological concept,[222] or even a theological one, like the "divine desolation" of which the German mystic Johannes Tauler (ca. 1300-1361) speaks in his sermon on the hidden nature of God:

> Then Man can see the quality of divine isolation in silent emptiness, in which no word in the essence is ever spoken in an essential way, nor is any work ever done. For there everything is so silent, so secret, and so empty.[223]

Nevertheless: within the narrative of the drama, Helena is conjured up,

---

[220]Curiously, both Jung and Rudolf Steiner do precisely this, seemingly unalert to the parodic complexity of Goethe's text, which he himself referred to (in his letter to Wilhelm von Humboldt of 17 March 1832) as "these very serious jokes" [*diese sehr ernsten Scherze*] (Goethe, *Briefe* [HA], vol. 4, p. 481).

[221]*Faust II*, ll. 6239-6246 (l. 6246); Goethe, *Faust*, trans. Arndt, p. 177.

[222]For Jung, this is what he means by "introversion"; see Bishop, *Analytical Psychology and German Classical Aesthetics*, vol. 1, pp. 66-67.

[223]Sermon 83 ("Audi, Israel"), in Johannes Tauler, *Die Predigten Taulers: Aus der Engelberger und der Freiburger Handschrift sowie aus Schmidts Abschriften der ehemaligen Straßburger Handschriften*, ed. Ferdinand Vetter (Berlin: Weidmann, 1910; reprinted Dublin and Zurich: Weidmann, 1968), p. 277; "*Denne mag der mensche an sehen die eigenschaft der goetlichen wuestenunge in der stillen einsamkeit, do nie wort in dem wesende nach weselicher wise inne gesprochen enwart noch werk gewürkt enwart; denne do ist es so stille, so heimelich und so wuest.*"

albeit only temporarily, for Faust, mistaking representation for reality (cf. ll. 6553-6554), intervenes in "the ghostly masque" (*das Fratzengeisterspiel*), and literally explodes the magical tableau. The structural significance of the entire sequence of scenes resides in the fact that it is repeated in Act 2, when Faust goes in quest of Helena—for a second time.

Within the symbolic economy of *Faust*, the figure of Helena represents what, in his essay on Winckelmann, Goethe called "the ultimate product of constantly self-intensifying nature" (*das letzte Produkt der sich immer steigernden Natur*).[224] That is to say, Helena represents the goal of creation, the work of the gods: the beautiful human being, complete in herself.[225] For Plotinus, the beauty of Helena was nothing less than the beauty of art itself. "Whence shone forth the beauty of Helena, battle-sought?" Plotinus asked in his *Enneads*, and he answered: "In all [cases of beauty] is it not the Idea, something of that realm but communicated to the produced from within the producer, just as in works of art [...] it is communicated from the arts to their creations?"[226] The "beautiful appearance" (*schöner Schein*) of art enables us, in the words of K. J. Obenauer, to forget the "abysses of the two worlds" of heaven and earth (that is, the ideal and the real). For the work of art is, at one and the same time, natural and supernatural, for "where material [*Stoff*], content [*Gehalt*], and form [*Form*] attain ideal reality, the primordial opposites of time and eternity, material and spirit, are overcome."[227]

Thus Faust's desire is nothing less than to realize the beauty of ancient Greece: "And shall I not, by passion's power, draw / Back into life that unique form I saw?" (*Und sollt' ich nicht, sehnsüchtigster Gewalt, / Ins Leben ziehn die einzigste Gestalt?*), he rhetorically asks in front of Chiron:

> Eternal, godlike being, tender as she
> Is noble, lovely in her sublimity!
> You saw her once—I have seen her *today*;
> She charms my eyes, she charms my heart away,
> She rules me now, my fixed, my guiding star:
> I cannot live till I find Helena!

---

[224]Goethe, "Winckelmann and His Age"; Goethe, *GE* 3, 103 [translation modified]; *Werke* [HA], vol. 12, p. 102.

[225]Obenauer, *Der faustische Mensch*, p. 105.

[226]*Enneads*, 5.8 [2]; in Plotinus, *The Enneads*, trans. Stephen MacKenna, abridged John Dillon (Harmondsworth: Penguin, 1991), p. 412.

[227]Obenauer, *Der faustische Mensch*, p. 106.

[*Das ewige Wesen, Göttern ebenbürtig,*
*So groß als zart, so hehr als liebenswürdig?*
*Du sahst sie einst;* **heut** *hab' ich sie gesehn,*
*So schön wie reizend, wie ersehnt so schön.*
*Nun ist mein Sinn, mein Wesen streng umfangen;*
*Ich lebe nicht, kann ich sie nicht erlangen.*][228]

Similarly, Goethe opts not to descend into the "Orphic darknesses," but
instead to elevate them into the sunlit fields of Arcadia.[229] This realization
of Faust's desire will lead him, in Act 3, to marriage with Helena, and to
her conception of their son, Euphorion—only for Euphorion to die, and
Helena to disappear again; and, in Act 5, to his union with the Eternal
Feminine, for just as Faust "draws into life" (*ins Leben zieht*), so the Eternal Feminine, in the final line of the poetic drama, "draws us on high"
(*zieht uns hinan*).[230] Far from being a descent to the depths (and Goethe
never actually wrote the scene where Faust encounters Persephone),[231]
Goethe's Orphic path leads instead up to the very heights of Apollonian
clarity.[232] This path takes the form of a spiral: a typically Goethean structure. For Goethe regarded the spiral as the archetypal pattern of all human
development, as "the circle," along which "all humankind must move," as he
wrote in his "Introduction" to his *History of the Doctrine of Color* (1810):

> Nothing stands still. In the case of all apparent steps backward
> humankind and science are still moving forward [...]. [...]
> The circle in which humankind has to run is sufficiently pre-
> cise, and despite the great standstill to which barbarism
> brought us, we have already run through it more than once. If
> one wishes to attribute a spiral movement to it, it still returns
> to the point through which it has already moved. In this way
> are repeated all true opinions and all errors.[233]

---

[228] *Faust II*, ll. 7438-7439 and 7440-7445; Goethe, *Faust: Part Two*, trans. Luke, pp. 91 and 91-92.

[229] Hiebel, *Goethe: Die Erhöhung des Menschen*, p. 213.

[230] *Faust II*, l. 12111; Goethe, *Faust: Part Two*, trans. Luke, p. 239.

[231] See Goethe, *Faust: Kommentare*, ed. Schöne, p. 527; see also Goethe's conversation with
Eckermann of 15 January 1827 (Eckermann, *Conversations of Goethe*, p. 149).

[232] Hiebel, *Goethe: Die Erhöhung des Menschen*, p. 214.

[233] Goethe, *Werke* [HA], vol. 14, p. 7; "*Nichts ist stillstehend. Bei allen scheinbaren Rückschritten
müssen Menschheit und Wissenschaft immer vorschreiten [...]. [...] Der Kreis, den die Menschheit
auszulaufen hat, ist bestimmt genug, und ungeachtet des großen Stillstandes, den die Barbarei machte, hat
sie ihre Laufbahn schon mehr als einmal zurückgelegt. Will man ihr auch eine Spiralbewegung zuschreiben,
so kehrt sie doch immer wieder in jene Gegend, wo sie schon einmal durchgegangen. Auf diesem Wege
wiederholen sich alle wahren Ansichten und alle Irrtümer.*"

Moreover, as at least two commentators have pointed out,[234] the developmental logic of "Primal Words. Orphic" exhibits a spiral structure. Just as Goethe's Orphic insight returns him to that fundamental conviction he expressed in his study of Winckelmann—"the beautiful individual as the greatest achievement of the cosmos, and the work of art as something that elevates [...] the human being above himself or herself, rounds off the circle of life and deeds, and deifies him or her for the present, in which the past and future are contained"[235]—so we find the image of a circle closing in upon itself in the final stanza of Goethe's poem "Permanence in Change" (*Dauer im Wechsel*) (1803), which anticipates, as we shall see, the conclusion of "Primal Words. Orphic":

> Let the start and end so fusing
> Join in One and unify!
>     [...]
> Thank the Muses for bestowing
> Favour of a lasting kind:
> Import from your heart outflowing
> And the form within your mind.

> [*Laß den Anfang mit dem Ende*
> *Sich in **eins** zusammenziehn!*
>     [...]
> *Danke, daß die Gunst der Musen*
> *Unvergängliches verheißt,*
> *Den Gehalt in deinem Busen*
> *Und die Form in deinem Geist.*][236]

In its essence, Goethe's Orphic doctrine is an aesthetic doctrine; concomitantly, the Orphic moment is precisely the moment in our lives when our need of art is greatest.

---

[234]Robert Petsch, "'Urworte. Orphisch,'" *Germanisch-Romanische Monatsschrift* 21 (1933): 32-45; Dietze, "Urworte, nicht sonderlich orphisch," p. 18, n. 16. For further discussion of the spiral structure of "Primal Words. Orphic" from *daimon* to *elpis*, see Hiebel, *Goethe: Die Erhöhung des Menschen*, pp. 36-40.

[235]Goethe, *GE* 3, 104 [translation modified]; *Werke* [HA], vol. 12, p. 103.

[236]Goethe, *Selected Poems*, trans. John Whaley (London: Dent, 1998), p. 87; *Werke* [HA], vol. 1, p. 248. For a commentary on this text, see William Stephan Davis, "Subjectivity and Exteriority in Goethe's 'Dauer im Wechsel,'" *The German Quarterly* 66 (1993): 452-466.

## ORPHISM, AND PRIMAL WORDS

For all his skepticism about the historical Orphic religion itself, Goethe found himself nothing less than inspired by its hymnic tradition and by its *hieroi logoi*, its four "holy words," which Hermann had discussed at some length in his correspondence with Creuzer, and to which Zoega had argued that a fifth should be added. The fruit of this inspiration is the poem "Primal Words. Orphic."

In the Orphic hymnary, as it has come down to us, Goethe would have found hymns dedicated "To the Daimon" (*daimon*), "To Fortune" (*tyche*), and "To Love" (*eros*),[237] while from the Orphic-Macrobian tradition, as he had found it in Zoega, Goethe took over directly the five "holy words" that stand as the titles for the five stanzas of his poem: ΔΑΙΜΩΝ, *Dämon* ("Daimon"); ΤΥΧΗ, *das Zufällige* ("Chance"); ΕΡΩΣ, *Eros* ("Love"); ΑΝΑΓΚΗ, *Notwendigkeit* ("Necessity"); ΕΛΠΙΣ, *Hoffnung* ("Hope"). Originally, when "Primal Words. Orphic" was first published in *Zur Morphologie* (On Morphology) in 1817,[238] the headings of the stanzas were in Greek alone. But when the text was republished in *Über Kunst und Alterthum* in 1820,[239] Goethe added the transliterations, and provided a commentary.[240] This commentary, helpful as it is (and, in the case of Goethe's work, rare[241]), does not "explain" the poems, or obviate the need for further interpretation. In his conversation with the historian Heinrich Luden on 19 August 1806, Goethe commented that "the poet should not be his own interpreter and dissect his poetry into everyday prose, for that way he would cease to be a poet. The poet sends his creation out into the world; it is the business of the reader, the aesthetician, the critic, to investigate what he intended with his creation."[242] (It has

---

[237] *The Mystical Hymns of Orpheus*, trans. Taylor, nos. 73, 72, and 58 (pp. 141, 139-140, and 117-120).

[238] See *Zur Morphologie* 1/2 (1820): 97-99.

[239] See *Über Kunst und Alterthum* 2/3 (1820): 66-78.

[240] In a handwritten version provided for the Grand Duchess Maria Paulowna, Goethe provided a slightly varying set of transliterations; see Hans Gerhard Gräf, "Zu dem Gedicht: Urworte. Orphisch," *Jahrbuch der Goethe-Gesellschaft* 2 (1915): 241-243; and Dietze, "Urworte, nicht sonderlich orphisch," pp. 15-16.

[241] For another example, see Goethe's commentary on "A Winter Journey in the Harz" [*Harzreise im Winter*] [1777] (Goethe, *GE* 1, 66-71), written during his visit to the Harz mountains in December 1777 (*Werke* [HA], vol. 1, pp. 392-400).

[242] Biedermann, *Goethes Gespräche*, vol. 1, p. 427; "*Der Dichter soll doch nicht sein eigener Erklärer sein und seine Dichtung in alltägliche Prosa fein zerlegen; damit würde er aufhören, Dichter zu sein. Der Dichter stellt seine Schöpfung in die Welt hinaus; es ist Sache des Lesers, des Ästhetikers, des Kritikers, zu*

even been suggested that, with his commentary on "Primal Words. Orphic," Goethe has, mischievously, concealed more than he has revealed.[243]) In a sense, a text such as "Primal Words. Orphic" poses a challenge to poet and reader alike: for, as Goethe suggested to Sulpiz Boisserée, "the admirer, connoisseur, interpreter has a completely free hand in discovering the symbols"—those symbols, that is, "which the artist, *consciously or unconsciously*, has embedded in his work."[244]

In his commentary, Goethe tells us that his poem tried "to compress, to present in a poetic-and-compendium-like, laconic manner" what had been "handed down from old and new Orphic doctrines."[245] It offers, then, a kind of quintessence of Orphism, new *and* old—an exercise, in other words, in cultural memory,[246] but one with existential implications. As far from being an academic exercise in historical philology as it is from being "a masterpiece of Orphic poetry," arising out an unconscious experience of illumination,[247] the poem is intended to be an exposition of living wisdom—"primordial, magic utterances on the fate of humans,"[248] a "primordial, concentrated depiction of human fate."[249] In it Goethe had sought, he told Boisserée, to "re-quintessentialize" a "diffuse antiquity"

---

*untersuchen, was er mit seiner Schöpfung gewollt hat.*" (Further on in this conversation Goethe is recorded as enunciating the following hermeneutic principle: "In poetry there are no contradictions. These can only be found in the real world, not in the world of poetry. What the poet creates must be accepted, as he has created it. Just as he made his world, so it is. What the poetic mind [*Gemüt*] produces must be received by a poetic mind. Cold analysis destroys poetry and does not produce any reality. There only remain shattered pieces, which are of no use and get in the way" [*Goethes Gespräche*, vol. 1, p. 430]).

[243]Hoffmeister, "Goethes 'Urworte-Orphisch,'" p. 179.

[244]Letter to Sulpiz Boisserée, 16 July 1818 [my emphasis]; *Briefe* [HA], vol. 3, p. 435; "*Dagegen hat der Liebhaber, Kenner, Ausleger völlig freie Hand die Symbole zu entdecken, die der Künstler bewußt oder unbewußt in seine Werke niedergelegt hat.*"

[245]Goethe, *Werke* [HA], vol. 1, p. 403; "*Was nun von älteren und neueren Orphischen Lehren überliefert worden, hat man hier zuammenzudrängen, poetisch-compendios, lakonisch vorzutragen gesucht.*"

[246]Schmidt, *Goethes Altersgedicht "Urworte. Orphisch,"* p. 27; cf. Jan Assmann, *Das Kulturelle Gedächtnis: Schrift, Erinnerung und Politische Identität in frühen Hochkulturen* (Munich: C. H. Beck, 1992). In turn, Assmann draws on the notion of a collective memory, proposed by the French philosopher and sociologist Maurice Halbwachs (1877-1945) in his *La Mémoire collective* (Paris: Presses universitaires de France, 1950).

[247]Thus the claim in Charles du Bos, *Der Weg zu Goethe*, trans. Conrad Fischer (Olten: Walter, 1949), pp. 33 and 42-43; cited in Dietze, "Urworte, nicht sonderlich orphisch," p. 14.

[248]Letter to Sulpiz Boisserée of 21 May 1818; *Werke* [WA], vol. IV.29, p. 180; "*uralte Wundersprüche über Menschen-Schicksale.*"

[249]Letter to C. G. D. Nees von Esenbeck of 25 May 1818; *Werke* [WA], vol. IV. 29, p. 185; "*dieser uralten concentrirten Darstellung menschlichen Geschickes.*"

and turn it into a "cup that refreshes the heart," to "freshen up" these "moribund ways of speaking" with his own "living experience."[250] His own "Orphica,"[251] as he called the poem, represents the sum of experience of an older man, whose mature age determines the perspectival point from which it was written.[252] (Max Kommerell is probably right when he suggests the poem's title was chosen "with an undertone of gentle irony."[253]) This emphasis on experience—on experience gained through life—is central to Goethe's intentions; rather than with the Orphic mysteries of ancient time, his concern is with the "mysteries and wonders" among which, he told Eckermann on 7 October 1827, we are all groping: "We all walk in mysteries. We do not know what is stirring in the atmosphere that surrounds us, nor how it is connected with our own spirit."[254] Rather than offering an initiation into the Orphic ancient mysteries, his poem uncovers the mysteriousness of life itself. This desire to reinterpret and, in this precise sense, to reawaken the mysteries of Orpheus, has continued to occupy poets and writers, among them Stéphane Mallarmé (1842-1898) and Rainer Maria Rilke (1875-1926), and constitutes the continuing appeal of Orphism in modern literature and thought.[255]

So much for the "Orphic" part of the title. What about its other part? Words.

Primal Words.

Primordial Words. *Ur-Worte.*

---

[250]Letter to Sulpiz Boisserée of 16 July 1818; *Briefe* [HA], vol. 3, p. 435; "*wenn man das diffuse Altertum wieder wieder quintessenzirt, so gibt es alsobald einen herzerquickenden Becher, und wenn man die abgestorbenen Redensarten aus eigener Erfahrungs-Lebendigkeit wieder anfrischt.*"

[251]Letter to Boisserée, ibid.; "*Orphika.*"

[252]Schmidt, *Goethes Altersgedicht "Urworte. Orphisch,"* p. 28.

[253]Max Kommerell, *Gedanken über Gedichte* [1943] (Frankfurt am Main: Klostermann, 1985), p. 200; "*vielleicht ist die Bezeichnung mit einem Unterton leiser Ironie gewählt.*"

[254]Eckermann, *Conversations of Goethe*, pp. 234, 233; "*wir tappen alle in Geheimnissen und Wundern* [...] *Wir wandeln alle in Geheimnissen. Wir sind von einer Atmosphäre umgeben, von der wir noch gar nicht wissen, was sich alles in ihr regt und wie es mit unserm Geiste in Verbindung steht.*"

[255]For a study of the continuing influence of Orphic ideas in modern literature and thought, see Elizabeth Sewell, *The Orphic Voice: Poetry and Natural History* (London: Routledge and Kegan Paul, 1961); Strauss, *Descent and Return* (for discussions of Gérard de Nerval, Mallarmé, and Rilke); and Robert McGahey, *The Orphic Moment: Shaman to Poet-Thinker in Plato, Nietzsche, and Mallarmé* (Albany, NY: State University of New York Press, 1994). Most recently, Terence Dawson has discerned in modern and postmodern literature and culture the existence of an "Orphic complex"; see Terence Dawson, "The Orpheus Complex," *Journal of Analytical Psychology* 45 (2000): 245-266; and "*Sliding Doors*, Orpheus, and the Spanish Inquisition," *Harvest: International Journal for Jungian Studies* 49/1 (2003): 40-57.

What *is* a "primal," or a "primordial," word? In one commentator's view, a possible response to this part of the title is "to imagine a mysterious time and place at which the utterance of words is a revelation of truth rather than a mere naming, and thus to experience a thrill of anticipation at what is to come: five oracular utterances, revealing aspects of how things are, from the depths of ancient wisdom."[256] And one German critic has responded in precisely this way, writing that "what alone matters is humankind's very own knowledge about itself, that flashes like a bolt of lightning and lights up the landscape of human life *sub specie aeternitatis*, brings it into the perspective of eternity."[257] Yet Goethe's real intention is, perhaps, less grand—and at the same time far more moving.

That some of humanity's most ancient words often have two antithetical meanings was noted by Freud in "The Antithetical Meaning of Primal Words" (*Über den Gegensinn der Urworte*) (1910).[258] In this paper, Freud took a statement in *The Interpretation of Dreams* (*Die Traumdeutung*) as his starting point for his discussion of the work of the philologist Carl Abel (1837-1906), who had shown that, in ancient Egyptian, certain words had two opposite meanings.[259] Freud concluded his paper by drawing an important link between historical linguistics and psychoanalysis, suggesting that "we psychiatrists cannot escape the suspicion that we should be better at understanding and translating the language of dreams if we knew more about the development of language."[260] (One such word, the term *pharmakon*, meaning both "poison" and "cure," is an example of an *Urwort* that has been discussed at length by Jacques Derrida [1930-2004] in his essay on Plato's *Phaedrus*.[261]) And in *Transformations and Symbols of the Libido*, Jung at one point uses the notion of *Urworte*, referring to the account of the development of lan-

---

[256]Minden, "'Urworte. Orphisch,'" p. 78.

[257]Gerhart Schmidt, "Goethes 'Urworte. Orphisch,'" *Zeitschrift für philosophische Forschung* 11 (1957): 37-53 (p. 38).

[258]Freud, *SE* 11, 153-161; *FGW* 8, 214-221. For further discussion, see Paul Gordon, "Freud's 'On the Antithetical Sense of Primary Words': Psychoanalysis, Arts, and the Antithetical Senses," *Style* 24/2 (Summer 1990): 167-186.

[259]Freud, *SE* 4, 318; *FGW*, 2/3, 323.

[260]Freud, *SE* 11, p.161; *FGW* 8, 331; "*als unabweisbare Vermutung drängt sich uns Psychiatern auf, daß wir die Sprache des Traumes besser verstehen und leichter übersetzen würden, wenn wir von der Entwicklung der Sprache mehr wüßten.*"

[261]Jacques Derrida, "La pharmacie de Platon" [1968], in *La Dissémination* (Paris: Editions du Seuil, 1972), pp. 69-198; "Plato's Pharmacy," in *Dissemination*, trans. Barbara Johnson (Chicago: University of Chicago Press, 1981), pp. 61-84.

guage by Wilhelm Wundt (1832-1920) in his *Grundriß der Psychologie* (Outline of Psychology) (1896, ⁵1902).²⁶²

It is true that, taken together, Goethe's Orphic words are indeed *antithetical* in nature, opposing chance and necessity, or individuality and collectivity. As we shall see (in chapter 4), the first stanza (*daimon*) concerns itself with the inner law that provides the individual with impetus, while the second (*chance*) and fourth (*necessity*) speak of the outside forces that engage, influence, and restrict, restrain, or retard us; stanzas three (*eros*) and five (*elpis*) speak of the forces that open up, liberate, and propel us forward again.²⁶³ Yet the *Ur*-element of the text is much closer to the sense in which Jung understands the primordial—that is, not so much in a chronological, as in a qualitative sense of the most intense, the most authentic experience possible. In a short essay published in the *Kölner Zeitung* in 1929, entitled "Freud and Jung: Contrasts," Jung insisted on the need for an authentic experience of the primordial, for what he called *Urerfahrung*: "We moderns are faced with the necessity of rediscovering the life of the spirit: we must experience it anew for ourselves [*Wir Modernen sind darauf angewiesen, den Geist wieder zu erleben, das heißt Urerfahrung zu machen*]. It is the only way in which to break the spell that binds us to the cycle of biological events."²⁶⁴ Likewise, in his 1932 lecture "Psychotherapists or the Clergy," he placed vigorous emphasis on the moment that, he assured his audience, "marks the beginning of the cure"—when "this spontaneous activity of the psyche often becomes so intense that visionary pictures are seen or inner voices heard," phenomena Jung describes as "a true, primordial experience of the spirit."²⁶⁵

So the "words" in Goethe's poem are "primordial" or "primal" in the sense that they represent the essential truth of what *is*. In his conversation with his secretary, the philologist Friedrich Wilhelm Riemer, on 10 May 1806, Goethe observed that, in earlier centuries, "the great ideas of life" had been expressed in "intuitions of fantasy," "in figures, in gods"; whereas, by contrast, we (the moderns) express them in "concepts."²⁶⁶ In

---

²⁶²Jung, *PU* §23; Wilhelm Wundt, *Grundriss der Psychologie*, 4th ed. (Leipzig: Engelmann, 1901), p. 366.

²⁶³Buck, *Goethe's "Urworte. Orphisch,"* p. 51.

²⁶⁴Jung, *CW* 4 §780.

²⁶⁵Jung, *CW* 11 §535.

²⁶⁶Biedermann, *Goethes Gespräche*, vol. 1, p. 409; "*Die frühern Jahrhunderte hatten ihre Ideen in Anschauungen der Phantasie; unseres bringt sie in Begriffe*. Die großen Ansichten des Lebens waren damals in Gestalten, in Götter gebracht; *heutzutage bringt man sie in Begriffe*."

"Primal Words. Orphic," one might say, his intention was to express "Orphic concepts."[267] By making use of the linguistic possibility in German of adding the prefix *Ur-*, Goethe indicates that the text embodies, in the words of the editors of the *Berliner Ausgabe*, "the quintessence of his own deepest convictions."[268] As such, the work is usually classed among Goethe's so-called *weltanschauliche Gedichte*—those later works of Goethe expressing a "world view" (or, more accurately, a "way of looking at the world").

In these forty lines, which embrace "a tiny cosmos,"[269] one critic has noted "the entirely free, emotionally musical construction of the whole and its separate parts."[270] In formal terms, the poem consists of five sections, each eight lines long—the traditional *ottava rima*, as used by Boccaccio, Ariosto, and Tasso, and deployed by Goethe in such other poems as "Why give us deep vision so far-sighted" (*Warum gabst du uns die tiefen Blicke*) (1776), "Dedication" (*Zueignung*) (1784), the "Dedication" (*Zueignung*) to *Faust* (1797), his "Epilogue to Schiller's 'The Bell'" (*Epilog zu Schillers "Glocke"*) (1805), as well as the incomplete epic, *The Secrets* (*Die Geheimnisse*) (1783-1784).[271] In the original German, each stanza consists of eight eleven-syllable lines, with an iambic rhyming pattern ( / x = unstressed / stressed). The lines form feminine (i.e., two syllable) rhymes, alternating in the following pattern with a final couplet: *ab ab ab cc*. (Only in one place—in the *b*-rhymes of the central stanza—does Goethe, following the contemporary poet J. J. Wilhelm Heinse [1746-1803] and, before him, Wieland, use a masculine, i.e., one syllabic, rhyme.[272]) According to one commentator, "the final couplet emerges from a pattern of rhythmical variations on the basic iambic metre as metrically perfectly regular, so that metre underlies rhythm as laws underlie apparent randomness,"[273] thus matching the theme of lawfulness or order-

---

[267] Cf. diary entry for 7 October 1817; Goethe, *Werke* [WA], vol. III.6, p. 119; "*Orphische Begriffe*."

[268] Goethe, *Poetische Werke; Kunsttheoretische Schriften und Übersetzungen* [Berliner Ausgabe], ed. Siegfried Seidel et al., 22 vols. (Berlin and Weimar: Aufbau-Verlag, 1965-1978), vol. 1, p. 395; cited in Buck, *Goethes "Urworte. Orphisch,"* p. 27; "*Quintessenz eigener Grundüberzeugungen*."

[269] Dietze, "Urworte, nicht sonderlich orphisch," p. 12.

[270] Petsch, "'Urworte. Orphisch,'" p. 36.

[271] See Buck, *Goethes "Urworte. Orphisch,"* p. 29. For further discussion, see Wolfgang Kayser, "Goethes Dichtungen in Stanzen," *Euphorion: Zeitschrift für Literaturgeschichte* 54 (1960): 229-241.

[272] Buck, *Goethes "Urworte. Orphisch,"* p. 30.

[273] Minden, "'Urworte. Orphisch,'" pp. 79-80.

liness (*Gesetzmäßigkeit*) in the poem; while another critic points out that the final couplets both conclude the stanza and provide a bridge to the next, expressing in concentrated form what has preceded and dialectically anticipating what follows.[274] The overall effect—impossible to capture fully in translation—is one of dignified sententiousness, authoritative pronouncement, and awe-inspiring, Delphic clarity.

The poem demands to be read as a whole, and *in the order in which its constituent stanzas are presented*; for "these few stanzas," Goethe commented, "contain much that is meaningful in a sequence which, when one recognizes it, makes easier for the mind the most important considerations."[275] Thus to each "primal word" there corresponds a stage in human life, and the poem as a whole surveys the whole of life from birth to old age.[276] One scholar has tried to map the different stages of life onto the stanzas of the poem, so that to *Daimon* corresponds birth; to *Chance*, youth; to *Eros*, maturity; to *Necessity*, full age; and finally, to *Hope*, old age.[277] Equally important, however, is the way in which each stage is considered not just from a biological, but from a philosophical, even psychological, perspective.[278] Taken together, these stanzas represent, in the words of Emil Staiger, "everything that the poet and scientist has ever said about human beings, compressed with great power into a few lines."[279] And in them, as Friedrich Hiebel has suggested, Goethe enters, borne along by his own, individual version of Christianity and by his morphological concept of the entelechy, into the realm of Orphism, into the realm of the ancient Greek Dionysian mysteries—territory into which previously he had not ventured, until prompted to do so by the controversy between Hermann and Creuzer.[280]

---

[274]Dietze, "Urworte, nicht sonderlich orphisch," p. 19.

[275]Goethe, *Werke* [HA], vol. 1, p. 403; "*Diese wenigen Strophen enthalten viel Bedeutendes in einer Folge, die, wenn man sie erst kennt, dem Geiste die wichtigsten Betrachtungen erleichtert.*"

[276]Hoffmeister, "Goethe's 'Urworte. Orphisch,'" p. 180.

[277]Wipf, *Elpis*, p. 131.

[278]Hoffmeister, "Goethe's 'Urworte. Orphisch,'" p. 180.

[279]Emil Staiger, *Goethe*, vol. 3, *1814-1832* (Zurich: Atlantis, 1959), p. 99.

[280]Hiebel, *Goethe: Die Erhöhung des Menschen*, p. 36.

CHAPTER 4

# Primal Words. Orphic

In his draft for a book about classical scholars, Nietzsche argued that one should "know" Greek culture, not simply for the sake of knowledge, but in order to "surpass" it. "Remember how much Goethe knew of the classical world," he observed, "surely less than a classicist, but yet enough to grapple with it with significant results."[1] "Primal Words. Orphic" (*Urworte. Orphisch*) supports Nietzsche's thesis, and offers evidence of a continuity of ideas across different times and cultures, in this case through Goethe's explicitly aesthetic appropriation of ancient Orphic wisdom. This poem represents a connecting point between the wisdom of the ancients and the tradition of German classicism, which lies at the heart of Jung's analytical psychology. Having examined the history of the idea of the midlife crisis, Jung's own contribution to this history, and the continuing interest in the ancient cult of Orphism from the age of Goethe to our own, let us now turn to the actual text of Goethe's poem and consider it in more detail.

---

[1] Friedrich Nietzsche, "We Classicists" (*Wir Philologen*), §167, trans. William Arrowsmith, in *Unmodern Observations*, ed. William Arrowsmith (New Haven and London: Yale University Press, 1990), pp. 305-387 (p. 382); *Sämtliche Werke: Kritische Studienausgabe*, ed. Giorgio Colli and Mazzino Montinari, 15 vols. (Berlin and New York: Walter de Gruyter; Munich: dtv, 1967-1977 and 1988), vol. 8, 5[167], pp. 88-89; *"Man denke, was Goethe vom Alterthum verstand; gewiß nicht soviel als ein Philologe und doch genug, um fruchtbar mit ihm zu ringen."*

## DAIMON

According to Macrobius, one of the four presiding deities at the birth of the individual is the *daimon*, and in the Orphic hymnary we find the following poem addressed to this figure:

> Thee, mighty ruling Daimon dread, I call,
> Mild Jove, life-giving, and the source of all:
> Great Jove, much wand'ring, terrible and strong,
> To whom revenge and tortures dire belong.
> Mankind from thee in plenteous wealth abound,
> When in their dwellings joyful thou art found;
> Or pass thro' life afflicted and distress'd,
> The needful means of bliss by thee suppress'd.
> 'Tis thine alone, endu'd with boundless might,
> To keep the keys of sorrow and delight.
> O holy blessed father, hear my pray'r,
> Disperse the seeds of life-consuming care,
> With fav'ring mind the sacred rites attend,
> And grant to life a glorious blessed end.[2]

The first stanza, "ΔΑΙΜΩΝ, Daimon"—and thus "Primal Words. Orphic" as a whole—opens with the following lines:[3]

> When you were granted here your brief admission,
> As suns and planets met that day they charted
> For evermore your growing to fruition
> According to the law by which you started.

> [*Wie an dem Tag, der dich der Welt verliehen,*
> *Die Sonne stand zum Gruße der Planeten,*
> *Bist alsobald und fort und fort gediehen*
> *Nach dem Gesetz, wonach du angetreten.*]

Whereas the Orphic hymn is addressed to Zeus Ploutodotes (the Giver of Wealth), Goethe's stanza is addressed to the reader. Its title offers a good example of the use Goethe (and, after him, Jung) made of mythological

---

[2] *The Mystical Hymns of Orpheus*, trans. Thomas Taylor, 2nd ed. (London: Dobell; Reeves and Turner, 1896), no. 73, p. 141. For a commentary, see *The Orphic Hymns*, trans. Apostolos N. Athanassakis (London: Scholars Press, 1977), pp. 138-139.

[3] The translation offered here is a composite one, based on the versions by Christopher Middleton (*GE* 1, 231-233) and John Whaley (Goethe, *Selected Poems* [London: Dent, 1998], pp. 123-125). For the German text of the poem, see Goethe, *Werke* [HA], vol. 1, pp. 359-360 (or *Werke* [WA], vol. I.3, pp. 95-96); and for the German text of Goethe's commentary, see *Werke* [HA], vol. 1, pp. 403-407 (or *Werke* [WA], vol. I.41, pp. 215-221).

motifs to explore psychological themes. Originally,[4] the term *daimon*, as used by Homer, meant "divider" or "allotter," referring to unexpected events that arose in human life; then, in Hesiod, it acquired the sense of "guardian" or "protector," and in this sense we read in Plato's *Phaedo* that each of us has a "guardian spirit [*daimon*], given charge over us in life," which guides us, after death, to the assembly where each is judged.[5] Elsewhere in the *Phaedo* we learn that "God gave the sovereign part of the human soul to be the divinity [*daimon*] of each one," and that since the wise man "is ever cherishing the divine power and has the divinity within him [*daimon*] in perfect order, he will be singularly happy."[6] In Plato's *Symposium*, the *daimon* refers to an intermediate being between the gods and the humans,[7] while in the *Republic* Socrates develops a veritable allegorical system involving not just the concept of the *daimon*, but also the notions of *ananke* and *tyche*.[8] In the *Laws*, the Athenian Stranger relates how Kronos, "the god who was a friend of humanity," set up as "kings and rulers within our cities," not human beings, but *daimons*—"the better species of daimons, who supervised us in a way that provided much ease both for them and for us," providing "peace and awe and good laws and justice."[9]

---

[4]See the entry on *daimon* in Simon Hornblower and Antony Spawforth, eds., *The Oxford Classical Dictionary*, 3rd ed. (Oxford and New York: Oxford University Press, 1996), p. 426. See, too, the discussions in Pierre Hadot, *The Inner Citadel: The "Meditations" of Marcus Aurelius* [1997], trans. Michael Chase (Cambridge, MA: Harvard University Press, 1998), pp. 76, 122-125, and 159-160; and *N'oublie pas de vivre: Goethe et la tradition des exercices spirituels* (Paris: Albin Michel, 2008), pp. 169-172.

[5]Plato, *Phaedo*, 107d, in *The Collected Dialogues*, ed. Edith Hamilton and Huntington Cairns (Princeton, NJ: Princeton University Press, 1963), p. 89.

[6]Plato, *Timaeus*, 90a and 90c, in *Collected Dialogues*, p. 1209.

[7]Plato, *Symposium*, 202d-203a, in *Collected Dialogues*, pp. 554-555. For further discussion, see Paul Friedländer, *Plato 1: An Introduction* [1928], trans. Hans Meyerhoff (London: Routledge and Kegan Paul, 1958), chapter 2, "Demon and Eros," pp. 32-58; and Karl Kerényi, "Der grosse Daimon des Symposion" [1942], in *Humanistische Seelenforschung* (Wiesbaden: VMA-Verlag, 1978), pp. 289-310.

[8]According to the tale of Alcinous, Lachesis (one of the Fates, the daughters of Necessity) addresses the souls that are about to be born with the following words: "No divinity shall cast lots for you, but you shall choose your own deity [*daimon*]. Let him to whom falls the first lot select a life over which he shall cleave of necessity [*ananke*]"—thus each of us chooses our own destiny, each chooses our own necessity—and woe betide us if we choose badly: whoever chooses a life of tyranny, for example, should be aware of the horrors it involves, but will, when it is too late, "blame [...] fortune [*tyche*] and the gods and anything except himself" (Plato, *Republic*, 617e and 619c, in *Collected Dialogues*, pp. 841 and 843).

[9]Plato, *Laws*, Book 4, 713d, in *The Laws of Plato*, trans. Thomas L. Pangle (Chicago and London: University of Chicago Press, 1980), p. 99.

The relation between the *daimon* and the individual is central to understanding the term's use in Goethe's text. According to Heraclitus, "the character of a person is his or her *daimon*,"[10] and in this sense, too, Socrates had his *daimonion*. The Stoic philosophers spoke of the *deus internus*, the "god within," and for Chrysippus, "to live according to virtue is the same thing as living according to one's experience of those things which happen by nature," because when "everything is done according to a harmony with the genius [or *daimon*] of each individual with reference to the will of the universal governor and manager of all things," one discovers "the virtue of the happy man" and attains "the perfect happiness of life."[11] In his *Meditations*, Marcus Aurelius bids himself (and the reader) "practice only to live the present which you are now living," with the goal of living "at peace with the divinity which is within you [*daimon*]."[12] (In ancient Roman culture, the equivalent of the *daimon* became the figure of the tutelary spirit or "genius." In his *Epistles*, for example, Horace refers to the genius as "that companion who rules our star of birth [*natale comes qui temperat astrum*], the god of human nature, though mortal for each single life," whom he described, as Jung noted with curious fascination, as "changing in countenance, white or black."[13])

Many centuries later, other thinkers still found the idea of the *daimon* a useful one. The substance of the exchange between Thoas and Iphigenie in Act 1, Scene 4, of Goethe's drama *Iphigenia on Tauris* (*Iphigenie auf Tauris*) (1779; 1787)—when Thoas states, "There speaks no god; what speaks is your own heart," to which Iphigenia replies, "They only speak

[10]Heraclitus, Diels-Kranz 22 B 119; see *Die Vorsokratiker*, ed. Jaap Mansfeld, 2 vols. (Stuttgart: Reclam, 1983-1986), vol. 1, pp. 274-275; *Les Présocratiques*, ed. Jean-Paul Dumont (Paris: Gallimard, 1988), p. 173; cf. p. 1242, for commentary on *daimon* here. Compare, too, with Nietzsche's remark in *Beyond Good and Evil [Jenseits von Gut und Böse]* [1886], §70: "If one has character one also has one's typical experience, which recurs repeatedly" (*Basic Writings of Nietzsche*, ed. and trans. Walter Kaufmann [New York: The Modern Library, 1968], p. 270); *"Hat man Charakter, so hat man auch ein typisches Erlebnis, das immer wiederkommt."*

[11]Diogenes Laertius, *The Lives and Opinions of Eminent Philosophers*, trans. C. D. Yonge (London: Bell, 1895), book 7, §83, p. 291.

[12]Marcus Aurelius, *Meditations*, book 12, §3 (*The Meditations*, trans. G. M. A. Grube [Indianapolis: Hackett, 1983], p. 123). See Hadot, *The Inner Citadel*, p. 123.

[13]Horace, *Epistles*, Book 2, Epistle 2 (in *Satires, Epistles and "Ars Poetica,"* trans. H. Rushton Fairclough [London: Heinemann; New York: Putnam, 1926], p. 439). For Jung's curiosity about the genius's "changing countenance," see "The Father in the Destiny of the Individual" [1909/1949], *CW* 4, §§693-744 (here: §744, n. 26). In the Orphic hymn to Melinoe, this mysterious figure, thought likely to be a female infernal *daimon*, is described as "partly black thy limbs and partly white, / From Pluto dark, from Jove etherial bright" (trans. Taylor, p. 138), "now plain to the eye, now shadowy, now shining in the darkness" (trans. Athanassakis, p. 95).

through our own heart to us"[14]—is reflected in the thought of the German Idealist philosopher, G. W. F. Hegel (1770-1831). He spoke of a dual aspect of individuals, distinguishing between their external life and their inner existence, and describing this "inner particularity" as one's *fate* (*Verhängnis*), for "this particularity of my interior is the oracle, on whose declaration all the decisions of the individual depend; it constitutes the objectivity which asserts itself from within the interior of the character."[15] Hegel's philosophical rival, Arthur Schopenhauer (1788-1860), quoted the entire opening stanza of "Primal Words. Orphic" in his prize essay *On the Freedom of the Will* (*Über die Freiheit des Wollens*) (1839), published in *The Two Fundamental Problems of Ethics* (*Die beiden Grundprobleme der Ethik*) (1841). For Schopenhauer, its lines expressed, "with equal accuracy and poetry," his own doctrine of "individual character," according to which "the presupposition on which the necessity of the effects of all causes rests is the inner essence of each and every thing," be that a natural power, its vital energy, or its will; a law that, in Scholastic philosophy, was summarized in the formula *operari sequitur esse* (i.e., functioning follows upon being, or action follows being).[16] And in an essay on the nineteenth-century Swiss novelist Gottfried Keller, the German aesthetician Friedrich Theodor Vischer (1807-1887) related the daimonic to the tragic, equating the former with "powers that burst forth from the unknown womb of Being or are unleashed from the dark depths of the soul, and weave the fate of Man."[17] (Vischer's novel *Auch Einer* [1878], to which *Memories, Dreams, Reflections* as well as one of Jung's *Black Books* make passing reference,[18] belongs to the important, if unrecognized, con-

---

[14]Goethe, *Werke* [HA], vol. 5, p. 20.

[15]G. W. F. Hegel, *Enzyklopädie der philosophischen Wissenschaften im Grundrisse (1830): Dritter Teil: Die Philosophie des Geistes mit den mündlichen Zusätzen* [*Werke*, vol. 10] (Frankfurt am Main: Suhrkamp, 1970), §405, Zusatz, pp. 131-132; *"Diese Besonderheit meines Innern ist das Orakel, von dessen Ausspruch alle Entschließungen des Individuums abhängen; sie bildet das Objektive, welches sich von dem Inneren des Charakters heraus geltend macht."*

[16]Arthur Schopenhauer, *Prize Essay on the Freedom of the Will*, ed. Günter Zöller, trans. Eric F. J. Payne (Cambridge: Cambridge University Press, 1999), pp. 50-51. For further discussion of Schopenhauer's essay, see the chapter entitled "The Mystery of Freedom," in Rüdiger Safranski, *Schopenhauer and the Wild Years of Philosophy*, trans. Ewald Osers (Cambridge, MA: Harvard University Press, 1990), pp. 307-326.

[17]*"Mächten, die geisterhaft aus unbekanntem Schosse des Daseins, oder wild aus schwarzen Tiefen des Gemütes hervorbrechen und des Menschen Schicksal flechten"*; F. T. Vischer, *Altes und Neues*, 3 vols. in 1 (Stuttgart: Bonz, 1881), vol. 2, pp. 135-216 [p. 190].

[18]Jung, *MDR*, p. 122; *ETG*, p. 109; and C. G. Jung, *The Red Book: Liber Novus*, ed. Sonu Shamdasani (New York and London: Norton, 2009), p. 286, n. 135. For further discussion of F. T.

texts of Jung's work, and it could well have exercised a larger influence on Jung than is usually thought.)

Drawing on this philosophical tradition, in both its ancient and modern guise, Jung observes in *Aion* that "when an inner situation is not made conscious, it happens outside, as fate."[19] Citing Diotima's words in the *Symposium* that "Eros, dear Socrates, is a mighty daimon,"[20] he describes the *daimon[ion]* as "a determining power which comes upon the individual from outside, like providence or fate." Yet, he adds, "the ethical decision is left to us," for "we must know, however, what we are deciding about and what we are doing," for then, "if we obey we are following not just our own opinion," and "if we reject it we are destroying not just our own invention."[21] Likewise, the classical scholar Walter Burkert (b. 1931) defines the term *daimon* as meaning "inscrutable power, something that motivates the human being, yet without an originator that can be named."[22] It is this sense that Goethe uses it here, glossing the word in his commentary as "the necessary, limited individuality of the person, immediately declared at the moment of birth, the characteristic thing by means of which the individual is differentiated from every other person, whatever similarities they share."[23] In fact, we can distinguish between three fundamentally different senses in which Goethe uses the term *daimon* (or, in German, *Dämon* [plural: *Dämonen*] or *das Dämonische* ["the daimonic"]),[24] which clarifies the meaning of the term in his poem.

---

Vischer's *Auch Einer: Eine Reisebekanntschaft*, see Ruth Heller, "*Auch Einer*: The Epitome of F. Th. Vischer's Philosophy of Life," *German Life and Letters* 8/1 (October 1954): 9-18; and Harvey W. Hewett-Thayer, "The Road to *Auch Einer*," *Publications of the Modern Language Association of America* 75/1 (March 1960): 83-96.

[19]Jung, *CW* 9/ii §126; "*wenn ein innerer Tatbestand nicht bewußtgemacht wird, dann ereignet er sich als Schicksal außen.*"

[20]*Symposium*, 202e; Plato, *Collected Dialogues*, p. 555.

[21]Jung, *CW* 9ii §51; "*eine von außen an den Menschen herantretende, bestimmende Macht aus, wie die der Vorsehung und des Schicksals. Dabei ist die ethische Entscheidung dem Menschen vorbehalten. Er muß aber wissen, worüber er entscheidet, und wissen, was er tut; wenn er gehorcht, so folgt er nicht bloß seinem eigenen Gutdünken, und wenn er verwirft, so zerstört es nicht bloß seine eigene Erfindung.*"

[22]Walter Burkert, *Griechische Religion der archaischen und klassischen Epoche* (Stuttgart, Berlin, Cologne: Kohlhammer, 1977), pp. 279-280; "*Daimon ist undurchschaute Macht, ein den Menschen Treibendes ohne benennbaren Urheber.*"

[23]Goethe, *Werke* [HA], vol. 1, p. 403; "*die notwendige, bei der Geburt unmittelbar ausgesprochene, begränzte Individualität der Person, das Charakteristische, wodurch sich der Einzelne von jedem andern bei noch so größer Ähnlichkeit unterscheidet.*"

[24]For these distinctions, see Karl Justus Obenauer, *Der faustische Mensch: Vierzehn Studien zum zweiten Teil von Goethes "Faust"* (Jena: Diederichs, 1922), p. 177; and Friedrich Hiebel, *Goethe: Die*

First, Goethe uses the term, usually in the plural, to refer to ambivalent, hostile, or even evil entities or powers that hamper, hinder, or otherwise restrict us. In his conversations with Eckermann in 1828 and 1829, for example, Goethe refers to the *daimons* that keep "tripping up" the "extraordinary individual," until he "falls at last"; "the world will not attain its goal so speedily as we expect and desire," he says, because "there are always retarding daimons, who start in opposition at every point"; it is difficult, he concedes, for "our better nature to maintain itself vigorously, and not to allow the daimons more power than is due"; and when Goethe wonders whether "the daimons, to tease and make sport with men, have placed among them single figures so alluring that everyone strives after them, and so great that nobody reaches them"—such as Raphael, Mozart, Shakespeare, or Napoleon—Eckermann wonders whether the *daimons* had "intended something of the kind with Goethe" himself, for Goethe was "a form too alluring not to be striven after, and too great to be reached."[25]

Yet it turns out these incorporeal beings can sometimes prove to be beneficent, especially when they appear in Goethe's works in the context of antiquity. The fourth of his *Roman Elegies* (*Römische Elegien*) (1788-1790; 1795), for instance, opens with the lines: "Lovers are pious: we worship all supernatural beings, / Gods and goddesses all, humbly their favour we beg" (*Fromm sind wir Liebende, still verehren wir alle Dämonen, / Wünschen uns jeglichen Gott, jegliche Göttin geneigt*).[26] In "The Second Sojourn in Rome" (1819-1828), Part Three of his *Italian Journey* (*Italienische Reise*), Goethe appended the following lines to the text of his poem "Cupid, you wanton, self-willed boy!" (*Cupido, loser, eigensinniger Knabe!*):[27]

> If the little poem quoted above is not taken literally, if my
> readers do not think here of the daimon we usually call Amor,

*Erhöhung des Menschen: Perspektiven einer morphologischen Lebensschau* (Berne and Munich: Francke, 1961), pp. 20-41.

[25]See Goethe's conversations of 11 March 1828, 23 October 1828, 2 April 1829, and 6 December 1820; Johann Peter Eckermann, *Conversations of Goethe*, trans. John Oxenford and ed. J. K. Moorhead [1930] (New York: Da Capo, 1998), pp. 252, 275, and 306. For a discussion of Goethe's conversations with Eckermann from a psychoanalytic perspective, see Avital Ronell, *Dictations: On Haunted Writing* (Bloomington: Indiana University Press, 1986).

[26]Johann Wolfgang von Goethe, *Erotic Poems*, trans. David Luke (Oxford and New York: Oxford University Press, 1997), p. 13; *Werke* [HA], vol. 1, p. 159.

[27]Goethe, *Selected Verse*, trans. David Luke (Harmondsworth: Penguin, 1964), pp. 108-109; *Werke* [HA], vol. 1, p. 237.

but imagine instead a group of active individuals who address
and challenge a person's innermost being, pull him this way
and that, and confuse him by dividing his interest, then, in a
symbolical manner, they will be participating in the situation
in which I have found myself [...]. It will be admitted that
great effort was required of me to maintain myself against so
many things, not to grow weary of active work, and not to become indolent about assimilating things.[28]

And the ambivalence of the *daimon* is captured well in a poem from Goethe's sketches for his *West-Eastern Divan* (*West-Östlicher Divan*) (1819):

> In your time you romped with wild,
> Daimonic-inspired young hordes,
> Then gently came, year on year, towards
> Those who are the wise, the godlike-mild.

> [*Du hast getollt zu deiner Zeit mit wilden*
> *Dämonisch genialen jungen Schaaren,*
> *Dann sachte schlossest du von Jahr zu Jahren*
> *Dich näher an die Weisen, Göttlich-Milden.*][29]

Whereas the divine is associated with the "mild," the *daimonic* is brilliant,
is inspired, is *genial—dämonisch genial*—and so we arrive at the second
meaning of the term.

This second sense is found when Goethe uses a substantival adjective,
*das Dämonische*—a concept to which the term *daimon* stands in a close,
albeit an oblique,[30] relation. Goethe's notion of the daimonic is a complex
matter in its own right,[31] defining it in Part Four, Book 20, of *Dichtung
und Wahrheit* as "something in nature (whether living or lifeless, animate
or inanimate) that manifested itself only in contradictions and therefore
could not be expressed in any concept, much less any word":

> It was not divine, for it seemed irrational; not human, for it
> had no intelligence; not diabolical, for it was beneficent; and

---

[28]Goethe, *GE* 6, 384; *Werke* [HA], vol. 11, pp. 478-479.

[29]Goethe, *Werke* [WA], vol. I.6, p. 283.

[30]Karl A. Wipf, for instance, disputes the existence of any relation (*Elpis: Betrachtungen zum
Begriff der Hoffnung in Goethes Spätwerk* [Berne and Munich: Francke, 1974], p. 132), but etymologically, as well as conceptually, there is an overlap between *Dämon* and *das Dämonische*.

[31]For discussion of Goethe's conception of the daimonic, see H. B. Nisbet, "*Das Dämonische*:
On the Logic of Goethe's Demonology," *Forum for Modern Language Studies* 7 (1971): 259-281; and,
most recently and most comprehensively, Angus Nicholls, *Goethe's Concept of the Daemonic: After the
Ancients* (Rochester, NY: Camden House, 2006).

not angelic, for it often betrayed malice. It was like chance, for it lacked continuity, and like Providence, for it suggested context. Everything that limits us seemed penetrable by it, and it appeared to dispose at will over the elements necessary to our existence, to contract time and expand space. It seemed only to accept the impossible and scornfully to reject the possible. This essence, which appeared to infiltrate all the others, separating and combining them, I called daimonic [*dämonisch*], after the example of the ancients and others who had perceived something similar. I tried to save myself from this fearful thing by taking refuge, as usual, behind an image [*hinter ein Bild flüchtete*].[32]

And in conversation with Eckermann on 2 March 1831, Goethe described the daimonic as "that which cannot be explained by reason or understanding," as something that "lies not in my nature, but I am subject to it."[33] As examples, Goethe cites Napoleon, or his friend, Duke Carl August of Sachsen-Weimar-Eisenach, which brings us to the third category: *the daimonic individual.*

Not just Napoleon and Carl August, but also Egmont, Mirabeau, Frederick the Great, Peter the Great, Lord Byron, Paganini, and even Cagliostro—these are all names mentioned by Goethe in connection with term (*the*) *daimon*[*ic*]. In his famous conversation with Eckermann of 11 March 1828, in which he also talks about need for "repeated puberty," or for psychological rebirth, Goethe exclaimed that "the darkening and illuminating of man make his destiny!" (*Des Menschen Verdüsterungen und Erleuchtungen machen sein Schicksal!*), and he commented further:

> The daimon ought to lead us every day in leading-strings, and tell us what we ought to do on every occasion. But the good spirit leaves us in the lurch, and we grope about in the dark. [...] For what is genius but that productive power by which arise deeds that can display themselves before God and nature, and are therefore permanent and produce results?[34]

And so Mozart, Phidias, Raphael, Dürer, Holbein, Luther, Lessing, Lorenz Oken, Alexander von Humboldt, and even Pierre Jean de Béranger, the writer of French popular songs, are said to occupy, inas-

---

[32] Goethe, *GE* 5, 597; *Werke* [HA], vol. 10, pp. 175-176.

[33] Eckermann, *Conversations of Goethe*, p. 392.

[34] Eckermann, *Conversations of Goethe*, pp. 245, 246.

much as they evince the qualities of genius, the role of *daimon* in the history of art, science, and literature.

A year or so before composing "Primal Words. Orphic," Goethe had evoked, in a letter to Carl Friedrich Zelter of 26 March 1816, the idea that "each of us has something special inside us, that we seek to develop, by letting it continue to work its effect," a "wondrous being that does its best for us day by day, and so one grows old, without knowing how or why."[35] This notion is closely related to Goethe's use of the Aristotelian concept of *entelechy*. According to Aristotle, each organism can be considered under a three-fold aspect: (i) its power, or its potential as possibility (*dynamis*); (ii) its energy, its actuality in reality (*energeia*); and (iii) its goal as the organism realizes it in itself (*entelecheia*).[36] Several years later, in conversation with Eckermann on 3 March 1830, Goethe affirmed the Aristotelian concept of *entelechy* and a related idea, the Leibnizian concept of the monad, remarking that "the obstinacy of the individual and the fact that man shakes off what does not suit him" was "a proof" that something like Aristotle's *entelechy* exists, and adding that Leibniz had had "similar thoughts about independent beings, and indeed what we term an entelechy he called a monad."[37]

In his commentary on "Primal Words. Orphic" Goethe commits himself, by speaking of "innate power and quality," "the unchanging nature of the individual," and "this firm, solid being, which can only develop from itself,"[38] to the notion of innate character; and although he was never explicit on this point, Jung probably shared this view. For example, in his lecture to the Kulturbund in Vienna on "The Inner Voice" (*Die Stimme des Innern*), later published as "The Development of the Personality" (*Vom Werden der Persönlichkeit*) (1934), Jung discusses what it means for the individual to have a vocation (*Bestimmung*).[39] "Any-

[35]Goethe, *Briefe* [HA], vol. 3, p. 347.

[36]According to Friedrich Hiebel, these three aspects can be mapped onto three different stages of life respectively, viz. (i) childhood as the age of possibility, of artistic potential; (ii) youth as the age of educative energy, the mastering of artistic skills; (iii) maturity, in which the artistic entelechy can reveal itself in full; see *Goethe: Die Erhöhung des Menschen*, p. 15.

[37]Eckermann, *Conversations of Goethe*, p. 353. Cited in Reinhard Schantz, "Goethes 'Urworte. Orphisch' in ihrer geschichtsphilosophischen Bedeutung," *Zeitschrift für Religions- und Geistesgeschichte* 3 (1951): 38-53.

[38]Goethe, *Werke* [HA], vol. 1, p. 404; *Werke* [WA], vol. I.41, p. 216; "*angeborne Kraft und Eigenheit; die Unveränderlichkeit des Individuums; dieses feste, zähe, dieses nur aus sich selbst zu entwickelnde Wesen.*"

[39]This is a richly evocative term in the German philosophical tradition, from J. G. Fichte's *Die*

one with a vocation," Jung declared, "hears the voice of the inner man: *he is called*":

> That is why legends say that he possesses a private daimon who counsels him and whose mandates he must obey. The best known example of this is Faust, and an historical instance is provided by the daimon of Socrates. Primitive medicine-men have their snake spirits, and Aesculapius, the tutelary patron of physicians, has for his emblem the Serpent of Epidaurus. He also has, as his private daimon, the Cabir Telesphorus, who is said to have dictated or inspired his medical prescriptions.[40]

Likewise, in *Memories, Dreams, Reflections* the term "daimon" is used to describe the "life instinct," which "comes to us from within, as a compulsion or will or command,"[41] and there is a lengthy passage about Jung's own "daimon."[42] (Indeed, on his stone at Bollingen, Jung chiselled an inscription to Telesphorus, the companion of Asclepius.[43])

Thus we might read the term "daimon," as it is used in "Primal Words. Orphic," as representing an internalization of what Goethe, elsewhere, understands as an external force. It signifies "the unchanging nature of the individual"[44]—the "in-dividual," that is, in its etymological sense of what is indivisible,[45] or in the sense that, in the words of the early Goethe, "the individual is inexpressible" (*individuum est ineffabile*).[46] Another

---

Bestimmung des Menschen (1800) to Nikolaj Berdjajew, *Von der Bestimmung des Menschen: Versuch einer paradoxalen Ethik* (1935).

[40]Jung, *CW* 17 §300; "*Wer* Bestimmung *hat, hört die* Stimme des Innern, *er ist* bestimmt. *Deshalb glaubt auch die Sage, daß er einen privaten Dämonen habe, der ihn berät und dessen Aufträge er auszuführen hat. Ein allbekanntes Beispiel ist das daimonion des Sokrates. Primitive Medizinmänner haben ihre Schlangengeister, wie auch Äskulap, der Schutzpatron der Ärzte, durch die epidaurische Schlange dargestellt war. Überdies hatte er als Privatdämon den Kabiren Telesphorus, der ihm anscheinend die Rezepte vorlas respektive eingab.*"

[41]Jung, *MDR*, p. 381; *ETG*, p. 351; "*den Lebenstrieb tritt uns von innen her als ein Muß oder Wille oder Befehl entgegen.*"

[42]Jung, *MDR*, pp. 389-390, cf. 377; *ETG*, p. 358, cf. 347.

[43]Jung, *MDR*, p. 254, cf. *MDR*, p. 38; *ETG*, p. 231, cf. 29.

[44]Goethe, *Werke* [HA], vol. 1, p. 404; "*die Unveränderlichkeit des Individuums.*"

[45]See Jochen Schmidt, *Goethes Altersgedicht "Urworte. Orphisch": Grenzerfahrung und Entgrenzung* (Heidelberg: Winter, 2006), p. 12.

[46]Goethe, letter to Lavater of 20 September 1780; *Briefe* [HA], vol. 1, p. 325. The exact source of this dictum, widely attributed to medieval Scholastic thought, is unknown. Meinecke used the part of Goethe's letter that features this phrase on the original title page of *Die Entstehung des Historismus* [1936], and attributed the thought to Herder (Friedrich Meinecke, *Historism: The Rise of a New Historical Outlook*, trans. J. E. Anderson [London: Routledge, 1972], p. 334); Wilhelm Dilthey used the

word for this aspect of the individual is character—"its first and original character."[47] In one of his last letters, written to Wilhelm von Humboldt on 17 March 1832, Goethe declared:

> The sooner the individual realizes that there is a craft, there is an art that can assist him in the regulated intensification of his natural aptitudes, the happier he is; what he receives from outside in no way damages his innate individuality. The greatest genius is one that gathers everything up into itself, that knows how to make everything its own, without it making even the slightest change to what is in the fundamental determination one calls character; rather, it is what uplifts it and enables its capacities.[48]

The astrological reference of the stanza's opening lines recalls the first page of Goethe's semiautobiographical work, *Poetry and Truth* (*Dichtung und Wahrheit*) (volume 1 of which was published in 1811). Here Goethe recounts the planetary constellation at the time of his birth, midday on 28 August 1749, in an arresting and dramatic opening paragraph:

> It was on the 28th of August, 1749, at the stroke of twelve noon, that I came into the world in Frankfurt on the Main. The constellation was auspicious: the Sun was in Virgo and at its culmination for the day. Jupiter and Venus looked amicably upon it, and Mercury was not hostile. Only the moon, just then becoming full, was in a position to exert adverse force, because its planetary hour had begun. It did, indeed, resist my birth, which did not take place until this hour had passed.[49]

---

phrase as the motto for his biography of Friedrich Schleiermacher (Wilhelm Dilthey, *Das Leben Schleiermachers*, vol. 1 [1870], in *Gesammelte Schriften*, vol. 13, ed. M. Redeker, 3rd ed. [Göttingen: Vandenhoeck und Ruprecht, 1979], p. 1), and elsewhere cites Humboldt's view that "individuality contains the secret of all existence" [*in der Individualität liegt das Geheimnis alles Daseins*] (*Die geistige Welt: Einleitung in die Philosophie des Lebens*, vol. 1, *Abhandlungen zur Grundlegung der Geisteswissenschaften* [*Gesammelte Schriften*, vol. 5], 8th ed. [Göttingen: Vandenhoeck und Ruprecht, 1974], p. 227).

[47]Goethe, *Werke* [HA], vol. 1, p. 404; "*sein erster und ursprünglicher Charakter.*"

[48]Goethe, *Briefe* [HA], vol. 4, p. 480; "*Je früher der Mensch gewahr wird daß es ein Handwerk, daß es eine Kunst gibt, die ihm zur geregelten Steigerung seiner natürlichen Anlagen verhelfen, desto glücklicher ist er; was er auch von außen empfange, schadet seiner eingebornen Individualität nichts. Das beste Genie ist das, welches alles in sich aufnimmt, sich alles zuzueignen weiß, ohne daß es der eigentlichen Grundbestimmung, demjenigen was man Charakter nennt, im mindesten Eintrag thue, vielmehr solches noch erst recht erhebe und durchaus nach Möglichkeit befähige*"; cited in Johannes Hoffmeister, "Goethes 'Urworte. Orphisch': Eine Interpretation," *Logos* 19 (1930): 173-212 (p. 193).

[49]Goethe, *GE* 4, 21; *Werke* [HA], vol. 9, p. 10.

Goethe's references to astrology here, as in "Primal Words. Orphic" and elsewhere, are ironic, but not entirely so, for they indicate his awareness of the cultural significance of astrology.[50]

For Goethe had no interest in astrology as something that is a matter of supposedly precise calculation, but rather as something that is felt.[51] "This immense clockwork," he wrote to Johann Caspar Lavater on 19 February 1781, "only interests me in its darkest intuition,"[52] and in his letter to Schiller of 8 December 1798, Goethe spoke of "astrological superstition" as "resting on the dark intuition of a world whole":

> Experience tells us that the nearest stars exercise a decisive in-
> fluence on weather, vegetation, etc., one only has to climb,
> step by step, and who can say, where this influence ceases? Af-
> ter all, the astronomer finds everywhere one planet disturbing
> another. And the philosopher is inclined—indeed, he is com-
> pelled—to asume an effect on what is furthest away. So the in-
> dividual in his self-assurance has only to go a bit further and
> extend this state of affairs to the moral, to good fortune and
> misfortune. I wouldn't even want to call this and similar delu-
> sions superstition, it lies so deep in our nature, it is as accept-
> able and pardonable as any belief.[53]

And Goethe's general skepticism toward astrology is reflected in his review of Schiller's *Die Piccolomini*, first performed in Weimar on 30 Jan-uary 1799, when he remarks, reflecting on Wallenstein's belief in astrol-ogy, that "anyone who asks the stars what he should do, clearly does not know what should be done" (*Wer die Sterne fragt, was er tun soll, ist gewiß nicht klar, was zu tun ist*).[54] This skepticism about a related doctrine, alluded to in his letter to Schiller, of *actio in distans*,[55] is reflected in his bal-

---

[50]For further discussion of Goethe's attitude to astrology, see J. Schiff, "Goethe und die Astrologie," *Preussische Jahrbücher* 210 (1927): 86-96; Eduard Spranger, "Die sittliche Astrologie der Makarie in *Wilhelm Meisters Wanderjahren*" [1939], in *Goethe: Seine geistige Welt* (Tübingen: Wunderlich; Leins, 1967), pp. 350-363; and Jean-Paul Deschler, *Die Astrologie in Goethes Weltschau: Ein Beitrag zur Gottesfrage in seinem Leben und Werk* (Berne: Lang, 2000).

[51]See Werner Danckert, *Goethe: Der mythische Urgrund seiner Weltschau* (Berlin: Walter de Gruyter, 1951), p. 148.

[52]Goethe, *Werke* [WA], vol. IV.5, p. 57; "*da dieses ungeheure Uhrwerck mich selbst nur in der dunckelsten Ahndung interessirt.*"

[53]Goethe, *Werke* [HA], vol. 2, p. 360.

[54]Goethe, *Werke* [WA], vol. I.40, p. 56.

[55]The doctrine of *actio in distans* (action at a distance) originally arose in the context of Newton's theory of gravity as a means of explaining the attraction and repulsion of noncontiguous bodies. In his *Metaphysical Rudiments of the Natural Sciences* [*Metaphysische Anfangsgründe der Naturwissenschaften*]

lad, "Action from a Distance" (*Wirkung in die Ferne*) (1815; probably written 1808).[56]

In his *History of the Doctrine of the Colors* (*Materialien zur Geschichte der Farbenlehre*) (1810), Goethe noted that both pure and applied mathematics alike were open to misuse. Arising out of astronomy as an application of a misuse of applied mathematics, he wrote, astrology "infers from the effect of known powers the effects of unknown ones, and treats them as equal."[57] Elsewhere in the *Doctrine of Colors*, Goethe wrote that "everyone's year of birth" contains its "natal prognostication," more in "the coincidence of earthly things, than in the effect on each other of heavenly stars."[58] In his research on optics, published under the title "Entoptic Colors" (*Entoptische Farben*) (1820), Goethe casts "a paradoxical sidelong glance at astrology," in which he interprets astrology as a kind of giant optical experiment. On this account, "the astrologers, whose doctrine was based on devout, untiring observation of the sky," anticipated Goethe's own theories on reflection, his "doctrine of how light is emitted, reflected, and dispersed" (*unsere Lehre von Schein, Rück-, Wider- und Nebenschein*).[59] In this way Goethe sought to reinvigorate astrology by supplying it with new meaning:

---

[1786] Kant defined *actio in distans* as "the action of one matter upon another outside of contact [...]. This action at a distance, which is also possible without the mediation of matter lying in between, is called immediate action at a distance, or the *action* of matters on one another *through empty space*" (Kant, *The Philosophy of Material Nature*, trans. James Ellington [Indianapolis, IN: Hackett, 1985], pp. 60-61). Later, in his postscript to the preface to the first edition of *On the World Soul* [*Von der Weltseele*] [1798], F. W. J. Schelling argued that the concept of *actio in distans* "rests entirely on the idealist conception of space": "For by this, two bodies at the greatest distance from each other can be regarded as touching, and conversely, bodies which (on the common notion) are actually touching can be seen as acting on each other from a distance. It is very true that a body only *acts where it is*, but it is equally true that it only *is where it acts*, and with this principle the last bastion of the atomistic philosophy is surmounted" (Schelling, *Ideas for a Philosophy of Nature*, trans. Errol E. Harris and Peter Heath [Cambridge: Cambridge University Press, 1988], p. 272).

[56] Goethe, *Werke* [HA], vol. 1, pp. 282-283. In the great hall, the queen commands her page to fetch her purse, lying on her bed table on the other side of the castle. One of the ladies of the court, drinking sorbet, spills her drink on her gown, and retires. In the corridor she meets the page on his way back, and the couple—secret lovers, it seems—seize the opportunity to embrace and kiss each other. On his return the queen notices the page's waistcoat is stained. The queen calls to the court mistress of ceremonies and points out—presumably with heavy irony—that the earlier dispute about *actio in distans* is now settled: for when the drink was spilt here in the hall, it was able to stain the page's waistcoat on the other side of the castle.

[57] Goethe, *Materialien zur Geschichte der Farbenlehre*, section 3, "Roger Bacon"; *Werke* [HA], vol. 14, p. 62.

[58] Goethe, *Materialien zur Geschichte der Farbenlehre*, section 5, "Allgemeine Betrachtungen"; *Werke* [HA], vol. 14, p. 96.

[59] Goethe, *Entoptische Farben*, §32, "Paradoxer Seitenblick auf die Astrologie"; Goethe, *Werke* [WA], vol. II.5, pp. 299-301 (p. 300). "Entoptical" colors, discovered by Thomas Johann Seebeck

The full moon does stand not opposed in enmity to the sun,
but is kind enough to send back to him his light, which he had
lent her; it is Artemis, who regards her brother, in a friendly,
yearning way. [...] Thus, for example, a birth that takes place
precisely at the time of the full moon, is to be considered as extremely fortunate: for the moon no longer appears as an adver-
sary, restricting and even abolishing the positive influence of
the sun, but as a friendly, gentle, helping assistant, as Lucina,
as a midwife.[60]

Yet by seeing astrology (and, for that matter, alchemy) as precursors of
modern science, Goethe—like Jung, or like Ernst Cassirer[61]—succeeded
in appreciating, not its scientific truth (for it has none), but rather the full
dimension of its symbolic significance.

The second line of this stanza, "As stood the sun to the salute of planets" (Middleton) or "As suns and planets met that day" (Whaley), recapitulates Goethe's account of his horoscope as it is presented at the
beginning of *Dichtung und Wahrheit*. There, as we have seen, the sun
stands, already at its zenith—as if Goethe's very birth was itself an Orphic
moment, a moment of crisis (and, indeed, Goethe tells us that he was fortunate to survive his first few hours). In this astrological nativity, so to
speak, we find an expression of Goethe's interest in the concept of "constellation" (*Konstellation*), expressed here in its sidereal aspect as a depend-
ency on the stars. This profound conviction of a need to honor the stars is
articulated in the third stanza of Goethe's Masonic poem, entitled
*Symbolum*, in the lines "above, the stars, / And below, the graves" (*oben die
Sterne / Und unten die Gräber*)[62]—an expression, in Werner Danckert's
view, of "a primordial experience of tellurism," that is to say, "the strange,
special form of cosmic ecstasy" that Ludwig Klages called "magical," and
depicted as "the dual relation to the distance of the night firmament and
to the realm of the dead."[63] According to J. J. Bachofen, a sense of depend-

---

[1770-1831], arise within a glass medium when suddenly cooled (see Goethe's letter to an unknown
correspondent of 24 April 1817; *Werke* [WA], vol. IV.28, p. 70).

[60]Goethe, *Werke* [WA], vol. II.5, pp. 300-301.

[61]See Jung, *CW* 8 §§88-91; and *CW* 5 §213 and §226. See, too, Ernst Cassirer, *The Philosophy of
Symbolic Forms*, vol. 2, *Mythical Thought* [1925], trans. Ralph Manheim (New Haven and London:
Yale University Press, 1955), pp. 66-67.

[62]Goethe, *Werke* [HA], vol. 1, p. 340. Goethe's poem draws a parallel between the stages of
Masonic initiation and the development of the individual's life; not least, then, for this reason we shall
return to this poem before the end of this chapter.

[63]Danckert, *Goethe*, p. 148. Danckert's source here is Ludwig Klages, *Vom kosmogonischen Eros*,

ency on the stars—Aristotle's principle that the movement of the planets is the cause of all phenomena—was a "primordial thought" of human-kind and governed the world-view of antiquity,[64] because (as Klages explains) "the distant images of the planets were in those days powerful *daimons*, and on the other hand the *daimons* were 'spirits' from a *primor-dial-original world-before-time*."[65] (Danckert calls this argument a "pan-daimonic" interpretation of "telluric-related stellar-worship."[66])

As Herbert Anton has remarked, the sun occupied an important posi-tion in the Orphic cult, in the shape of Eros-Phanes, the "shining one," one of the earliest attested figures of Orphic worship.[67] Phanes, "the one who makes [or is] manifest," was also known as Protogonos, "the First-born," and under this name he was addressed in an Orphic hymn: "O mighty first-begotten, hear my pray'r, / Twofold, egg-born, and wand'ring thro' the air; / Bull-roarer, glorying in thy golden wings, / From whom the race of Gods and mortals springs."[68] Certainly, there is an underlying congruence between the narrative of auto-procreation and destruction embodied in the figure of Phanes, the central Orphic myth of

---

2nd ed. (Jena: Diederichs, 1926), p. 76; "*die* [...] *Doppelbeziehung zur Ferne des nächtlichen Firmaments und zum Totenreich.*"

[64]J. J. Bachofen, *Versuch über die Gräbersymbolik der Alten*, 2nd ed., introd. Carl Albrecht Bernoulli, preface Ludwig Klages (Basel: Helbing und Lichtenhahn, 1925), p. 282; "*ein Urgedanke der Menschheit, der die Anschauungsweise der alten Welt völlig beherrschte.*" Cf. "*der Umlauf der Planeten bringt alle Erscheinungen hervor*" = Aristotle, *Metaphysics*, Book 12 chapter 8: "all the spheres combined are to explain the observed facts" (Aristotle, *The Basic Works*, ed. Richard McKeon [New York: Ran-dom House, 1941], p. 883).

[65]Klages, *Vom kosmogonischen Eros*, p. 146; "*weil die Fernbilder der Gestirne damals mächtige Dämonen waren und die Dämonen hinwieder 'Geister' einer* uranfänglichen Vorwelt."

[66]Danckert, *Goethe*, p. 149; "*die 'pandämonistische' Deutung einer tellurisch gebundenen Gestirn-verehrung.*"

[67]Herbert Anton, "'Urworte. Orphisch,'" in *Gedichte von Johann Wolfgang Goethe*, ed. Bernd Witte [*Literaturstudium: Interpretationen*] (Stuttgart: Reclam, 1998), pp. 169-185 (p. 171); see, too, Theodor Gomperz, *Greek Thinkers: A History of Ancient Greece*, trans. Laurie Magnus, 4 vols. (Lon-don: Murray, 1906-1912), vol. 1, pp. 84 and 92; and Sara Rappe, *Reading Neoplatonism: Non-discur-sive Thinking in the Texts of Plotinus, Proclus, and Damascius* (Cambridge: Cambridge University Press, 2000), pp. 145 and 149-152. The figure of Phanes was significant for Jung: in *Transformations and Symbols of the Libido*, he discusses "the Orphic figure of Phanes" as a god of light and love, identical to Priapos and to Dionysos *(PU* §223); in the *Red Book*, and in the *Black Books* on which it is based, Jung attaches great significance to ΦΑΝΗΣ (i.e., Phanes) as "the newly-appearing God" (*der neuerscheinende gott*), to whom ΦΙΛΗΜΩΝ (i.e., Philemon) introduces him (Jung, *The Red Book*, p. 301, and see fn. 211); while in the *Systema Munditotius*, which Jung began to elaborate in his *Black Books* in 1917, Phanes (or Erikapaios) is depicted at the top as a young boy in a winged egg (*The Red Book*, p. 364).

[68]See the entry on "Phanes" in Hornblower and Spawforth, eds., *The Oxford Classical Dictionary*, p. 1153; *The Mystical Hymns of Orpheus*, trans. Taylor, no. 6, p. 18.

crisis—descent—reascent or ritual death—dismemberment—reconstitution, and the solar myth.

In the second of treatises on classical archaeology, Jörgen Zoega quotes Macrobius to the effect that "the daimon is the sun, the father of the spirit, of warmth and light" (whereas the Orphic deity of the next stanza, *tyche*, is "the moon, with which the bodies under the moon wax and wane, and whose always changing path accompanies the multiple changes of mortal life").[69] For Goethe, too, the cosmological figure of the sun has great psychological, even ethical, significance. In another of his late poems, "Testament" (*Vermächtnis*) (1829), the image of an internal sun, in juxtaposition to the external, cosmic sun, is used by Goethe to denote the central point of moral orientation in the individual:

> Thank now the sage, O child of earth,
> Who showed her and her kin the path
> For circuiting about the sun.
>
> Now turn yourself about, within:
> Your centre you will find therein,
> No noble soul can this gainsay.
>
> [*Verdank es, Erdensohn, dem Weisen,*
> *Der ihr die Sonne zu umkreisen*
> *Und dem Geschwister wies die Bahn.*
>
> *Sofort nun wende doch nach innen,*
> *Das Zentrum findest du da drinnen,*
> *Woran kein Edler zweifeln mag.*][70]

In "Testament of Old Persian Faith" (*Vermächtnis altpersischen Glaubens*) in the *West-Eastern Divan*, we find the injunction:

> When the new-born's sacred hands have motion
> Turn him quick towards the sun's devotion,
> Mind and body bathe in fire's healing!
> Grace of every dawn shall form his feeling.
>
> [*Regt ein Neugeborner fromme Hände,*
> *Daß man ihn sogleich zur Sonne wende,*
> *Tauche Leib und Geist im Feuerbade!*
> *Fühlen wird es jedes Morgens Gnade.*][71]

---

[69]Georg Zoega, "ΑΓΑΘΗ ΤΥΧΗΙ: Tyche und Nemesis," in *Abhandlungen*, ed. Friedrich Gottlieb Welcker (Göttingen: Dieterich, 1817), pp. 32-55 (pp. 39-40).

[70]Goethe, *GE* 1, 267 [trans. Christopher Middleton]; *Werke* [HA], vol. 1, pp. 369-370.

[71]Goethe, *Poems of the West and East: West-Eastern Divan—West-Östlicher Divan: Bi-Lingual*

And in the first part of "Trilogy of Passion" (*Trilogie zur Leidenschaft*) (1823-1824) the sun is associated with a paradise of personal identity that is, only all too quickly, threatened by ourselves and by those around us, particularly through sexuality:

> Yet we, in such a paradise begun,
> Enjoy but briefly the amazing sun,
> And then the battle's on: vague causes found
> To struggle with ourself, the world around.
>
> [*Und wir, gepflanzt in Paradieses Wonne,*
> *Genießen kaum der hoch erlauchten Sonne,*
> *Da kämpft sogleich verworrene Bestrebung*
> *Bald mit uns selbst und bald mit der Umgebung.*][72]

Thus, within the economy of these texts, the sun retains, in accordance with the traditional hierarchy of myth, its "logocentric superiority"—yet this superiority is simultaneously challenged by Goethe and Jung alike. By Goethe, inasmuch as he speaks positively in *Dichtung und Wahrheit* (Part Three, Book 13) of "the twofold gleam of both celestial lights" (*Doppelglanz der beiden Himmelslichter*),[73] thus according to both sun (= *daimon*) and moon (= *tyche*) an equal respect. And in another poem from the *West-Eastern Divan*, the sun appears surrounded by a crescent moon—how is this possible? asks Suleika in the opening stanza:

> The sun appears! Such splendour sighted!
> The sickle moon wraps round it now.
> Who could have this pair so united?
> This puzzle, how explain it? How?
>
> [*Die Sonne kommt! Ein Prachterscheinen!*
> *Der Sichelmond umklammert sie.*
> *Wer konnte solch ein Paar vereinen?*
> *Dies Rätsel, wie erklärt sich's? Wie?*]

Her lover, the poet Hatem, sees in the conjunction of sun and moon a

---

*Edition of the Complete Poems*, trans. John Whaley (Berne; Berlin; Frankfurt am Main: Peter Lang, 1998), p. 421; *Werke* [HA], vol. 2, p. 105.

[72]Goethe, *GE* 1, 243-245 [trans. John Frederick Nims]; *Werke* [HA], vol. 1, p. 380; cited in Hoffmeister, "Goethes 'Urworte. Orphisch,'" p. 196.

[73]Goethe, *GE* 4, 414; *Werke* [HA], vol. 9, p. 562. The erotic context of this remark is the following: "It is a very pleasant sensation to have a new passion stir in us before the old one has completely died away. Thus at sunset it is good to see the moon rise on the opposite side, and one can revel in the twofold gleam of both celestial lights."

symbol of the sultan's power, and he hastens to reassure her in the third and final stanza:

> Our bliss is imaged here the clearest!
> Now you and me again I see,
> Your sun you call me, you my dearest,
> Come close, sweet moon, enclosing me!
>
> [*Auch sei's ein Bild von unsrer Wonne!*
> *Schon seh' ich wieder mich und dich,*
> *Du nennst mich, Liebchen, deine Sonne,*
> *Komm, süßer Mond, umklammre mich!*][74]

(Of course, the opposition of light-and-darkness continues to structure Goethe's thought, as it does much Western thought in general; after all, Goethe considered himself, not least as a scientist and researcher into color, as someone who had, as it were, "seen the light."[75]) From Jung, too, the superiority of the sun is subject to challenge, inasmuch as he interrogates the meaning of life *after* the sun has reached its zenith at midday—What is the purpose of the second half of life? is the question that he poses.

In line 4 of stanza 1, the notion that the life upon which the individual embarks at birth is "lawful" (*Nach dem Gesetz wonach du angetreten*) anticipates Jung's idea in his paper "The Stages of Life" that these various stages are governed by corresponding laws, the "law" of the morning and the "law" of the evening.[76] In an earlier poem, "The Divine" (*Das Göttliche*) (1783), Goethe had spoken of the laws that govern our lives and bring it full circle:

> Following great, bronzen,
> Ageless laws
> All of us must
> Fulfill the circles
> Of our existence.
>
> [*Nach ewigen, ehrnen,*
> *Großen Gesetzen*
> *Müssen wir alle*

---

[74]Goethe, *Poems of the West and East*, trans. Whaley, p. 265; *Werke* [HA], vol. 2, p. 67.

[75]See his comment to Eckermann of 4 January 1824: "I discovered light in its purity and truth, and I considered it my duty to fight for it" [*Ich erkannte das Licht in seiner Reinheit und Wahrheit, und ich hielt es meines Amtes, dafür zu streiten*] (Eckermann, *Conversations of Goethe*, p. 35).

[76]Jung, *CW* 8 §787.

*Unseres Daseins*
*Kreise vollenden.*][77]

These laws exercise an influence on the individual from the moment of birth on, and for the rest of his or her life: here, Goethe emphasizes that the development of the human individual is a task that requires a life-time.[78] This development, or so Goethe's commentary suggests, remains true to its etymological sense: "this firm, tough being, this being can only develop out of itself," it "un-ravels" (*ent-wickelt*) itself from a predetermined core,[79] much as Jung saw the life of the individual in terms of process, speaking of the "individuation process" or *Individuationsprozess*. This line, together with the next (line 5) that urges the individual— whom, throughout this stanza, the poem directly addresses, using the informal second-person form in German, *du*—not to try and flee from its own self, touches on the theme of freedom and necessity, the dialectical relationship of determining constellation and free self-development,[80] which the second stanza explores in further detail. The final lines of the first stanza, however, affirm, with reference to authorities both pagan (the sibyls) and biblical (the prophets), the autotelic nature of the individual, its time-and-space-transcending potential—

> Thus must you be, from self there's no remission,
> Thus long have sibyls, prophets this imparted;
>
> [*So mußt du sein, dir kannst du nicht entfliehen,*{[81]}
> *So sagten schon Sibyllen, so Propheten;*]

—while the concluding couplet of the first stanza thus relates the two notions of "self" and life (*lebend*) through the idea of shaping, forming, and trans-forming. For all that the self is "torn apart" (*zerstückelt*), like the mythical figure of Orpheus or the the god Dionysos was, it can never—again, like Orpheus and Dionysos—be "torn to pieces" and destroyed:

---

[77]Goethe, *GE* 1, 80 [trans. Vernon Watkins]; *Werke* [HA], vol. 1, p. 148.

[78]Theo Buck, *Goethes "Urworte. Orphisch" interpretiert und mit einer Dokumentation versehen* (Frankfurt am Main, Berlin, Berne: Lang, 1996), p. 35. Recall the title of the study by Marie de Hennezel and Bertrand Vergely, *Une vie pour se mettre au monde* (2010).

[79]Goethe, *Werke* [HA], vol. 1, p. 404; "*Dieses feste, zähe, dieses nur aus sich selbst zu entwickelnde Wesen.*" On this point, see Schmidt, *Goethes Altersgedicht "Urworte. Orphisch,"* p. 18.

[80]Buck, *Goethes "Urworte. Orphisch,"* p. 35.

[81]In *The Red Book*, Jung appears to allude to this line when he writes: "But you cannot flee from yourself" [*du kannst dir aber nicht entfliehen*] (Jung, *The Red Book*, pp. 233-234).

No time there is, no power, can decompose
The minted form that lives and living grows.

[*Und keine Zeit und keine Macht zerstückelt*
*Geprägte Form, die lebend sich entwickelt.*]

This developmental perspective, indebted to Herder's organological thought,[82] was one that Goethe applied widely. He wrote of himself (in the third person) in "Self-Description" (1797) that "an ever more active poetic, formative drive, both inwards and outwards, constitutes the nodal point [*Mittelpunkt*] and basis of his existence; once one has understood that, then all other apparent contradictions resolve themselves."[83] And at the end of *Faust*, as Faust's "entelechy" is borne up into heaven, so the "more perfect" angels sing:

When spirit-energy
Captures the physical
Elements powerfully,
No force angelical
Can loose the subtle bond
That has allied them:
Only the love beyond
Time can divide them.

[*Wenn starke Geisteskraft*
*Die Elemente*
*An sich herangerafft,*
*Kein Engel trennte*
*Geeinte Zwienatur*
*Der innigen beiden,*
*Die ewige Liebe nur*
*Vermag's zu scheiden.*][84]

This "unified twin-nature" of the self is, at this stage of "Primal Words. Orphic," however, still in the process of formation. And yet, as we shall see, love will have its part to play here, too.

[82]See Schmidt, *Goethes Altergedicht "Urworte. Orphisch,"* p. 18. For an (old, but helpful) account of Herder's thought, see Hans Kern, *Von Paracelsus bis Klages: Studien zur Philosophie des Lebens* (Berlin: Widukind; Alexander Boss, 1942), pp. 60-74; and for a recent (and stimulating) account, see John H. Zammito, *Kant, Herder, and the Birth of Anthropology* (Chicago and London: Chicago University Press, 2002).

[83]Goethe, *Werke* [HA], vol. 10, p. 529; *"Immer tätiger, nach innen und außen fortwirkender poetischer Bildungstrieb mach den Mittelpunkt und die Base seiner Existenz; hat man den gefaßt, so lösen sich alle übrigen anscheinenden Widersprüche."*

[84]Goethe, *Faust II*, ll. 11958-11965; *Faust: Part Two*, trans. Luke, p. 235.

## CHANCE

Found in Hesiod and in the Homeric Hymns associated with him,[85] the figure of Tyche, translated by Thomas Taylor as "Fortune" but meaning "Chance" or "Lot," is addressed in the Orphic hymn to her as follows:

> Approach, queen Fortune, with propitious mind
> And rich abundance, to my pray'r inclin'd:
> Placid and gentle Trivia, mighty nam'd,
> Imperial Dian, born of Pluto fam'd,
> Mankind's unconquer'd endless praise is thine,
> Sepulch'ral, widely wand'ring pow'r divine!
> In thee our various mortal life is found,
> And some from thee in copious wealth abound;
> While others mourn thy hand averse to bless,
> In all the bitterness of deep distress.
> Be present, Goddess, to thy vot'ries kind,
> And give abundance with benignant mind.[86]

Where the Orphic poet turns to the divine figure of the sublunary goddess, Diana, in the second stanza of "Primal Words. Orphic," entitled "TYXH, Chance," Goethe broadens his consideration of the individual as an objective of transformation (in German, as *ein Wandelndes*),

> But easing change gets round that stern constriction
> As with and round us change is all-imbuing.
>
> [*Die strenge Grenze doch umgeht gefällig*
> *Ein Wandelndes, das mit und um uns wandelt.*]

What is chance, what is *tyche*? For the Greeks, *tyche* was an outside force (rather than an internal one, like the *daimon*) that influenced human beings, one of the great concepts of fate.[87] Whereas the *daimon* was, in a sense, morally neutral, there were two kinds of chance or luck: a positive kind, or good luck (*eutychia*), and (inevitably) a negative kind, or bad luck

---

[85]Hesiod, *Theogony*, l. 360, and "To Demeter," l. 420, in *Hesiod, The Homeric Hymns and Homerica*, trans. Hugh G. Evelyn-White (Cambridge, MA: Harvard University Press; London: Heinemann, 1914), pp. 105 and 319. The fame of the Homeric Hymns in the German tradition is reflected, for example, in the translation of a selection of them by Eduard Mörike (see his *Sämtliche Werke*, ed. Herbert G. Göpfert [Munich: Hanser, 1958], pp. 1234-1256).

[86]"To Fortune," in *The Mystical Hymns of Orpheus*, trans. Taylor, no. 72, pp. 139-140. For a commentary, see *The Orphic Hymns*, trans. Athanassakis, p. 138.

[87]For a helpful, clarificatory discussion of the concept of *tyche* in relation to *fortuna, heimarmene, fatum,* and *moira,* see Anton Anwander, "'Schicksal'-Wörter in Antike und Christentum," *Zeitschrift für Religions- und Geistesgeschichte* 1 (1948): 315-327 and 2 (1949/1950): 48-54 and 128-135.

(*dystychia*).[88] For Pindar, in particular, *tyche* was a daughter of Zeus, one of the most powerful goddesses of fate.[89] According to Roman mythology, *tyche* was the goddess Fortuna, and it was to her manifestation as the smiling goddess, or Agathe Tyche, that Goethe dedicated an "altar," his "stone of good fortune," in his garden in Weimar in 1777.[90]

Conceived as a plan on 25 December 1776 (not just Christmas Day, but also the birthday of Charlotte von Stein), as his diary entry shows,[91] this "altar" consists of a sphere, standing on a cube: interpreted variously as a representation of the division in the human being between individuality (the cube) and the happiness of external circumstances (the sphere), or as an emblem of mobility (the sphere) supported by an emblem of stability (the cube).[92] As Wilhelm Heckscher has suggested, the juxtaposition of cube and sphere recalls an emblem in a collection by Otto Vaenius (c. 1556-1629), his *Emblemata sive Symbola* (1624), which bears the title *Mobile fit fixum* ("what is mobile becomes immobile"), and there is an extensive emblematic tradition behind this image.[93] On one level, according to Pierre Hadot, the monument symbolizes the autobiographical situation in which Goethe found himself, now that his *tyche* had led him to stay in Weimar and to devote himself to Charlotte;[94] indeed, the dialectical relationship of inner and outer, *daimon* and *tyche*, forms the theme of a passage translated by Goethe from the *Golden Sayings*, a Greek text inspired by the

[88]See Schmidt, *Goethes Altersgedicht "Urworte. Orphisch,"* p. 18. See Simplicius's commentary on Aristotle's *Physics*, book 2, §81, cited in *The Mystical Hymns of Orpheus*, trans. Taylor, pp. 139-140.

[89]Pindar, *Olympian Odes*, no. 12: "Daughter of Zeus the Deliverer! thou saving goddess, Fortune! I pray thee to keep watch around mighty Himera; for, at thye bidding, swift ships are steered upon the sea, and speedy decisions of war and counsels of the people are guided on the land" (Pindar, *The Odes*, trans. John Sandys [London: Heinemann; New York: Putnam, 1927], p. 129). See Buck, *Goethes "Urworte. Orphisch,"* p. 39.

[90]See Goethe's letter to Lavater of 3-5 December 1779; *Briefe* [HA], vol. 1, pp.287-289.

[91]See Goethe, *Werke* [WA], vol. III.1, p. 29. Cf. the entry for 5 April 1777; *Werke* [WA], vol. III.1, p. 37.

[92]Nicholas Boyle, *Goethe: The Poet and the Age*, volume 1, *The Poetry of Desire (1749-1790)* (Oxford and New York: Oxford University Press, 1991), p. 286.

[93]For discussion of the iconographic significance of Goethe's *"Stein des guten Glücks,"* see William S. Heckscher, "Goethe im Banne der Sinnbilder: Ein Beitrag zur Emblematik," *Jahrbuch der Hamburger Kunstsammlungen 7* (1962): 35-54; reprinted in Sibylle Penkert, ed., *Emblem und Emblematikrezeption: Vergleichende Studien zur Wirkungsgeschichte vom 16. bis 20. Jahrhundert* (Darmstadt: Wissenschaftliche Buchgesellschaft, 1978), pp. 355-385, and in *Art and Literature: Studies in Relationship*, ed. Egon Verheyen (Durham, NC: Duke University Press; Baden-Baden :Valentin Koerner, 1985), pp. 217-236.

[94]Hadot, *N'oublie pas de vivre*, pp. 202-206.

school of Pythagoras, in part of a letter he wrote to Charlotte on 8 September 1780:

> And when you have achieved it,
> You will recognize the unchanging nature of the gods and Man,
> In which everything moves and by which all is surrounded,
> Gently contemplate nature, which is ever always the same,
> Not hope for the impossible, but be satisfied with life.

> [*Und wenn du's vollbracht hast,*
> *Wirst du erkennen der Götter und Menschen unänderlich Wesen*
>                                       {= *dämon*}
> *Drinne sich alles bewegt und davon alles umgränzt ist* {= *tyche*},
> *Stille schaun die Natur sich gleich in allem und allem*
> *Nichts unmögliches hoffen und doch dem Leben genug seyn.*][95]

At the same time, the monument—best viewed from an upper garden, where the viewer is invited to rest on a stone bench by its inscription, the poem, "Chosen Rock" (*Erwählter Fels*) (1782)[96]—constitutes "the purest plastic expression of enclosure and containment," as "the cube—which is both a conventional pedestal fixed in the earth and an abstract torso—supports the sphere—which is poised to roll off in all directions" and which also, as "an abstract head, implies through its infinite radii, movement away from its own centre and outward."[97]

---

[95]Goethe, *Briefe* [HA], vol. 1, p. 316; see the remarks in Wipf, *Elpis*, p. 101. Compare with the following translation: "When thou hast made this habit familiar to thee, / Thou wilt know the constitution of the Immortal Gods and of men. / Even how far the different beings extend, and what contains and binds them together. / Thou shalt likewise know that according to Law, the nature of this universe is in all things alike, / So that thou shalt not hope what thou ought'st not to hope [...]" (*The Golden Verses of Pythagoras, and Other Pythagorean Fragments*, ed. Florence M. Firth, introd. Annie Besant [London and Benares: Theosophical Publishing Society, 1905], pp. 5-6). For further discussion of the importance of the sayings for Goethe, see Adolf Beck, "Der 'Geist der Reinheit' und die 'Idee des Reinen': Deutsches und Frühgriechisches in Goethes Humanitätsideal," *Goethe: Viermonatsschrift der Goethe-Gesellschaft* 7 (1942): 160-169 (pp. 165-166) and 8 (1943): 19-57.

[96]"Here, in silence, the lover thought of his beloved, / Full of cheer he said: 'Become my witness, o stone! / But do not get up, you have so many companions; / To each rock of the meadow, that nourishes me, the happy one, / To each tree of the forest, which I, as I wander, embrace, / Remain a memorial of bliss! I cried, dedicating in joy. / But a voice I lend only to you, as from the many / One the Muse chooses to kiss, as her friend, on the lips'" [*Hier im stillen gedachte der Liebende seiner Geliebten; / Heiter sprach er zu mir: Werde mir zeuge, du Stein! / Doch erhebe dich nicht, du hast noch viele Gesellen; / Jedem Felsen der Flur, die mich, den Glücklichen, nährt, / Jedem Baume des Walds, um den ich wandernd mich schlinge! / Denkmal bleibe des Glücks! ruf' ich ihm weihend und froh. / Doch die Stimme verleih' ich nur dir, wie unter der Menge / Einen die Muse sich wählt, freundlich die Lippen ihm küßt*] (Goethe, *Werke* [HA], vol. 1, p. 204).

[97]Clark S. Muenzer, "Wandering Among Obelisks: Goethe and the Idea of Monument," *Modern Language Studies* 31/1 [Remembering Goethe: Essays for the 250th Anniversary] (Spring, 2001): 5-34 (pp. 30-31).

Yet from the seemingly abstract (Pythagorean) concepts of fate, chance, or contingency, Goethe develops the concrete notion of chance-as-circumstance. Like chance, circumstances can be propitious, or deleterious. Goethe once noted that "as soon as the world catches sight of the single individual who strives, immediately there sounds a general cry to oppose him," and "all those above and around him are intensely concerned to surround him with barriers and limits, to slow him down in every way, to make him impatient, morose, and not just from without but also from within to bring him to a halt";[98] and, as we have seen, he knew of the existence of "retarding demons," thanks to whom, "although the whole progresses, it is but slowly."[99] In this second stanza and in his commentary on it, Goethe both extends the theme of transformation, and begins to consider the molding effect of social interchange on the individual:

> No more alone, you grow through social friction
> And do such deeds as any man is doing.
> This life's an ebb and flow, a contradiction,
> A toy that's toyed with, play for our pursuing.
>
> [*Nicht einsam bleibst du, bildest dich gesellig*
> *Und handelst wohl so, wie ein andrer handelt:*
> *Im Leben ist's bald hin-, bald widerfällig,*
> *Es ist ein Tand und wird so durchgetandelt.*]

Thus the force of chance becomes associated with the realm of society; in his commentary, Goethe extends the persistence of the personality beyond the human individual to "nations, tribes, and families," discussing how, in the course of education, the laws and customs of the locality, in the form of the wet nurse and carer, the father or guardian, teacher or attendant, are all inculcated in the individual. (In Freudian terms, this process corresponds to the development of the superego.) Yet the individual's *daimon* tries to hold out against the force of chance, and Goethe offers us his own version of Freud's doctrine of "the return of the repressed," when he writes how "the old Adam, or whatever one wants to

[98]Goethe, *Materialien zur Geschichte der Farbenlehre*, section 5, "Allgemeine Betrachtungen"; *Werke* [HA], vol. 14, p. 97; "*sobald die Welt den einzelnen Strebenden erblickt, sobald erschallt ein allgemeiner Aufruf, sich ihm zu widersetzen. Alle Vor- und Mitwerber sind höchlich bemüht, ihn mit Schranken und Grenzen zu umbauen, ihn auf jede Weise zu retardieren, ihn ungeduldig, verdrießlich zu machen und ihn nicht allein von außen, sondern auch von innen zum Stocken zu bringen.*"
[99]Conversation with Eckermann of 23 October 1828; *Conversations of Goethe*, p. 275.

call it," will always, "however often one drives it out, always return more invincible."[100]

Thus the sense of "chance"—in German, *das Zufällige*—is a threefold one. First, it can mean just that: chance—pure contingency—or (in the words of a former British Prime Minister, Harold Macmillan) "events, dear boy, events." Second, it can mean what happens to us (in German, *uns zu-fällt*)—the events, historical and personal, that, subtly and not so subtly, affect our lives. And third, it can mean what we have to do (in German, what is *zufällig für uns*)—our social, legal, moral obligations, our obedience to the law. In his commentary, Goethe speaks compellingly of the continuing influence of the *daimon*, which whispers in the individuals's ear and tells him or her what to do,[101] and he cites Socrates as an example.[102] Correspondingly, in his discussion of the "determination" (*Bestimmung*) of the individual, Jung uses a closely related image—and an identical example—in his lecture on "The Development of Personality":

> Someone who has a vocation *must* obey his own law, as if it were a daimon whispering to him of new and wonderful paths. Anyone with a vocation hears the voice of the inner man: he is *called*. [{*Der, der Bestimmung hat,*} *muß dem eigenen Gesetze gehorchen, wie wenn es ein Dämon wäre, der ihm neue, seltsame Wege einflüstert. Wer Bestimmung hat, hört die Stimme des Innern, er ist bestimmt.*] That is why the legends say that he possesses a private daimon who counsels him and whose mandates he must obey.[103]

Jung uses Socrates as an example, but also Faust (whose *daimon* appears in the form of Mephistopheles)—as well as Napoleon, and even Goethe himself:

---

[100]Goethe, *Werke* [HA], vol. 1, p. 405; "*der alte Adam, und wie man es nennen mag, der, so oft auch ausgetrieben, immer wieder unbezwinglicher zurückkehrt.*"

[101]Goethe, *Werke* [HA], vol. 1, p. 405; "*der ihm gelegentlich ins Ohr raunt, was denn eigentlich zu tun sei.*"

[102]See *The Apology*, 31c-d: "You have often heard me say before on many occasions—that I am subject to a divine or supernatural experience [*daimonion*] […]. It began in my early childhood—a sort of voice which comes to me, and when it comes it always dissuades me from what I am proposing to do, and never urges me on" (Plato, *Collected Dialogues*, p. 17).

[103]Jung, *CW* 17 §300. Compare with Bertrand Vergely's distinction between "the voice of our ego" (*la voix de notre moi*) and "the voice of life" (*la voix de la vie*), "a tiny interior voice which guides us, which explains things to us, which warns us, which rejoices when we rejoice, which becomes sad when we become sad, which sometimes also becomes sad when we rejoice about certain things, and sometimes, inversely, which rejoices when we become sad about certain things" (Marie de Hennezel and Bertrand Vergely, *Une vie pour se mettre au monde* [Paris: Carnets Nord, 2010], p. 93).

The best known example of this is Faust, and an historical instance is provided by the daimon of Socrates. [...] The original meaning of "to have a vocation" is "to be addressed by a voice" [*Bestimmung haben heißt im Ursinn: von einer Stimme angesprochen sein*]. The clearest examples of this are to be found in the avowals of the Old Testament prophets. That it is not just a quaint old-fashioned way of speaking is provided by the confessions of historical personalities such as Goethe and Napoleon, to mention only two familiar examples, who made no secret of their feeling of vocation.[104]

Whereas Edmund Bergler sees the *daimonion* as an essentially negative figure, for Jung it is a far more positive force.[105]

Further on in this lecture, Jung declares that "only the man who can consciously assent to the power of the inner voice becomes a personality," for "it is able to cope with the changing times, and has unknowingly and voluntarily become a *leader* [*Führer*]."[106] This remark, apt to be misunderstood as an ill-conceived, even mischievous, and potentially politically compromising remark, is, however, seen in its context here, an echo of the Pythagorean idea of the *hegemonikon* (ἡγεμονικόν), the "governing," "guiding," or "leading principle," found in the writings of such pre-Socratic thinkers as Alcmaeon and Philolaus,[107] and referred to in his diary by Goethe.[108] For what we are, who we are, belongs to our innermost nature; how we exercise our capacities and realize our potential depends on the historical moment in which we find ourselves, our social standing, our access to resources, financial and intellectual. In the words of one of Goethe's commentators, Eduard Spranger (1882-1963), this second stanza concerns itself with our "receptive experience, in which we first begin to discover ourselves," with the dialectic of "receptive experience"

---

[104]Jung, *CW* 17 §§300-301. Moreover, according to Eckermann's account of his conversation with Goethe of 3 May 1827, the French literary critic Jean-Jacques Ampère (1800-1864) was right to discern, in "the scorn and the bitter irony" of Mephistopheles, a part of Goethe himself (*Conversations of Goethe*, p. 199).

[105]"Socrates had in mind a malignant spirit operating within the personality. His description was sheer mythology, but his observations were correct" (Edmund Bergler, *Divorce Won't Help* [New York and London: Harper, 1948], p. 62).

[106]Jung, *CW* 17 §308, §306.

[107]See *Les Présocratiques*, ed. Dumont, pp. 220, 223 (Diels-Kranz A 8 and 13), 498, 506 (Diels-Kranz A 17 and 11).

[108]See his entry for 26 March 1780; Goethe, *Werke* [WA], vol. III.1, p. 112. For further discussion, see Beck, "Der 'Geist der Reinheit' und die 'Idee der Reinen,'" pp. 20-22.

and "active intervention in the external world,"[109] or, as one of Goethe's
aphorisms puts it, of "metamorphosis in the higher sense"—"taking and
giving, winning and losing."[110]

This sense of continuous activity, of to-ing and fro-ing, is well captured in Goethe's language in this stanza: "in life," he says, "it's all back
and forth" (*bald hin-, bald widerfällig*), and his commentary's account of
the individual's life, particularly the transition from youth to mature
adulthood, is accompanied by a sense of further change to come, "as the
day goes on, there develops a more serious disquiet, a more profound
yearning," and "the advent of a new god is expected"[111]—

> Full circle come the years, the end is sighted,
> The lamp awaits the flame, to be ignited
>
> [*Schon hat sich still der Jahre Kreis geründet,*
> *Die Lampe harrt der Flamme, die entzündet*]

—and this god is Eros. In a sense, we are already in a moment of psychological crisis, as the "strict limit" becomes the "full circle" of years. The
"dialectical correlation" of (daimonic) entelic law and the play of chance,
as one commentator puts it,[112] acquires the contours of a crisis. Only this
crisis is the one between childhood and youth; this is not yet the midlife
crisis. The Orphic moment has not yet come. But with his introduction
of the theme of sexual love, Goethe opens the way to a fuller, richer

---

[109]Eduard Spranger, "Goethes Weltanschauung" [1932], in *Goethe: Seine geistige Welt*, pp.
275-317 (pp. 304-305); "*das empfangende Erleben, an dem wir uns erst selbst kennen lernen; das tätige
Eingreifen in die Außenwelt.*"

[110]Goethe, *Maxims and Reflections*, ed. Hecker, §96; *Werke* [HA], vol. 12, p. 501. According to
Goethe, this "metamorphosis" was superbly depicted in Dante (see *Inferno*, Canto 25, ll. 49-141).
When presenting the literary-historical background (above all, Hamann and Klopstock) of the *Sturm
und Drang* in the context of his own life in Part Three, Book 12, of *Dichtung und Wahrheit*, Goethe
writes: "This reciprocal harassment and incitement, which could grow excessive, had a good influence
on each of us in his own way. And out of this creative whirl, this desire to live and let live, this
give-and-take [*diesem Nehmen und Geben*] within a group of unbuttoned youths recklessly following
their individual innate characters without any theoretical guidance emerged that famous, much discussed and decried literary epoch in which a throng of young geniuses burst forth with all the boldness
and arrogance peculiar to their years. By using their abilities well, they brought about much joy and
good; but by misusing them they caused much vexation and evil. It is precisely the effects and
countereffects arising from this source that will be the main theme of this book" (Goethe, *GE* 4, 384;
*Werke* [HA], vol. 9, p. 520).

[111]Goethe, *Werke* [HA], vol. 1, p. 405; "*Da entsteht denn mit dem wachsenden Tage eine ernstere
Unruhe, eine gründlichere Sehnsucht; die Ankunft eines neuen Göttlichen wird erwartet.*"

[112]Buck, *Goethes "Urworte. Orphisch,"* p. 41; "*Entelechische Gesetzlichkeit und Spiel des Zufalls
wirken als Korrelate dialektisch zusammen.*"

understanding of the archetypal force of Eros, and its life-enhancing, transformative power.

## EROS

For a third time, there is a correspondence between, on the one hand, the "holy words" of Orphic tradition and the Orphic hymns, and, on the other, Goethe's poem. In the Orphic hymnary, Eros (or Love) is addressed as follows:

> I call, great Love, the source of sweet delight,
> Holy and pure, and charming to the sight;
> Darting, and wing'd, impetuous fierce desire,
> With Gods and mortals playing, wand'ring fire:
> Agile and twofold, keeper of the keys
> Of heav'n and earth, the air, and spreading seas;
> Of all that Ceres' fertile realms contains,
> By which th' all parent Goddess life sustains,
> Or dismal Tartarus is doom'd to keep,
> Widely extended, or the sounding deep;
> For thee all Nature's various realms obey,
> Who rul'st alone, with universal sway.
> Come, blessed pow'r, *regard these mystic fires*,
> And far avert unlawful mad desires.[113]

Just as this Orphic hymn is anything but erotic, so Goethe's stanza on Eros is anything but mystical. At the beginning of "ΕΡΩΣ, Love," we have been awaiting this new god, so central to Orphic cosmogony and Platonic (and Neoplatonic) philosophy alike, and because—

> And come it must!

> [*Die bleibt nicht aus!*]

—we do not have to wait long:

> —He plunges earthwards winging
> Who from the timeless void to heaven once sped,
> On airy pinions hovering and swinging
> All springtime's day around the heart and head,
> Away and back again forever springing,
> Then woe is weal, there's sweet delight in dread.

---

[113]"To Love," in *The Mystical Hymns of Orpheus*, trans. Taylor, no. 58, pp. 117-120. For a commentary, see *The Orphic Hymns*, trans. Athanassakis, p. 133.

—[*Er stürzt vom Himmel nieder,*
*Wohin er sich aus alter Öde schwang,*
*Er schwebt heran auf luftigem Gefieder*
*Um Stirn und Brust den Frühlingstag entlang,*
*Scheint jetzt zu fliehn, vom Fliehen kehrt er wieder,*
*Da wird ein Wohl im Weh, so süß und bang.*]

In this third stanza, Goethe introduces the god of sexual love, consistent with the ancient iconographical depiction of Eros as a young boy with wings. Of course, this same god was used by Freud to represent sexual libido as one of the two basic drives, according to psychoanalysis.[114] At first sight, Goethe's recognition of the importance of love stands in contrast to the almost complete absence of discussion of sexuality in Jung's essay on "The Stages of Life." Indeed, Jung hardly ever explicitly discussed sexual issues, with one major exception, his lecture on "The Love Problem of a Student" (*Das Liebesproblem des Studenten*) (1928).[115]

In "The Stages of Life," however, Jung does note that "psychic birth, and with it the conscious differentiation from the parents, normally takes place only at puberty, with the eruption of sexuality,"[116] while later on he refers to the idea that the psychic components of masculinity and femininity might be used, during the first half of life, in an unequal way, requiring compensation in the second half.[117] And towards the end of *Memories, Dreams, Reflections*, its author sings an extraordinary paean to Eros, praising it as "a *kosmogonos*, a creator and father-mother of all higher consciousness."[118] *Memories, Dreams, Reflections* places Eros in its classical context, describing it as a *daimon*, whose paradoxical nature defies description:

> In classical times, when such things were properly understood, Eros was considered a god whose divinity transcended our human limits, and who could therefore neither be comprehended nor represented in any way. I might, as many be-

[114]See Freud, *Outline of Psychoanalysis* (*Abriß der Psychoanalyse*) (1938); *SE* 23, 148; *FGW* 17, 70-71.

[115]Jung, *CW* 10 §§197-235. This is, of course, not to say that sexuality is not an important issue for Jungian psychology. For further discussion, see Paul Bishop, "The Holy Grail of Sexuality: Jung and Wagner," in *Spring: A Journal of Archetype and Culture* 69 (2002): 115-132.

[116]Jung, *CW* 8 §756; "*die seelische Geburt und damit die bewußte Unterscheidung von den Eltern erfolgt normalerweise erst mit dem Einbruch der Sexualität im Pubertätsalter.*"

[117]Jung, *CW* 8 §§782-783.

[118]Jung, *MDR*, 386; *ETG*, 356.

> fore me have attempted to do, venture an approach to this daimon, whose range of activity extends from the endless spaces of the heavens to the dark abysses of hell; but I falter before the task of finding the language which might adequately express the incalculable paradoxes of love.[119]

The passage expands the topos of unsayability, appealing repeatedly to experience and to the paradoxical nature of Eros alike to insist on its essential inexpressibility:

> In my medical experience as well as in my own life I have again and again been faced with the mystery of love, and have never been able to explain what it is. [...] Here is the greatest and smallest, the remotest and nearest, the highest and lowest, and we cannot discuss one side of it without also discussing the other. No language is adequate to this paradox. Whatever one can say, no words express the whole. To speak of partial aspects is always too much or too little, for only the whole is meaningful.[120]

Not only linguistically and conceptually, but emotionally and existentially, we are defeated by Eros. Yet Eros also expresses, so *Memories, Dreams, Reflections* argues, our deepest desire to be whole, to be unified, to be as (at) one with ourselves:

> We are in the deepest sense the victims and the instruments of cosmogonic "love." I put the word in quotation marks to indicate I do not use it in its connotations of desiring, preferring, favouring, wishing, and similar feelings, but as something superior to the individual, a unified and undivided whole. Being a part, human beings cannot grasp the whole. They are at its mercy. They may assent to it, or rebel against it; but they are always caught up by it and enclosed within it. They are dependent on it, and are sustained by it. Love is their light and darkness, whose end they cannot see.[121]

Ultimately, so *Memories, Dreams, Reflections* concludes, we cannot name love, we cannot understand it, we can only acknowledge it in its unknowability, and accord it the status of the divine:

> Human beings can try to name love, showering upon it all the

[119] Jung, *MDR*, 386; *ETG*, 356.
[120] Jung, *MDR*, 386; *ETG*, 356.
[121] Jung, *MDR*, 386; *ETG*, 356.

names at their command, and still they will involve themselves in endless self-deceptions. If human beings possess a
grain of wisdom, they will lay down their arms and name the
unknown by the more unknown, *ignotum per ignotius*—that
is, by the name of God. This is a confession of their subjec-
tion, their imperfection, and their dependence; but at the
same time a testimony to their freedom to choose between
truth and error.[122]

This is a powerful rhetorical performance, but in the end, it amounts to
no more than an admission of defeat. Perhaps sexuality remains an aporia
in Jungian thought, after all? Tellingly, however, Goethe's discussion is
more complex, and more sophisticated, than this exposition in *Memories,
Dreams, Reflections.*

To begin with, Goethe's Eros is cunningly ambiguous in its gender.
The first line contains two pronouns, one feminine (*sie*), one masculine
(*er*); grammatically speaking, the first refers back to the feminine noun,
the flame (*die Flamme*) awaited by the candle, while the second refers forward to the masculine noun, *Eros*. Conceptually, however, both refer to
(masculine) Eros, whose German transliteration, love (*die Liebe*), is feminine. Through its use of the German language, Goethe's poem engenders
Eros as both a feminine, as well as a masculine, deity.[123]

According to Hesiod, Eros—"fairest among the deathless
gods, who unnerves the limbs and overcomes the mind and wise counsels
of all gods and all men within them"—arises, along with the Earth, out of
the primeval chaos,[124] and Hesiod's myth is expressly endorsed by
Phaedrus in the *Symposium.*[125] In *Faust*, Part Two, the Classical
Walpurgisnacht ends on the Rocky Shores on the Aegean Sea, where
Homunculus's glass retort shatters, he returns to the elements, and the
Sirens sing:

What fiery wonder transfigures the sea?
The waves splinter and glitter, what storm can this be?
All shining and swaying, a progress of light,
Those bodies aglow as they move through the night,

---

[122]Jung, *MDR*, 387; *ETG*, 365.

[123]Buck, *Goethes "Urworte. Orphisch,"* p. 45.

[124]Hesiod, *Theogony*, ll. 121-122, in *Hesiod, The Homeric Hymns and Homerica*, trans.
Evelyn-White, p. 87.

[125]*Symposium* 178b; in Plato, *Collected Dialogues*, p. 532. See Hoffmeister, "Goethes 'Urworte.
Orphisch,'" p. 197; and Schmidt, *Goethes Altersgedicht "Urworte. Orphisch,"* p. 20.

And the whirl of the fire all about and around!
Now let Eros, first cause of all, reign and be crowned!

[*Welch feuriges Wunder verklärt uns die Wellen,*
*Die gegeneinander sich funkelnd zerschellen?*
*So leuchtet's und schwanket und hellet hinan:*
*Die Körper, sie glühen auf nächtlicher Bahn,*
*Und ringsum ist alles vom Feuer umronnen;*
*So herrsche denn Eros, der alles begonnen!*][126]

Similarly, in "Primal Words. Orphic," Eros swoops out of the dreariness and desolation of everyday life, and suddenly, unexpectedly—with a flutter of his wings—transforms it into an erotic oasis, a sexual springtime. Eros leads us into an unending universe of pleasure—but also of pain, "so great, so wonderful, and so all-embracing is the power of Love," says (in Plato's *Symposium*) Eryximachus, who distinguishes, like Pausanias, between Uranian (heavenly) Love and Pandemic (earthly) Love, between "the regulating principle of Love" that "brings together those opposites [...] and compounds them in an ordered harmony," and "that other Love" that brings "mischief and destruction," due to "the uncontrolled and the acquisitive in that great system of Love which the astronomer observes when he investigates the movements of the stars and the seasons of the year."[127] The oxymoronic complexity of Eros never ceases (to amaze): it is both "painful and pleasurable," in Sappho's phrase [γλυκύπικρου] "bitter-sweet,"[128] in Ovid's *dulce malum*,[129] in Petrarch's

---

[126]Goethe, *Faust II*, ll. 8474-8479; *Faust: Part Two*, trans. Luke, p. 123. For a commentary on this scene, see Karl Kerényi, *Das Ägäische Fest: Die Meergötterszene in Goethes Faust II* (Amsterdam: Pantheon, 1941); revised in the third edition as *Das ägäische Fest: Erläuterungen zur Szene "Felsbuchten des Ägäischen Meers" in Goethes Faust II* (Wiesbaden: Limes, 1950). Jung greatly admired this book (see his letter to Kerényi of 18 January 1941; *Letters*, vol. 1, p. 291), and claimed it had inspired him to write *Mysterium Coniunctionis* (see *GW* 14, p. xiii).

[127]See *Symposium*, 185c – 189b (Plato, *Collected Dialogues*, p. 541; cf. Hoffmeister, p. 198).

[128]See fragment 130: "Once again limb-loosening Love makes me tremble, / the bitter-sweet, irresistible creature" (*Greek Lyric*, vol. 1, *Sappho; Alcaeus*, trans. David A. Campbell [Cambridge, MA; London: Heinemann, 1982], pp. 146-147). For further discussion, see Heinz Martin Müller, *Erotische Motive in der griechische Dichtung bis auf Euripides* (Hamburg: Buske, 1980), pp. 99-101, 142; and Anne Carson, *Eros the Bittersweet: An Essay* (Princeton: Princeton University Press, 1986). According to Bachofen, Sappho's home, Lesbos, was "one of the great centers of the Orphic mystery religion" (*Mother Right*, "Introduction," in J. J. Bachofen, *Myth, Religion, and Mother Right: Selected Writings of J. J. Bachofen*, trans. Ralph Manheim [Princeton, NJ: Princeton University Press, 1973], p. 90); see also his discussion of Lesbos and Orphism (*Myth, Religion, and Mother Right*, pp. 201-207; J. J. Bachofen, *Der Mythus von Orient und Occident: Eine Metaphysik der alten Welt*, ed. Manfred Schröter, introd. Alfred Baeumler [Munich: Beck, 1926], pp. 491-508).

[129]See *Amores* II, ix.b: "'Lay aside thy loves,' should some god say to me, 'and live without them,' I

*dolce amaro.*[130] At its most extreme, Eros is sado- or masochistic (or both), as Jungian analysts have come to realize;[131] even more extreme, in another sense, is Goethe's realization in his commentary on this stanza that love marks the point of coincidence between individual destiny and circumstantial contingency:

> This term refers to everything one can think of, from the merest inclination to the most passionate madness; here, the individual *daimon* and seductive *tyche* meet each other; the individual seems only to obey himself or herself, to let his or her will prevail, to indulge his or her drives, and yet contingent events impose themselves, alien things distract him or her from the path; he or she thinks of himself or herself as hunting, yet is the prey, believes himself or herself to have won, and is already lost.[132]

This central position of Eros in life is mirrored by the central position of the stanza—a centrality in line with Leo Strauss's "rule of forensic rhetoric."[133] This centrality is matched by the rich polysemy of the final word in the concluding couplet of this stanza:

> Some hearts away in general loving float,
> The noblest, yet, their all to one devote.
>
> [*Gar manches Herz verschwebt im Allgemeinen,*
> *Doch widmet sich das edelste dem Einen.*]

---

would pray him not ask it—even so sweet an evil are the fair" [*"Vive" deus "posito" siquis mihi dicat "amore!" / deprecer—usque adeo dulce puella malum est*] (Ovid, *Heriodes and Amores,* trans. Grant Showermann [London: Heinemann; New York: Putnam, 1931], pp. 408-409); see Schmidt, *Goethes Altersgedicht "Urworte. Orphisch, "* p. 21.

[130] See the *Canzoniere,* no. 129: "In the high mountains and harsh woods I find / some peace; and every habitable place / is for my eyes a mortal enemy. / With every step I take comes a new thought / about my lady which often will turn / to pleasure torment that I bear for her. / And on the verge of changing the bitter-sweetness of this life of mine / I say 'Perhaps it is Love saving you / for better days; perhaps, / you're loathsome to yourself but dear to her.' / Then to another thought I pass and sigh: / 'Now could this be the truth? But how? But when?'" [*Per alti monti et per selve aspre trovo / qualche riposo: ogni habitato loco / è nemico mortal degli occhi miei. / A ciascun passo nasce un penser novo / de la mia donna, che sovente in gioco / gira 'l tormento ch'i' porto per lei; / et a pena vorrei / cangiar questo mio viver dolce amaro, / ch'i' dico: Forse anchor ti serva Amore / ad un temp migliore; / forse, a te stesso vile, altrui se' caro. / En in questa trapasso sospirando: / Or porrebbe esser vero? or come? or quando?*] (Petrarch, *Selections from the "Canzoniere" and Other Works,* trans. Mark Musa [Oxford and New York: Oxford University Press, 1985], p. 47; *Canzoniere,* ed. Roberto Antonelli, Gianfranco Contini, Daniele Ponchiroli [Turin: Einaudi, 1992], p. 179); see Schmidt, *Goethes Altersgedicht "Urworte. Orphisch, "* p. 21.

[131] See Lyn Cowan, *Masochism: A Jungian View* (Dallas, TX: Spring Publications, 1982). For further discussion, see Anita Phillips, *A Defence of Masochism* (London and Boston: Faber and Faber, 1998).

[132] Goethe, *Werke* [HA], vol. 1, pp. 405-406.

[133] Buck, *Goethes "Urworte. Orphisch, "* pp. 47 and 51. As Leo Strauss argues in "How to Study

What is "the One" (*das Eine*)? This word, and the significance of the couplet, can be read in at least four different ways.[134] First, in the Pythagorean, Platonic, and ultimately Neoplatonic tradition, the One is the primal source of Being, the originary monad, the Unity underlying the Infinite Variety of the All.[135] The "noble heart" (*cor gentil*)—a motif associated with Dante, and the Neoplatonic convictions of the *dolce stil nuovo*, the Renaissance reflowering of "courtly love"[136]—dedicates itself to the one, in the sense that the goal of its erotic devotion is the Neoplatonic transcendent "One," *to Hen*, of which Plotinus speaks. We could call this, following Jochen Schmidt, the "esoteric" sense of the word.[137] Or, second, we could read it in a more prosaic sense, in line with Goethe's "exoteric" interpretation of the line in his commentary. Here a dedication to one (person) is taken to mean something quite simple—marriage. (Goethe expands on the social ramifications of the decision to marry, deriving from it the origin of the family, of society, and, ultimately, of the law. We shall return to Goethe's commentary below.) Or, third, it could mean Nature, in the sense that Goethe wrote in another poem, "And it is the One Eternal / Multiply self-manifest" (*Und es ist das ewig Eine, / Das sich vielfach offenbart*).[138] Or, finally, we could read "the one" as a commitment to the principle of "one-ness," to the principle of "in-dividuality." It is, in the words of another critic, "not the result of the ultimate vision, but the principle of one's attitude to one's environment."[139]

In Goethe's vocabulary, as in Jung's, the terms "individual" ("individuation"), "personality," and "self" are virtually interchangeable, and are different ways of articulating this notion of "oneness." In an autobio-

---

Spinoza's *Theological-Political Treatise*," the center is, compared with the beginning and the end, the "least exposed" part of a text, and so he directs his attention to the center of a text (*Persecution and the Art of Writing* [1952] [Chicago and London: University of Chicago Press, 1988], p. 185).

[134]Schmidt, *Goethes Altersgedicht "Urworte. Orphisch,"* p. 21.

[135]In one of Plato's dialogues, Parmenides sets out the doctrine of the One (*Parmenides*, 137c – 142e; in *Collected Dialogues*, pp. 931-936). For further discussion, see John Bussanich, "Plotinus's Metaphysics of the One," in *The Cambridge Companion to Plotinus*, ed. Lloyd P. Gerson (Cambridge: Cambridge University Press, 1996), pp. 38-65.

[136]Schmidt, *Goethes Altersgedicht "Urworte. Orphisch,"* p. 14. See also Milad Doueihi, *A Perverse History of the Human Heart* (Cambridge, MA, and London: Harvard University Press, 1997), pp. 56-62.

[137]See *Enneads*, 3.8, "Nature, Contemplation, and the One" (Plotinus, *The Enneads*, trans. Stephen MacKenna, abridged John Dillon [Harmondsworth: Penguin, 1991], pp. 233-247).

[138]"Parabase" (c. 1820); Goethe, *GE* 1, 154; *Werke* [HA], vol. 1, p. 358.

[139]Hoffmeister, "Goethes 'Urworte. Orphisch,'" p. 202.

graphical sketch, Goethe defends the individual against the general, and the right of the individual to pursue (in Nietzsche's words) a sacred "self-ishness":

> The individual gets lost; the memory of him disappears, and yet it is in the interest of him and others that it be preserved. Each person is only an individual and can in fact only be interested in what is individual. The general takes care of itself, imposes itself, preserves itself, increases itself. We use it, but we do not love it. We love only what is individual [...].[140]

Reflecting, in Part Two, Book 6, of *Dichtung und Wahrheit*, on his departure from Frankfurt for Leipzig, Goethe embraces the decision "to live for one's own self," which takes various forms according to the different stages of life. "Thus at certain junctures children detach themselves from parents, servants from masters, and protégés from patrons," he writes, "and such attempts to stand on one's own feet, to be independent, to live for one's own self, whether successful or not, are always in keeping with nature's will."[141] At the end of Part Two, Book 10, of *Dichtung und Wahrheit*, Goethe reflects that "a human being is really only required to be effective in the present," and that "a human being's personality is what affects his fellow man most."[142]

In one of his late poems, collected in a cycle known as the *Zahme Xenien*, Goethe writes of himself, in relation to his environment and to his inner entelechy, as constituting an essential unity, of being "one" (*der Eine*):

> Life is what I cannot share,
> What's inside or what's out there,
> Everything must be a whole,
> Which dwells in me and with you all.
> All I've ever written shows you
> What I think, and what I feel.

---

[140]"Bedeutung des Individuellen," in Goethe, *Werke* [WA], vol. I.6, p. 276; "*Das Individuum geht verloren; das Andenken desselben verschwindet und doch ist ihm und andern daran gelegen, daß es erhalten werde. Jeder ist selbst nur ein Individuum und kann sich auch eigentlich nur für's Individuelle interessiren. Das Allgemeine findet sich von selbst, dringt sich auf, erhält sich, vermehrt sich. Wir benutzen's, aber wir lieben es nicht. Wir lieben nur das Individuelle.*"

[141]Goethe, *GE* 4, 186; *Werke* [HA], vol. 9, p. 242. See the analysis of the "lemniscate"-like (or symmetrically intersecting) rhetorical structure of this sentence in Hiebel, *Goethe: Die Erhöhung des Menschen*, p. 44.

[142]Goethe, *GE* 4, 330; *Werke* [HA], vol. 9, p. 447.

Thus I split myself, my loved ones,
And yet it is as One I'm real.

[*Teilen kann ich nicht das Leben,*
*Nicht das Innen noch das Außen,*
*Allen muß das Ganze geben,*
*Um mit euch und mir zu hausen.*
*Immer hab' ich nur geschrieben,*
*Wie ich fühle, wie ich's meine,*
*Und so spalt' ich mir, ihr Lieben,*
*Und bin immerfort der Eine.*][143]

Thus "the One" (*das Eine*) is "the One" (*der Eine*); even though in another poem Goethe describes himself as being, like the gingko biloba, "one and double" (*eins und doppelt*) (see below),[144] Goethe nevertheless remains "the one."

## THE NECESSITY OF LOVE; OR, EROTIC NECESSITY

In the third of the Orphic hymns, dedicated "To Night," we find the line "Dread Necessity"—*ananke*—"governs all things," more elaborately rendered by Taylor as: "For dire Necessity, which nought withstands, / Invests the world with adamantine bands."[145] This idea informs Goethe's commentary on the Eros-stanza, and in the next stanza itself, entitled "ΑΝΑΓΚΗ, Necessity," he develops further the complex dialectic of freedom and necessity.[146] In the experience of Eros, Goethe writes, "the individual *daimon* and the temptations of *tyche* are bound together": we think we are fulfilling our own desires but, in reality, chance circumstances have intervened, and diverted us from our true path. Yet, Goethe continues, "there can be no end of erring," for "the path itself is error."[147] Here Goe-

---

[143] Goethe, *Werke* [HA], vol. 1, p. 320.

[144] Goethe, *Poems of the West and East*, p. 261 [trans. modified]; *Werke* [HA], vol. 2, p. 66. For a fascinating discussion of the question of totality, of *coincidentia oppositorum*, in the "Prologue in Heaven" in Goethe's *Faust I* and Balzac's *Séraphita* (1834-1835), one of the "Études philosophiques" of the *Comédie humaine*, see Mircea Eliade, *The Two and the One* [*Méphistophélès et l'androgyne*] [1962], trans. J. M. Cohen (London: The Harvill Press, 1965), pp. 78-124.

[145] *The Orphic Hymns*, trans. Athanassakis, p. 9; *The Mystical Hymns of Orpheus*, trans. Taylor, p. 15.

[146] On the notion of the transformation of chance into necessity, compare with Zarathustra's statement: "We are still fighting step by step with the giant Chance, and hitherto the senseless, the meaningless, has still ruled over mankind [...] All 'it was' is a fragment, a riddle, a dreadful chance—until the creative will says to it: 'But I willed it thus!'" (Friedrich Nietzsche, *Thus Spake Zarathustra*, trans. R. J. Hollingdale [Harmondsworth: Penguin, 1969], pp. 102 and 163).

[147] Goethe, *Werke* [HA], vol. 1, p. 406.

the restates his notion of the beneficial aspect of error expressed elsewhere in his works; for example, in his *Maxims and Reflections*: "Error is related to truth as sleep to waking. I have observed that after erring, a man turns again to truth as if refreshed."[148] Nevertheless, the concluding lines of the Eros stanza, Goethe assures us, "give a decisive indication of how one can escape this error and come to obtain a lifetime's security."

A lifetime's security? Truly, Goethe's Orphic teachings promise much! And yet this commentary reveals Goethe's concerns with the concrete circumstances—the familial, the social, the legal circumstances—of the individual, not a pseudo-spiritual transcendence into a mystical never-never land. On the contrary, Goethe concerns himself with the necessities that arise through the erotic encounter, or the necessity of love.

When the individual decides to exercise his or her will upon the world, so (and experience provides ample evidence of this) the world frequently resists that will. In Goethe's phrase, *tyche*—chance circumstance—"gets in the way."[149] But through this experience the individual becomes aware that (s)he is "not only determined and formed"—Goethe's actual expression is "stamped," *gestempelt*—"by nature," but that (s)he "perceives inwardly" that (s)he "can determine" herself or himself.[150] In other words, in the erotic encounter with the Other, the individual believes (s)he has won (the Beloved), whereas, in fact, (s)he really *is* lost. Through the experience of being determined by the Other, however, the individual grasps the possibility of self-determination: "Now he or she perceives inwardly that he or she can determine himself or herself."[151] What chance sends the individual, (s)he can not only grasp, but can make his or her own, and (s)he can embrace another being, like himself or herself, with "eternally indestructible" desire.[152]

Thus, for Goethe, only the truly "free" individual can make the "free"

---

[148]Goethe, *Maxims and Reflections*, ed. Hecker, §391; *Werke* [HA], vol. 12, p. 410.

[149]Goethe, *Werke* [HA], vol. 1, p. 406; *"wenn Tyche da oder dort in den Weg trat."*

[150]For Goethe, we feel we are free, in the sense that Spinoza writes, "we feel and know by experience that we are eternal" (*Ethics*, part 5, proposition 23, scholium; *Selections*, ed. John Wild [London: Scribner, 1928], p. 385). Of course, Goethe uses freedom in the Leibnizian sense of, not the freedom to choose among alternatives, but the freedom—to be one's self (see Frederic Will, "Goethe's Aesthetics: The Work of Art and the Work of Nature," *The Philosophical Quarterly* 6 [1956]: 53-65 [p. 56]).

[151]Goethe, *Werke* [HA], vol. 1, p. 406; *"jetzt wird er in seinem Innern gewahr, daß er sich selbst bestimmen könne."*

[152]Goethe, *Werke* [HA], vol. 1, p. 406; *"daß er den durchs Geschick ihm zugeführten Gegenstand nicht nur gewaltsam ergreifen, sondern auch sich aneignen und, was noch mehr ist, ein zweites Wesen eben wie sich selbst mit ewiger, unzerstörlicher Neigung umfassen könne."*

decision to give up, precisely, his or her "freedom";[153] this decision constitutes the basis of Goethe's controversial doctrine of renunciation. Yet, by
dedicating herself or himself to just one man or to just one woman, the
"noble" individual raises his or her desire out of mere generality, devotes it
to one individual in particular, and thus realizes the universality of love:

> So many soaring hearts are dissipated,
> The noblest to the One is dedicated.
>
> [*Gar manches Herz verschwebt im Allgemeinen,*
> *Doch widmet sich das edelste dem Einen.*]

We might call this necessity of devotion to one Other, which can also be
read as the Other that is one's (so far) unrealized self, the necessity of love.
From it, Goethe evolves nothing less than an entire theory of society.

In the I-Thou relationship (to use Martin Buber's terms)[154] of love,
flesh and spirit are inextricably intermingled: "two souls should become
one body, two bodies become one soul," Goethe writes in his commentary. To this intermingling, this "reciprocal loving necessity,"[155] is added
(in fact, there arises from it) a Third. There is a child. And as the child is
born, so the family is born, too. Parents and children must "form a totality,"[156] Goethe writes, a cause of "common satisfaction"; ever the realist,
however, he adds that "even greater is the need."[157] Families, as Goethe
sees them, are both "desirable" and "necessary," so that "the advantages
attract everyone, and one is content with accepting the disadvantages."[158]
Families join with families to form clans, clans join with clans to form a
nation; the dialectic of love and necessity provides Goethe with an entire
anthropology, and on this dialectic, too, the law is based. Rather than
being passed down from heaven, rather than being commanded by God
through a prophet, the law is founded on the transformation of "loving
inclination" into "duty," expressed through the contracts and ceremonies
of the church and the state. (Indeed, in one of his aphorisms, Goethe

---

[153]Goethe, *Werke* [HA], vol. 1, p. 406; "*so ist durch freien Entschluß die Freiheit aufgegeben.*"

[154]See Martin Buber [1878-1965], *Ich und Du* (Berlin: Schocken, 1922); *I and Thou*, trans. Ronald Gregor Smith (New York: Scribner, 1937).

[155]Goethe, *Werke* [HA], vol. 1, p. 406; "*zu wechselseitiger liebevoller Nötigung.*"

[156]Goethe, *Werke* [HA], vol. 1, p. 406; "*sich abermals zu einem Ganzen bilden.*"

[157]Goethe, *Werke* [HA], vol. 1, p. 406; "*groß ist die gemeinsame Zufriedenheit, aber größer das*
*Bedürfnis.*"

[158]Goethe, *Werke* [HA], vol. 1, p. 406; "*so wünschenswert als notwendig ; der Vorteil zieht einen*
*jeden an, und man läßt sich gefallen, die Nachteile zu übernehmen.*"

defines duty [*Pflicht*] as "where one loves, what one commands one-self."[159]) Goethe's vision of humanity thus embraces the political. And at the core of Goethe's theory of the state lies the notion of the contract, placing him in a political tradition that reaches back, via Rousseau (and, before him, Hobbes), to Epicurus.[160]

Although this stanza is dedicated to the god Eros, it is hard not to think of another god, too—the god under whose name the entire poem is placed, Orpheus. For Orpheus embarks on his journey to the under-world, to the realm of Persephone, to Hades, in order to regain his beloved wife, Eurydice. Thus Orpheus's love survives death, just as Orpheus himself survives both Eurydice's return to the underworld, when he is unable to resist turning round to look at her, and his own death, when his head travels, still singing, across the seas to Lesbos, giving rise to that island's traditions of music and poetry.

## The Necessity of Necessity; or, Necessary Necessity

In a paper on the transference, Freud alludes to the *hieroi logoi* that occur in Goethe's poem, arguing that two of them, the powers of *daimon* and *tyche*—"daimon" and "chance," inner disposition and external cir-cumstance—together determine "the fate of the individual," and only rarely, perhaps never, just one of them alone.[161] Freud's view here, as elsewhere, is essentially deterministic; Goethe's is, as we shall see, more complex.

In the second half of this stanza on necessity, Goethe explores the idea of "seeming freedom" (*scheinfrei*), in which capricious whim (*Willkür*) bows to purposeful will (*Wollen*); and, in turn, the will complies with necessity. In the actual language of the stanza (*wollten, Wille, Wollen, sollten, Willen, Willkür*), Goethe embodies this dialectic of freedom and necessity; and, in his commentary, he explains more discursively the involvement of the individual in the implications of love, family, and society. We might compare Goethe's commentary with Jung's use of the

[159]*Maxims and Reflections*, ed. Hecker, §829; Goethe, *Werke* [HA], vol. 12, p. 518; "*Pflicht: wo man liebt, was man sich selbst befiehlt.*"

[160]See Michel Onfray, *Les sagesses antiques* [*Contre-histoire de la philosophie*, vol. 1] (Paris: Grasset, 2006), pp. 221-224.

[161]Freud, "The Dynamics of Transference" [*Zur Dynamik der Übertragung*] [1912]; *SE* 12, 97-108 (p. 99); *FGW* 8, 374 (pp. 364-365). See, too, his remark about necessity or *ananke* as "frustra-tion by reality" or "the pressure of vital needs" in the twenty-second of his *Introductory Lectures on Psy-cho-Analysis* (*SE* 16, 355; *FGW* 11, 368).

term "necessity" in "The Stages of Life," when he discusses the psychological problems of youth: "In all this there is something of the inertia of matter; it is a persistence in the previous state [*ein Beharren im bisherigen Zustand*] whose range of consciousness is smaller, narrower, and more egoistic than that of the dualistic phase. For here the individual is faced with the necessity of recognizing and accepting what is different and strange as a part of his own life, as a kind of 'also-I' [*das andere, das Fremde ebenfalls als sein Leben und als ein Auch-Ich zu erkennen und anzunehmen*]."[162]

In his commentary on this fourth stanza, Goethe says that it requires "no comments," for there is "no-one whom experience does not provide with sufficient annotations to such a text,"[163] and the opening lines of the stanza run as follows:

> Then back once more, to what the stars had fated:
> Conditioning and law; and wish from willing
> Can only come since we are obligated,
> Our will then all our fitful fancies killing.

> [*Da ist's denn wieder, wie die Sterne wollten:*
> *Bedingung und Gesetz; und aller Wille*
> *Ist nur ein Wollen, weil wir eben sollten,*
> *Und vor dem Willen schweigt die Willkür stille.*]

To understand this stanza, we can try to disentangle the various terms that constitute Goethe's taxonomy of the will. In his *History of the Doctrine of Colors*, Goethe distinguishes between the will (*der Wille*) and wanting (*das Wollen*).[164] The (good) will—"the main fundament of ethics"—is, Goethe writes, "in its nature directed only toward what is right," and so the will itself "belongs to freedom, it applies to the inner individual."[165] By contrast, what one wants—"the main fundament of character"—is, as Nietzsche would say, "beyond good and evil," inasmuch as this form of willing has "no regard to right and wrong, to good and evil, to truth and error";

---

[162]Jung, *CW* 8 §764; "*des Stoffes, dessen Bewußtheit kleiner, enger, egoistischer ist als die Bewußtheit der dualistischen Phase, in welcher das Individuum vor die Notwendigkeit gestellt ist.*"

[163]Goethe, *Werke* [HA], vol. 1, p. 407; "*Keiner Anmerkungen bedarf wohl diese Strophe weiter; niemand ist, dem nicht Erfahrung genugsame Noten zu einem solchen Text darreichte.*"

[164]See Schantz, "Goethes 'Urworte. Orphisch' in ihrer geschichtsphilosophischen Bedeutung," p. 45.

[165]*Materialen zur Geschichte der Farbenlehre*, Section 6, "Newtons Persönlichkeit"; Goethe, *Werke* [HA], vol. 14, p. 173; "*seiner Natur nach nur aufs Rechte gerichtet [...] Der Wille gehört der Freiheit, er bezieht sich auf den innern Menschen.*"

for (the condition of) wanting "belongs to nature and relates to the external world."[166] In the face of our (ethical) will, our (capricious) will (*die
Willkür*) gives way or, as the stanza says, "falls silent." We might not want
what we will, but we should not will everything that we want. (Although
he argues without specific reference to the will, Jung seems to know of
similar difficulties when he writes that it is not only "the contradiction
between subjective assumptions" and "external facts" that can "give rise to
problems," for "even when things run smoothly in the outside world," he
says, "inner, psychic difficulties" may arise.[167])

So in this stanza Goethe directly confronts the dialectic of freedom
and necessity that has, right from its opening (to whose astrological imagery the first line of this stanza alludes) onward, dominated its main argument. And it is a theme on which Goethe has much to say elsewhere.[168]
For example, in one of his early poems, one of whose versions is entitled
"To Fate" (*Dem Schicksal*) (1776), Goethe ponders—

> How strangely a deep fate guides us,
> And, alas! I feel how, silently, we
> Are prepared for new scenarios.
>
> [*Wie seltsam uns ein tiefes Schicksal leitet,*
> *Und, ach, ich fühl's, im stillen werden wir*
> *Zu neuen Szenen vorbereitet.*]

—an idea which, in its later version, entitled "Restriction" (*Einschränk-
ung*) (1789), he rewrites as—

> How strangely does fate lead me;
> And alas, I feel, close and far away
> How much is still prepared for me.
>
> [*Wie seltsam mich das Schicksal leitet;*
> *Und ach, ich fühle, nah und fern*
> *Ist mir noch manches zubereitet.*][169]

We find this sense of inevitability expressed in one of Goethe's letters to

---

[166]Goethe, *Werke* [HA], vol. 14, p. 173; "*das entschiedene Wollen ohne Rücksicht auf Recht und
Unrecht, auf Gut und Böse, auf Wahrheit oder Irrtum; das Wollen gehört der Natur und bezieht sich auf die
äußere Welt.*"

[167]Jung, *CW* 8 §762.

[168]For further discussion, see in particular Schantz, "Goethes 'Urworte. Orphisch' in ihrer
geschichtsphilosophischen Bedeutung," pp. 44-46; and Johannes A. E. Leue, "Goethes 'Urworte.
Orphisch," *Acta Germanica* 2 (1968): 1-10 (pp. 7-8).

[169]Goethe, *Werke* [HA], vol. 1, p. 132.

Charlotte von Stein, in which he laments "how restricted" the individual is "now in understanding, now in strength, now in force, now in will,"[170] as well as in the text "On Nature," also dating from this early period: "We obey her laws, even in resisting them; we work with her, even in working against her."[171] And in a diary entry for 25 May 1797 we find the following terse, aphoristic observations: "The law makes Man[,] not Man the law. The great necessity exalts[,] the small one humbles Man."[172]

In these formulations, Danckert wonders, can we detect an echo of an "ancient, even pre-ancient" sensibility, an echo or "a paraphrase of that primordial sense of fate," according to which, even when we are reluctant to act, we inevitably bring about what we seek to avoid?[173] In Egmont's lament,[174] Danckert finds the source of the phrase that Bachofen, in his inaugural lecture on natural law, would proclaim as the maxim of his own, deep sense of world-historical feeling.[175] For "primordial religion" (*die Urreligion*), as Carl Albrecht Bernoulli (1868-1937) put it, is "fulfilled in the feeling of fate."[176]

This dialectic between freedom and necessity exists on many levels in Goethe's works. First, there is the dialectic in its historical dimension. In his tribute to Shakespeare (1771), Goethe claims that the English dramatist's plays all revolve around "an invisible point, which no philosopher has discovered or defined, and where the characteristic quality of our being, our presumed free will, collides with the inevitable course of the whole."[177] Second, there is the dialectic in its existential dimension. In

[170]Letter to Charlotte von Stein of 9 June 1784; *Werke* [WA], vol. IV.6, p. 295; "*Wie eingeschränckt ist der Mensch bald an Verstand, bald an Krafft, bald an Gewalt, bald an Willen.*"

[171]Goethe, *GE* 12, 4; *Werke* [HA], vol. 13, p. 47; "*Man gehorcht ihren Gesetzen, auch wenn man ihnen widerstrebt, man wirkt mit ihr, auch wenn man gegen sie wirken will.*"

[172]Goethe, *Werke* [WA], vol. III.2, p. 70; "*Das Gesetz macht den Menschen / Nicht der Mensch das Gesetz. // Die große Nothwendigkeit erhebt / Die kleine erniedrigt den Menschen.*"

[173]Danckert, *Goethe: Der mythische Urgrund seiner Weltschau*, p. 142.

[174]"Men think that they direct their lives and are in control of themselves; yet their inmost selves are irresistibly pulled towards their destinies" [*Es glaubt der Mensch, sein Leben zu leiten, sich selbst zu führen; und sein Innerstes wird unwiderstehlich nach seinem Schicksale gezogen*] (Act 5, final scene); Goethe, *GE* 7, 149 [trans. Michael Hamburger]; *Werke* [HA], vol. 4, p. 451.

[175]J. J. Bachofen, *Selbstbiographie und Antrittsrede über das Naturrecht*, ed. Alfred Baeumler (Halle an der Saale: Niemeyer, 1927), p. 59; compare with Danckert, *Goethe: Der mythische Urgrund seiner Weltschau*, p. 145.

[176]Carl Albrecht Bernoulli, *Johann Jakob Bachofen und das Natursymbol: Eine Würdigungsversuch* (Basel: Schwabe, 1924), p. 515; "*Die Urreligion wird erfüllt vom Gefühl des Schicksals.*" Compare with Danckert, *Goethe: Der mythische Urgrund seiner Weltschau*, p. 152.

[177]Goethe, *GE* 3, 165; *Werke* [HA], vol. 12, p. 226; "*den geheimen Punkt (den noch kein Philosoph*

Part Four, Book 16, of *Dichtung und Wahrheit*, Goethe considers the proposition that "nature operates according to eternal, necessary laws, which are so divine that the Divinity itself cannot alter them. Unconsciously," he adds, "all human beings are in perfect agreement about this"—"Just consider how any natural phenomenon astounds and actually horrifies us if it hints at understanding, reason, or merely free will."[178] Hence, Goethe continues, "when animals evince something like reason, we cannot get over our astonishment, for as close as we are to them, they still seem to be separated from us by an infinite gulf, and to be relegated to the realm of necessity. Consequently," he concluded, with a dig at Descartes (and later philosophers who approach the world in mechanical terms), "it is little wonder that some thinkers have explained the expert but strictly limited skills of these creatures entirely in terms of mechanics."[179] (Later, Nietzsche will define the difference between animals and humans in relation to the capacity for the perception of time, or memory;[180] likewise, Jung concurs that animals, in contrast to human beings, do not have problems.[181])

Elsewhere in *Dichtung und Wahrheit* (Part Three, Book 11) Goethe reflects on the principle that few biographies can depict an individual's progress as "pure, calm, and steady," for—

> our lives, like the context in which we live, are an incomprehensible mixture of freedom and necessity. Our desires proclaim in advance what we will do under any set of circumstances. These circumstances, however, control us in their own way. The "what" is within us, the "how" rarely depends on us, the

---

gesehen und bestimmt hat), in dem das Eigentümliche unsres Ichs, die prätendierte Freiheit unsres Wollens, mit dem notwendigen Gang des Ganzen zusammenstößt."

[178]Goethe, *GE* 5, 524; *Werke* [HA], vol. 10, p. 79; "*Die Natur wirkt nach ewigen, notwendigen, dergestalt göttlichen Gesetzen, daß die Gottheit selbst daran nichts ändern könnte. Alle Menschen sind hierin, unbewußt, vollkommen einig. Man bedenke, wie eine Naturerscheinung, die auf Verstand, Vernunft, ja auch nur auf Willkür deutet, uns Erstaunen, ja Entsetzen bringt.*"

[179]Goethe, *GE* 5, 524; *Werke* [HA], vol. 10, p. 79; "*Wenn sich in Tieren etwas Vernunftähnliches hervortut, so können wir uns von unserer Verwunderung nicht erholen: denn ob sie uns gleich so nahe stehen, so scheinen sie doch durch eine unendliche Kluft von uns getrennt und in das Reich der Notwendigkeit verwiesen. Man kann es daher jenen Denkern nicht übelnehmen, welche die unendlich kunstreiche aber doch genau beschränkte Technik jener Geschöpfe für ganz maschinenmäßig erklärten.*"

[180]*Untimely Meditations*, no. 2, "On the Uses and Disadvantages of History for Life," §1; Friedrich Nietzsche, *Untimely Meditations*, trans. R. J. Hollingdale (Cambridge: Cambridge University Press, 1983), pp. 60-61.

[181]Jung, *CW* 8 §753.

"why" we dare not enquire about, and therefore we are correctly referred to the *quia*[182]

—*quia* here being "the 'because,'" or what emerges from this conjunction of the individual and his or her circumstances, a "because" that is more than purely causal. A related thought is given expression in his *Maxims and Reflections*, where Goethe reflects that "whatever lives has the gift of adapting itself to the most diverse requirements of external influences, while nevertheless not surrendering a certain definite independence."[183] In another aphorism, originally from his notebooks on science (1823), Goethe introduces the image of a gameboard: Nature gives us the pieces, so now it is for us to play:

> Nature has given us the chessboard, outside of which we neither can nor want to operate, she has given us the pieces, whose value, movement, and abilities gradually become clear to us: now it is for us, to make the moves, with which we hope to win the game [...].[184]

Or as he wrote to Carl Friedrich Moritz von Brühl on 23 October 1828, "if we consider ourselves in every stage of our life, we will find that we are determined from outside, from our first breath to our last; but that, nevertheless, we retain the highest freedom [*die höchste Freiheit*] to cultivate ourselves within ourselves in such a way [*uns innerhalb unsrer selbst dergestalt auszubilden*] that we chime in harmony with the ethical order of the world"—and so that, moreover, "whatever hindrances may present themselves, we thereby can come to be at peace with ourselves."[185]

---

[182]Goethe, *GE* 4, 355; *Werke* [HA], vol. 9, p. 478; "*Es sind wenig Biographien, welche einen reinen, ruhigen, steten Forschritt des Individuums darstellen können. Unser Leben ist, wie das Ganze, in dem wir enthalten sind, auf eine unbegreifliche Weise aus Freiheit und Notwendigkeit zusammengesetzt. Unser Wollen ist ein Vorausverkünden dessen, was wir unter allen Umständen tun werden. Diese Umstände aber ergreifen uns auf ihre eigne Weise. Das Was liegt in uns, das Wie hängt selten von uns ab, nach dem Warum dürfen wir nicht fragen, und deshalb verweist man uns mit Recht aufs Quia.*"

[183]Goethe, *Maxims and Reflections*, ed. Hecker, §1253; *Werke* [HA], vol. 12, p. 369; "*Das Lebendige hat die Gabe, sich nach vielfältigsten Bedingungen äußerer Einflüsse zu bequemen und doch eine gewisse errungene entschiedene Selbständigkeit nicht aufzugeben*"; cited in Buck, *Goethes "Urworte. Orphisch,"* p. 56.

[184]Goethe, *Maxims and Reflections*, ed. Hecker, §420; *Werke* [HA], vol. 12, p. 420; "*Die Natur hat uns das Schachbrett gegeben, aus dem wir nicht hinauswirken können noch wollen, sie hat uns die Steine geschnitzt, deren Wert, Bewegung und Vermögen nach und nach bekannt werden: nun ist es an uns, Züge zu tun, von denen wir uns Gewinn versprechen [...]*"; cited in Schantz, "Goethes 'Urworte. Orphisch' in ihrer geschichtsphilosophischen Bedeutung," p. 46.

[185]Goethe, *Briefe* [HA], vol. 4, p. 306; "*Betrachten wir uns in jeder Lage des Lebens, so finden wir, daß wir äußerlich bedingt sind, vom ersten Atemzug bis zum letzten; daß uns aber jedoch die höchste*

Which leads to the third aspect of the freedom-necessity dialectic—to
the dialetic in its aesthetic dimension, which is Goethe's answer to the
entire problem of freedom and necessity. In an entry in the *Italian Journey*
dated 6 September 1787, Goethe writes that he is applying the
(Spinozistic) principle—ἐν καὶ πᾶν, *hen kai pan*—to his study of nature,
*and* to his study of art. "Every time I apply it, I become convinced of the
correctness of my principle for explaining artworks," he noted, "and elu-
cidating all at once what artists and connoisseurs have been seeking and
studying in vain"; with this "master key," he claimed, "I have opened the
door, and am standing on the threshold"—or the *propylaeum*[186]—and he
declared that "this much is certain":

> The ancient artists had as great a knowledge of nature as
> Homer, and just as sure a notion as he of what can be de-
> picted, and how it must be depicted. [...] These sublime
> works of art are also the sublimest works of nature, created by
> men following true and natural laws. Everything arbitrary, ev-
> erything imaginary crumbles away, there we have necessity,
> there we have God [*Alles Willkürliche, Eingebildete fällt
> zusammen, da ist die Notwendigkeit, da ist Gott*].[187]

This final line echoes a similar sentiment, expressed much earlier—in his
letter of 3 October 1779 to Charlotte von Stein—in the course of a journey to Switzerland, where Goethe, overwhelmed by the natural landscape, proclaimed: "One feels profoundly that nothing here is arbitrary,
that all is slowly moving, eternal law" (*man fühlt tief, hier ist nichts
willkührliches, alles langsam bewegendes ewiges Gesez*).[188]

These remarks on, first, art; and, second, nature—and Goethe's
entire argument is that, at some level, nature and art are related, indeed,
are identical[189]—take us to the heart of the philosophical dialectic of
necessity and freedom. In "Significant Help Given by an Ingenious Turn
of Phrase" (*Bedeutende Fördernis durch ein einziges geistreiches Wort*)
(1823) Goethe observed that he had "long been suspicious" of the famous

---

Freiheit übriggeblieben ist, uns innerhalb unsrer selbst dergestalt auszubilden, daß wir uns mit der sittlichen
Weltordnung in Einklang setzen und, was auch für Hindernisse sich hervortun, dadurch mit uns selbst zum
Frieden gelangen können."

[186] *Die Propyläen*, the Greek term for the entrance to a temple, was the name given by Goethe to
the art journal he founded in 1798.

[187] Goethe, *GE* 6, 316; *Werke* [HA], vol. 11, p. 394.

[188] Goethe, *Briefe* [HA], vol. 1, p. 276.

[189] See Will, "Goethe's Aesthetics."

injunction of the Delphic Oracle, "the great and important-sounding task: 'know thyself.'" For this imperative, he continued, had always seemed to him to be "a deception practised by a secret order of priests who wished to confuse humanity with impossible demands, to divert attention from activity in the outer world to some false, inner speculation."[190] Goethe's suspicion is justified, for the command of the Delphic Oracle only really makes sense alongside another ancient Greek imperative, Pindar's γένοι' οἷος ἐσσί μαθών[191]—restated by Nietzsche as *werde, der du bist!* "become who you are!"[192]—and Plotinus's injunction, "always work at sculpting your statue." (In his notes for the fourth volume of *The Philosophy of Symbolic Forms,* Cassirer seems to suggest that these two imperatives are closer than one might think, when he offers a Goethean reading of the Delphic Oracle's commend.[193])

As Goethe has made clear in his commentary, the existence of the individual is (always) (already) situated within a preexisting cosmos of parental-familial, social, and ultimately political circumstances (not to mention biological, physiological predispositions) that (pre)structure the relation of the individual self to him/her self and to others. The only way out of the paradox of necessity and freedom—that is, the (lack of) freedom to be (other than) what one is—is by means of what, in one of his Caen seminars, Michel Onfray has called a "metaphysical pirouette," a move that consists in understanding that freedom lies in the consent to

---

[190]Goethe, *GE* 12, 39; *Werke* [HA], vol. 13, p. 38; "*Hiebei bekenn' ich, daß mir von jeher die große und so bedeutend klingende Aufgabe: erkenne dich selbst, immer verdächtig vorkam, als eine List geheim verbündeter Priester, die den Menschen durch unerreichbare Forderungen verwirren und von der Tätigkeit gegen die Außenwelt zu einer innern falschen Beschaulichkeit verleiten wollten.*"

[191]Pindar, *Pythian Odes,* no. 2, l. 72: "Become true to thyself, now that thou hast learnt what manner of man thou art" (Pindar, *The Odes,* trans. Sandys, p. 179).

[192]See Friedrich Nietzsche, *Die fröhliche Wissenschaft* [1882; 1887], §270, in *The Gay Science,* trans. Walter Kaufmann (New York: Vintage Books, 1974), p. 219; *Also sprach Zarathustra,* part 4, chapter 1, in *Thus Spake Zarathustra,* trans. Hollingdale, p. 252; and *Ecce Homo: How One Becomes What One Is,* trans. R. J. Hollingdale (Harmondsworth: Penguin, 1992), [subtitle], p. 1. Both the advice of the Delphic oracle and the Pindaric command are related to Goethe's conception of the self (*Selbstigkeit*) by Adolf Beck, "Der 'Geist der Reinheit' und die 'Idee des Reinen,'" p. 164.

[193]"Socrates begins with the Delphic oracle's call of *gnothi seauton,* but as Goethe correctly saw, he grasped this in a quite different sense. […] This call now means: know your *work* and know 'yourself' *in* your work; know what yo u do, so you can do what you know. Give shape to what you do; give it form by starting from mere instinct, from tradition, from convention, from routine, from *empeiria* [i.e, 'experience'] and *tribe* [i.e., 'habituation'] in order to arrive at 'self-conscious' action—a work in which you recognize yourself as the sole creator and actor" (Ernst Cassirer, "On Basis Phenomena" [c. 1940], in *The Philosophy of Symbolic Forms,* vol. 4, *The Metaphysics of Symbolic Forms,* ed. John Michael Krois and Donald Phillip Verene, trans. John Michael Krois [New Haven and London: Yale University Press, 1996], pp. 185-186).

necessity.[194] On this model, to consent to what is necessary (about one's self) involves knowledge of what that necessity entails, and through one's knowledge, and then one's consent, being free.[195] The creation of (one's own) freedom through consent to (one's own) necessity implies that, to execute the dual manoeuvre of first knowing, and then consenting to, what one is, knowledge and creation of self are fused: the construction of subjectivity and the attainment of freedom through consent-to-necessity thus go hand in hand.

Such is the sense that Spinoza gave to freedom, when he located it, not in "free decision," but in "free necessity"; an understanding he expounded at length in his *Ethics*, at the beginning of which he defined something as being "free" when it "exists solely by the necessity of its own nature."[196] Nor was Hegel's conception any less dialectical when he defined freedom as insight into necessity, declaring that "the truth of necessity is freedom."[197] For, as Eugen Drewermann has explained, Kant argued that actual science excludes freedom (inasmuch as freedom is not a scientific category), yet he nevertheless believed one must *postulate* freedom. For Hegel, necessity and freedom may (and do) *contradict* each other, but they do not *exclude* each other. And so the necessity that I can recognize can be transformed into freedom, by means of a process of recognition, of which psychotherapy constitutes an outstanding example, which is not necessarily executed intellectually.[198] (These ideas find confir-

[194]Cf. Michel Onfray, *La résistance au christianisme (2)* (Paris: Frémeaux; France-Culture; Grasset; Université populaire de Caen, 2005), CD 8, track 9.

[195]Compare with Goethe's idea, following Leibniz, of a "freedom of necessity," since—both in the case of the *nisus formativus* in animals, and the "inner drive, divine mission" [*innerer Drang, göttlicher Auftrag*] of human beings—true freedom is the freedom to be one's being (see Will, "Goethe's Aesthetics," p. 56; and Alexander Rueger, "The Cultural Use of Natural Knowledge: Goethe's Theory of Color in Weimar Classicism," *Eighteenth-Century Studies* 26 [1992-1993]: 211-232).

[196]Spinoza, letter to G. H. Schuller, October 1764, in *On the Improvement of the Understanding: The Ethics; The Correspondence* [*Works of Spinoza*, vol. 2], trans. R. H. M. Elwes (New York: Dover, 1955), p. 390; and *Ethics*, part 1, definition 7 (ibid., p. 46). Compare with Michel Onfray, *Les libertins baroques* [*Contre-histoire de la philosophie*, vol. 3] (Paris: Grasset, 2007), pp. 265 and 272.

[197]In *The Science of Logic* [*Die Wissenschaft der Logik*, 1812-1816], Hegel writes that *"freedom* is the *truth of necessity"* [*die Freiheit {ist} die Wahrheit der Notwendigkeit*] (G. W. F. Hegel, *Werke*, ed. Eva Moldenhauer and Karl Markus Michel, 20 vols. [Frankfurt am Main: Suhrkamp, 1986], vol. 6, *Wissenschaft der Logik II*, p. 249; cf. p. 246); and compare with his *Enzyklopädie der philosophischen Wissenschaften im Grundrisse* [1830], I, §158: "This *truth* of *necessity* is thus *freedom*" [*Diese Wahrheit der Notwendigkeit ist somit die Freiheit*] (*Werke*, vol. 8, p. 303).

[198]See Eugen Drewermann's interventions on the edition of *Funkhausgespräche* entitled "Schuld—Gibt es die? Die Hirnforschung und der Freie Wille," broadcast 27 March 2007 (repeated 25 June 2008) on WDR 5; the "Podiumsdiskussion" between Eugen Drewermann and Gerhard Roth

mation of a sort in the conclusions drawn in the 1970s from Benjamin Libet's investigations of readiness potential and volitional acts,[199] and recent experiments conducted at the Max Planck Institute for Human Cognitive and Brain Sciences in Leipzig, which suggest that, several seconds before we consciously make a decision, its outcome can be predicted from unconscious activity in the brain.[200])

Ultimately, however, Goethe's position can be related to a tradition that both precedes and succeeds him. In *La Sagesse tragique* (2006), Michel Onfray explicitly links the idea of consent to necessity with Nietzsche's doctrine of *amor fati*,[201] defining the Pindaric-Nietzschean injunction-invitation to "become who one is" as "to want the will that wills us" (*devenir ce que l'on est, c'est vouloir le vouloir qui nous veut*)—in other words, it is "to understand that freedom exists only in necessity, that no choice is possible except in accepting what is plainly the case"; from which, Onfray concludes that "to want what the will wants" (*vouloir ce que veut la volonté*) is the final word of "tragic wisdom" (*la sagesse tragique*).[202] Or, in the terms used by Bertrand Vergely with reference to the Stoic philosopher Epictetus, the power of consciousness when faced with nature allows it to mitigate the dominance of the latter over the individual in a physical sense by delivering the individual from nature in a moral sense.[203] (The essence of Epictetus's thought may be found in one of the maxims in his *Enchiridion*—"Require not things to happen as you wish, but wish them to happen as they do happen, and you will go on well"[204]—and his

---

organized by *Nordwest vor Ort*, Nordwestradio (Radio Bremen), held on 24 February 2008 in the Haus der Wissenschaft, Bremen; and the edition of *Redefreiheit* entitled "Die Unfreiheit des freien Willens," broadcast on Nordwestradio (Radio Bremen), 23 February 2008.

[199] Benjamin Libet, Anthony Freeman, Keith Sutherland, eds., *The Volitional Brain: Towards a Neuroscience of Free Will* (Thorverton: Imprint Academic, 1999); and Benjamin Libet, *Mind Time: The Temporal Factor in Consciousness* (Boston, MA, and London: Harvard University Press, 2004).

[200] Chun Siong Soon, Marcel Brass, Hans-Jochen Heinze, John-Dylan Haynes, "Unconscious determinants of free decisions in the human brain," *Nature Neuroscience*, http://www.nature.com/neuro/journal/vaop/ncurrent/abs/nn.2112.html. Accessed 15 April 2008. For further discussion, see Michael Pauen, *Illusion Freiheit? Mögliche und unmögliche Konsequenzen der Hirnforschung* (Frankfurt am Main: Fischer, 2004); and "Does Free Will Arise Freely?" *Scientific American* [Special Edition], 14/1 (January 2004): 40-47.

[201] Michel Onfray, *La Sagesse tragique: Du bon usage de Nietzsche* (Paris: Le Livre du Poche, 2006), pp. 21 and 161; p. 126.

[202] *Ibid.*, pp. 127-128.

[203] Bertrand Vergely, *Pascal ou l'expérience de l'infini* (Toulouse: Milan, 2007), p. 17.

[204] Epictetus, *Enchiridion*, §8 (*The Moral Discourses of Epictetus*, trans. Elizabeth Carter [London: Dent; New York: Dutton, 1910], p. 258). According to Bertrand Vergely, this dictum serves to sum-

222 READING GOETHE AT MIDLIFE

allusion to an earlier Stoic, Cleanthes: "Conduct me, Jove, and thou, O Destiny, / Wherever your decrees have fixed my station. / I follow cheerfully; and, did I not, / Wicked and wretched, I must follow still."[205]) That is to say, fate—or exterior constraint—can be transformed into destiny—or interior freedom.[206]

In his recent book, coauthored with Marie de Hennezel, entitled *Une vie pour se mettre au monde* (2010), Vergely finds in Epictetus an emblem of fulfilment and, in his dictum, a solution to the otherwise insoluble problem of freedom and determination, reflected in the opposition of chance (*le hasard*; in Orphic terms, *tyche*) and destiny (*le destin*; or *fatum, fortuna, heimarmene*).[207] We get nowhere, Vergely asserts, in declaring that chance does not exist or fate does not exist, but it is astounding, he believes, to discover that one has a destination (or, to put it another way, that one is going somewhere), that "something is not fateful without nevertheless being by chance, and that something is not by chance without nevertheless being fateful": here, "another dimension of life" opens up.[208] Nor is it interesting, he avers, to know whether or not one is free *a priori*. If I am free *a priori*, but I have never tasted freedom, what does it matter? And what does it matter if, not being free, I nevertheless feel myself to be free? For anyone who knows himself or herself to be free knows more about freedom and more about life than a theory that proclaims them to be an illusion.[209] The solution lies in the creative aspect of responsibility, the source of which lies in our interiority.[210] The "great paradox of freedom," according to Vergely, lies in "wanting the life one has not wished for."[211]

And with specific reference to Goethe (in a recent study of the great poet and the ancient tradition of "spiritual exercises"), Pierre Hadot has suggested that "the ultimate meaning of the Goethean attitude toward the present" amounts—by means of "a concentration on the present, on the

---

marize the secret of true freedom according to Stoicism (de Hennezel and Vergely, *Une vie pour se mettre au monde*, p. 185).

[205]Epictetus, *Enchiridion*, §53 (*The Moral Discourses of Epictetus*, p. 274); compare Seneca, *Letters to Lucilius*, no. 107; cited by St. Augustine in *The City of Go*d, book 5, chapter 8; alluded to by Nietzsche in *Dawn*, §195; see Hadot, *N'oublie pas de vivre*, p. 262.

[206]Vergely, *Pascal*, p. 17.

[207]De Hennezel and Vergely, *Une vie pour se mettre au monde*, pp. 182 and 179.

[208]*Ibid.*, p. 179.

[209]*Ibid.*, p. 183.

[210]*Ibid.*, pp. 180 and 182.

[211]*Ibid.*, p. 182.

existence that we only attain in the instant moment"—to "the sense of joy and a duty to exist in the cosmos, a profound feeling of participation in, of identification with, a reality that transcends the limits of the individual."[212] Precisely this attitude, he argues, is the fruit of a "spiritual exercise" (*exercice spirituel*) characterized by "a movement of detachment from the self that transforms our thought and our actions, a transformation of our relation to reality, a 'transformation of the everyday.'"[213] This transformation is wrought by adopting a perspective "from on high," which places the destiny of the individual within "the perspective of the All, of the Cosmos, of universal existence," and leads to "an acquiescence in existence considered as the supreme value, to the total consent to the will of God-Nature"—to that "joyful fatalism" (*freudiger Fatalismus*) for which Nietzsche so admired Goethe,[214] and is expressed in the lines of Lynceus the Watchman in *Faust*, Part Two—

A beauty eternal
In all things I see,
And the world and myself
Are both pleasing to me.
Oh blest are these eyes,
All they've seen and can tell:
Let it be as it may—
They have loved it so well!

[*So seh' ich in allen*
*Die ewige Zier,*
*Und wie mir's gefallen,*
*Gefall' ich auch mir.*
*Ihr glücklichen Augen,*
*Was je ihr gesehn,*
*Es sei, wie es wolle*
*Es war doch so schön!*][215]

---

[212]Hadot, *N'oublie pas de vivre*, p. 83.

[213]*Ibid.*, p. 232; cf. Goethe, *Notes and Essays on the West-Eastern Divan;* "*ein verklärtes Alltägliche*" (*Werke* [HA], vol. 2, p. 206).

[214]Hadot, *N'oublie pas de vivre*, p. 233; cf. Nietzsche, *Twilight of the Idols*, "Expeditions of an Untimely Man," §49; Friedrich Nietzsche, *Twilight of the Idols; The Anti-Christ*, trans. R. J. Hollingdale (Harmondsworth: Penguin, 1968), p. 103.

[215]Goethe, *Faust II*, ll. 11296-11303; *Faust: Part Two*, trans. Luke, pp. 214-215. According to one reading, as Hadot points out, the word *Zier* corresponds here to the Greek term *kosmos*, which means both "order" and "ornament" (Hadot, *N'oublie pas de vivre*, p. 132; Theodor Friedrich and Lothar J. Scheithauer, *Kommentar zu Goethes "Faust"* [1959] [Stuttgart: Reclam, 1989], p. 274; cf.

—as it is also in the conclusion to the poem "The Bridegroom" (*Der Bräutigam*), "Let life be as it will, yet it is good" (*Wie es auch sei das Leben es ist gut*).[216] For this reason, Hadot argues that the symbol of Hermes's caduceus, which Goethe would have found in a passage of Macrobius cited by Zoega (see Chapter 3), serves as a kind of "key" to unlock the secret structure of "Primal Words. Orphic," inasmuch as the twin serpents of *daimon* and *tyche* intertwine round the rod of *ananke*, knotted together by *eros*, and lifted into the air—as we shall see—by the wings of *elpis*.[217]

These considerations help clarify the seemingly obscure remarks made by Goethe in his conversation with Friedrich von Müller of 28 March 1819, where he appears—in the context of a discussion of the common ground between Islam and Protestantism—to make a distinction between "inner" and "outer" aspects of fate:

> Mistakes of individuality as such would be permitted and forgiven by the moral world-order; each person should come to terms with them and punish himself or herself for them [= inner fate], but where one goes beyond the bounds of individuality—causing sacrilege, disturbance, untruth—there Nemesis should, soon or later, impose appropriate external punishment [ = external fate].[218]

According to Werner Danckert, "in Goethe's spherical cosmos there is

---

Goethe, *Faust-Dichtungen*, ed. Ulrich Gaier, 3 vols. [Stuttgart: Reclam, 1999], vol. 2, *Kommentar* I, p. 1068). In Goethe's use of the mythical figure of Lynceus (one of the Argonauts, and hence associated with Orpheus), Ulrich Gaier detects an echo of Plotinus's famous *Ennead* on intellectual beauty: "In our realm all is part rising from part and nothing can be more than partial; but There each being is an eternal product of a whole and is at once a whole and an individual manifesting as part but, to the keen vision There, known for the whole it is. The myth of Lynceus seeing into the very deeps of the earth tells us of those eyes in the divine. No weariness overtakes this vision [...] [and] to see is to look the more, since [...] to continue in the contemplation of an infinite self and of infinite objects is but to acquiesce in the bidding of their nature. [...] [A]ll the Principles of this order, dwelling There, are as it were visible images projected from themselves, so that all becomes an object of *contemplation to contemplators immeasurably blessed*" (Plotinus, "On the Intellectual Beauty," *Enneads* 5.8 [4]; in Plotinus, *The Enneads*, trans. MacKenna, pp. 414-415). For the italicized passage, see Plato, "a sight for the eyes of the blessed" (*Phaedo*, 111a; in *Collected Dialogues*, p. 92). In the case of Goethe, however—and in this respect one might disagree with Hadot (cf. pp. 226-227)—the beauty admired is not intellectual, but the kind of perception in which he is interested is preeminently aesthetic (as Hadot elsewhere recognizes; cf. pp. 264-265).

[216]Goethe, *Werke* [HA], vol. 1, p. 386; *Selected Verse*, trans. Luke, p. 333.

[217]Hadot, *N'oublie pas de vivre*, pp. 176, 215-217. See Macrobius, *Saturnalia*, book 1, chapter 19, §§16-18 (see below).

[218]Flodoard von Biedermann, ed., *Goethes Gespräche*, 5 vols. (Leipzig: Biedermann, 1909-1911), vol. 2, p. 434.

only one primordial sacrilege—to go beyond the confines of one's own being."[219] Conversely, and more positively, this idea is expressed (by Goethe) in the following aphorism (and by one of his characters, Ottilie, in her notebook): "One only has to declare oneself to be free, in that moment one feels oneself as limited. But if one dares to declare oneself to be limited, one feels oneself to be free."[220] For Danckert, the "highest freedom" (as understood by Goethe) realizes itself "not in deeds, but in the inner formation of self through submission to the rhythm of the cosmos."[221]

So how are we to explain the coexistence in Goethe's thinking of, on the one hand, the emphasis on (self) control, on individual and social responsibility, on a "hard 'Must'" (dem harten Muß), and, on the other, the "elementary pathos" (Danckert) of his attitude towards necessity? On Danckert's account, the complexity of this "vital-original attitude" undoubtedly springs from "a fundamental feeling of being bound up with the universe," which presupposes "a structure of selfhood" that could be described as "a sympathetic world-feeling," or (in Freudian terms) as "the superior value of the *id* over against the *ego*" (or perhaps, in Jungian terms, the superiority of the Self over the ego).[222] What C. A. Bernoulli, in the context of Bachofen's feeling for religious experience, called "ego-free fatalism" (*ich-entspannter Fatalismus*), could thus also be applied to Goethe. Such an outlook would, in the eyes of Ludwig Klages, be characteristic of "the basic feeling of the Pelasgian experience of fate," of which he wrote that "humankind and its fate seem to be like two sides of a higher unity, and the necessity of what happens appears to us to be the expression of a being, in which we are involved and of which we are a part."[223] Indeed, Goethe himself wrote in an aphorism that "the rational world is to be considered as a great immortal individual, that incessantly brings about what is necessary and thereby masters even chance"[224]—herewith reformulating the idea in the *Timaeus* that "the world came into being" as "a living creature truly endowed with soul and intelligence by the providence of

[219]Danckert, *Goethe: Der mythische Urgrund seiner Weltschau*, p. 145.

[220]Goethe, *Maxims and Reflections*, ed. Hecker, §44; Goethe, *Werke* [HA], vol. 12, p. 520; cf. *Elective Affinities* (*Die Wahlverwandtschaften*) (1809); *Werke* [HA], vol. 6, p. 397.

[221]Danckert, *Goethe: Der mythische Urgrund seiner Weltschau*, p. 142.

[222]*Ibid.*, p. 151.

[223]Ludwig Klages, *Der Geist als Widersacher der Seele*, 6th ed. (Bonn: Bouvier, 1981), p. 547.

[224]*Maxims and Reflections*, ed. Hecker, §444; *Goethe's Maximen und Reflexionen: A Selection*, ed. and trans. R. H. Stephenson (Glasgow: Scottish Papers in Germanic Studies, 1986), p. 121; *Werke* [HA], vol. 12, p. 366.

God,"[225] and the claim of Anaxagoras that "mind" or "reason" (*Nous*) constitutes the universal organizing principle, having "arranged everything—what was to be and what was and what now is and what will be."[226]
(Here Goethe's rhetoric, as R. H. Stephenson has pointed out, reinforces
his thought.[227])

Aside from this ancient, holistic conception of the world, Goethe's
thinking articulates a link, at which the cult of Orpheus hints, between
fate and the feminine. The association of the feminine and the idea of fate
belongs, according to Bachofen, to the deepest and most primordial form
of religion.[228] One thinks, not just of the figure of *tyche* or Fortuna, but
also of the Moirae, the Parcae, the Horae, and so on—variants of the
Great Mother (or Magna Mater) figure of antiquity. "The idea of a fate
that strictly rules everything and leads what has become to its decline is
joined as a necessary supplement to the idea of the mother," Bachofen
wrote, "and shows the life-giving power of nature in the light of the great
Moira, who intertwines into the fabric of every earthly existence the
thread of death."[229] And *ananke*, for the Greeks, was above all the necessity
of nature, the workings of natural law. This held true in particular for the
Orphic tradition, as interpreted by Zoega. "The Orphics say that the
demiurge," Zoega wrote, "is fed by *adrastea*"—that is to say, by fate—
"lives with *ananke*, and produces destiny [*das Fatum*]."[230] (Zoega also
notes the interchangeability of the different names for fate, but distinguishes between *themis* [universal law], *dike* [the being of perfect justice],
*adrastea* [when depicted in the beauty of the firmament], *ananke* [neces-
sary and unchanging], and *tyche* [apparent chance, changeable].[231]) For his
part, Goethe hints at the relation between *ananke* and *tyche*, inasmuch as

---

[225] *Timaeus*, 30c; Plato, *Collected Dialogues*, p. 1163.

[226] Anaxagoras, Diels-Kranz fragment B 12, in Jonathan Barnes, *Early Greek Philosophy* (Harmondsworth: Penguin, 1987), p. 228. For further discussion, see R. S. Peters, ed., *Brett's History of Psychology*
(London: Allen and Unwin; New York: Macmillan, 1953), pp. 41-43.

[227] Goethe's thought is "given aesthetic articulation by the homoeoteleuton"—the rhetorical device of using a series of words with identical or similar endings—"in 'vernünftige-Notwendige-
Zufällige'" (Stephenson, *Goethe's "Maxims and Reflections,"* p. 158); "*Die vernünftige Welt ist als ein
großes unsterbliches Individuum zu betrachten, das unaufhaltsam das Notwendige bewirkt und dadurch
sich sogar über das Zufällige zum Herrn macht.*"

[228] See the extensive discussion of this point in Klages, *Der Geist als Widersacher der Seele*, pp.
544-550.

[229] Bachofen, *Versuch über die Gräbersymbolik der Alten*, p. 315.

[230] Zoega, "ΑΓΑΘΗ ΤΥΧΗΙ: Tyche und Nemesis," in *Abhandlungen*, p. 41.

[231] *Ibid.*, p. 54.

the sociability evoked in the third line of stanza two now appears in the idea of social convention, or social compulsion, explored in this stanza.

In the next two lines of stanza four, Goethe explores the notion that freedom can be found in the rejection of caprice, and that, much as in the Christian formulation, obedience to (the will of) God is "perfect freedom," we transcend necessity through accepting it:[232]

> Its dearest from the heart is extirpated,
> Hard "Must" prevails, both will and fancy stilling.
>
> [*Das Liebste wird vom Herzen weggescholten,*
> *Dem harten Muß bequemt sich Will' und Grille.*]

What is "loveliest" to the individual is pushed away from his or her heart; even more radically, what is "loveliest" to him or her is pushed away by the heart itself, just as inclination in turn submits to the acceptance of necessity. We shall return to the theme of the transcendence of necessity through its acceptance in our discussion of the next (and final) stanza, but the concluding lines of "ΑΝΑΓΚΗ, Necessity" offer a powerful expression of just how grim Goethe's vision has become:

> It only seems we're free, years hem us in,
> Constraining more than at our origin.
>
> [*So sind wir scheinfrei denn nach manchen Jahren*
> *Nur enger dran, als wir am Anfang waren.*]

All this effort, all this development, all this struggle—and to what end? Our progress, it seems, has only been illusory, for after all these years we only "appear" to be free. Furthermore, the sense of futility is heightened by an awareness of the structural element of repetition within our lives—we are "even more constrained," as Goethe puts it, than we were when we started; when we embarked on the journey of our life, which seems to be been leading us in nothing but a circle.[233] Yet within these

---

[232]See the second collect for peace in the Order for Morning Prayer in *The Book of Common Prayer*, based on a Latin prayer in the Sacramentary of Gelasius and found in the Sarum Breviary.

[233]Compare with Verena Kast's comments on how "life exists in relationship to the structural element of repetition": "This repetition has much in common with ordinary life, with the experience that we cannot constantly climb the highest peaks, that 'peak experiences' are not a constant part of the human condition," and "repetitions increase the older people get, because repetition is a function of time." For forty-year-olds, she adds, "the beginning of perceptible aging is painful because so much repeats itself and so often this repetition involves starting over from the beginning"—in other words, "this experience of the Sisyphean always involves the question of meaning" (*Sisyphus: The Old Stone—A New Way, A Jungian Approach to Midlife Crisis* [1986], trans. Norman M. Brown

lines there is also an anticipation of what might, in the final stanza, give us hope.

By the end of the fourth stanza, chance has had conferred on it the status of necessity, and the individual has come to terms with the need for determination (*Bedingung* [l. 26]), for limitation (*Grenze* [l. 33]), and for obedience to the law (of life) (*Gesetz*); at the same time, however, this limitation threatens to become *too* limiting (*Nur enger dran als wir am Anfang waren*), and the individual runs the risk of becoming excessively restricted—in the next stanza Goethe will speak of "confines," "iron walls," "repulsive gates." So we have reached a moment of crisis—a crisis which, as he comments, would lead "many persons to despair, when the present thus holds them prisoner."[234] In his commentary, Goethe seems hardly able to bear to speak of this moment of crisis, when capitulation to the necessities of life seems inevitable; indeed, such capitulation has already taken place. This is not just a moment of crisis; this is the midlife crisis; it heralds the Orphic moment of death—*and renewal.*

For the Orphic moment presages the moment of release, of something new, of something different. Like Eurydice, we are hemmed in on all sides, blocked in, surrounded by death, but from this prison we shall, like Eurydice, be released (even if ultimately, like to Eurydice, we shall eventually return to Hades again...); like Orpheus, we are ripped apart and torn to shreds, but we shall continue to sing... (until we are silenced, only for our lyre to become a constellation in the firmament...). In the midst of crisis, Goethe offers us an extremely ambiguous solution, yet the only one there is: hope.

---

[Einsiedeln: Daimon, 1991], p. 29). For Murray Stein, the "vicissitudes of the soul during midlife liminality" include precisely the sense of setback experienced by Odysseus and his companions at the end of the *Odyssey*, Book 10. "Just as," he writes, "the drifting and wandering seem to be drawing to an end and some resolution comes into sight, there is a critical loss of consciousness, and it's back to square one all over again"; an experience which is "as commonplace as it is distressing: in this phase of the midlife transition there is much repetition of the same patterns, recycling, blowing back and forth, covering the same ground all over again" (*In Midlife: A Jungian Perspective* [Dallas, Texas: Spring Publications, 1983], p. 87). Yet, Stein argues, these repetitions are, in fact, *regressions*; and, on the basis that "the favoring of retrograde movement" is a characteristic of Hermes, who "brings about a reconnection to the different complexes, the different parts of one's history and memory" (pp. 41-42; cf. Rafael López-Pedraza, *Hermes and His Children* [Zurich: Spring Publications, 1977], pp. 31-32), Stein interprets such experiences as "regressions in the service of the Self: they lead consciousness downward to its sources in the unconscious" (p. 87).

    [234]Goethe, *Werke* [HA], vol. 1, p. 407; "*gar mancher, der verzweifeln möchte, wenn ihn die Gegenwart also gefangen hält.*"

## HOPE

In addition to the four "holy words" depicting the deities attendant on the birth of the individual—Δαιμων [*daimon*], Tυχη [*tyche*], Eρως [*eros*], and Aναγκη [*ananke*]—there should be added, Zoega argued, a fifth—Eλπις [*elpis*]. Goethe concurred, and "Primal Words. Orphic" ends with a fifth stanza that brings its Neoplatonic (or neo-Neoplatonic) argument to a conclusion. Now, to write about the history of the concept of hope, and the role hope plays in Goethe's outlook, lies outside the scope of this study, for it would require another volume altogether. So let us here consider just one approach, from a thinker we have already mentioned (see Chapter 2), Otto Friedrich Bollnow.[235]

Drawing on his earlier discussion in the *Protagoras*,[236] in the fourth book of his *Republic* Plato discusses the four cardinal virtues of wisdom (*sophia*), courage (*andreia*), moderation (*sophrosyne*), and justice (*dikaiosyne*).[237] To these pagan virtues, the Christian tradition added—as Bollnow has pointed out—the three cardinal virtues of faith, love, and: hope.[238] In opposition to Martin Heidegger's characterization of human existence in terms of the moods of care (*Sorge*) and anxiety (*Angst*), Bollnow introduced as a second, polarizing force, the category of hope.[239] For Bollnow, the human being is essentially the being that has hope (*das hoffende Wesen*).[240] In the experience of hope, he explains, the human being "experiences something else that supports," an experience of "being accepted" and "being taken up" by "a power that is not our own."[241] For

---

[235] See Ralf Koerrenz, *Otto Friedrich Bollnow: Ein pädagogisches Porträt* (Weinheim and Basel: Beltz, 2004), "Die gestimmte Erziehungswirklichkeit," pp. 60-78.

[236] Plato, *Protagoras*, 349b (*Collected Dialogues*, p. 341), where Socrates lists five virtues: wisdom, moderation, courage, justice, and holiness. In the *Laws*, the Athenian Stranger insists on the need for justice to be apparent: "If there is one human being, or some oligarchy, or a democracy, whose soul is directed to pleasures and desires, and needs to be filled with these, and retains nothing, but is sick with endless and insatiable evil—if such a one rules a city or some private individual, trampling underfoot the laws, there is [...] no device of salvation" (Book 4, 714a; *The Laws*, trans. Pangle, p. 100).

[237] Plato, *Republic*, book 4, 427e; *Collected Dialogues*, p. 669.

[238] Otto Friedrich Bollnow, *Wesen und Wandel der Tugenden* (Frankfurt am Main: Ullstein, 1958), pp. 24-25.

[239] See Otto Friedrich Bollnow, *Neue Geborgenheit: Das Problem einer Überwindung des Existentialismus*, 4th ed. (Stuttgart: Kohlhammer, 1979), p. 116.

[240] Bollnow, "Selbstdarstellung," in Ludwig J. Pongratz, ed., *Pädagogik in Selbstdarstellungen*, 4 vols. (Hamburg: Meiner, 1975-1982), vol. 1, pp. 95-144 (p. 122).

[241] Hans-Peter Göbbeler and Hans-Ulrich Lessing, eds., *Otto Friedrich Bollnow im Gespräch* (Freiburg im Breisgau and Munich: Alber, 1983), p. 33; "*dass in der Hoffnung dem Menschen etwas*

"the essence of hope" resides in the following fact: "That I do not imagine
what is going to happen and how it is going to happen, but that I switch
off my own will and abandon myself to what approaches me as offering
support."[242] Furthermore: to hope, Bollnow emphasizes, does not mean
adopting a *laissez-faire* attitude, because hope involves both the desire to
shape what is to come, as well as an acceptance of it. And so in hope, as
Bollnow understands it, we encounter seemingly abstract philosophical
issues of free will and determinism on an existential level. Ultimately,
hope is "what makes life possible as life, as an acting and striving toward
the future," and in this sense hope is nothing less than "the foundation of
the soul."[243]

Bollnow's discussion of hope provides us with a useful framework to
approach the final stanza of Goethe's "Primal Words. Orphic," entitled
precisely "ΕΛΠΙΣ. Hope":

> But such a confine, such a wall immuring
> In odious chafe, is breached and left ungated
> Though like the timeless crags it seems enduring!
> A Being rises light and liberated:
> Through showering rain and cloud and mist obscuring
> She lifts us up, we soar on wings elated:
> You know her well, to nowhere she's confined—
> A wingbeat—aeons vanish far behind!

> [*Doch solcher Grenze, solcher ehr'nen Mauer*
> *Höchst widerwärt'ge Pforte wird entriegelt,*
> *Sie stehe nur mit alter Felsendauer!*
> *Ein Wesen regt sich leicht und ungezügelt:*
> *Aus Wolkendecke, Nebel, Regenschauer*
> *Erhebt sie uns, mit ihr, durch sie beflügelt;*
> *Ihr kennt ihr wohl, sie schwärmt durch alle Zonen;*
> *Ein Flügelschlag—und hinter uns Äonen.*]

---

*andres als tragend entgegenkommt. Dieses Angenommenwerden und Aufgefangenwerden von einer andern
Kraft, die nicht die unsre ist, das ist mir das Entscheidende.*"

[242]Bollnow, "Selbstdarstellung," p. 67; "*Zum Wesen der Hoffnung; dass ich mir keine Vorstellung
von dem mache, was kommen soll und wie es kommen soll, sondern dass ich dabei den eignen Willen
ausschalte und mich ganz dem überlasse, was mir als tragend entgegenkommt.*" Compare with Bollnow's
claim that the chief expression of hope is "a tranquil, trusting relationship to the future" [*ein gelassen
vertrauendes Verhältnis zur Zukunft*].

[243]Bollnow, *Neue Geborgenheit*, p. 116; "*die Hoffnung* [*ist*] *dasjenige, was das Leben als Leben, als
in die Zukunft gerichtetes Handeln und Streben, allererst ermöglicht. Die Hoffnung wäre also der letzte
Grund der Seele.*"

This stanza begins with an intensification, if it were possible, of the moment of crisis—the sense of confinement, of restriction, of suffocation becomes palpable, almost painful. In the desperate scenario Jung paints in "The Soul and Death," we are alone, "it is night and so dark and still that one hears nothing and sees nothing but the thoughts which add and subtract the years, and the long row of those disagreeable facts which remorselessly indicate how far the hand of the clock has moved forward, and the slow, irresistible approach of the wall of darkness which will eventually engulf everything I love, possess, wish for, hope for, and strive for, [...] and fear envelops the sleepless one like a smothering blanket."[244] Even our hopes and desires, it seems, can turn against us, as Goethe's character Wilhelm Meister suggests when he reflects that "the desires and hopes that a man cherishes in his heart would seem to be what he knows best; and yet, when they suddenly appear before him and are, as it were, pressing in upon him, he retreats from them, not recognizing them for what they are"[245]—a notion referred to by Ernst Bloch as "the melancholy of achievement" (*Melancholie der Erfüllung*).[246] And yet—as Elizabeth Sewell recognized, these lines are a tribute to Goethe's conception of "metamorphoses" as a fundamentally synthetic method: "Here a mind passionately interested in the dynamics of life, in the individual organism, in nature at large, in human beings and in his own thinking and feeling and acting self, having tried to evolve a dynamic of nonmathematical thought as a means of interpreting life, brings this home, centrally and finally, to words, poetry and myth," she wrote in *The Orphic Voice* (1960): "Metamorphosis was for Goethe not just a phenomenon; it was a working discipline."[247]

In the final stanza of "Primal Words. Orphic," the "borders" that constrict us are insurmountable, the walls that hem us in are "made of iron," the tall gates that impinge upon us are, in German, *widerwärtig* (deriving from the Old High German, *widarwertig*—"inimical," "hostile").[248] And yet—the gates can be unbolted, the door can be opened, the

---

[244] Jung, *CW* 8, §796.

[245] *Wilhelm Meister's Apprenticeship (Wilhelm Meisters Lehrjahre)*, Book 4, chapter 19; Goethe, *GE* 9, 165; *Werke* [HA], vol. 7, p. 276.

[246] See Ernst Bloch, *Das Prinzip Hoffnung* [1959], 3 vols. (Frankfurt am Main: Suhrkamp, 1980), vol. 1, p. 343.

[247] Elizabeth Sewell, *The Orphic Voice: Poetry and Natural History* (New Haven: Yale University Press, 1960), p. 274.

[248] See Wipf, *Elpis*, p. 138.

walls can be traversed. From the moment of midlife crisis, as Goethe understands it, there is an exit, and the moment of transition—the moment of deepest, darkest, bleakest despair, *and* the moment of over-coming, of renewal, of rebirth—*is* the Orphic moment. And this exit, this moment of transition, this triumphant Orphic moment is placed under the sign of the goddess—hope.[249]

For among these gloomy clouds, this fog and mist, these squalls and showers, something, someone, is moving, light and "unchecked," "un-reined-in." This being lacks "reins," yet in fact it bears them,[250] on its back—in the shape of its wings, which lift it (and with it, us) into the air. In the view of the Orphics, according to Zoega's account, nothing can resist *ananke* (necessity), which is the same as *tyche* (chance), except "the unchecked daring of the human mind, which we call, to use another expression, hope."[251] Uplifted and, as it were, "given new wings," we do not stand still, but continue, so to speak, onward and "upward."

To understand how hope can exercise this transformative effect, we need to consider the final stanza of "Primal Words. Orphic" in the light of Goethe's earlier poem, "My Goddess" (*Meine Göttin*) (1780). In this poem, the poet's goddess turns out to be *Phantasie*—in other words, the imagination. In the final lines of this work in praise of *Phantasie*, Goethe refers to her sister goddess as hope:

> Yet I know her sister,
> The elder, less flighty one,
> My quiet friend—
> O may she only turn
> Away from me when
> The light of this life does,

---

[249]For further discussion of the function of the concept of hope in Goethe's later writings, see Wipf's study of *Elpis*; as well as Joachim Müller, "Bild und Sinnbild der Hoffnung in Goethes Werk," in *Wirklichkeit und Klassik: Beiträge zur deutschen Literaturgeschichte von Lessing bis Heine* (Berlin: Verlag der Nation, 1955), pp. 349-365; and Bruno Hillebrand, *Die Hoffnung des alten Goethe* [*Abhandlungen der Klasse der Literatur*, 1983, no. 5] (Wiesbaden: Steiner, 1983); and for further dis-cussion of this stanza in particular, see Wilhelm Flitner, "Elpis: Betrachtungen über Goethes 'Urworte. Orphisch,'" *Goethe: Viermonatsschrift der Goethe-Gesellschaft* 4 (1939): 128-147; and Ar-thur Hübscher, "Das fünfte Urwort," in *Versuche zu Goethe: Festschrift für Erich Heller zum 65. Geburtstag am 27.3.1976*, ed. Volker Dürr und Géza von Molnár (Heidelberg: Stiehm, 1976), pp. 133-140.

[250]Wipf, *Elpis*, p. 139.

[251]Zoega, "ΑΓΑΘΗ ΤΥΧΗΙ: Tyche und Nemesis," in *Abhandlungen*, p. 40; "*dem unbezähmten Erkühnen des menschlichen Geistes, das wir mit einem andern Ausdruck Hoffnung nennen.*"

She who nobly impels
And comforts us: Hope!

[*Doch kenn' ich ihre Schwester,*
*Die ältere, gesetztere,*
*Meine stille Freundin:*
*O daß die erst*
*Mit dem Lichte des Lebens*
*Sich von mir wende,*
*Die edle Treiberin,*
*Trösterin, Hoffnung!*][252]

Hope, "the eternal encourager in effort and comforter in sorrow,"[253] is thus associated with the goddess *Phantasie.* The role of the imagination in the psychic life of the individual was recognized, too, by Goethe, as his remarks in a letter of 1817 show:

> The imagination is the fourth principal faculty in our intellectual being, it supplements sensuousness, in the form of memory, it lays the perception of the external world before the understanding, under the form of experience, it moulds or finds forms for the ideas of reason and thus enlivens the whole human unit which without it would necessarily sink into barren incapacity.[254]

The relation between the Imagination and its sister, Hope, explains the mechanism by which Hope can offer us help.

For the "beat of the wings" that carries us upward is associated, through its iconography, with another wingèd, mythological creature, with Pegasus, the symbol of poetry and, by extension, art.[255] This mythical creature, according to Greek legend, sprang from the blood of the Gor-

---

[252]Goethe, *GE* 1, 79 [trans. Michael Hamburger]; *Werke* [HA], vol. 1, p. 146.

[253]See James Boyd, *Notes to Goethe's Poems,* 2 vols. (Oxford: Basil Blackwell, 1966-1867), vol. 2, p. 221.

[254]Letter to Maria Paulowna of 3 January 1817 (Goethe, *Briefe* [HA], vol. 3, p. 385).

[255]Pierre Hadot compares this symbolism of Pegasus—an image of which was chosen by the Berlin sculptor Johann Gottfried Schadow (1764-1850) to decorate the reverse side of the commemorative coin he designed in honor of Goethe in 1816 (Buck, *Goethes "Urworte. Orphisch,"* p. 60, n. 124)—with the wingèd horse, Buraq, on whom, according to tradition, Mohammed was carried during his Night Journey to Jerusalem (see Sura 17:1 of the Qur'an); Goethe alludes to this image when, in his *Notes and Essays on the West-Eastern Divan,* he writes that "a transfigured everyday lends us wing to attain the higher and the highest" [*ein verklärtes Alltägliche verleiht uns Flügel, zum Höheren und Höchsten zu gelangen*] and asks: "What is there to prevent the poet from mounting Mohammed's miraculous horse and soaring up into the heavens?" (*Werke* [HA], vol. 2, p. 206; cf. Hadot, *N'oublie pas de vivre,* p. 232).

gon, Medusa, when Perseus cut off her head. From the horror (of life) that we cannot contemplate arises art (which we can contemplate)—art, which transforms that life (and its horror) into beauty. Pegasus gave the Muses, the goddesses of art and poetry, the very source of inspiration, when with his hooves he made the waters of the spring, Hippocrene, flow freely. (This is why, in German, "to climb onto Pegasus" is a synonym for writing poetry, and the image of Pegasus as the symbol of poetic inspiration informs other works of German classical verse, including Schiller's early poem, "Pegasus in Harness" [*Pegasus im Joche*] [1796].)[256]

This moment is one we may well call Orphic, because Orpheus himself was an artist—a singer and poet, whose song could bring the world alive, and entrance the creatures in it. The famous third-century mosaic in the Archaeological Museum in Palermo shows him doing precisely this. Orpheus descended to Hades, yet returned to the land of the living: the ultimate "comeback kid" of the ancient cult, whose timeless rituals celebrated the deepest mysteries of life and death. With one beat of its wings, *elpis*—which itself knows no restrictions of place or space—carries us through time itself, across the aeons.

Goethe's understanding of the salvific power of art is tied up with his view of its relation to time. The relation is evoked in the final line of the poem—"aeons vanish far behind" (*und hinter uns Äonen*). Behind the German word *Äon* lies the Greek, *aion* (αἰών), the name of a god as well as a philosophical concept.[257] As a deity, Aion is the Greek god of eternity, of time itself—sometimes in its linear, sometimes in its cyclical aspects. One of its identifications was with the sun, *helios*; and in this representation, Aion was present right at the beginning, in the very first stanza, of "Primal Words. Orphic." Iconographically, Aion is represented as a lion-headed man with four wings on his back, carrying keys and a scepter, his head encircled by a serpent (as we shall see, elements of this image recur in the figure of the caduceus).[258] As a concept, *aion* is the power of

---

[256]Friedrich Schiller, *The Minor Poems*, trans. John Herman Merivale (London: Pickering, 1844), pp. 72-76; *Sämtliche Gedichte und Balladen*, ed. Georg Kurscheidt (Frankfurt am Main and Leipzig: Insel, 2004), pp. 83-85.

[257]On the figure and concept of *aion*, see the entry by Henriette Harich-Schwarzbauer and Rémi Brague on "Aion," in *Religion in Geschichte und Gegenwart: Handwörterbuch für Theologie und Religionswissenschaft*, ed. Hans Dieter Betz, 4th ed., 8 vols. (Tübingen: Mohr Siebeck, 1998-2005), vol. 1, p. 234.

[258]Brian P. Copenhaver, ed., *Hermetica: The Greek "Corpus Hermeticum" and the Latin "Asclepius" in a new English translation with notes and introduction* (Cambridge: Cambridge University

life itself. For the "obscure" Heraclitus, life-or-time—*aion*—is "a child at play, playing draughts."²⁵⁹ In Gnostic thought, Aion was sometimes identified with the Barbelo, the second principle of the classic Gnostic myth, sometimes as three, four, five, or as many as ten separate entities "emanating" from that principle.²⁶⁰ In the Hermetic tradition, the Aion (or eternity) is created by God, in turn the Aion makes the cosmos, which in turn makes time, which in turn makes coming-to-be.²⁶¹ And in the tradition of Neoplatonism, Plotinus defines *aion* as life itself, for Eternity means "Ever-Being" (αἰών = ἀεὶ ὄν), "the Life—instantaneously entire, complete, at no point broken into period or part."²⁶²

In his important study entitled *Aion: Contributions to the Symbolism of the Self* (*Aion: Beiträge zur Symbolik des Selbst*) (1951), Jung uses the word in at least three senses, referring to Epiphanius's account of the "Korion," the celebration of the birth of Aion from the virgin, Kore, in Alexandria on the night of the Epiphany (5-6 January);²⁶³ to the Gnostic myth (found, for example, in Valentinus) of Aion as the Autopator (i.e., self-originater), "the ageless Aion, eternally young, male and female, who contains everything in himself and is [himself] contained by nothing";²⁶⁴ and the *aion* as period of time, and in this sense he refers to the "Christian aion."²⁶⁵ True, the line *hinter uns Äonen*, read literally, means we should put time behind us—and don't look back! For, just as it was Orpheus's mistake (as Manto reminds Faust) to "look back" at Eurydice, thereby losing her forever, so it is a big mistake for us to "look back" at the past—and thereby risk losing our future. There is, however, an even more precise way of reading this line.

In Zoega's fifth treatise, "On the Original God of the Orphics" (*Über den uranfänglichen Gott der Orphiker*), the figure of Aion is identifed with

---

Press, 1992), pp. 167-168. For a discussion of Aion in Orphic literature, see M. L. West, *The Orphic Hymns* (Oxford: Clarendon Press, 1983), pp. 219-120 and 230-231.

²⁵⁹Heraclitus, Diels-Kranz 22 B 52 (Barnes, *Early Greek Philosophy*, p. 102).

²⁶⁰See *The Gnostic Scriptures*, trans. Bentley Layton (London: SCM Press, 1987), pp. 12-13; but see also further detailed references in the index to this collection.

²⁶¹See the dialogue between Mind (Nous) and Hermes in *Corpus Hermeticum*, no. 11, in Copenhaver, *Hermetica*, p. 37.

²⁶²*Enneads*, 3.7 [4]; in Plotinus, *The Enneads*, trans. MacKenna, p. 216.

²⁶³Jung, *CW* 9/ii §164; cf. Epiphanius of Salamis, *Against Heresies* [*Aversus Haereses*] or the *Panarion*, 51.22.

²⁶⁴Jung, *CW* 9/ii §298; cf. Epiphanius, *Against Heresies*, 31.5.

²⁶⁵Jung, *CW* 9/ii, p. ix.

(Eros) Phanes and equated with "measurable time" (or diachronic time) in the "real world," in opposition to Chronos, representing "unlimited time" (or synchronic time) in the "absolute world."[266] Now, in Goethe's thinking the aim of art is to transcend this opposition, and to bring the eternal into our transitory experience of life; to inject eternity, so to speak, into the everyday. Thus the transformation of the Now into the Eternal is central to Goethe's conception of art. In his poem "The Divine" (*Das Göttliche*) (1783) Goethe wrote, invoking the idea of "the impossible" that Manto throws as an accusation in the face of Faust:

> Yet man alone can
> Achieve the impossible:
> He distinguishes,
> Chooses, and judges;
> He can give lasting
> Life to the moment.

> [*Nur allein der Mensch*
> *Vermag das Unmögliche:*
> *Er unterscheidet,*
> *Wählet und richtet;*
> *Er kann dem Augenblick*
> *Dauer verleihen.*][267]

And this aesthetic outlook, transferred to life itself, is celebrated in his late poem, already mentioned, "Testament" (*Vermächtnis*):

> Be moderate when blessings flow,
> Good sense in every detail show
> Where life is in its ecstasies;
> Then bygone time gives permanence,
> The future lives, and in advance:
> Eternity the moment is.

> [*Genieße mäßig Füll' und Segen,*
> *Vernunft sei überall zugegen,*
> *Wo Leben sich des Lebens freut.*
> *Dann ist Vergangenheit beständig,*
> *Das Künftige voraus lebendig,*
> *Der Augenblick ist Ewigkeit.*][268]

---

[266]Zoega, *Abhandlungen*, pp. 211-264 (pp. 211 and 254-255); compare with Dietze, "Urworte, nicht sonderlich orphisch," p. 26, n. 32.

[267]Goethe, *GE* 1, 81 [trans. Vernon Watkins]; *Werke* [HA], vol. 1, p. 148.

[268]Goethe, *GE* 1, 269 [trans. Christopher Middleton]; *Werke* [HA], vol. 1, p. 370.

This idea—the Eternity of the Moment—is a common one in Goethe's later thought; in his letter to Auguste von Bernstorff of 17 April 1823, for example, he remarks that "if only the eternal [*das Ewige*] would remain present at every moment [*jeden Augenblick*], we would not suffer from time's transitoriness";[269] and in his conversation with Eckermann of 3 November 1823, he observed that "every situation—nay, every moment [*jeder Augenblick*] is of infinite worth; for it is the representative of a whole eternity [*einer ganzen Ewigkeit*]."[270]

This link between here-and-now and the aesthetic for-ever forms the basis of one of Goethe's less well known poems, entitled "Today and Eternity" (*Heut und ewig*), and published in 1820 in the same edition of *Kunst und Altertum* that contained "Primal Words. Orphic."[271] This poem also takes "the impossible" as its starting-point, but in the context of our everyday experience, and uses the same image of wing-borne flight as the *elpis* stanza:

> It can't be done—to show the day the day,
> One confusion in another is reflected,
> Each person thinks: I'm right in what I do and say,
> No self-control: critique on others is deflected.
> In that case, one's advised silent to stay,
> And let the spirit ever higher be elected.
> From yesterday, there's no tomorrow: but in time
> The ages sometimes sink, and sometimes shine.

> [*Unmöglich ist's den Tag dem Tag zu zeigen,*
> *Der nur Verworrnes im Verworrnen spiegelt,*
> *Und jeder selbst sich fühlt als recht und eigen,*
> *Statt sich zu zügeln, nur am andern zügelt;*
> *Da ist's den Lippen besser daß sie schweigen,*
> *Indeß der Geist sich fort und fort beflügelt.*
> *Aus Gestern wird nicht Heute; doch Äonen,*
> *Sie werden wechselnd sinken, werden thronen.*][272]

This poem forms a diptych with a much earlier text, consisting of lines originally composed in 1784 for the incomplete epic, "The Mysteries" (*Die Geheimnisse*), but not published until 1820; in this poem, "For Ever" (*Für ewig*), Goethe writes:

---

[269] Goethe, *Briefe* [HA], vol. 4, p. 63; cited in Anton, "'Urworte. Orphisch," p.182.

[270] Eckermann, *Conversations of Goethe*, p. 19.

[271] See Karl Borinski, "Goethes 'Urworte. Orphisch,'" *Philologus* 69 (1910): 1-9 (p. 9).

[272] Goethe, *Werke* [WA], vol. I.3, p. 163.

For what man within his earthly limits
Of happiness can grant the name of gods—
Loyal harmony, that no change of mind permits
The friendship, that lasts against the odds;
Light, which from wise men lonely thoughts elicits,
And in poets as beautiful images unfolds.
All that I had in my best hours discovered
In eternity—and for myself uncovered.

[*Denn was der Mensch in seinen Erdeschranken*
*Von hohem Glück mit Götternamen nennt,*
*Die Harmonie der Treue, die kein Wanken,*
*Der Freundschaft, die nicht Zweifelsorge kennt;*
*Das Licht, das Weisen nur zu einsamen Gedanken,*
*Das Dichtern nur in schönen Bildern brennt,*
*Das hatt' ich all in meinen besten Stunden*
*In ihr entdeckt und es für mich gefunden.*][273]

We might compare this concrete version of *aion* as eternity with another
key intertext—arguably *the* key intertext for Goethe's writings—*Faust.* In
the momentous words of the antepenultimate scene, Faust (nearly?)
repeats the words of his original wager with Mephistopheles—the story
"arc" that has spanned over ten thousand lines of text—and boldly
declares his political—and personal—vision:

Yes! to this vision I am wedded still,
And this as wisdom's final world I teach:
Only that man earns freedom, merits life,
Who must reconquer both in constant daily strife.
In such a place, by danger still surrounded,
Youth, manhood, age, their brave new world have founded.
I long to see that multitude, and stand
With a free people on free land!
Then to the moment I might say:
Beautiful moment, do not pass away!
Till many ages [*Äonen*] shall have passed
This record of my earthly life shall last.
And in anticipation of such bliss
What moment could give me greater joy than this?

[*Ja! diesem Sinne bin ich ganz ergeben,*
*Das ist der Weisheit letzter Schluß:*

[273]Goethe, *Werke* [WA], vol. I.3, p. 44.

*Nur der verdient sich Freiheit wie das Leben,*
*Der täglich sie erobern muß.*
*Und so verbringt, umrungen von Gefahr,*
*Hier Kindheit, Mann und Greis sein tüchtig Jahr.*
*Solch ein Gewimmel möcht' ich sehn,*
*Auf freiem Grund mit freiem Volke stehn.*
*Zum Augenblicke dürft' ich sagen:*
*"Verweile doch, du bist so schön!*
*Es kann die Spur von meinen Erdetagen*
*Nicht in Äonen untergehn. – "*
*Im Vorgefühl von solchem hohen Glück*
*Genieß' ich jetzt den höchsten Augenblick.*][274]

With these words, Faust sinks back—into his grave, which the lemurs, those skeletal ghosts of the dead, have been digging—only to rise (in entelic form, in the concluding "Mountain Gorges" scene of the poetic drama), onward and upward to his encounter with the Magna Mater in the figure of the Mater Gloriosa.

But how does art achieve the status of the eternal? "Primal Words. Orphic" itself illustrates Goethe's intentions, as does his letter to his daughter-in-law, Ottilie von Goethe, of 21 June 1818, in which he discusses his recent literary production. Here he writes that the intention of the *West-Eastern Divan* is "to free us from the present that determines us and to place us in a boundless freedom, as far as feeling is concerned, for the moment."[275] Whereas the poems in this cycle "expand the feelings, the imagination" (*das Gefühl, die Einbildungskraft*), the purpose of "Primal Words. Orphic," he added, "was to open up infinite space to reflection [*dem Nachdenken*] and to allow everything we have experienced to be seen again, as if in a thousand mirrors."[276] (In these remarks, Jochen Schmidt sees an anti-Romantic thrust, inasmuch as "Primal Words. Orphic" constitutes a "poetry of reflection" [*Reflexionspoesie*] that is not "abstractly independent, conceptually autonomous," but is based on concrete experience of life and limits itself—"None proves a master but by limitation"[277]—in its return to that experiential

---

[274]*Faust II*, ll. 11573-11586; *Faust: Part Two*, trans. Luke, p. 223; *Werke* [HA], vol. 3, pp. 347-348.

[275]Goethe, *Briefe* [HA], vol. 3, p. 431.

[276]Goethe, *Briefe* [HA], vol. 3, p. 431.

[277]"Nature and Art" (*Natur und Kunst*) (c. 1800; pub. 1807); Goethe, *GE* 1, 165 [trans. Michael Hamburger]; *Werke* [HA], vol. 1, p. 245.

starting point.[278]) Rightly considered, this expansion of mind and feeling gives us, within our limited earthly life, at least a taste of the infinite: and of no more of the infinite can we, with our limited capacities, actually know. Art might not, in the absolute sense, be unending: but inasmuch as "Primal Words. Orphic" offers a "conceptually systematic thought" that turns into "living thought that can never reach a conclusion," because we enter thereby into "the irrevocable dialectic of limitation and expansion,"[279] it becomes unending *for us*. Our life might reach a conclusion (in the sense of an ending), but our thinking on life never reaches a conclusion (in the sense of a final judgement), and it is only extinguished, still incomplete, with our biological demise.

Another intertext that casts light on the conclusion to "Primal Words. Orphic," and explains its grounds for hope, is "Permanence in Change" (*Dauer im Wechsel*) (1803), whose concluding stanza runs:

> Let the start and end so fusing
> Join in One and unify!
> Swifter than the things you're losing
> You must let yourself go by!
> Thank the Muses for bestowing
> Favour of a lasting kind:
> Import from your heart outflowing
> And the form within your mind.
>
> [*Laß den Anfang mit dem Ende*
> *Sich in **eins** zusammenziehn!*
> *Schneller als die Gegenstände*
> *Selber dich vorüberfliehn.*
> *Danke, daß die Gunst der Musen*
> *Unvergängliches verheißt,*
> *Den Gehalt in deinem Busen*
> *Und die Form in deinem Geist.*][280]

In the end, we arrive back at the beginning; the circle is closed when it reaches its starting-point, and "all of us must / Fulfill the circles / Of our existence." Referring to the ancient symbol of the ouroboros, Goethe once commented that "for a symbol of eternity one uses a serpent, that

---

[278]Schmidt, *Goethes Altersgedicht "Urworte. Orphisch,"* p. 30. Schmidt contrasts Goethe's ambition with the mirror metaphor of Friedrich Schlegel's aim "to increase reflection again and again, as multiplying it in an *infinite* series of mirrors" (*Athenäum Fragments*, no. 116).

[279]Schmidt, *Goethes Altersgedicht "Urworte. Orphisch,"* p. 32.

[280]Goethe, *Selected Poems*, trans. Whaley, p. 87; *Werke* [HA], vol. 1, p. 248.

curls round in a circle," but he regarded this as symbol instead of "a like-ness of happy temporality [*glücklichen Zeitlichkeit*]." For "what more can someone want than that he is allowed to join his end to his beginning?" Goethe asked in his letter of 5 January 1814 to Friedrich Wilhelm Hein-rich von Trebra (1740-1819), adding that this can only happen through "the lasting nature of affection, of trust, of love, of friendship."[281]

The serpent occurs in another ancient symbol: the caduceus, the wand carried by the winged messenger-god Hermes (or Mercury), round which two serpents are entwined: and the winged figure of the Sol-Mercurius is, surely, iconographically present in the lines of this con-cluding stanza.[282] In his *Saturnalia*, Macrobius explains the relationship between the sun, Mercury, and the symbol of the caduceus, in a complex passage that deserves to be quoted in its entirety:

> Another clear proof that it is the sun that we worship under the name of Mercury is the caduceus, which the Egyptians have designed as the sacred staff of Mercury. It shows a pair of serpents, male and female, intertwined; the middle parts of the serpents' coils are joined together as in a knot, called the knot of Hercules; their upper parts are bent into a circle and complete the circle as they meet in a kiss; below the knot their tails rejoin the staff at the point at which it is held, and at that point appear the wings with which they are provided.[283]

In his interpretation of the figure of the caduceus, Macrobius explains the wings as a reference to the passing of time,[284] while the kiss of the two ser-pents represents love, and their intertwining, necessity.[285] As a symbol of transcendence-within-immanence the mercurial caduceus will return as a serpent coiled around the neck of an eagle, as a serpent coiled around a

[281]Goethe, *Briefe* [HA], vol. 3, p. 251.

[282]See Macrobius, *Saturnalia*, book 1, chapter 19, §16; Borinski, "Goethes 'Urworte. Orphisch,'" pp. 2-3; Anton, "Urworte. Orphisch," pp. 183-184. For further discussion of the symbol of the caduceus, see Pierre Hadot, "Emblèmes et symboles goethéens: Du caducée d'Hermès à la plante archétype," in *L'art des confins: Mélanges offerts à Maurice de Gandillac*, ed. Annie Cazeneuve and Jean-François Lyotard (Paris: Presses universitaires de France, 1985), pp. 431-444.

[283]Ambrosius Aurelius Theodosius Macrobius, *The Saturnalia*, trans. Percival Vaughan Davies (New York: Columbia University Press, 1969), book 1, chapter 19, §16, p. 135.

[284]*The Saturnalia*, §18: "Why the wings are added has already been explained [as a symbol of the swift movement of the sun; see §8], and of the above-mentioned attributes the coiled bodies of the ser-pents have been specially chosen, as illustrating the serpentine course of each of the two stars [i.e., the sun and the moon]" (Macrobius, *Saturnalia*, p. 136).

[285]*The Saturnalia*, §17: "This kiss of the serpents is the symbol of Love; and the knot is the sym-bol of Necessity" (Macrobius, *Saturnalia*, p. 136).

sun on the golden haft of a staff, and as "the ring of rings" (the ring of eternal recurrence) in Nietzsche's *Zarathustra*...[286] And the interrelationship of love and necessity—love *of* necessity—is reformulated in Nietzsche's concept of *amor fati*...

In the final stanza of "Permanence in Change," the end represents a return to the beginning, just as the end of life represents a return to its beginning. Using a related image to the one of flight found in "Primal Words. Orphic," the self "speeds over" (*vorüberfliehn*) itself faster than over objects—and faster than objects "speed over" it. In other words, the self is interacting with the world, but is undergoing an internal process of change as well. The references to the Muses—originally goddesses of memory, and later goddesses of artistic inspiration—as well as the vocabulary of "import" (*Gehalt*) and "form" (*Form*) suggest that the "everlasting favour" to which the final lines refer is *aesthetic* in nature. Goethe is suggesting that we transform the past—and so open up the way to the future—through *art*, and so the conclusions of "Primal Words. Orphic" and its two intertexts, "My Goddess" and "Permanence in Change," could be summarized as an aesthetic claim about the relation between memory, imagination, and hope. What gives us hope is the ability of our imagination to prevent us from becoming "stuck in the past" of memory and instead, by means of the aesthetic imagination, to transform time—and ourselves.

## CONCLUSION

Just as Orpheus descends to the depths of Hades, there to release his beloved, Eurydice, so we must descend to the depths of our (unconscious) being, in order to release from the clutches of all that is deathly, stultifying, and life-denying, the self. Orpheus, as Manto reminds Faust, failed in his task. We must not in ours.

The mechanism for the exploration, release, construction, and cultivation of the self is the same as the (re)shaping of self in relation to self, to others, and to time: it is the imagination, or *Phantasie*. For Jung—as for Goethe[287]—imagination (*Phantasie*) represents the crucial aspect of the

---

[286]See "Zarathustra's Prologue," §10; "Of the Bestowing Virtue," §1; and "The Seven Seals (or: The Song of Yes and Amen)," §1, in Nietzsche, *Thus Spake Zarathustra*, trans. Hollingdale, pp. 52-53, 100, 244.

[287]For further discussion of Goethe's concept of the imagination, see Eduard Spranger, "Goethe über die Phantasie" [1945], in *Goethe: Seine geistige Welt*, pp. 364-391.

psyche, and in *Psychological Types* (*Psychologische Typen*) (1921), he defined it in the following extravagant terms, which underscore its immense significance:

> Fantasy is just as much feeling and thinking; as much intuition as sensation. There is no psychic function that, through fantasy, is not inextricably bound up with the other psychic functions. Sometimes it appears in primordial form, sometimes it is the ultimate and boldest product of all our faculties combined [*Sie erscheint bald als uranfänglich, bald als letztes und kühnstes Produkt der Zusammenfassung alles Könnens*]. Fantasy, therefore, seems to me the clearest expression of the specific activity of the psyche. It is, pre-eminently, the creative activity from which the answers to all answerable questions come; it is the mother of all possibilities, where, like all psychological opposites, the inner and outer worlds are joined together in living union. Fantasy it was and ever is which fashions the bridge between the irreconcilable claims of subject and object, introversion and extraversion. In fantasy alone both mechanisms are united.[288]

For the German classicists (such as Goethe, and Schiller, but also Herder, or Wieland), the chief vehicle for the aesthetic was the *symbol*. In his treatise *On the Aesthetic Education of Humankind in a Series of Letters* (*Über die ästhetische Erziehung des Menschen in einer Reihe von Briefen*) (1795), Schiller worked out a complex theory of the symbol or, as he called it, "living form" (*lebende Gestalt*). Put briefly, Schiller posited two drives, the sensuous drive (or *Stofftrieb*) and the form drive (or *Formtrieb*)—

> The object of the sense-drive [...] we call *life*, in the widest sense of this term: a concept designating all material being and all that is immediately present to the senses. The object of the form-drive [...] we call *form*, both in the figurative and in the literal sense of this word: a concept which includes all the formal qualities of things and all the relations of these to our thinking faculties.

—out of the reciprocal interaction of which arises the third drive, the ludic drive (or *Spieltrieb*):

> The object of the play-drive, represented in a general schema, may therefore be called *living form* [*lebende Gestalt*], a concept

[288]Jung, *CW* 6 §78.

serving to designate all the aesthetic qualities of phenomena
and, in a word, what in the widest sense of the term we call
*beauty* [*Schönheit*].[289]

In his discussion of Schiller's treatise in *Psychological Types*, Jung equated
Schiller's "living form" with his own concept of the symbol, arguing that
"the object of the mediating function" is "'living form'" (*lebende Gestalt*),
for "this would be precisely a symbol in which the opposites are
united"—and "the third element, in which the opposites merge, is fantasy
activity, which is creative and receptive at once [*die einserseits schöpferische
und anderseits rezeptive Phantasietätigkeit*]."[290] What, then, for Jung, is the
symbol? It is "a product [*ein Gebilde*] of an extremely complex nature,
since data from every psychic function have gone into its making":

> It is, therefore, neither *rational* nor *irrational*. It certainly has a
> side that accords with reason, but it has another side that does
> not; for it is composed not only of rational but also of irratio-
> nal data supplied by pure inner and outer perception. The
> profundity and pregnant significance of the symbol appeal
> just as strongly to *thinking* as *feeling*, while its peculiar plastic
> imagery, when shaped into sensuous form, stimulates *sensa-
> tion* as much as *intuition* [*Das Ahnungsreiche und Bedeutungs-
> schwangere des Symbols spricht ebensowohl das Denken wie das
> Fühlen an, und seine eigenartige Bildhaftigkeit, wenn zu
> sinnlicher Form gestaltet, erregt die Empfindung sowohl wie die
> Intuition*].[291]

Moreover, he described the "function" (*Funktion*)—"being here understood not as a basic function but as a complex function made up of other
functions"—of the "symbol" as "transcendent" (*transzendent*), but as
transcendent in this specific sense, "not as denoting a metaphysical quality but merely the fact that this function facilitates a transition from one
attitude to another."[292]

> From the activity of the unconscious there now emerges a new
> content, constellated by thesis and antithesis in equal measure
> and standing in a *compensatory* relation to both. It thus forms

---

[289]Letter 15, §2, in Friedrich Schiller, *On the Aesthetic Education of Man in a Series of Letters*, ed.
and trans. Elizabeth M. Wilkinson and L. A. Willoughby, 2nd ed. (Oxford: Clarendon Press, 1982),
p. 101.

[290]Jung, *CW* 6 §171.

[291]Jung, *CW* 6 §823.

[292]Jung, *CW* 6 §828.

the middle ground on which the opposites can be united. [...]
If the mediatory product remains intact, it forms the raw material for a process not of dissolution but of construction, in
which thesis and antithesis both play their part. In this way it
becomes a new content that governs the whole attitude, putting an end to the division and forcing the energy of the opposites into a common channel. The standstill is overcome and
life can flow with renewed power towards new goals. [...] The
raw material shaped by thesis and antithesis, and in the shaping of which the opposites are united, is the living symbol [*das
lebendige Symbol*]. Its profundity of meaning is inherent in the
raw material itself, the very stuff of the psyche, transcending
time and dissolution; and its configuration by the opposites
ensures its sovereign power over all the psychic functions [*In
seinem für eine lange Epoche nicht aufzulösenden Rohstoff liegt
sein Ahnungsreiches, und in der Gestalt, die sein Rohstoff durch
die Einwirkung der Gegensätze empfängt, liegt seine Wirkung
auf alle psychischen Funktionen*].[293]

As is clear from these extracts, Jung's theory of the symbol, despite his use
of such terms as "transcendent," is far removed from mystical metaphysics, just as is the aesthetic theory of German classicism—to which, in formulation and conception, Jung's intellectual proximity is astonishing.[294]
Indeed, Jung's position may justly be compared with that of Herbert
Marcuse (1868-1979), one of his contemporaries, who turns out to be
another inheritor of this classical tradition. In *Eros and Civilisation*
(1956), a work that discusses Schiller's *Aesthetic Letters* in some detail,
Marcuse puts forward Orpheus, together with Narcissus, as figures representing, through self-contemplation and death, the liberation of the self.
These figures, Marcuse admits, "have not become the culture-heroes of
the Western world," for "theirs is the image of joy and fulfillment; the
voice which does not command but sings; the gesture which offers and
receives; the deed which is peace and ends the labor of conquest; the liberation from time which unites man with god, man with nature." But
their image has been preserved in literature (Rilke's *Sonette an Orpheus*
[1923], André Gide's *Le Traité du Narcisse* [1891], Paul Valéry's "Narcisse

[293]Jung, *CW* 6 §825, §827, §828.

[294]In one of a series of lectures on "The Theory of Psychoanalysis" (1913), first given at Fordham
University, New York, in 1912, Jung is explicit that we may talk about the "non-conscious" [*das
"Nichtbewußte"*] as "the unconscious" [*das "Unbewußte"*], "without attributing to it any mystical sig-
nificance" [*ohne damit irgendeinen mysteriösen Sinn zu verknüpfen*] (Jung, *CW* 4 §255).

parle"...).[295] In the association of Orpheus with homosexuality found in
the classical tradition, Marcuse sees a rejection of "the normal Eros, not
for an ascetic ideal, but for a fuller Eros," and the negation by Orpheus
and Narcissus of the Promethean world-order reveals, Marcuse argues, a
"new reality, with an order of its own, governed by different principles":

> The Orphic Eros transforms being: he masters cruelty and
> death through liberation. His language is *song*, and his work is
> *play*. Narcissus' life is that of *beauty* and his existence is *con-*
> *templation*. These images refer to the *aesthetic dimension* as the
> one in which their reality principle must be sought and vali-
> dated.[296]

One might almost say: the (Marcusean) Eros of Orpheus give us cause for
(Goethean) Hope...

And so, for all his rhetoric of the primordial, and the misleading confusion of symbols with Kantian ideas,[297] Jung's remarks about the importance of symbols at the end of his paper "The Stages of Life" ultimately
deserve to be read in the context of the aesthetic theories of German classicism. What gives us hope (*Elpis*) is the power of the imagination (*Phan-*
*tasie*) to create the symbols required to transcend the midlife crisis:

> Do we ever understand what we think? We only understand
> that kind of thinking which is a mere equation, from which
> nothing comes out but what we have put in. That is the
> working of the intellect. But besides that there is a thinking
> in primordial images, in symbols [*ein Denken in urtümlichen*
> *Bildern, in Symbolen*] which are older than the historical
> man, which are inborn in him from the earliest times, and,
> eternally living, outlasting all generations, still make the
> groundwork of the human psyche [*ewig lebendig die*
> *Untergründe unserer Seele erfüllend*]. It is only possible to live

---

[295]Herbert Marcuse, *Eros and Civilisation: A Philosophical Enquiry into Freud* (London:
Routledge and Kegan Paul, 1956), p. 162; see Strauss, *Descent and Return*, p. 11.

[296]Marcuse, *Eros and Civilisation*, p. 171.

[297]Jung writes that "One of these primordial thoughts [*Urgedanken*] is the idea of life after death"
(*CW* 8 §794). In the first Critique, Kant referred to the three Ideas of God, Freedom, and Immortal-
ity; but Jung's terminological confusion here—*urtümliches Bild, Symbol, Urbild, Urgedanke,*
*Idee*—cannot be resolved so easily. For Goethe's thoughts on immortality, see his conversations with
Eckermann of 2 May 1824 and 4 February 1829 (*Conversations of Goethe*, pp. 60 and 287). The tenor
of Goethe's comments here on the idea of immortality is remarkably similar to comments in *Memories,*
*Dreams, Reflections* in the chapter entitled "On Life after Death" (Jung, *MDR*, 330-358; *ETG*,
302-329).

the fullest life when we are in harmony with these symbols;
wisdom is a return to them.[298]

Thus what matters, in the end, is not (conscious) knowledge but (archetypal) wisdom. In one of his *Zahme Xenien*, Goethe writes:

Stop bragging and boasting about wisdom,
Modesty would suit you better;
Hardly have you committed the mistakes of youth,
You must make the mistakes of old age.

[*Hör' auf doch mit Weisheit zu prahlen, zu prangen,*
*Bescheidenheit würde dir löblicher stehn:*
*Kaum hast du die Fehler der Jugend begangen,*
*So mußt du die Fehler des Alters begehn.*][299]

Socrates' knowledge lies in knowing that he knows nothing; Goethe's
wisdom lies in wising up to not being wise. Thus ancient wisdom,
obscured by Orphic mist, becomes available, made transparent, for today.
By relating Yesterday and Tomorrow to Today and the (Here-and-)Now
of Art, we find, so Goethe tells us in another of his *Zahme Xenien*, the
source of hope:

When yesterday lies clear and open
Your powers today are free,
You can hope for a tomorrow
That will no less happy be.

[*Liegt dir Gestern klar und offen,*
*Wirkst du heute kräftig frei,*
*Kannst auch auf ein Morgen hoffen,*
*Das nicht minder glücklich sei.*][300]

This is why the final stanza of "Primal Words. Orphic" is placed under
the patronage of *elpis*; why Goethe's poem on fate (*Dem Schicksal*), from
which we have already quoted (see above), ends with hope—

You have chosen for us the right measure,
And wrapped us in a gloom that's pure,
So that we, with living power full,
In the tender present hope for the dearest future.

[298]Jung, *CW* 8 §794.
[299]Goethe, *Werke* [WA], vol. I.3, p. 234.
[300]Goethe, *Werke* [HA], vol. 1, p. 308.

*[Du hast für uns das rechte Maß getroffen,*
*In reine Dumpfheit uns gehüllt,*
*Daß wir, von Lebenskraft erfüllt,*
*In holder Gegenwart der lieben Zukunft hoffen.]*[301]

—and why his Masonic poem, *Symbolum*, concludes with "the voices of
the spirits, / The voices of the masters" (*Die Stimmen der Geister, / Die
Stimmen der Meister*), who call to us:

Do not neglect to exercise
The powers of good.

Here laurels are wound
In silence eternal,
They'll richly reward
The active among you!
We urge you to—hope.

[*"Versäumt nicht zu üben*
*Die Kräfte des Guten.*

*Hier winden sich Kronen*
*In ewiger Stille,*
*Die sollen mit Fülle*
*Die Tätigen lohnen!*
*Wir heißen euch hoffen."]*[302]

In the darkness, chaos, and confusion of the Orphic moment, the
moment of death and stasis before a new cycle of life begins, we need hope
to begin the next stage of our journey. Where do we find hope? In art—no
longer do we need to sacrifice animals, undergo mystic initiation, or
invoke the deity (for, as Jung reminds us, "called or not called, the god is

---

[301] Goethe, *Werke* [HA], vol. 1, p. 132. For discussion of the meaning of *dumpf*, see Adolf Beck,
"Der 'Geist der Reinheit' und die 'Idee des Reinen,'" p. 162, n. 3.

[302] Goethe, *Werke* [HA], vol. 1, pp. 340-341. The concluding line of the final stanza also brings to
a close the account of the rise of National Socialism and the causes of the Second World War offered by
the eminent German historian, Friedrich Meinecke (1862-1954). In the final chapter of *The German
Catastrophe: Reflections and Recollections* [*Die deutsche Katastrophe: Betrachtungen und Erinnerungen*]
[1946], Meinecke proposes, as an antidote to the tendencies unleased in the Third Reich, the creation
of "Goethe Communities," which would regularly meet on Sundays to read the work of great German
writers and listen to great German music. "Lyrical and thoughtful poetry," he wrote, "could then form
the kernel of such festal hours. Lyrics of the wonderful sort, reaching their peak in Goethe and Mörike
where the soul becomes nature and nature the soul, and sensitive, thoughtful poetry like that of Goethe and Schiller—these are perhaps the most essentially German parts of our literature. He who steeps
himself in them will detect something indestructible—a German *character indelibis*—in the midst of
all the destruction and misfortune of our Fatherland" (*The German Catastrophe: Reflections and Recollections*, trans. Sidney B. Fay [Boston: Beacon Press, 1963], pp. 120-121).

present"); Goethe's message, using the language of ancient wisdom, reformulates the psychological truth of the Orphic cult for his time, and ours. Just as Schiller learned from Goethe that, "confronted with excellence, there is no other freedom than love,"[303] and Bertrand Vergely has spoken of "the duty to hope,"[304] so we might say that, in the midlife crisis, there is no alternative to hope. We shall, like Don Fernando at the end of Heinrich von Kleist's short story, "The Earthquake in Chili" (*Das Erdbeben in Chili*), simply have to resign ourselves to being happy.[305] Far from being esoteric, despite its Orphic wrapping, Goethe's advice is eminently pragmatic: and it sums up the richly intuitive insights of Jung's model of the stages of life.

---

[303] Schiller to Goethe, 2 July 1796 (*Werke: Nationalausgabe*, ed. on behalf of the Goethe- und Schiller-Archiv, the Schiller-Nationalmuseum, and the Deutsche Akademie, 43 vols. [Weimar: Böhlau, 1943-], vol. 28, p. 235); "*daß es dem Vortrefflichen gegenüber keine Freiheit gibt als die Liebe.*"

[304] Bertrand Vergely, *Petit traité sur le devoir de bonheur* (Toulouse: Milan, 2004).

[305] Heinrich von Kleist, *Sämtliche Erzählungen, Anekdoten, Gedichte, Schriften*, ed. Klaus Müller-Salget (Frankfurt am Main: Deutscher Klassiker Verlag, 2005), pp. 189-221 (p. 221).

# *Index*

9 781630 518288